Speaking Out

Speaking Out

IDEAS THAT WORK FOR CANADIANS

Jack Layton

KEY PORTER BOOKS

MAY 11 2004

National Library of Canada Cataloguing in Publication Data

Layton, Jack, 1950–
   Speaking out: ideas that work for Canadians / Jack Layton.

Includes index.
ISBN 1-55263-577-5

1. Canada—Social conditions—1991–   2. Canada—Economic conditions—1991– 3. Canada—Politics and government—1993– I. Title.

FC635.L39 2004   971.064'8   C2003-907309-2

The publisher gratefully acknowledges the support of the Canada Council for the Arts and the Ontario Arts Council for its publishing program. We acknowledge the support of the Government of Ontario through the Ontario Media Development Corporation's Ontario Book Initiative.

We acknowledge the financial support of the Government of Canada through the Book Publishing Industry Development Program (BPIDP) for our publishing activities.

Key Porter Books Limited
70 The Esplanade
Toronto, Ontario
Canada M5E 1R2

www.keyporter.com

Text design: Jack Steiner
Electronic formatting: Jean Lightfoot Peters

Printed and bound in Canada

04 05 06 07 08 09 6 5 4 3 2 1

To Olivia Chow, and Sarah and Michael Layton
And in memory of Dan Leckie and Robert E.J. Layton

"If we do not change our direction, we are liable to end up where we are headed."
—CHINESE PROVERB

Contents

Preface   9

1. Why Does Politics Matter?   13

2. Sharing Our World   44

3. Sustaining Our Lives   76

4. A Caring Society   113

5. Reawakening Our Communities   151

6. Building the New Prosperity   187

7. Building a Just Society   236

   A Call to Action   265

   Index   283

Preface

My father always said to the four of us kids, "You wouldn't want to miss an opportunity!" He said it most often at the end of a family dinner. We'd groan...then clear the dishes.

But sometimes, usually one-on-one, or with Mom alongside, he'd share his counsel when we faced tougher choices in our lives. In these more serious discussions, I always drew strength from Dad's focus on taking the opportunity to serve. He saw a problem, or someone would bring one to him, and he'd want to pull people together to develop ideas that would work. He'd call on people to take the opportunity to serve their community, putting the best ideas into action.

Now I find myself with a wonderful opportunity to serve. I wish Dad were still here to advise me. I do get regular e-mails from my mother, who, of course, was always the one with the best advice on practical matters anyway. Lately she's been telling me that one of our best new constituencies as New Democrats is to be found among "informed seniors." To quote her: "They're not only worried about themselves and the future of things like health care, Jack," she writes. "They're worried about the air their grandchildren breathe." According to a Toronto Board of Health report prepared by Dr. Sheela Basrur, the medical officer of health widely regarded as the most sane voice during Toronto's SARS crisis in 2003, each year in Toronto alone, one thousand people, mostly children and seniors, die before their time because of smog.

I've always found it immensely rewarding to join with others in speaking out about issues and collaborating with people to find ideas that work and to put these solutions in place. Over the twenty years I've spent in public life, working in local government and in Canada-wide organizations, I've had hundreds of these opportunities. Now, as leader of the New Democratic Party of Canada, I have a chance to infuse into our national dialogue a full range of positive ideas and strategies for solving the serious problems we face as a nation.

The NDP is a great place to pursue this work because it has always been about building a better world, taking positive action together. Think of Tommy Douglas bringing medicare into being as the first provincial premier to carry our political banner (at the time it was the Cooperative Commonwealth Federation, or CCF). Or think of Manitoba premier Gary Doer putting into place a remarkable sustainable energy strategy for the twenty-first century that will reduce pollution and at the same time strengthen the economy of the province. The NDP's focus is to tap that positive energy that Canadians have in abundance. And to draw on their best ideas and make them work.

This book isn't about the NDP platform. We have election campaigns for that. It's about the experiences I've had—as a city councillor, community activist, and Federation of Canadian Municipalities president—that make me believe that by working together, citizens can be the catalysts for the adoption of good ideas in government at all levels.

Over the past two decades, however, political debate has been about how we should accomplish less together, not more. Whether it's tax cuts that effectively download responsibility for paying for good ideas onto individuals through user fees; or whether it's trade deals that restrict governments' capacity to act in their citizens' interests; or whether it's handing over the collective role of government to corporations through privatization, we've been taught to abandon the concept that we can build together.

I reject that analysis because I'm a pragmatist who's seen good ideas in action. This book shares just some of those ideas and solutions, and the role they played in making me believe federal politics matters. All politicians speak with hope about the future. But I believe that experience—where someone has been, the choices he or she has made, his or her solutions to problems—is equally important. Rhetoric is easy. Results are what counts.

Friends suggested to me that I should share some of these experiences with a broader range of Canadians. I'd like to tell you a bit about where I've been, the people I've met, and some of the ideas I'm proud to have put in effect.

We have opportunities to make our world a better place. The question is, Are we going to take them? I know what Dad would have said.

Good ideas come from many directions. Since I started working on this book, many people have generously shared their ideas with me. I want to single out the following: Greg Allen, David Bell, Lisa Caton, Martha Friendly, Michael Hough, Phil Jessup, Richard Johnston, Gordon Laird, Hugh Mackenzie, Burkhard Mausberg, Michael Rachlis, Wayne Roberts, Mary Rowles, Michael Shapcott, Rick Smith, Jim Stanford, Ross Sutherland, Dan Tatroff, Ralph Torrie, Mel Watkins, Michael Wiggin, Armine Yalnizyan, and Peter Zimmerman.

I could not have completed this project without George Ehring and Dennis Mills (the editor, not the MP), and my team in Ottawa, especially Franz Hartmann, Jamey Heath, Donne Flanagan, Bruce Cox, and Chris Watson. Others who have been instrumental in the project are Jim Laxer, Alison Reid, and Marjan Farahbaksh. Pierre Ducasse, Karl Belanger, and André Cardinal have assisted me in various ways with the French edition, prepared by the superb translator, Isabelle Allard. I also want to thank my French publisher, Guy Saint-Jean, for his patience and faith.

Various friends encouraged me to write this book but some went further and offered me their homes as getaways. Svend Robinson and his partner Max Riveron provided a haven on Parker Island, and Pat Martin and his wife Barbara loaned us their Salt Spring Island farmhouse for secluded writing.

Serendipity intervened when I called Key Porter's Meg Taylor at a moment she had been considering calling me. Little did she know that at the behest of her astonishingly demanding and supportive employer, Anna Porter, she would be compelled to virtually move in to my home to supervise the completion of the book, which otherwise might well still be on the go.

Olivia Chow devoted the better part of two erstwhile holidays to organizing ideas and editing drafts—with constant encouragement and creativity.

To all of these and to the many hundreds of friends and acquaintances who have shared their good ideas with me over the years, I offer my deepest thanks. Any shortcomings in capturing the full extent of the possibilities embodied in their ideas are mine alone.

CHAPTER 1

Why Does Politics Matter?

Politics matters. Ideas matter. Democracy matters, because all of us need to be able to make a difference. This book is about politics, ideas, and democracy. The chapters that follow are about ideas—ideas that work. If you'll bear with me, I'd like to start with politics and democracy. And as outrageous as it sounds for me to say, politics is too important to leave just to politicians. That's where you come in. You, the Canadian citizen, or someone who is on the way to becoming one. Canada is your country. Democracy should ensure your engagement in setting the course for your country. You should feel right at the centre of the political process, but you are being pushed out, because when politicians linked closely to their corporate friends tell you that politics doesn't matter, what they really mean is that they want you to stay out of it and leave it to them. Power has been slipping away from Canadians. Have you noticed? I remember the optimism of Canadian politics years ago—we could build together and were proud of it. We built health care systems for all, the best affordable housing in the world, great education systems for our kids, railways and public transit systems, communities where quality of life was second to none. But now we feel that slipping. Even as communities across Canada are showing the way with local solutions, grabbing every opportunity that comes within their grasp, our federal government has cynically slipped into the role of naysayer.

For at least ten years, we've being told we cannot build anymore because we have no financial capacity to do so. As we turn away, discouraged, from voting, from participating, from building together, the vacuum that's created allows powerful elites to be free to negotiate the deals behind closed doors, even though those deals could cost you your job. They want to sell off our public resources without your knowledge. There is a CEO atmosphere around government these days, the direction of the country established in Bay Street board-rooms, out of the range of pesky questions. Powerful interests want to spend your money on astoundingly expensive Star Wars missile defence programs, for instance, and the less that Canadians have a chance to say anything about it the better.

There's another reason why so many people come to believe that politics doesn't matter. Sociologists call it "feeling alienated," left outside, as though there is nothing that we can do about the problems we face. It's sad. I've met Canadians, across the country, who refer to Ottawa not as a place but as a bad idea. These folks think that government, with its complex processes and shenanigans, doesn't represent them, or speak for them, or act on their behalf. The recent Liberal sponsorship scandal and other debacles have rubbed more salt in the wounds. People's confidence is further shaken when governments act to dismantle public services or social programs that people rely on. But think about it—shouldn't our alienation be driving us to be *more* involved in politics, not less? People should be working with their neighbours, their co-workers, and with others who share their concerns, coming together to make sure their voices are heard, their interests protected, and their ideas and concerns treated seriously.

For two decades at least, corporate think-tanks and the politicians that promote their messages have been telling Canadians, essentially, that citizens do not matter in the political process because they lack the capacity to build the country of their dreams. This feeds a sense of alienation. With every election, fewer people turn out to vote. That's just as well from the point of view of the corporate players. According to them, the country we dream of is possible only if we leave the decision making to the private sector. They promise prosperity but then dismantle the public sector for corporate profit, at heavy cost to all of us.

It's time to build again. I'm a typical Canadian in that I've always loved building. Canadians are builders. But year after year, we've been taking apart what we built: medicare, affordable housing, industrial strategies, and public power systems. The past ten years have been all about tax cuts. These years have focused on privatizing our public services and on empowering the corporations through trade deals that handcuff citizens wanting to build better communities. I intend to show in this book that we can once more build to achieve a new prosperity for Canadians, even a prosperity for those corporations who have been maximizing their success when people are poor.

In the world of 9/11, SARS, mad cow disease, forest fires and floods, the need for collective action has been brought into sharp relief. We can almost see the faces of those courageous nurses, firefighters, and peacemakers.

After the terrible health crises of 2003, Canadians recognize the need for public services and the taxes that pay for them. Let's face it: our taxes pay for nurses on SARS wards, for our soldiers on peacekeeping and peacemaking missions, for forest-fire fighters, for childcare workers, and much more. As the American jurist Oliver Wendell Holmes said a century ago, "Taxes are what we pay for civilized society." Or, as my disarmingly insightful wife, Olivia Chow, put it so clearly on national TV (as she provided commentary on a CTV panel during our NDP leadership convention), "Taxes are what we put on the table, to do the things we want to do in common."

When the private sector fails to provide affordable housing, and people wind up homeless, on the street, it is not time to advocate less government.

I have always found it interesting that not one politician who is caught up in this corporate drift says "We should privatize or do more with less" when it's about the military. Why, then, do these same people say we should privatize and cut health care, education, or environmental protection? It's because corporations want it that way, and their powerful influences have permeated government much too extensively.

The end result has been to teach Canadians to expect less, as a way of life. Do not expect solutions now for cities, for long-term or home care, for childcare, or for assisting the people afflicted by desperate poverty and disease around the world. Lower your expectations, you Canadians. Abandon your dreamy ways, your optimism, your capacity to construct the future you wish for in communities, in Canada, in the world. What a sad and demoralizing message it has been. No wonder people do not want to be associated with politics at all and stay home when voting time comes.

That's why so many Canadians have turned to completely different ways of challenging the way things are and building what they believe in. Community organizations, non-government organizations, movements of citizens have sprung up related to peace, the environment, sovereignty, health care, human rights, education, worker safety and salaries, international development assistance, equality. These groups, said General Romeo Dallaire, as he spoke to journalists working for free speech in the fall of 2003, are the places where hope for the future resides. It's called "civil society," society outside the traditional governmental/electoral processes, and it is rising up. I'm not the only one to have said that "a new superpower is emerging"—people in communities around the world, connecting in novel ways, exercising their aspirations in positive initiatives locally and globally. These are the builders of the future. Let's become part of that process, and turn politics on its head.

When Canadians get up in the morning, we turn on the tap, and without thinking about it, we expect safe, clean water to come out. That water is treated and delivered by public sector workers toiling away for a public utility. We flush the toilet, and without thinking about it, we expect the sewage to disappear and be properly treated by yet another publicly owned utility. We drive to work on public highways or ride there on public transit. Our children go to public schools. In most of Canada, the electricity that powers our workplaces and our homes has been generated and delivered to us by a public utility. In the rest of the country, our power is publicly regulated. We expect police officers to maintain law and order. We expect firefighters to protect our communities. If we need health care, we expect doctors and nurses to minister to us in public hospitals. All these services (and hundreds of others) are provided to us in one way or another by our government. What's really unthinkable is that we would ever want to do without public services. But our governments are now selling them off to private companies or creating cozy-sounding "public-private partnerships" (P3s). Can that be good?

Fortunately, the message that private multinational corporations bring us closer to the divine has worn a little thin. The past two decades have been the Era of Corporate Corruption, aptly demonstrated in the United States by Enron and WorldCom, and in Italy by Parmalat, and by so many others. For those who still believe that corporations are reliable and trustworthy, every week brings a new tale of CEOs raking in multimillion-dollar salaries, while their corporations lose money and lay off workers—Nortel is the most insidious example because it's ostensibly a Canadian company—plus pension-fund rip-offs, insider trading, "cooked" accounting books, and profits diverted to offshore tax havens.

For a number of very good reasons, many aspects of our economy and society are better delivered by government than by the private sector. That's because governments are typically more transparent, accountable, and efficient than the private sector. Many others are better left to the private sector, and, when they are, we should let them be. It's important for us to find the balance—and to know the difference. However, if we think it's best for the private sector to deliver certain goods or services, we, the people, need to make sure that we have good regulation and oversight to protect us and our environment. I don't think that government needs to run a mine, but we must not rely on the mining company to tell us it's safe for workers—the families of the dead Westray miners can testify to that. Thankfully, the families and the Steelworkers never gave up and pressed the Canadian government to adopt laws with penalties in situations where worker safety is jeopardized. They did so with the help of our NDP MPs Alexa McDonough and Yvon Godin, a miner.himself. I don't have a problem with private trucking, but I think someone else ought to make sure that drivers have received their certification only as a result of excellent training, and that the trucks are reliable and inspected for safety so people don't get killed by flying tires on highways. When it comes to food safety, I trust someone employed by the public rather than meat-packing company executives to inspect their products.

When people in Walkerton, Ontario, died or succumbed to painful illnesses because the provincial government had decimated its water inspection services, it is not the time to advocate less government.

When hospital waiting lists grow to unacceptable and dangerous lengths because we underfund the health care system and fail to provide adequate numbers of trained nurses, doctors, and other medical staff, it is not the time to advocate less government.

We need to advocate for positive change. To move from opposition to proposition. To build instead of diminish. I came by this belief in many ways. One of the pathways has deep family roots.

An early memory for me—providing an important political lesson—is hearing about the work of my great-grandfather, Philip E. Layton, who had been blinded as a teenager in a woodcutting accident. After otherwise recovering from that, he immigrated to Canada from England and settled in Montreal. Then he did something very romantic: he sailed back to England to marry the young nurse who had cared for him there, and they returned in 1887 to make their lives together in Montreal.

He was dismayed that blind children had no opportunity for schooling, and that blind adults had nowhere to work. He was appalled at the meagre lives blind people eked out, too many of them reduced to selling pencils on street corners. Once, his two sons—both notorious pranksters—grabbed his dark glasses as he napped, took his white cane and a cup, pretended to be poor blind kids, and collected coins at the corner of Guy and Sherbrooke, near their little house. They were caught and given a talking-to they never forgot. The world of those with disabilities is not to be made fun of or exploited. It is, rather, a world of people who deserve every right and opportunity of any citizen. My great-grandfather and his wife, Alice, were determined to not only provide for their family but to improve the plight of blind people in Canada. Although he became a successful piano tuner and salesman, his real achievement was in organizing members of the blind community to fight for themselves.

Just after the turn of the century, Philip and Alice found a farm property west of the city (on what is now Sherbrooke Street West) that they hoped to buy in order to build a school and workshop. They began a fundraising drive, using networks of volunteers to hold Montreal's first "tag day," selling tags that could be hung off coat buttons in support of the cause. Out onto Montreal streets they flooded to sell their tags, young people, boys and girls—yes, including blind girls! scandalous at the time—all to build a dream.

In 1908, that dream became a reality, and Montreal's blind people had a lending library, sheltered workshop, and social club. Soon after, a school was built, and thousands of Montreal's blind children have studied there for almost a century. My great-grandfather's vision became the Montreal Association for the Blind (MAB). For blind people themselves, the project provided an early step toward full participation in the community, realizing their rights of citizenship.

Even though I never knew my great-grandfather, I will not forget his lesson of organizing people and empowering them. And several of Philip's descendants became involved in politics. My grandfather Gilbert became a cabinet minister in a government formed by newly elected reformers determined to throw out the arrogant and corrupt Liberal government of the day. They called themselves the Union Nationale and were led by Maurice Duplessis. The premier was an ardent French-Canadian nationalist who, some years later, opposed forced participation of young francophone Quebeckers in the Second World War, which he regarded as Britain's conflict. My grandfather had resigned his cabinet post and his seat in

1938 and later broke with the party over this "conscription crisis," believing that all Canadian young people should fight the fascists. He then returned to Montreal to follow in his father's footsteps as director of the MAB. Gilbert's brother, George, won a seat on Montreal's city council. My father, Robert, served as chair of the MAB. My sister, Nancy, now serves on the board, carrying on the family tradition. That people can advocate for change and actually make it happen has been an essential part of that tradition.

My path grew out of the tumultuous days of the October Crisis. It was 1970. Quebec's Quiet Revolution had moved to a much more active and aggressive form of protest against inequality. Self-determination movements were forming and gaining support. I was an early supporter of a community movement in my neighbourhood. FRAP stood for Front d'Action Politique, a democratic municipal political organization concerned about good planning, affordable housing, the environment, and local democracy in the era of the autocratic mayor of Montreal, Jean Drapeau. It was exciting, canvassing and building support among low-income tenants for the idea that their neighbourhoods should be protected from ruthless plans to evict them and tear down their homes. We knocked on doors, talked to residents, and built a movement to save old affordable housing. It was really my first direct local politics experience. I thought of it as a real life version of the democracy I was studying in my political science courses. A few years later, renamed the Montreal Citizens' Movement, this municipal party became the elected majority government of the Montreal City Council, under the leadership of my friends mayor Jean Doré and the deputy mayor Thérèse Daviau.

Sadly, some political movements in Quebec at the time, however, moved far beyond the kind of protest that a democracy can accept. Over several months, terrorist bombings of

Westmount mailboxes by the Front de Libération du Québec (FLQ) had escalated into the kidnapping of the British trade commissioner, James Cross, and the murder of the Quebec labour minister, Pierre Laporte.

I was in my last year of studying politics, economics, and philosophy at McGill University, and when Laporte was murdered I found myself at first agreeing with the popular sentiment calling for drastic action in response to the threat the FLQ seemed to represent. When Prime Minister Pierre Trudeau said he would suspend civil liberties through the use of the War Measures Act, I was inclined to go along with the vast majority of Canadians and even Quebeckers behind the get-tough plan.

Then a parliamentarian, Tommy Douglas, leader of the New Democratic Party of Canada, gave a widely reported speech decrying the suspension of civil rights. I said to myself, That's a very unpopular position this NDP leader is taking. Still, as I listened to his powerful arguments and his brilliant capacity to deliver them, I realized that this unpopular stance was right. Eloquence, logic, and passion for his ideals were displayed in a way I had never heard before. Here's just some of what Douglas said that influenced me so strongly. The words are from his address to the House of Commons during the crisis on October 16: "We are prepared to support the government in taking whatever measures are necessary to safeguard life and to maintain law and order in this country. But, Mr. Speaker, we are not prepared to use the preservation of law and order as a smokescreen to destroy the liberties and the freedom of the people of Canada. The government, I submit, is using a sledgehammer to crack a peanut!"

In the subsequent three weeks, as many as 424 people were detained under the War Measures Act. Most of them were never charged. Jean Marchand, Pierre Trudeau's

Quebec lieutenant, accused all kinds of groups of being terrorist suspects. Some of the people arrested were from
FRAP, the very group that was contesting the municipal election—I had canvassed on behalf of their local candidate. As
developments were reported to the House on November 4,
Douglas made an impassioned plea for human rights: "I
think it is significant that to date most of those detained
seem to be members of either FRAP or the Parti Québécois.
Although I disagree with the separatists, it is not a crime to
be one as long as they do not seek to use violence or uncon-
stitutional means to advance their objectives. We in the New
Democratic Party recognize the need for prompt and energetic steps to stamp out terrorism, but we have insisted from
the beginning that in the process of stamping out terrorism
we must not abridge the freedoms that our people and our
forefathers have won for us over the years."

I joined the NDP at the very next opportunity.

Just a few months ago, I met the organist at the Anglican
church where my uncle was being memorialized. He said to
me that he supported the work I was doing as leader of the
NDP. As we chatted, the conversation turned to how it was
that I had joined the NDP. Then he said, "Perhaps it is significant that I was one of those arrested and jailed without
charge during the October Crisis in Quebec." It turned out
that he was a South African who had moved to Canada and
was working on justice issues, including working to end
apartheid. Travelling in these circles evidently made him suspicious to the Canadian military and RCMP. Under the War
Measures Act, no reasons were needed to scoop him up and
detain him for questioning, without any of the normal protections granted to Canadians.

• • •

Events of the sixties and seventies were formative for me: protesting against the Vietnam War, riding one of many buses to the U.S. border to denounce the testing of nuclear weapons, joining the march down Sherbrooke Street in Montreal as part of the "McGill français" demonstration to make the big English-language university bilingual, studying political philosophy with Charles Taylor while he was writing his magnum opus on Hegel and dialectics. Taylor's book *The Pattern of Politics* laid out the idea that debate and conflict can produce positive transformations. I had never thought of it that way. Compromise had been the watchword of Canadian politics, especially among the elites; Taylor told us that this was the politics of status quo and privilege. He encouraged us to "challenge the way things are."

With Taylor's urging, I headed to Toronto to broaden my academic horizons. At York University, young professors turned me on to all manner of new thinking. I met and studied under Jim Laxer, a young leader of the Waffle movement. The Waffle was the name chosen by a group on the left within the New Democratic Party that felt the party was waffling on fundamentals like socialism and Canadian independence, hence the tongue-in-cheek moniker. I found very compelling the concept that Canadians on the left had to be much more clear in our denunciation of certain government policies and more ambitious in our work to prevent Canada from being swallowed up by the United States and its multinational corporations. The well-known Canadian economist Mel Watkins had been writing about the need to place controls on foreign investment to protect our ability to make decisions in Canada that represented our values, rather than those of the U.S. administration and its supporters in corporate America. By the time I had become immersed in my doctoral studies, I decided to study how nations had attempted to influence and restrain the movement of foreign capital to achieve national goals—like employment, research and development, environmental benefits, regional economic development, and the like. As I was beginning the work, the NDP won sufficient seats in the 1972 election to create a minority government for the Liberals. Prime Minister Trudeau now needed the support of the new leader of the NDP, David Lewis, in order to govern. Lewis supported Trudeau's Foreign Investment Review Agency (FIRA), which tried to make transnational corporate expansion in Canada more palatable. I ended up completing my doctoral thesis on the operations of this agency. After studying the thousands of foreign takeovers that were approved by FIRA and the very few that were refused, I concluded that this instrument of public policy had largely failed because of a lack of will on the part of the federal government to insist that its objectives be met. In the process, I developed an early appreciation of the growing power of multinational corporate capital flows in determining the shape of national societies, even undermining democratic institutions. Years later, the concern about this globalization process reached a fever pitch as a growing movement of young people, environmentalists, social justice advocates, and international development proponents rose up against the whittling away of people's power through trade deals of all sorts. My early assessment of the threats to sovereignty that globalization could pose has proven, sadly, to be all too true. We'll come back to this key challenge in later chapters of this book.

At the same time as I was researching the global, my professor of urban studies at York immersed me in the local. Professor Michael Goldrick, a friendly mentor in my early days at the windswept school, brought me into contact with the ideas of thinkers like Jane Jacobs and the activism of a young lawyer and Toronto city councillor named John Sewell. Theirs was exciting, hands-on work that focused on stopping bad projects like the Spadina Expressway and promoting livable communities through affordable co-operative housing and neighbourhood preservation policies. Goldrick became a candidate in the famous 1972 municipal election in Toronto, the one that elected the "tiny perfect mayor," David Crombie, and his reform council. I threw myself into the campaign with a vengeance and learned about street-to-street electoral politics and community organizing from some of the best in the city. The win was unpredicted, huge, and very exciting.

I was hooked on local politics and neighbourhood engagement. After that election, I became involved in many urban reform movements and coalitions that formed around fair transit fares, that pursued community policing to reduce harassment of minorities and gays, that worked for rent controls to protect tenants from being gouged by unscrupulous landlords, and much more. We won some of these long struggles. Perhaps the most significant was the effort to build a rent control system in Ontario, where tenants were being hammered with massive rent increases they simply couldn't afford. They had virtually no rights to protect themselves. I learned about how to help tenants to organize to protest impossible rent increases and poor maintenance of their rented homes and apartments. The key concept I was taught by people like Norm Brudy, who had been empowering tenants for years, was to help tenants understand that by acting collectively they could be much more effective. Step by step, we would walk through the process of building a tenant association, taking on the landlord by together withholding rents, pressing governments to insist that landlords enforce basic building standards, and forming the Federation of Metro Tenants' Associations to ultimately convince political parties to establish rent controls and the media to be supportive. I will never forget the powerful speeches of Stephen Lewis, then the young leader of the Ontario NDP, who relentlessly took the sad stories of the tenants to the public forum of the Legislature. The combination of grassroots organization and a political party that would present their case effectively was a potent mixture. Rent controls came into place as a result of the combined pressure. Nightly meetings and weekend rallies and conventions were piled on top of my duties as a professor in the Politics Department at Ryerson Polytechnical Institute. I taught classes in local government, Canadian government and politics, and political theory to a succession of budding journalists, social workers, public health inspectors, engineers, and librarians.

My first wife, Sally, and I lived in North York, fiefdom of its outspoken mayor, Mel Lastman, who later became the first mayor of the megacity. Our children, Sarah and Michael, were born there, and we became involved in trying to preserve the quiet family neighbourhood from Lastman's big developer friends who wanted to overrun the communities with high-rises. A trip to North York today will demonstrate that we weren't entirely successful.

By 1982, we had moved to downtown Toronto, and I decided to put my years of political theory into direct action. I ran for Toronto City Council and won in what *The Toronto Star* reported was the big upset of the election. Our huge team of volunteers took on a much-touted incumbent conservative alderman named Gordon Chong, who had huge financial backing from the business elites on Bay Street. We were given no chance to win, but the hundreds of tenants who had worked with us for fair and affordable housing over the past few years turned out to help. We ended up with six hundred volunteers. On election night, when some pundits declared me defeated as the early returns came in, only to eat crow later as the big apartment buildings' votes piled in, I remember saying, "Six hundred workers can beat $60,000 anytime!" I learned that democracy could be about people, not money. It's a lesson we need to relearn periodically.

The next twenty years as a city councillor would show me every day how much politics matters to people in very down-to-earth ways. Sometimes the issues had an impact on only a limited number of people: a community garden, a bicycle repair service run by formerly homeless men, an income-generating recycling program in Toronto's oldest public housing neighbourhood. Yet even these "small" issues were important and worthwhile to the people involved. Other times, the scope was larger. With other councillors, I helped initiate Toronto's first blue-box curbside recycling program to pick up glass, plastic, and cans. I also chaired the Toronto Board of Health for many years, with its $50 million budget involving six hundred-plus health care professionals, helped put in place Canada's first AIDS Defence Plan, and assisted in developing a labour-business-city partnership to retrofit building spaces, which created jobs, saved energy, cut costs, and reduced pollution. Some projects took a long time, like the seventeen years to try to persuade city council to remove the ugly Gardiner Expressway in the part of the port lands that I represented and replace it with a tree-lined boulevard, bike lanes, and public art. Others projects were elegantly simple ones that community groups can achieve, as long as they have some political support, like the installation of an elegant wind turbine on Toronto's waterfront. In that case, I was able to help the turbine come into being as the vice chair of the $2 billion-a-year publicly owned energy company known as Toronto Hydro.

It surprises many people, but municipal governments all across the country are putting together some of the most progressive, innovative solutions to practical problems facing their residents. You will read about lots of examples in this book. Cities, towns, and villages have the power to build programs that really work to meet people's immediate needs, implement ideas, and create change, and they are doing it now, from coast to coast. Local democracies and community governments are where the real innovations are happening; the best ideas are being originated with public participation and creativity. The problem? No money! It's that simple. But the federal government is so awash in revenue that it can afford to give tax cuts to the corporate world with abandon. At the same time, community governments must put needed projects and creative initiatives on hold while having to raise taxes just to tread water. Changing this unfortunate reality was a key motivation for me when I decided to move to federal politics and leave behind the exciting world of local government and its emphasis on direct contact with people and their ideas and solutions. I want community democracy to be able to flourish, so I headed to Parliament Hill, apparent fount of our national aspirations but too often the problem rather than the solution.

I desperately worry that at the national level the Canadian government is losing, or giving away, its ability to act on behalf of its citizens.

During those same twenty years I served on Toronto City Council, the federal government signed away significant democratic and sovereign powers in international trade deals like the North American Free Trade Agreement (NAFTA) and through the World Trade Organization. Why would our government do this? The goal was to create a legal environment globally that would make it easier for governments to reduce services while opening the door to their corporate replacements: to shrink the public provision for people's needs while enshrining a legal latticework that would facilitate multinational corporate expansion. Just look at how services like care for seniors, drinking water supply, and even our energy utilities have come under the growing influence of multinational corporations instead of public institutions or community organizations. This transition from a mixed economy to one where privatizations are increasing and public services are sent into tailspins was mandated by trade arrangements that were never approved by democratic processes. A better set of ideas for trade in the context of well-functioning and just democracies needs to be constructed.

During the same period, the federal government and our chartered banks have facilitated the foreign takeover of thousands and thousands of Canadian companies. Think about this: from 1985 to 2002, foreign corporations applied to Industry Canada's Investment Review Division for the takeover of 10,052 Canadian companies. Not a single takeover was rejected. Not one.

Of the new foreign investment spending in Canada during that time, only 3.4 per cent was actually used for new business investment in real machinery or factories or buildings. A staggering 96.6 per cent went for corporate takeovers. Is this really what we mean when we talk about encouraging investment in Canada?

In his new book, Vanishing Country, Mel Hurtig describes this takeover scene and the threats to Canada's independence. He and writers like Linda McQuaig, Maude Barlow, Tony Clarke, and others have chronicled the wholesale sell-out of Canada, and it is very alarming.

Not to put too fine a point on it, my fellow Canadians, but global corporate powers are taking over our country and threatening our independence, and using their friends in federal and provincial governments as their "business partners." Our governments are allowing this takeover through downsizing and privatizing, through the more attractive packaging called public-private partnerships and through abdication of democratic decision making such as we find in the NAFTA's Chapter 11, which blithely gives foreign corporations the right to sue Canadian governments for lost profits if our legislation limits their freedom in Canada. (Canadian companies, however, do not have this right.) As Hurtig says, "The potential for future U.S. corporate claims relating to health care, education, social services, municipal water delivery, federal and provincial resources and cultural policies are real and ominous."

Perhaps the most symbolic example has been the decision of the federal Liberal government, in the fall of 2003, to turn over the Canadian census-taking job to Lockheed Martin, the world's largest munitions manufacturer. Asked why an American multinational was contracted to count Canadians, the hapless minister responsible at the time cited the provisions of trade agreements as the reason this couldn't be prevented. As NDP MP Bill Blaikie put it in yet another of his wonderful contributions to parliamentary debate, "In just which corner of the Pentagon will the Canadian vital statistics be stored?"

All this has to change if Canadians are to be able to create solutions in our own interests. In the end, this is why Canadian independence is important. Politics is about people, not just corporations. Sovereignty lets people decide. And we are losing our sovereignty.

I know that sounds dramatic. But the fact that we are losing our independence ought to concern every Canadian. At the local level, we still have the power to put in place community gardens so people can grow their own food. At the national level, however, our agricultural policies are subject to scrutiny by foreign governments. Community decisions in a whole range of policy areas are based on Canadian values, determined by our democratic processes, as awkward as they can be. International trade arrangements are jeopardizing our ability to make these decisions and are increasingly turning over the direction of our society to huge corporate entities that do not necessarily share our values.

What values? Let's start with the idea that Canadians believe that communities are places where we help one another. We don't just leave people to fend for themselves when it comes to health care, to housing, to education, or to safe communities. That's why Canadians say they are proud of our health care system. In fact, for many of us, it's what we cite first when asked about what makes us different. We also highlight our diversity and the welcome we give to people from everywhere. The diversity and welcome are founded on public services that help people adjust and make their way in a new land while also ensuring that they can preserve as well as celebrate their cultural communities in enduring ways. These public services need support, including financial support. Yet another value is our belief in peace. Canadians support their soldiers abroad by citing their key role in pursuing peace. Blessed are the peacemakers. Ask Canadians what the proudest achievement of 2003 was, and the most frequent answer is that we refused to participate in the invasion of Iraq.

So Canadians have their values, but our recent governments, which have pushed international trade deals that sacrifice democratic rights and accountability and give even more rights to already powerful and profitable multinational corporations, have been out of touch with the Canadian bedrock. We need to confront this challenge directly. We need federal and provincial governments that put the interests of Canadians first. That's why, when I was president of the Federation of Canadian Municipalities (FCM), I created the team of municipalities that challenged the unbridled implementation of the General Agreement on Trade in

Services (GATS). It was going to lock municipalities into a decision-making straitjacket. The most dramatic example happened at the Greater Vancouver Regional Council. To save some money, some councillors were getting ready to agree to a plan by a huge multinational water company to build a treatment plant. But then council discovered that if the voters and their elected representatives were ever unhappy with the private operator and wanted to bring the water system back into the public realm, it would have to pay compensation for lost profits to the multinational corporation and might well have to bid competitively for its own water system against other giant companies. Vancouver sought out the help of the FCM, which just so happened to have a president (me) who was very concerned about the situation. FCM's worries about the implications for local democracies were forcefully expressed to flummoxed federal trade bureaucrats who treated us with patronizing contempt. As a result, municipal opposition to the trade deals grew, along with the protests by community groups and young people in the streets.

Though we have already signed over far too much of our sovereignty, it is not too late to get it back. But the clock is ticking.

In case there are any doubts about urgency, let's remember that Canada has already been forced to pay a penalty to the U.S.-based manufacturer of the toxic gasoline additive MMT. This additive is not permitted in the U.S., but because of the wording of the NAFTA rules, the manufacturer was able to successfully sue Canada for prohibiting its sale. Their case was that Canada had to pay the forgone profits of the company. In other words, when Canadians wanted to prevent a toxic compound from being used here, we had to pay a penalty to the U.S.-based multinational firm! Imagine if something similar happened with hundreds of decisions made by Canadian democracies—from local governments and provinces to the federal government? Well, that's the future we have in store. Unless we act. Unless we transform our politics.

The final approach to politics that I want to present here is about connections. Connections of people and connections of processes and systems. The incarnation of the best politics would point out the great extent to which our economy, our environment, our health, our social safety net, our democracy, and, yes, our independence itself are all connected. How can we even think about building a healthy society without thinking about what we eat, what kind of housing we have, how much income we earn, the quality of the air we breathe? And so on. Every one of these affects the other.

Let me take a simple example. We all want to live in safe neighbourhoods. When we say "safe," that brings up the subject of crime. But a neighbourhood downwind from a polluting, coal-fired generating station is not safe. A community that draws its drinking water from a polluted river is not safe. A one-industry town is not safe. A society that neglects its children will not be a safe place for long.

We all need to think more about how interconnected we are, how much we depend on the environment and on the economic and social systems that weave society's fabric together. That's why in this book, when I talk about public health, for example, I hope you will be thinking not just about prenatal services, preventing the spread of AIDS, or community clinics. We also need to realize that public health is also about the air we breathe, which causes asthma in tens of thousands of people; it's about designing communities and encouraging transportation alternatives so people don't always have to rely on using cars to get around; and it's about eliminating the chemicals in our surroundings that cause cancer in so many people.

We can't think about the economy without thinking about its environmental impacts—and vice versa. The disappearance of some of our fisheries on both the Atlantic and Pacific coasts is a perfect example of the connection between environment and economy. So is the way we generate the energy we need and dispose of the waste we create.

It's all about the choices we make as a community. We can choose to build nuclear power plants and import toxic waste—which we do, by the tonne: between 1987 and 1999, toxic waste imports into Canada grew from 129,476 tonnes to 660,000 tonnes! Or we could retrofit buildings and improve public transit. We can make choices that respect the links between our economy and our environment and society. Or we can carry on making choices that create the appearance of prosperity now, passing on the problems to our children and their children. So what is this alternative vision of the economy interconnected to environment and to society?

It's a vision that reflects the reality of a complex twenty-first-century economy. It recognizes that the fundamental goals of an economy are to simultaneously create financial well-being, improve environmental quality, increase social equity, and promote human development. It is no longer exclusively about making profits. In the business community, this is being called the "Triple Bottom Line" approach: economic progress, environmental protection, and social equity. I believe we should add human development, including human rights for all, from childhood to old age, as a fourth bottom line, as Dr. Trevor Hancock has suggested. Others who have been using this approach for a long time call it sustainable development.

Businesses have always been motivated by the financial bottom line, the last line in the accounting statements, showing the profit or loss for the year. This one-dimensional approach has limited our possibilities. If we added bottom

lines for our social and environmental well-being and measured our success accordingly, we would be making the
connections that need to be considered if our world and our
societies within it are to be sustainable for the long term.
Canada should adopt this approach in its policy making.

A successful twenty-first-century economy will capture
the truth that public and private organizations should be
structured to use capital efficiently, improve environmental
quality, contribute to solving social inequities (not increase
them), create good-quality and safe jobs, practise true corporate responsibility, extend human rights, enhance democracy,
and invest in products and services that people want and
need. These organizations can be large or small, organized as
non-profits, public sector entities, or privately owned firms.
What matters is that we create a context within which all of
us have the opportunity to help meet the Quadruple Bottom
Line goals. This vision celebrates instead of denigrates the
idea that democratically elected and sovereign government
by the people can provide the flexible and purposeful framework for our economy.

What do I mean? Here's a for instance. The public sector
has to provide many essential services because only elected
government has the potential to be directly accountable to
the people. I say "potential" because true accountability
requires a democracy that works well. I join most Canadians
in putting education, health care, key community services
like water and childcare, energy, and some transportation
into this "public sector" category. Moreover, our government
has to invest in social and physical infrastructure, the nuts
and bolts, because elected and engaged governments can
reflect the balance and interconnectedness needed to reflect
the priorities of the public. Someone has to look out for the
common good, challenged, as it almost always is, by private
greed. Who better to take responsibility for this than all of us

together, through our votes and through our engagement in our communities?

This multiple bottom line vision is not mine alone. Such new thinking is, happily, sprouting up here and there, often in places least expected. I am simply acknowledging what is already happening on the ground every day. Consider what Bill Hunter, president and CEO of Alberta-Pacific Forest Industries, one of the largest pulp mills in North America, was quoted in The Globe and Mail, December 1, 2003, as saying: "There is a new wave of CEO thinking about the triple bottom line [profit, environment, and social effects]. It's ethical; it's moral; it's access to raw materials in the long term. Society should demand that and will demand that."

It is a vision that no longer accepts the black-and-white division of the economy into the public and private sectors. It is a vision that has a much more sophisticated view of the economy—it sees it in full colour.

Thinking outside the box, and considering multiple simultaneous benefits, also opens doors to new ways of looking at things. An NDP member, a jeweller in a resource town, told me a few months back about his dad, who used to berate the business leaders of the community when they griped about the workers wanting higher wages. The jeweller told them that when those workers don't have a few dollars left over from their pay packets after necessities, they don't buy jewellery. That means he can't hire sales staff, who then would have shopped in local stores. So giving raises to workers not only helps their quality of life, it spreads economic activity through a community as well.

Quadruple-bottom-line sustainability

- **encourages everyone to live by four "bottom lines" simultaneously;**

- **rewards businesses that truly practise the quadruple bottom line;**
- **penalizes businesses that sacrifice environment, social equity, and human development for personal or institutional greed.**

In short, what differentiates this vision from the status quo is not public versus private: it's the new multiple-bottom-line economy versus the unidimensional greed economy. We can draw some hope from some of the leading businesses and corporations that are beginning to "get it" and are trying to adopt a new approach to measuring corporate success. We can also draw hope from those catalysts for change that emerge from local community democracies.

In fact, the story that is unfolding today is about conflicting visions of collective goals, even conflicting visions of whether there is such a thing as collective goals (versus individual objectives). Parroting eighteenth-century theorists, to many corporate think-tanks, their tribunes, and representatives, the true goal of an economy is only the maximizing of profits. They continuously lobby governments and support political parties to develop and maintain laws and tax policies that affirm their concept of the greed economy. Why? Greed breeds Growth and is therefore Good. These interests don't want to share their power with the rest of us, so they are actually just as happy when other people do not turn out to vote because that way they can continue hoarding their wealth with the help of government policies. Declining democracy is beneficial to this agenda.

The worst nightmare of the greed economy is the quadruple-bottom-line economy—a successful, just, green, and equitable economy in which humanity develops and flourishes in a sustainable equilibrium with nature. A truly balanced economy. Such a positive vision of the economy would redirect the existing huge government subsidies away from the unbridled acquisitive economy toward one in which businesses and government activities are truly focused on all the interconnected bottom lines that make up a harmonious community of communities and ecosystems. If effectively transformed into policy, this vision could unleash our collective capacities, our "commonwealth," through community action, the enhancement of the health of ecosystems and the plants and animals that inhabit them, as well as through innovation and wealth creation.

Much of this book is therefore about relationships, both short term and long term. Thirty million people live in Canada, in different circumstances and facing different obstacles. I've tried to focus on some of the issues that have the greatest impact on the greatest number of people. I raise some issues that, it seems to me, people aren't thinking all that much about. I want to get people thinking. I hope this book stimulates discussion. And I've chosen innovative solutions that are working, to encourage discussion.

No matter how vast a country we occupy, we all live together—a point so obvious that we forget its implications. What we do affects each other in ways that we've lost sight of. People want to be connected—with each other, in their communities, and with a government that they feel is responsive to their concerns and able to help them achieve their goals. Like the issues, people are connected to each other in ways that are both obvious and subtle.

When we talk about the love that connects us to our partners, our parents, and our children, we know what we mean. We want their world to be a better place, somewhere they can live their lives in justice and dignity, a place where their dreams can come true. We hope for a place where they don't suffer hardships, where they grow and prosper, and where the future is a little brighter than the past.

We also talk about loving our country. That's a different kind of passion. But like everything else, the future of our country and the future of the people who live in it depend on each other. Ultimately it's the love of humanity, of all people, that should drive us forward. Canada is a natural breeding ground for such a powerful perspective. That's why all of us have to be involved, making a difference.

Things are beginning to change in Canada, even affecting the holy mantra of the right—tax cuts above everything. Canadians understand that when they stopped being described as citizens and started being defined as taxpayers, they lost something. Canadians understand even better than corporate leaders that there's no free lunch. That you can't keep cutting taxes without paying the price in reduced public services. Canadians understand that high-quality public services—public infrastructure, liveable cities, excellent education and training—are the keys to success in the new economy. It is clear to most Canadians now that, thanks to tax cuts, our governments at the federal, provincial, and municipal level across the country no longer have the resources they need to provide the services that we as Canadians require from our governments, and that Canada needs to secure its future.

From one end of the country to the other, people are rebelling against the mantra that everything government does is bad, and everything the corporate sector does is good. Over and over again, people tell pollsters that they would be prepared to pay taxes to buy improvements in public services. Over and over again, from provincial elections in Saskatchewan, Manitoba, Nova Scotia, New Brunswick, and Ontario to municipal elections in Vancouver, Toronto, and Montreal, to name just a few, voters are rejecting the siren call of tax cuts in favour of a return to responsible, progressive government—government committed to public service.

Politicians who cling to the old tax-cut mantra—like Paul Martin and the Conservative/Alliance amalgam—are stuck in a time warp. And by steadfastly refusing to see the downside of tax cuts and downsizing, they are standing in the way of the new prosperity.

Canadians have been losing faith in their politicians. Election after election, they voted for progressive ideas yet received a doctrinaire dose of precisely the opposite. As Canadians conclude that their voices are not reflected in election results, they drop out, stay home. Voter turnout is falling rapidly. Soon we'll have caught up with the poorest performer among the G-8 countries when it comes to democratic participation—the U.S., with turnout at or below 50 per cent. In this book, I'll touch on some of the ideas that can turn this around, that can rejuvenate our democracy from the federal level to the local community level. From proportional representation in our national elections to enhanced funding and powers for local governments and the community sector, there are solutions that can work.

And just in case someone is holding on to the view that politics does not matter, remember that Canada stayed out of the war in Iraq because people decided they wanted to make a difference. Into the streets they poured, by the thousands, saying no to the war. From the 250,000 people gathered in Montreal to the Grade 7 class I met in Moose Jaw that started the ball rolling for a community protest and anti-war website, Canadians decided to make a difference. And we did!

I had been the leader of the party only for about a month when Jean Chrétien decided to agree with Canadians, and with us, and refuse to join George W. Bush's invasion. It was a highlight of my first year. I knew the New Democratic Party had made a difference on that important issue. And we made a difference because we worked with the peace movements across the country. We set up Advocacy Teams in our caucus. One of them was the Peace and International Development Team, which I asked Alexa McDonough to lead. She has been our Peace Advocate. She and I pulled together the peace groups and said, "How can we help you achieve your goals?" We went to them—a reversal of the usual relationship between political parties and groups in the broader civil society. Non-government organizations (NGOs) are usually compelled to come on bended knee to the politicians. We decided to change that dynamic by going to them first. It's a new way of doing politics, and it's going to be much more effective.

Olivia Chow was the source from whom I shamelessly cribbed the concept for our six caucus "advocates"—for Peace, Health, Diversity, Democracy, Sustainability, and Communities. She had developed the concept and process that supported her invention of the Child and Youth Advocate on Toronto City Council, allowing her to move from opposition to proposition effectively, with many well-informed partners in the community. The result for her was astounding: council began supporting initiatives, including spending, for children and youth. It was so positive. It was about making a difference, not just spouting off for the cameras. This, I thought, was politics as it should be.

We duplicated this kind of work on other key issues with our various Advocacy Teams. In addition to the Women's Caucus, these teams brought the power of positive vision and practical proposals to our daily work: proportional representation, softwood lumber policy, the green car manufacturing strategy, a national pharmacare program, the inquiry into Maher Arar, the "once in a lifetime" bill to help immigrant extended families reunite in Canada, the modernization of marriage laws to give human rights to same sex couples, and much more. In working through the teams, with active partners in the NGO and civil society organizations, our tiny group in the House of Commons was making a difference.

And people across Canada noticed. Many have joined with us in the building project. I welcome you too.

Let's make it a habit to make a difference. That's why politics matters.

Sharing Our World

In summer, when a fisherman in St. John's, Newfoundland, wakes up at dawn and gets ready to head out to sea, the sun has just set within the hour at the western edge of Canada. From east to west, this country spans more than 5,500 kilometres, in six different time zones. North to south, we cover nearly half of the Northern Hemisphere.

Most people in the world love their country. Canadians love their countryside. And although many have never seen the Arctic tundra, an old-growth forest, a teeming marsh, Canadians identify with those landscapes—and with good reason. We are fortunate enough to inhabit some of the most magnificent natural environments in the world. And it is our responsibility to protect this natural heritage.

But instead of being a leader in environmental stewardship, we are actually laggards. Canadians use more energy per capita than almost all other countries—including the United States—and we can't just blame our northern climate. We use significantly more energy per person than the people in Finland or Sweden. We produce the third-highest per capita emissions of carbon dioxide, after the even-more-wasteful U.S. and Australia. More than 750,000 square kilometres of our country are covered by fresh-water lakes and rivers, but every year Canadians are subject to at least six hundred boil-water orders.

Over half of our land area is covered by forests, but each year we cut trees that cover more than 10,000 square kilometres—nearly twice the size of Prince Edward Island—and about 90 per cent of the logging in our boreal forest is clear-cut, causing soil erosion and loss of biodiversity. Solutions such as certified, sustainable logging and the creation of secondary wood-based manufacturing so that we don't just export raw logs and jobs are lagging badly.

When it comes to garbage, we have little to be proud of. Only 15 per cent of the waste we generate is recycled or composted, 5 per cent is incinerated, and 80 per cent of it winds up in landfills. Our national government does little to help change this situation.

On the most important environmental issue of our time, global climate change, Canada has not led the way it should. I attended the worldwide "Conference" of the "Parties" in Bonn, Germany, in the summer of 2001 and was distressed to see the Canadian delegation adopting positions that potentially threatened the very viability of the Kyoto Protocol. The official policy of the Liberal Party, laid out in its 1993 Red Book, called for Canada to improve energy efficiency and increase the use of renewable energies, with the aim of cutting carbon dioxide emissions by 20 per cent from 1988 levels by the year 2005. Instead of meeting these targets, the Liberal government dithered and watched emissions increase over 18 per cent above 1990 levels! We were one of the last countries to ratify the Kyoto Protocol on the reduction of greenhouse gases. And Paul Martin has raised serious doubts about his commitment to the protocol. In December 2003, days before he became prime minister, the press reported that Martin refused to say he would follow through on Canada's Kyoto commitment should the deal die. Instead, according to press reports, he said, "What I have said very clearly is you need a plan to determine whether in fact you can meet those targets....That plan is going to determine our capacity to do so [meet targets], our ability to do so and really what are the very important steps. And we have not yet developed that plan, certainly not to my satisfaction." He's had ten years since making the Red Book commitment to devise a plan to deal with the biggest environmental issue facing our time. To date, the best he can do is complain that no plan has been developed, as if the blame for this lies elsewhere. The federal government is lagging behind the people. Individual Canadians are committed to protecting the environment. In poll after poll, Canadians have said that they consider the environment among their highest priorities, and that they are prepared to spend money to protect it.

As if to demonstrate their level of personal commitment, in communities and neighbourhoods, in households and on farms, Canadians are working hard to improve their own environmental performance. And they're showing that this can be done while at the same time they are enhancing economic activity and strengthening our social relations.

Examples abound of Canadians doing the right thing. As I will describe later, my hometown of Hudson, Quebec, led the way in battling multinational chemical companies to reduce pesticide use. In Halifax and Guelph incredible strides in waste reduction and composting have been made. In Calgary, the city council endorsed the building of a new rapid-transit line extension, and they contracted with a wind-power manufacturer to provide all the electricity needed to run it. In a marketing masterstroke, they call it Ride the Wind. That initiative will get people out of their cars and into public transit; more important, the wind power will reduce carbon dioxide (CO_2) emissions by 26,000 tonnes a year. When you ride Calgary's C-Train, it's like sailing—the wind is pushing you along, with no pollution at all. Now, if Calgary, the oil capital of Canada, can pull this off, anyone can. And there are countless more projects like these that improve our environment.

It's time—well, it's long past time—that we took control

of our environmental future, building on best practices and carving out exciting new approaches to public policy. We have to free local communities to innovate. We should facilitate their exchange of winning ideas. We should be encouraging municipalities to act as catalytic agents for environmental rehabilitation. And we should be applauding those people who walk softly on the planet and rewarding those who create economic opportunity while widening the spaces for nature to thrive.

The country is full of ideas that work. Let's promote them. Let's open our imagination and dare to take new directions. At our recent NDP leadership convention, my friend Pierre Ducasse put it well: "To have the results you have never had, you must do what you have never done."

Renewing our resources

Like a lot of kids these days, especially those who live in cities, our son, Mike, has asthma. When he reached his teens, we were lucky that he could go to camp as a counsellor for a few weeks every summer.

A few years ago, we were looking forward, as always, to the time when he came home. Within a day of his return from the clean air of Northern Ontario, I was standing beside him in an emergency ward while the doctor put the third oxygen mask on his face. His mother, Sally, had experienced this moment many times, too. The smog had brought his asthma to a critical level. It was the most terrifying moment any parent could have.

The doctor looked at me and said, "You're lucky you brought him in here in time." Not long before, a Scarborough teenager, struggling to breathe, was rushed to hospital, but the first emergency ward had been full, and by the time he arrived at a hospital that could care for him, they couldn't save the boy's life. This is not something you forget.

But because we have not acted, the horrors return. When my mom went to the funeral home recently to pick up the ceremonial urn containing my dad's ashes, she saw, in the corner of the director's office, a child's bike. Attempting a light-hearted aside in the awkwardness of the moment, she said, "That's an odd way to commute to work."

"Oh no, Mrs. Layton," soothed the funeral home manager. "The bicycle was the favourite toy of the five-year-old we buried today. He died from asthma only a day after the city's last smog alert."

That story made something burn deep inside me. This is the injustice of pollution, the uncounted cost. A bike leaning against a funeral home director's office wall. A child choking to death. Parents and doctors unable to save him. All because we pollute as we recklessly burn fossil fuels in spite of the public's desire to use existing technologies to do better.

Health Canada reports that every year more than 5,000 Canadians die prematurely as a result of air pollution. Other government estimates put the figure as high as 16,000 a year. In 2000, the Ontario Medical Association estimated that air pollution resulted in 9,800 hospital admissions and 13,000 visits to emergency rooms in that province alone. Most of the fatalities are among children and the elderly, the people whose respiratory systems are the most fragile. The OMA report *Ontario's Air: Years of Stagnation* also notes: "These serious health effects that we are now experiencing in Ontario at current levels of air pollution also have significant economic impacts. Annually, air pollution is estimated to cost Ontario over $1 billion a year from hospital admissions, emergency room visits and absenteeism. When the pain and suffering and loss of life from polluted air are added into these costs, then the total annual economic loss from polluted air was estimated at $10 billion a year."

Needless to say, if we spent just a fraction of that amount addressing the causes of air pollution rather than the health effects caused by it, we would save both lives and money.

Around the world, people have recognized the urgent need to clear the air. This call for action finally resulted in the signing of the Kyoto Protocol in 1997, which set national targets for the reduction of greenhouse gases. Canada's original target was a mere reduction of 6 per cent from 1990 levels. But because the federal government has dithered, our emissions have increased during the past seven years, now over 18 per cent higher than 1990 levels and going up.

THE KYOTO PROTOCOL

Faced with record world temperatures, increasing air pollution, and unusually severe weather, the United Nations created the International Panel on Climate Change (IPCC) in 1988. That panel brought together leading scientists from around the world to study if, how, and why our climate was changing. In that same year, Toronto hosted one of the world's first major scientific conferences on climate change. The Changing Atmosphere Conference called for a 20 per cent reduction from 1988 greenhouse gas emissions by 2005.

Two years later, the IPCC issued its first report, which said that the planet was warming, and that human activity was causing it. The IPCC called for further study.

In 1992, another Earth Summit met in Rio de Janeiro. (The first had been held twenty years earlier, in Stockholm.) This summit resulted in the Rio Convention, which called on nations to stabilize

greenhouse gas emissions at 1990 levels by 2000.
Canada and the United States both agreed to the Rio
Convention, which recognized that developing nations
would be able to increase their emissions.

In 1995, the IPCC issued its second report, now
concluding that the best scientific evidence pointed to
a "discernable human influence on the global climate
system."

In 1997, representatives from more than 160
nations met in Kyoto, Japan, to review new targets for
greenhouse gas emissions. The Kyoto Protocol was
signed, including by Canada and the United States.
The accord set global targets for reduction of 1990
emissions by 5 per cent between 2008 and 2012.
Canada's target was set at a reduction of 6 per cent.
Many poor and developing nations did not have targets set in the first phase because these would have
prevented even modest efforts to improve living conditions, an exclusion supported even by George Bush Sr.

Further meetings were held (in Bonn in 1999,
and The Hague and Ottawa in 2000) to devise more
specific mechanisms for the reduction of emissions.
These meetings failed because the world's leading
nations could not agree on a number of important
issues.

Finally, on July 29, 2001, in Bonn, the meeting I
attended, 180 countries agreed to new rules for implementing the Kyoto Protocol. These rules will become
legally binding only after the protocol is ratified by at
least 55 countries, covering at least 55 per cent of the
emissions from developed nations. Significantly, the
United States and Australia, the countries with the
highest per capita emissions, have refused to ratify.
Most recently, Russia has been equivocating, which

could mean the death of Kyoto and therefore the death of the most significant worldwide collective effort to deal with the earth's biggest environmental challenge. This would be tragic because we know that such international initiatives can work. The Montreal Protocol on CFCs, for example, has helped to reduce our emissions of ozone-depleting chemicals.

The government of Canada ratified the Kyoto Protocol on December 10, 2002, bringing the number of signatories to more than one hundred. (Both the Canadian Alliance and Progressive Conservative parties voted against it.) But with the refusal of the United States and Australia to opt in, the pact is still not in force. It will take Russia's ratification to put the deal over the 55 per cent threshold, and I hope they will decide to come on board. In 2001, Canada's greenhouse gases exceeded 1990 levels by 18.42 per cent. Therefore, for Canada to meet its goal of a 6 per cent reduction from 1990 levels, it must reduce total greenhouse gas emissions by 21 per cent by the year 2012. The terms of the pact allow individual countries to develop their own plans for reducing emissions. With a greater commitment to the use of hydroelectric power and other renewable energy sources, the production of more fuel-efficient vehicles, and modest, practical efforts by corporations and individuals to use less energy, these goals can certainly be achieved.

The Canadian unions whose workers are most likely to be affected by implementation of the Kyoto Protocol—the Communications, Energy & Paperworkers Union, the Canadian Auto Workers, and the Steelworkers Union—all support the Kyoto Protocol.

Yet Kyoto represents only the first step toward

resolving climate change issues. In order to stabilize the earth's carbon cycle, leading scientists worldwide agree that reductions in greenhouse gasses of up to 60 per cent or more will be necessary. According to the IPPC, global greenhouse gas (GHG) emissions will likely rise somewhere between 47 and 164 per cent from 1990 levels by 2100. That means the concentration of GHGs in the atmosphere could approach 1,000 parts per million (ppm) by 2100, compared with about 370 ppm in 2000 and 280 ppm in the preindustrial era. Climate models predict that the global temperature will rise, as a result, in the range of 1.4° to 5.8° Celsius by the year 2100, leading to possibly abrupt, unwanted changes in the earth's physical and biological systems.

Already, say scientists studying biodiversity, numerous changes in the distribution and abundance of species has occurred over the past thirty years, owing to climate change in the past. A recent study published by *Nature* magazine predicts that 15 to 37 per cent of species in the geographical sample studied will be "committed to extinction" under the various climate scenarios.

Reducing greenhouse gas emissions will slow down and reduce damage caused by climate change. Kyoto is only a start. Far more dramatic reductions are required. In order to stabilize GHG emissions at, say, 450 ppm in the atmosphere, human emissions would have to drop below 2000 levels in a few decades and eventually decline to a very small fraction of current emissions.

Such dramatic reductions are doable. A David Suzuki Foundation and Torrie Smith Associates study indicates that Canada can reduce its GHG emissions by almost 50 per cent by 2030, putting the country on a trajectory to reduce emissions even further in the longer term. The study suggests that by a smart use of best available technology and innovative regulatory measures and financing, Canada can dramatically reduce its emissions. And we can begin realizing the huge job potential and cost savings that come from a green economy.

In 1903, petroleum supplied 2 per cent of the world's energy needs. That's just about what the worldwide supply of renewable energy provides today. Thankfully, renewable energy supply is on the rise. Here are just a few examples of how Canadian communities are leading the way in fighting pollution.

Edmonton brought in a Fuel Sense Program and worked with the 1,000 municipal employees who had logged the highest fuel consumption in city vehicles. Employees were trained to drive for better fuel efficiency, and the results worked. Then the program was expanded to the city's transit operators' training program. In one year, fuel consumption was down by 10 to 20 per cent, double the city's original goal. The program also produced savings of $175,000 and lower vehicle emissions. No doubt heath costs from respiratory disease fell, too.

In St. John's, Newfoundland, the city councillors approved plans to renovate their city hall and other municipal buildings, and they paid for the work entirely out of energy savings. They anticipate annual reduced energy costs of $600,000, along with better air quality, improved workplace lighting and comfort, and lower maintenance costs. Far from the economy "suffering," as the opponents of the Kyoto Protocol contend, the economy was enhanced.

Toronto has made an early start. Inspired by the

Changing Atmosphere Conference, the city council approved an emission reduction target of 20 per cent in 1990, the first municipality in the world (along with Hanover, Germany) to do so. In 1991, the council established the Toronto Atmospheric Fund (TAF) to finance community projects to reduce greenhouse gas emissions. Council endowed TAF with $23 million from the proceeds of a profitable sale of property. At about the same time, council established the Office of Energy Efficiency to further spearhead local greenhouse gas reductions.

In 1997, I had the honour of being president of TAF, a position I held until I was elected leader of the federal NDP in January 2003. TAF is the only municipal agency in the world today dedicated to combating global warming, though the model is now being considered by Vancouver and a number of European jurisdictions. TAF-sponsored projects have brought multiple benefits to the city, including cumulative CO_2 emissions reductions of upward of 250,000 tonnes and energy savings in city operations of over $2.7 million annually. (For more about the Toronto Atmospheric Fund, go to www.toronto.ca/taf.)

In 1993, I was involved in bringing together an association of private-sector companies, leaders of construction unions, bankers, municipal agencies, publicly owned energy companies, and community representatives to develop a plan to retrofit building stock in Toronto and save money and energy in the process. We called it the Better Buildings Partnership (BBP). This program is an example of sustainable economics. It creates jobs, helps businesses be more efficient, saves governments and consumers money, makes heating more affordable (especially for low-income people), and reduces pollution—all at the same time.

Here is how the program works. A building owner is offered the possibility of having renovations done, essentially at no cost because the type of work done reduces the building's energy use significantly, thus saving money. For example, insulation, windows, lights, motors, heating, ventilation and cooling systems, and control systems are all upgraded with much more energy-efficient materials and technologies. The energy reductions produce a financial saving that repays over an agreed period of time the cost of the work. Investors are found who are interested in predictable and moderate rates of return to put up the cash. (That's why such a project holds great promise for pension funds.)

Initially, the BBP was a pilot project with a target of retrofitting 2 per cent of all the buildings in Toronto. The pilot exceeded our hopes, and the city decided to expand it and has set a target to retrofit 40 per cent of industrial, commercial, and institutional floorspace in Toronto by 2010. To date, the partnership has retrofitted 32 million square feet of space in 467 buildings, creating 3,800 person years of employment, with a local economic impact of $126 million. At the same time, the owners of those buildings (private and public) reduced their annual operating costs by $19 million and cut CO_2 emissions by 132,000 tonnes a year. Hundreds of workers had good jobs. Buildings were made more energy efficient, which reduced their heating and cooling costs, which in turn produced lower greenhouse gas emissions. (For more information on the Better Buildings Partnership, go to www.toronto.ca/bbp.)

Imagine if cities around the world all pledged themselves to retrofit on such a scale. Work would be created for millions, pollution reduced by huge quantities, and all our buildings—our physical capital—would be in better shape. That's why I've proposed that Canada take the lead and develop a national energy retrofit program, which I'll describe in more detail in Chapter 6.

Another innovative community initiative in Toronto that

will cut pollution, create jobs, and save building owners money is called Deep Lake Water Cooling. Air conditioning is becoming increasingly important as the temperature rises. It's also really rough on the environment. From the huge chilling machines on big buildings to the small noisy air conditioners in home windows, cooling the air uses lots of electricity and heats up the planet. A brilliant engineer by the name of Bob Tamblyn convinced me that we should use the cold water at the bottom of Lake Ontario to cool our buildings instead of burning tonnes of coal to create electricity to power our air conditioners. I was skeptical at first. How could taking cold water from the lake be good for the environment? The trick is to use the cold water in the lake—instead of burning fossil fuels—to chill the air in office buildings. Here's how his proposal works.

Downtown office towers need a constant supply of "coolth" to cool the air that is circulated through the buildings. This is done with heat exchangers, remarkably simple devices that transfer heat from the air to water. Like a furnace in reverse, an exchanger passes warm air over a radiator full of cold water. Thanks to the immutable laws of thermodynamics, heat flows from the hotter to the cooler medium so that the water gets warmer as the air gets cooler. The cooled air is then circulated back through the building, and the warm water is sent off to get cooled again.

And how does this water that just chilled the air get cool again? This is where Lake Ontario comes into the equation. Lake Ontario is very cold—just ask anyone who has tried to swim in it. Because it's so deep, the water at the bottom of the lake is only 4° C. Tamblyn proposed to draw this very cold water through a large pipe into a special facility near Toronto's downtown office towers. There, the lake pipe containing cold water would meet the pipe from the office towers. This large heat exchanger would, once again following thermodynamic principles, transfer the coolness from the water in the lake pipe to the water in the pipe leading back to the office towers, water that would once again cool the air that is circulated through the office towers. And the warmer water from the lake would still be cool enough to be used for municipal drinking water.

The beauty of Deep Lake Water Cooling is that the natural cooling of the lake that takes place during the winter—not the burning of fossil fuels—air conditions our buildings.

The challenge to turn Bob Tamblyn's idea into reality was to convince all kinds of people—from big-building owners to public works officials in several levels of government to environmental groups in the city to politicians at all levels—that replacing polluting air conditioners with environmentally advanced central cooling using cold water as the basic cooling source was technically workable, economically viable, and politically achievable. I have to admit some ideas seem to take a long time to be put into place. The first meeting I convened on this topic, with then councillor Richard Gilbert, was in 1989. Thirteen years later, I stood on a stage with Robert Kennedy Jr. to announce that the project was going ahead on Toronto's waterfront. (To find out more about this, go to www.enwave.com.)

Overall, Toronto has achieved a million-tonne reduction in greenhouse gas emissions from city government operations, helping to bring Canada's biggest city a third of the way toward Kyoto compliance. City government cut its emissions by 42 per cent, helping Toronto achieve a 2 per cent citywide decrease in greenhouse emissions between 1990 and 1998.

Sudbury has announced a joint venture with a private-sector company to study the feasibility of developing at least 50 megawatts of wind power. The project expects to put in place 66 wind turbines, each producing 750 kilowatts, by the end of 2004. That would provide power to about 40 per cent of the city's residents, all of it non-polluting. The city is even considering a wind turbine assembly operation built in the community as a part of the deal.

Sequoia Energy, a company in Victoria, B.C., is negotiating with Manitoba Hydro to build the country's largest wind farm near St. Leon, in central Manitoba. It would produce as much as 100 megawatts of energy, enough to power 40,000 homes. They've been testing the winds for the past year, and working with a renewable energy company from San Diego and a German turbine assembler, they're close to getting the go-ahead. If so, it would generate more electricity than the wind farm in southern Alberta that powers Calgary's light-rail transit. That wind farm produces 75 megawatts, currently Canada's largest.

Believe it or not, few of the components required to build wind turbines are manufactured in Canada. That's why it's easier to import windmills from Europe at a cost of over $1 million for each one, plus $100,000 for each windmill in transportation costs.

And that's why I've been meeting with Bombardier officials and the leadership of the Canadian Auto Workers union. They are considering how we could meet some of the rapidly growing demand for turbines (thousands a year in Canada and the U.S.) by building them here. After all, the arms of wind turbines are like airplane wings set vertically. We know how to build planes in Canada, so let's get going.

Some countries have the national will to make a real effort to counteract global climate change. Denmark already produces 21 per cent of its electrical power by wind generation. (Canada's percentage is less than 1, but increasing.) Today, wind turbines supply electricity to forty million Europeans.

Germany, which has a goal of reducing its carbon emissions by 40 per cent by 2020, is the world's leader in wind generation. In 2003, that nation passed its 2010 goal by producing 12,500 megawatts of wind power. It has done this in part by restructuring its tax system to encourage alternative energy and discourage the use of fossil fuels.

After studying wind resources, Greenpeace and the European Wind Energy Association concluded that our planet's wind-generating potential is twice as great as the entire world demand for electricity projected for 2020. Meanwhile, the cost of generation continues to decline. The Greenpeace–Wind Energy Association study predicts that the average cost per kilowatt hour of wind-generated electricity will drop to 3.4 cents (Canadian) by 2010, and to 2.7 cents by 2020 (from its current 8 to 12 cents per kilowatt hour). In addition to these huge savings, there are no more pollution costs. And once the turbine is paid for, the fuel is free.

Another renewable energy resource that is commercial today is geothermal. Heat pumps tap into the earth's natural temperature, which remains relatively the same throughout the year, to provide both heating and cooling for buildings. In winter, when the ground is warmer than the air, underground pipes pump up the earth's heat to provide warmth. In the summer, when the earth is cooler than the air, the reverse happens. Today there are only 10,000 homes across Canada with geothermal heat pumps—the systems remain fairly expensive. Manitoba and Manitoba Hydro plan to promote installation of the system in 13,000 new homes, including Canada's first entirely geothermal subdivision. While heat pumps use some electricity to operate, they are incredibly efficient when compared with furnaces and air conditioners because they use renewable energy from the earth. Except for Manitoba, governments aren't doing enough to promote this overlooked technology.

One of the other renewable energy sources we should be plugging into is the oldest one available—the sun. Imagine if we could use the immense power of the sun right away rather than the solar energy stored in fossilized hydrocarbons created millions of years ago, the coal, oil, and natural gas we burn today. My dad, a heating and air-conditioning engineer, urged my brothers and me to consider these possibilities thirty years ago. My mom, an avid swimmer, had convinced Dad to put a narrow pool in the backyard so she could get her exercise by swimming lengths. The problem was the weather. The Ottawa River valley is cool for a good part of the spring and summer. If we could heat the pool, said my dad, then Mom could swim longer (and so could we). "What if you boys set up a system so that the pool water could be heated by the sun, keeping the pool swimmable longer each season?" My younger brothers, Rob and Dave, were the inventive ones and produced four systems on the roof for heating the water. We installed all four systems and compared their costs and effectiveness, and a coil of black plastic pipe did the best job: the pool's water was pumped into a tight coil of two-inch-diameter black pipe. The sun heated the black pipe and the heat was transferred to the cooler water inside. The result? We all swam in the pool—from May to October.

None of this surprised Dad, always an innovator. He was, after all, one of those who helped install wind turbines on the Gaspé Peninsula and on P.E.I.'s west coast after the oil crisis in the mid-1970s. His firm also pioneered a strategy for putting water on the huge, flat roofs of industrial buildings so that evaporation, caused by the sun's energy, would cool them in the summer and reduce the need for air conditioners.

The sun's energy can be used to heat water, or it can be used to create electricity. This all came nicely together in a story that the former NDP leader Alexa McDonough told me about the morning after hurricane Juan hit Nova Scotia in the fall of 2003. All the electricity in her neighbourhood was blacked out. That morning, she took a hot shower, a routine practice. Then she thought, Wait a minute! How come I have hot water? I've got no electricity for the hot water tank. The eureka moment came when she realized that her solar hot-water heater system on the roof was still working, of course. It had fully stocked her water tank with cozy H_2O. Wires falling down couldn't stop her solar system from providing needed energy.

We had the same experience at our house during the big summer blackout earlier in the year, because we have a similar heater on our roof.

Two lessons here: first, small-scale and local production of energy is more resilient than huge central energy plants connected through incalculable lengths of transmission wires. Second, renewable energy sources work better during crises.

The technology for producing electricity from solar power is still expensive, but with improvements—and expanding acceptance and use—costs are dropping. Sales of solar photovoltaic cells increased by 21 per cent a year from 1995 to 2001, which means that the costs will likely decrease even faster in the future.

In many villages in developing countries, where connecting to the electrical grid isn't feasible or is too costly, solar cells are already competitive for residential lighting. Families pay for the installation and then draw power essentially for free; the initial investment pays for itself in a couple of years (by not having to pay for kerosene or candles). Almost one-third of the world's population is not connected to an electrical grid. Solar energy is the best source for hundreds of millions of these people. And in these more remote locations, solar power provides a direct health benefit in two ways. First, it provides electricity to refrigerate vaccines and other medicines. Second, it reduces the amount of indoor smoke from open flames, which create numerous health risks. When Olivia and I travelled through the Yunnan province of China a few years ago, we found ourselves choking on that very smoke as seniors stirred the coals and generously poured us hot tea in the dark, dense air. We both thought, There has to be a role in Canada here. Canada could be a leader in developing a multiplicity of solar technologies, but we have no effective national plan.

Even in major urban centres, solar-powered electricity is a source not only for the future, but for today.

Japan is the world's leader in solar photovoltaics—driven by a smart national program of incentives, a desire to reduce their dependence on imported fossil fuels, and a commitment to cleaning up their air. The Japanese government introduced a 70,000 Roofs Program in 1996, subsidizing domestic, solar photovoltaic systems by 50 per cent. In 2001, Japan installed 120 megawatts of new solar generation, and the amount is steadily increasing.

Meanwhile, the United Kingdom has committed to source 10 per cent of its energy supply from renewable energy by 2010. In addition, the U.K. government is providing $728 million to support renewable energy projects to 2006. Funds to support solar energy are administered by the Energy Savings Trust, and some 40,000 photovoltaic panels have been installed on the roofs of U.K. homes.

A few years ago, the electrical utility in Sacramento, California, began to sell solar-electric systems to homeowners. These roof-top systems are connected to the grid, and the utility buys back the electricity they produce. On rainy days and at night the homeowners draw power from the grid, eliminating the need for batteries to store the energy. On sunny days, when the demand for electricity is the greatest (primarily because of air conditioning), the solar panels provide electricity to the utility company, and the consumer reaps the benefit.

A community I visited in the Netherlands, Eindhoven, is powered entirely by such a solar-energy swap. The people there, several thousand of them, reap the benefits of the sun's energy every day.

In 2003 a new apartment building was unveiled in downtown Manhattan that used photovoltaic cells to generate electricity as part of its basic design. Canada could have been a real leader in this area. In 1992 a consortium of Canadian companies came together to design and build the most advanced energy-efficient apartment building in the world. The group included Greg Allen and his partner, Mario Kani, innovative Canadian designers; the Green Catalyst Group, a small business I created to bring together some of the best minds, nationally and internationally, to develop advanced building and community design; Quadrangle Architects; and Windleigh Developments, as well as the Peel Non-Profit Housing Company. Our building was actually constructed in Mississauga and was cited by the United Nations Habitat program as a world leader several years ago.

Greg Allen took this award-winning design and added many new features similar to those found in the Manhattan building. The project would have been built already and housing hundreds in need of affordable accommodation had Mike Harris, the Conservative premier of Ontario at the time, not cancelled this and all other social housing projects in 1995.

Through energy efficiency and renewable energy sources, we can meet most of our power needs. Canada already produces about 58 per cent of its electricity from hydro power.

We could also be a leader in wind, geothermal, and solar energy.

The job-creation potential for green energy production and energy efficiency is enormous. But the reality is that jobs will also be lost in the fossil fuel sector. As a nation, we have a responsibility to ensure the transition to a green energy future is a just one so that all workers and communities share the benefits.

The Communications, Energy and Paperworkers (CEP) union, which represents tens of thousands of energy sector workers in Canada, has developed a comprehensive and innovative strategy that will smooth the way to what they call a just transition to sustainable development. Unlike much of the oil and gas industry, the CEP embraced the ratification of the Kyoto Protocol and rolled up its sleeves to figure out how its members and Canadians could benefit from the opportunities opened up by ratifying Kyoto. This proactive, solutions-based attitude is at the heart of the Just Transition strategy: "solutions to environmental problems address the interests of workers and the communities where they live. The cost of change should be fairly distributed throughout society. No worker should be asked to choose between his/her livelihood or the environment. Sustainable employment must be part of the solution along with a sustainable economy and healthy ecosystems. Just Transition is about planning for these changes in a fair and equitable way." Key elements of the strategy include

- taking advantage of the knowledge and skills that energy sector workers have by involving them in defining the problems and developing solutions to reducing energy use;
- ensuring that government plans for meeting our Kyoto targets include a detailed analysis of employ-

ment impacts as well as funded programs for
employment adjustment;

- requiring employers to include local employment
  adjustment plans, in particular for projects with limited lifespans such as mines;
- making sure communities—and their municipal
  leaders and local labour leaders—are part of any
  local Just Transition plan;
- working with all levels of government, local employers, and various community leaders to develop
  economic strategies that are truly environmentally
  sustainable;
- providing government support for research and
  development into sustainable businesses;
- making education and training available and economically accessible to all those who need them,
  especially workers displaced by job loss in the fossil
  fuel sector.

The good news is that the funding for the Just Transition
strategy could be paid for by using less than half of the federal tax revenue generated by all the new jobs and economic
activity created by a national energy retrofit program (about
$100 million a year over ten years)!

This sort of innovative policy or idea put into practice
would ensure that Canada has a secure energy future. But
our federal government is not willing to listen. It doesn't
want to annoy the big fossil fuel and nuclear power producers. In fact, the situation is worse. Paul Martin's budgets
have provided at least $250 million a year in tax benefits to
these very producers.

Unless you happen to be George W. Bush or a lobbyist
for fossil fuel corporations, chances are pretty good that you
believe climate change is already affecting the planet in

serious ways. Around the world, people are responding to that challenge. They are doing so internationally, with accords like the Kyoto Protocol. They are doing it nationally, with a whole variety of incentives, disincentives, policies, and programs. And people are doing it locally, in dozens of imaginative and practical ways. I know this from the work I've done at the Federation of Canadian Municipalities over the years. I also know this from my work as part of a federal government process to develop a climate change response plan, known as the National Climate Change Process (NCCP). I was privileged to be one of the 400-plus specialists involved in the NCCP. Many good ideas were thoroughly developed and investigated as part of this three-year process. The problem is that our government has not had the political will to move aggressively and take advantage of the opportunities to lead.

- **New electrical capacity brought on line in 2001 by wind power, in megawatts: 6,700**
  By nuclear power: 1,505
- **Potential cost of restarting four mothballed nuclear reactors in Pickering, Ontario, that would supply 2,060 MW of electricity: $4 billion**
  Estimated cost of building 2,667 1 MW wind turbines that would harness roughly 27 per cent of current viable wind energy potential in Canada: $4 billion
- **Number of compact fluorescent lamps in use worldwide in 2001: 1.8 billion**
  Number of coal-fired generation stations not needed because of the energy the lamps saved: 40
- **Percentage change in carbon emissions in the United States between 1990 and 2000: +18.1**
  In Europe: −1.8

If the earth were the size of an apple, our atmosphere would be much thinner than the peel. That's pretty fragile. You think we'd be more careful with it. What this country needs is a comprehensive strategy for energy that captures the possibilities for a truly sustainable approach to energy economics, environment, job-creation potential, and human well-being, all at the same time. I will have more to say about the shape of such a plan when I discuss new prosperity for Canada in Chapter 6.

Waste not, want not

In nature, there is no such thing as waste. Organisms consume; extract what they need for survival, growth, and reproduction; and discharge or leave behind what they cannot use. What remains becomes food for other organisms. This cycle means that someone's waste is another's resource.

But human beings have managed to think our way out of this cycle. The idea of human "domination" of nature—not to mention domination of other humans—combined with an oversimplified, linear idea of "progress" has taken us to new levels of arrogance about our place at the pinnacle of creation. Instead of using our capacity to think about coexistence, to take us to places of humility, inquiry, and wisdom, we have used it to become utterly unparalleled masters of wasteful consumption.

For a magnificent example of this arrogance of waste, we need look no further than my own city, Toronto.

Most Canadians have heard about Toronto's "big idea" to ship a trainload of its garbage every day, six hundred kilometres north, to Kirkland Lake, Ontario. The brilliant scheme involves dumping a million tonnes of green-bagged refuse into the deep lake that was formed in an abandoned hollowed-out iron mine. That lake sits at the top of one of the highest points in the great ridge that runs down the middle of the Canadian Shield. Yes, Toronto looked for the biggest hole it could find, far away from its own territory, so that it could dump garbage into it—with impunity. With impunity, yes, but not free. The city was prepared to pay $50 a tonne, for at least twenty years. That's $1 billion!

Torontonians would pay $1 billion to have someone else live with the stinking pile of garbage generated by Canada's most profligate city. It's no wonder that Canadians think Toronto is arrogant.

The proposed landfill threatened fisheries, border waters between Ontario and Quebec, and First Nations lands and communities, all legitimate and clear reasons for a federal environmental assessment. The Liberals refused to act.

The good news is that once the people of the city learned more about this idea—as a result of a brilliant, community-based coalition of Toronto environmentalists and a farmer/Aboriginal alliance from the North—and once people had half a chance to think about the absurdity of the scheme, the citizens of the city rejected the madness.

How this turnaround happened is a wonderful tale of democracy, toiling as it should—from the grassroots up. The full saga would take a book, or a mini-series, with sequels. Heading the brown team: Texas-based Waste Management, reportedly the largest garbage company in the world—with every high-paid lobbyist in town conscripted to its service. Close at hand were several local politicians, including the former mayor of Toronto Mel Lastman and the chair of the Works Committee. They were joined by business interests from Kirkland Lake, a community devastated by mine closures and struggling with high unemployment.

On the green team: Northerners who relied on the pristine environment—plus dairy farmers, ecological tourism operators, people who drank Adams Ale from the Kirkland

Lake water table, and First Nations communities who relied on traditional fishing and hunting. Add to those groups the Torontonians who wanted to compost their waste, recycle packaging, and reduce garbage—the Toronto Environmental Alliance and a broad network of citizens and groups. I represented the green team on the Works Committee and at city council, with lots of help from then councillor, now mayor, David Miller.

This titanic struggle, as the hockey broadcaster Danny Gallivan used to put it, raged over three years—and near the end we thought we had been beaten, but we were wrong. The green team triumphed. This happened for two reasons.

First, at the last minute, we were able to force a secret document onto the table, which showed that city council bore responsibility for most of the environmental liabilities. Even Mel Lastman admitted that this condition had to be removed. Waste Management withdrew its offer—it was not willing to take the "business risk," as their lawyers put it in a letter.

Second, the green side had gone beyond mere opposition to the folly. We laid out an alternative strategy for treating waste as a resource. The proposal included building recycling plants and large composting factories to turn kitchen and restaurant waste into nutrient-rich soils for gardens and produce energy at the same time. All this was based on the wonderful work of citizens and city councils in Halifax, Guelph, and Edmonton, which had variously put in place these advanced models of waste resource management.

A classic model for merging environmental and economic goals was created by the visionary citizens. First, ask Toronto's citizens to do some work—separate wet kitchen waste and allow the city to collect it in green boxes. Then take this beautiful muck to composting plants right in the city, instead of shipping the putrefying mass to far-off landfill sites or dumps in Canada's North, or down Highway 401 and across the border to Michigan. (There it would rot for decades to come, releasing methane gas into the atmosphere, each molecule doing twenty-one times the damage to the environment as carbon dioxide.) Our plan would use the gases from the composting plants to create energy, reducing our dependence on fossil fuels piped in from thousands of kilometres away. The composted material would be used on gardens in the city, avoiding the need to manufacture and ship artificial fertilizers over great distances to feed the city's plants.

We predicted that Torontonians would embrace these new ideas enthusiastically. Bureaucratic and political naysayers forecast doom and gloom. Yet faced with no mine, no cheap dump, and nothing else to offer, council was forced to implement the citizens' plan. Still, narrow thinking led the bureaucrats to propose a high price for collecting the compost and recycling materials.

That's when some councillors joined me in suggesting a radical idea: let's use market mechanisms to reward good behaviour and have bad behaviour incur a higher price! So council adopted our plan to have compost and recycling collected at no charge at all, while having a high price set for the collection of unsorted bags of garbage beyond a fixed minimum. Do the right thing, and you'll save money!

Lo and behold, Torontonians embraced the plan. Small businesses put out their composting in much greater quantities than the "experts" had predicted. Ditto, citizens. The latest numbers show that people are putting out so much of their waste as sorted, compostable material that the city is having to build or purchase more composting plants, creating even more local jobs.

In Halifax, the city council put in place a new waste-resource management strategy that diverted about 40 per cent of its solid waste through recycling and composting in just its first nine months of operation. The program saves energy, reduces waste sent to a landfill, produces useable compost, reuses materials through recycling, and reduces greenhouse gas emissions by half a megatonne. As a result, Halifax is one of the world's leading cities in solid-waste management. And in that city, citizen power also made it happen.

> In eighteenth-century Boston, when refuse in the streets threatened to impede the flow of traffic and the speed of commerce, the city's first "paved" roads were built: wooden planks placed on top of the garbage. —Molly O'Meara, *Reinventing Cities*

If single-celled organisms can be efficient...

Treating waste once it's produced is one thing; reducing waste in the first place is even more important. It's all about efficiency. Natural ecosystems constantly redefine themselves to become more and more efficient. The best examples I've seen close up are found in the astounding coral reefs. Constant adaptation over millennia produces more efficiency and specialization of the species in the reefs. Nature has been rather wise about such things. In nature, inefficient organisms usually die.

Human activity, at least our economic activity, is different. When humans are inefficient, the short-term consequences sometimes seem "profitable." Usually, the costs of the inefficiencies are passed on to others and all too often do not show up in the accounting books at all. Costs of fraud, of pollution, of unsafe workplaces, of below-poverty wages are all borne by others. The price is paid, but not by the firm. Such profits are false profits!

For example, if pollution goes up the smokestack or down

the river, the costs of addressing the harmful effects never appear on the balance sheet of the offending corporation. People toss old batteries into the "garbage," and they're toted off to landfills, where, years later, the chemicals leak out into the groundwater. The battery producer, the retailer, and the happy flashlight owner never have to pay the price for pollution caused later. However, the price is paid eventually—by future generations, by other organisms with which we share this degraded planet, and by our fellow citizens who get cancer. (Then, as taxpayers, we also pay for the health care costs.) But nowhere do all these costs ever become attached to the producer or seller of the battery or to the flashlight user.

Economists call these uncosted effects "externalities." Well, they're not external at all—they're just outside the profit-and-loss statements of the corporations that produce and sell the goods. When you don't have to pay the costs, you'll carry on with inefficiencies. That's what we do. But that's what we have to stop doing. We can use market principles to address some of these issues, to shift markets and product design. We can also steer product management toward waste reduction and recycling, and create more jobs.

Recycling costs more in the short run, but it creates jobs, in turn generating more economic activity and a more robust community—not to mention a healthier and more efficient one—and, therefore, one more likely to succeed. Polluters always object by saying that if we force them to do these things, they'll have to close down.

Mandating original product manufacturers to take responsibility for the goods they produce is called Extended Producer Responsibility (EPR). A national EPR system in Canada would be a step in the right direction toward reducing and recycling millions of tonnes of material that now becomes "waste."

EPR policy shifts the responsibility upstream, to the producer, away from municipalities and consumers. EPR provides incentives to producers to take environmental considerations into the design of their products. Consequently, the environmental impacts of production are reduced at the initial stage. "Polluter pays" is the underlying principle.

The Netherlands, for example, approved a National Environmental Policy Plan in 1989. Through the plan, companies voluntarily enter into covenants with the government; the provisions of the covenants are then enforceable by law. There are now more than one hundred such covenants in place in the Netherlands.

Dutch industry and government worked together to reduce packaging significantly, eliminate any hazardous materials (e.g., heavy metals) in packaging, prohibit the disposal of packaging in landfills, and develop recycling capacity. They have already exceeded their targets.

A 1998 OECD study of the Dutch experiences concluded that "the competitiveness of the Dutch industry neither increased nor decreased because of the packaging measures, while the competitiveness of the food production sector increased....The available results regarding market trends may indicate that packaging overall has only a marginal role in terms of competitiveness."

That is just one example. At least twenty-eight countries (and the number is growing) have mandatory rules for packaging. Another sixteen have laws that require the recovery of batteries. An increasing number of countries have implemented recycling and EPR laws to deal with the wide variety of electronics—including Switzerland, Taiwan, the Netherlands, Italy, Japan, and Norway—and others have such laws in the works. It makes environmental sense. It also makes economic sense.

IBM has opened a number of Routinization and Materials

Recovery Centers around the world to reclaim computer parts and reuse the electronics. In 1999, these centres processed more than 59,000 tonnes of equipment. Over 90 per cent was recycled; less than 3.7 per cent wound up in landfills.

Nike shoes (whose Asian sweatshops have rightly brought the company a lot of justifiable criticism) created a reuse-a-shoe program, which provides for the recycling of used athletic shoes. The outer rubber sole and inner foam are ground up and reused in running tracks, courts, gym floors, soccer fields, and playgrounds. The cloth upper part is turned into carpet underpadding. The program diverts at least ten million outworn shoes from landfills.

Xerox saves at least $200 million a year by recovering and remanufacturing used copiers.

In the United Kingdom, DuPont, which manufactures the paint used by Ford, is paid by how many cars are painted, not by how much paint they sell. Because DuPont and Ford split the savings, they both have an incentive to develop paint applications that minimize waste from the painting process. DuPont has increased its market competitiveness because other companies don't offer this service.

The materials in used cars themselves have long been recycled; commonly, about 75 per cent of a car, measured by weight, is reused or recycled. Still, in the United States, between ten and eleven million cars are scrapped—every year—and what isn't being recycled represents about 75 per cent of a car, when measured by volume. This includes much of the plastics, fibres, foams, glass, and rubber. In the U.S., it amounts to about 500,000,000 cubic feet of waste headed to the landfill—enough to fill 55,125 garbage trucks!

In Europe, they don't allow this environmental nightmare.

In 1996, German vehicle manufacturers voluntarily accepted responsibility for the return of their cars, no matter how many owners they may have had. It's the "polluter pays" principle: you made it, you take it back. The European Union recently approved what they call the End of Life Vehicle (ELV) Directive. The ELV Directive calls for the recovery of 85 per cent of all automobiles now, and 95 per cent by 2015. And the EU also expects automakers to cut back or eliminate the use of lead, mercury, cadmium, and other toxic metals.

In Canada, no such mandatory legislation is in place, and the automakers are only studying ways to improve the reuse and recycling of materials. But the Canadian Auto Workers (CAW) union is urging Canadian automakers to accept Extended Producer Responsibility. Why? Because the CAW knows it's good for the environment, and because it creates jobs.

The amount of waste that we generate is staggering. But with careful product design, proper corporate responsibility, and increased consumer awareness, we can dramatically reduce the amount of "garbage" we create. And we can learn to reuse and recycle it much more efficiently. If single-celled organisms can be efficient, so can we.

Sustaining Our Lives

Canada is graced with an abundant, and you might think inexhaustible, supply of fresh water. In fact, Canada's lakes and rivers contain enough water to cover our entire country (about ten million square kilometres) to a depth of two metres! That's a lot of water. However, fresh water represents less than 3 per cent of all the world's water, and of that 3 per cent, two-thirds is locked in glaciers and the polar ice caps. The world's available fresh water amounts to less than one-half of 1 per cent of all water or about one teaspoon a litre.

With climate change, glaciers and ice caps are rapidly melting. All of Canada's glaciers south of the territories will have melted by 2030. As a consequence, rivers such as the North and South Saskatchewan and the Bow will lose much of their volume because of depleted headwaters. Bob Hawkesworth, a Calgary alderman, told me that water in the Bow River is expected to be reduced by as much as 40 per cent during late summer, when the Bow River Glacier melts in ten years. This 644-kilometre-long river supplies irrigation water to more than 200,000 hectares and provides drinking water for many communities in southern Alberta.

You might think we'd be more careful with the water we all depend on. Without water, there's no life; without clean water everyone's health is at risk. But, as with air, we are polluting water with little regard for future generations or the big environmental picture. Some analysts predict that water will be the most important economic and environmental issue of the twenty-first century—one that will force dramatic decisions about growing and importing food, put great pressure on water-rich countries like Canada to export their water, and even provoke wars. As a recent World Bank report notes, "Water is vital for life, human life, life of our ecosystem, economic and social well-being. With water resources threatened in so many parts of the globe, and especially in developing countries, life itself is threatened. Action is, therefore, needed worldwide to reverse this trend and to better manage our water."

Worldwide, about two-thirds of all fresh water is used to irrigate crops. To grow a tonne of wheat requires about 1 million litres of water; one kilo of potatoes requires about 1,000 litres of water. Food supply and water supply are inextricably linked. One recent study suggests that in about twenty years, water scarcity will cause annual global losses of 350 million tonnes of food—slightly more than the entire current U.S. grain crop. Water-parched areas will be forced to import foods they once grew because there just won't be enough water to irrigate local crops.

And climate change will likely intensify this devastation. The world's breadbaskets (Canada's prairies, the U.S. southern plains, China's north plain, and India's Punjab region) are expected to suffer from increasingly hot and dry weather, which will significantly reduce their ability to grow staples like grain. In recent years, the world's grain harvest has been declining, partly because of a warmer climate and partly because of water shortages. With worldwide water consumption doubling every twenty years, a crisis of Malthusian proportions may be just around the corner. For some people, the lack of clean water is already a dire fact of everyday life.

Lest you think this is alarmist rhetoric, here are a few dry facts about the state of the world's fresh water:

- **In developing countries, about 80 per cent of all illnesses are water related. Every year, three million** children under the age of five die from diarrhea.

- More than one billion people lack access to safe water, and 2.4 billion—over one in three of the world's population—don't have adequate sanitation facilities.

- Clean water is so scarce in Mexico's maquiladora zones that babies and children are drinking Pepsi and Coca-Cola instead.

- About 90 per cent of the developing world's waste water runs untreated into local rivers and streams.

- Eighty per cent of China's rivers no longer support fish life.

- In 1972, China's Yellow River failed to reach the sea for the first time in thousands of years of recorded history. Since 1985, it has run dry every year.

- Three-quarters of Poland's rivers are so polluted by chemicals, sewage, and agricultural runoff that the water is unfit even for industrial use.

- In 1999, a federal government study revealed that one-third of Ontario's rural wells were contaminated by *E. coli* bacteria—and in that same year, the provincial government dropped testing for *E. coli* from its Drinking Water Surveillance Program. In 2000, the same government dropped the entire pro-gram. In June of that year, seven Ontarians died, and more than two thousand people became seriously ill in Walkerton, Ontario, because of *E. coli* bacteria in their drinking water.

- Every year, Canadians suffer through hundreds of boil-water orders, particularly in rural communities. Canadians should be shocked to learn of polluted waters in hundreds of communities in pristine P.E.I. and in Newfoundland and Labrador, not to mention British Columbia, with its snow-fed streams. Living

in our water-rich country, most Canadians are barely
aware of the consequences. But then, Canada has no
strategy for the stewardship of its fresh water, over
which we have been blessed with custodianship.
Shouldn't this change?

Friends of the Don

Let me return to the Great Lakes for a moment. One in every
three Canadians depends on them for fresh water, and they
constitute a major underpinning of our economy—in agriculture, transportation, industrial uses, and much more.

Pollution is killing this natural habitat and seriously
affecting people's health. Lake sediment contains polychlori-
nated biphenyls (PCBs) about a hundred times higher than
safe levels. Alien invasive species like zebra and quagga mus-
sels, sea lampreys, and more than 150 other non-native
species continue to invade and destroy this environment and
negatively affect the economy. Mercury (the greatest source
of which is atmospheric pollution from coal-fired generating
stations) continues to work its way up the food chain, causing cancer, reproductive and neurological diseases, and
immunological abnormalities; and despite years of efforts to
reduce toxic industrial releases, they are actually increasing.
Health authorities estimated that some 1,000 premature
deaths and at least 40,000 hospitalizations occurred along
the Ontario side of the Detroit River between 1986 and 1992
alone. Evidence of thyroid gland disorders in young women
in Windsor is twice as high as in Ontario as a whole.

While scientists continue to study contamination of the
lakes and issue dire reports about its consequences, we need
a national commitment to take action to restore one of our
most essential natural resources. As always, our environment, our economy, and our health are all intertwined.

Cleaning up the Great Lakes will take time and money, as well as a real international commitment. The International Joint Commission (made up of representatives from Canada and the U.S. to oversee the Great Lakes and the St. Lawrence River) calls upon the governments to "complete the cleanup of all known sites [of major sediment pollution] in the basin by 2025." That goal is achievable. And though cleanup cost would likely reach into the hundreds of millions of dollars, those costs are certainly less than treating generations of sick people or dealing with the destruction of so many industries and jobs.

In 1990, my right hand at city hall, the brilliant Dan Leckie, came into my office with mud on his boots. He was raving about a wonderful citizens' group called Friends of the Don, whose members had been hauling out tires, engine blocks, and other junk from this river that runs through Toronto. (A photography student once developed film in water taken straight out of the Don, just to show the level of chemical contamination.) Before long, working with city councillors Marilyn Churley and Barbara Hall, who represented the neighbourhoods near the Don, we sent out a letter that started with these lines: "Have you ever imagined swimming in the Don River?" We included photos of people swimming in the once-great recreational river half a century before. "Have you ever imagined fishing in the Don River?" More photos, then we asked, "Have you ever imagined *drinking* the water of the Don River?" It flows into Lake Ontario—the source of Toronto's drinking water, so even if people can't imagine it, they're doing it, every day! "If you don't think we're nuts yet," the letter went on, "we are inviting you to a public meeting to talk about the river and how it could be restored."

Being optimists, we prepared for a modest group of ten to twenty people at city hall. When lineups reached down the corridor, we shifted to a larger space. We had touched a nerve. Within two meetings, we had a full committee with vision documents, budgets, proposals, and a step-by-step initiative to bring city council on side. Some councillors wanted to leave all matters relating to the flow of water to the engineers. Incredible as it may seem, the engineers' plans included a $1 billion scheme to put most of the watershed's storm water into large pipes *under* the river valley, exacerbating the problems of stress on the watershed's ecosystems. Fortunately, many citizens with diverse expertise were part of that revitalization movement, and city council accepted our proposals over the objections of some senior bureaucrats and councillors.

In the years since, that community project has involved more than 10,000 volunteers, schoolchildren, local businesses, and service clubs like my own Rotary Club, who have planted about 30,000 native trees, shrubs, and wildflowers. Marshes have been created, which have reduced pollution-laden runoff and brought countless species back to the valley. Cycling and walking trails have opened up the area to tens of thousands of city dwellers. Salmon have been documented in the river for the first time in decades. Pollution sites have been cleaned up. Now songbirds, foxes, muskrats, and herons all make their homes there, right in the heart of the city.

Perhaps best of all, the Bring Back the Don Task Force concept was infectious. Across Canada, a network of watershed councils sprung up, mobilizing citizens, all of them linked to similar groups. Imagine what could have been done had the nation's government rolled up its sleeves and provided significant resources towards these projects.

However, not even an army of dedicated volunteers could restore the 10,000 kilometres of the Great Lakes' shorelines or clean up the thousands of tonnes of contaminated sediment. This is the painful lesson we've learned with the Great Lakes Water Quality Agreement, a Canada-U.S. pact to clean up the Great Lakes. The agreement focuses on so-called Areas of Concerns, some forty-two communities identified as hot spots. Citizens were asked to participate, preparing Remedial Action Plans to clean the areas up. By all accounts, the citizens were keen and excited, and after millions of volunteer hours identified many practical and doable solutions.

During this time a whole network of citizens organized under an umbrella group called Great Lakes United (GLU) to share their solutions, learn from each other, and propose cost-effective and successful cleanups. For years the people of Canada and the U.S. were ready to implement these solutions, but a lack of meaningful federal funding meant solutions were never properly implemented. The International Joint Commission, an independent, joint Canada-U.S. agency, repeatedly criticized the federal government for its funding inaction. But purse strings weren't loosened. What should have been a flow of funds to harness citizen volunteer involvement ended up being a trickle. And as a consequence volunteers became frustrated, disillusioned, and lost interest.

The lesson is clear: the only hope to restore the shores of the Great Lakes is a well-funded international program that involves local communities and volunteer groups who are empowered to speed up and enhance the work of governments.

Once again, while restoration is essential, the key is preventing pollution in the first place. That means stringent controls on the use of agricultural chemicals, further and tough limits on toxic industrial output, reduction of coal-fired generating stations, strict management of the dumping of ballast water from ocean-going ships (which introduces non-native species into the lakes), widespread bans on pesticides for lawns and gardens, and phasing out (then banning) municipal waste incinerators. We don't need more Love Canals. But we do need more people like Lois Marie Gibbs. For those too young to remember, the Love Canal was a chemical dump in Niagara Falls, N.Y., over which a housing subdivision was built. In 1978 the New York State Department of Health declared a state of emergency at Love Canal after a lengthy battle with residents about how to respond to the many health problems facing residents. A huge class-action lawsuit was launched, President Jimmy Carter called the Love Canal a national disaster, and the residents were eventually evacuated. Today, the neighbourhood remains a ghost town.

Had it not been for the courageous efforts of Lois Marie Gibbs, a resident of Love Canal, people might still be living and dying in the Love Canal. A wife and mother who had no previous political or activist experience, Gibbs mobilized her neighbours and turned the injustices facing residents of the Love Canal into a national issue. And thanks to her, an entire generation of grassroots environmental activists have been inspired to fight toxins before they are produced.

Preventing toxic pollution is another reason for governments to enact Extended Producer Responsibility (EPR) legislation—getting manufacturers to eliminate toxins from the waste stream in the first place, and putting the burden on them for all recovery costs associated with their products, even taking their products back when consumers are finished with them.

These strategies should be used across the country, of course, not just in the Great Lakes basin. Groundwater supplies about 90 per cent of rural Canadians with their drinking water—including everyone on Prince Edward Island—and once an aquifer is polluted, it can be decades, or lifetimes, before restoration makes the water safe to drink.

I've already mentioned the hundreds of boil-water orders that Canadians endure every year. Remember, we have *no* federal standards for drinking water quality and *no* federal water policy. Incredible. (Some would use stronger words.)

As usual, innovative solutions to reducing water use and providing clean water are available—and in effect now—around the world.

In developed countries like Canada, addressing the world's shortage of fresh water is often a matter of public education and public policy. People can vastly reduce their own use of water simply with low- or no-cost, common-sense remedies and by changing their habits. Don't let the tap run while you brush your teeth or wash the dishes. Install low-flush toilets and low-flow shower heads. Using soaker hoses or drip systems in your garden saves as much as 80 per cent of the water. People have it in their power to save millions of litres of water every year.

Because of our normally abundant rainfall, about 70 per cent of water used in Canada is for industrial, rather than agricultural, purposes. Significant reductions in water use will mean that industrial practices have to change.

Treating water and pumping it to households is a major part of every urban infrastructure in Canada. But only about 3 per cent of treated water is used for drinking. At great public expense, we bring water up to drinking quality—and use massive amounts of energy to deliver it—only to flush it down toilets (the biggest personal use of water), to wash cars, to cool machinery or heat radiators, and in countless industrial processes. In the summer, about half of our treated water is used on lawns and gardens.

The most effective way we can reduce the costs of water treatment systems—and save water along the way—is to reduce the amount of water that's treated and delivered in the first place. Let's talk about something as basic as a shower head. If you use a low-flow shower head in your home, you save water, and that's good. But, more important than saving water, you also save the energy required to heat the extra water and pump it to your shower. People usually don't think about how much energy is needed to move water from its source to a shower. So imagine carrying several buckets of water from wherever your community draws its potable supply all the way to your bathroom. A pretty good workout, right? That gives you some idea of the energy used by our cities and towns to make sure you've got your shower on demand. If you use half the number of buckets by changing that shower head, half the energy is used. You also save the money used to produce that energy. Your own hydro bill goes down. Great. When an entire city of people use low-flow shower heads, the public utility that generates electricity can save tens of millions of dollars by not having to build extra capacity, not to mention the environmental benefits from less fossil fuel pollution or fewer nuclear power stations

It's in a city's interest to *give* people low-flow shower heads because they save the city money—not to mention that when a city orders a huge number of shower heads, it can get a very good price. It's also in a manufacturer's interests, of course, and lots of jobs can be created.

The brilliant environmentalist Amory Lovins has a strategy for distributing the shower heads to people. He suggests we put a box of them on every street corner with a sign that says "Government Property. Do Not Steal."

So here's a choice. On the one hand, government can spend millions of dollars to build a generating station that pollutes the environment, and use the energy it produces to pump water. The people will use more energy to heat the water for their showers and watch it go down the drain. Alternatively, government can spend less money by buying shower heads from (preferably) a local manufacturer and giving them away, or making shower-head replacement part of a comprehensive water-saving retrofit program for communities, and continue to reap the benefits in reduced energy costs.

The city of Barrie, Ontario, chose such an alternative. Faced with a rapidly growing population and a proposal for a huge new brewery that would need lots of water (to be converted to a very useful purpose!), the city needed to consider the options for additional water supply and treatment. The "logical" way was to build a $41 million addition to its treatment plant and draw more water from Lake Simcoe by constructing a new $27 million intake facility. (This itself would have required a further $20 million to upgrade later.) But Barrie thought outside the box. The city installed low-flush toilets, plus low-flow shower heads and aerator faucets in about 11,000 homes. This option saved about 1,800 cubic metres of water a day, and at least $9.3 million over the construction option. Additional energy savings to homeowners, which came from having to heat less water, amounted to another $18.4 million. On top of that, about 2,400 new jobs were created (800 more than building new facilities), virtually all of them local.

The mayor of Santa Monica, California, told me the recent history of his city's terrible water shortage. It looked as if they could not construct any more homes or apartment buildings because there was no more water. Then they came up with an idea: a new building could be built, but only if it effectively used no water. Not possible? Well, it turned out that the existing wasteful faucets, shower heads, and toilets in the homes and apartments of the good citizens of Santa Monica held the key. Developers wanting to build new units would approach owners of older buildings and ask, "Can we take out your old toilets and faucets and give you free new ones that use less water? Oh, yes, we'll pay for all this work. You'll see the savings on your water bill." Just about everyone said yes. So the new buildings went up at the same time as the installation of the efficient water appliances—with no net increase in water use at all. Bingo!

"Now that's thinking outside the pipe," I told the mayor, and I looked for a similar opportunity in my own city. Not long afterwards, Toronto officials brought forward a plan to expand the city's water treatment plant—and a $1 billion expansion to the sewage treatment plant to provide water for suburban sprawl spreading over the agricultural lands north of the city. Some of us said, "Wait a minute." What would it cost to replace a million old-fashioned, water-wasting toilets (twenty-four litres) with models that used 75 per cent less water (six litres)? And could we also avoid all the new pipes and pumps—and the energy to move water through them and treat it all when it's contaminated? Would it make sense to give Torontonians a million new "thrones," all paid for, plus savings on their energy and water bills? In that way, the water not flushed could be diverted to the suburbs, without a single new pipe or pump. Naturally, the city council's conventional thinkers attacked my million-toilets plan. Some said that the low-flow toilets didn't work or that they usually had to be flushed twice. I pointed out that all of Western Europe was using them, with little social breakdown. But then, water is more scarce there and much more expensive. Here, we are profligate wasters, and water is cheap, so why change? To roars of derision and amusement from the media gallery, I invited the doubting councillors to visit our home and try out three different types of low-flow toilets. (We had no takers. Even Toronto politicians avoid some publicity!)

Nevertheless, the commissioner of the Works Department and a few of his more-creative staff saw potential in the idea. They tried a pilot project, replacing 40,000 toilets in apartment buildings. The owners loved the scheme; they saved water and pumping costs. Tenants liked the new fixtures. And the savings far exceeded the conservative projections. Now the council is involved in a multi-year program to replace almost a million toilets. In addition to the energy savings (from not pumping the extra water), the results include lower demand on the coal-burning electricity plants, thus reducing smog and climate-changing gas emissions. Not only that, but the toilet manufacturing business got a boost, and plumbers installing all the new fixtures were hiring apprentices to keep up with the demand. This is sustainability—the new prosperity.

The Federation of Canadian Municipalities' Green Municipal Funds are advancing this kind of thinking. Now we need an industrial strategy related to water and municipal infrastructure that ties together the opportunities to enhance our economic and environmental capital simultaneously.

I confess that it's fun to see policies of governments, big and small, change for the better, especially when the ideas have been initially laughed off. There's something special about last laughs.

Yet all these innovative conservation ideas flowing from local communities could be undermined if the federal government fails to protect the public ownership of our precious water resource. Thanks to the excellent work of Maude Barlow and the Council of Canadians, people from across the country are becoming aware of how federal inaction may very well result in transnational private corporations controlling and depleting our water supply if nothing is done to stop bulk exports of fresh water. As Barlow eloquently outlined in 2003, giant transnational corporations want to export Canada's fresh water to the rest of the world. They want to turn our precious resource into a commodity to be sold to the highest bidder. Barlow writes: "So far, Canada has not allowed these exports. But if we do allow them it will be impossible to stop them. (Yes, you read correctly: impossible)...Canada is bound by the North American Free Trade Agreement (NAFTA). And the NAFTA deal clearly says that once we start exporting water we cannot stop. Furthermore, Canadian and American corporations will have the actual legal right to come in and buy as much of our lake water as they want—without restriction. And if our government tries to pass a law prohibiting these exports, corporations can sue our government for lost revenue."

Canadians are not sitting idly by as federal government inaction threatens our water. They are telling the federal government in no uncertain terms that water is not like a soft drink. It should not be controlled by private, unaccountable transnational corporations. It should not be bought and sold to make a profit. As Maude Barlow rightly points out, water belongs to the earth and its species and should be declared a basic human right.

- **Litres of water used in a five-minute shower with a regular shower head: 100**
  With a low-flow shower head: 35
- **Litres of water used by the average Canadian household annually: 500,000**

Living machines

The smallest and most natural water treatment plant is literally that—a plant. Wetlands filter water, their vegetation cleans the air, and marshes provide an environment for wildlife. Canada has about a quarter of the world's wetlands, covering about 16 per cent of our country's land area. As with so many other resources, we are truly fortunate.

The small town of Roblin, Manitoba, created its own

engineered wetland. It's only sixteen hectares, but it manages water flow and reduces flooding and chemicals on irrigated land. A water-fowl habitat developed. Nutrients from the wetlands' effluent feeds crops. And the town has potential revenue from the sale of timber, which also benefits from the effluent.

Private companies can make their own wetlands. Around the world, businesses are adopting "living machines"—systems of shallow ponds and plants in greenhouses in which bacteria treat waste water that is then recycled for reuse.

During my time as an environmental consultant with my Green Catalyst Group, I had a chance to work with and promote an astonishing Canadian biologist, John Todd, who developed the living machine concept. The Body Shop, Ben & Jerry's, and a growing number of other companies have installed living machines in their own commercial spaces, treating their own water and reusing it.

Living machines vary in size. The city of Burlington, Vermont, built a living machine that treats 80,000 gallons (300,000 litres) of municipal sewage a day—and the effluent quality far exceeds standards and targets. That living machine produces no odours, and it fits into a residential environment. By the way, the system's greenhouses are manufactured by one of the most advanced firms in the field, located in Hamilton, Ontario. It's yet another Canadian exporter to the United States that's underappreciated in Canada.

As John Todd and I sat in the lush greenhouse environment of the living machine in Frederick, Maryland, he explained: "We don't know exactly why, but the water purification via the natural organism is so complete that it's removing trace elements that cannot be removed by traditional technologies." He laughed and added, "The snails. We think it has something to do with the snails, but we're not sure what!" For me, Todd was underlining the sense of mystery that we—especially decision makers—should have about natural systems. A little humility and respect for nature might serve us well, instead of behaving like "the dominant species."

John Todd made a recent return visit to Toronto from his posting at Harvard University. In a lecture about our waterfront, he outlined a vision for the role that living machines and natural systems could play in a sustainable urban future: we could lead the world using natural processes to purify waters we had polluted and keep ecosystems in better balance. We could rise to the challenge and the opportunity to use waste as a resource, to convert sewage and industrial discharges into useful plants and organisms rather than spreading them on farmland or incinerating them into our atmosphere. Our federal government should embrace and encourage such innovation. But water is such a provincial concern, say the constitutional gurus. A national will would be required. And I believe that Canadians would jump at the chance to become leaders in the world in the preservation and purification of fresh water. There would be no problem establishing that mandate for our national government if only the people of the country were asked. They could become engaged and excited at the prospect, given half a chance. Then the federal government could announce support for a cross-country engagement: strategies and community-based projects, new industrial development, job creation in the field of the enhancement of watercourses, wetlands, moraines, and threatened aquamarine environments. What an exciting prospect. Gary Doer's NDP government in Manitoba recently announced a water initiative that is capturing the imagination of Manitobans. Imagine if the entire country were enlisted in such a challenge. Canadians would excel—doing good things for the whole planet, starting here at home and sharing our knowledge abroad.

From the ground up

If the polluter pays principle applies to the products we manufacture, it should certainly apply to the cleanup of toxic chemicals that corporations leave in our soil.

Contaminated industrial lands litter our cities. These sites, called brownfields, total about 30,000 in Canada. In many situations they pose enormous health hazards, and cleanup costs are often very expensive. All too often, the companies that contaminated that land take no responsibility for cleaning up the mess they've left behind. Area residents suffer the health consequences; taxpayers suffer the economic consequences. However, as recently as October 2003, in a case brought by Quebec against Imperial Oil, the Supreme Court of Canada upheld the right of provincial governments to sue corporations based on the principle of polluter pays. This landmark case makes clear that corporations are liable for the messes they leave behind.

Ironically, most brownfields are now valuable real estate and on strategically located places near downtowns or along rivers or waterfronts. Once located on industrial lands that were formerly on the periphery of smaller cities, they are now, because of urban growth, close to downtown areas. These days, corporations seriously consider cleaning up brownfields, especially when limits on liability and taxpayer subsidies can be negotiated.

Cities are often interested in these projects for several good reasons. They create tens of thousands of jobs, add millions of dollars in property tax, revitalize neighbourhoods, allow for planned communities or facilities, reduce urban sprawl, and rehabilitate toxic or waste land, thereby reducing or eliminating the health hazard. Canada has many success stories of rehabilitated brownfields.

False Creek, in Vancouver, is an early example. Begun in

the 1970s on thirty-two hectares of decaying industrial land, False Creek, created on the designing table with the participation of city planners, became a benchmark for new communities. This planned community now provides housing for mixed ages and incomes, both market and non-market, with co-operatives and condominiums, rental and ownership.

The Moncton Shops Project in New Brunswick is another. For nearly a century, the soils on the 115-hectare site had been polluted by industrial contaminants from Canadian National Railways' repair shops. This site, when restored, will comprise 44 hectares of recreational area (including ten baseball diamonds, two football fields, and four soccer fields), a sportsplex with four NHL-sized hockey rinks, 26 hectares of residential units, and 24 hectares for a business and technology park. By the time it is finished—construction is expected to last about ten years—the project will have created about 2,100 person years of employment. An additional 5,000 permanent jobs are anticipated in the business and technology park, and the potential property tax base is almost $9 million a year.

In Montreal, more than 485 hectares of former Canadian Pacific Railway lands are being rehabilitated, and in Voisey's Bay, Argentia, in Newfoundland and Labrador, 3,600 hectares of an earlier military base are also being cleaned up for industrial and commercial use. Dozens of smaller projects are under way across the country.

However, brownfield redevelopment requires careful planning and thorough cleanup. The residential community of Lynnview Ridge, in Calgary, illustrates why.

For fifty years, Imperial Oil operated a refinery on the site. That closed down in the 1970s, and the land was later rezoned for residential use. Now, two-thirds of the property's soil has lead levels several times higher than the allowable provincial guideline of 140 parts per million—and dust in Lynnview homes has lead levels up to ten times higher than homes elsewhere in Calgary. In 2001, Imperial Oil offered owners a buyout package of 120 per cent of the homes' market value. To date, about 135 of the 160 homeowners have accepted the deal.

Imperial Oil says the lead comes from topsoil brought onto the site after they closed down by a development company that no longer exists. The Alberta government and the Lynnview homeowners aren't buying that story. The government sued Imperial Oil and won its case. Imperial Oil has appealed. Meanwhile, the remaining residents worry about their health and watch the ongoing legal battle with dismay.

Although local and provincial initiatives are a good start, we must do better. As the National Roundtable on Environment and Economy (NRTEE) has been suggesting for a while, it's time the government of Canada, steward to a magnificent land, took a leadership role in cleaning up brownfields. In May 2002, the NRTEE convened a taskforce, with the FCM as one of its members, and produced important recommendations on how to deal with brownfields. These included changing the federal tax system to remove disincentives to redevelopment, expanding Canada Mortgage and Housing Corporation's mandate so that they can provide mortgage insurance to qualified sites, providing grants to municipal governments to fund brownfield redevelopment, and creating a revolving loan fund for brownfield redevelopment.

As I found out during my years at the FCM, leadership is not hard to find in local communities on this issue, but a significant investment fund needs to be created nationally to stimulate action and capture a share of the benefits of remediation of polluted sites over the long term. Canadians want to invest in making their country a better place, if only their government would enlist their support and create the investment vehicles to do so. Revolving funds and investment bonds designed to achieve such exciting goals as cleaning up and restoring polluted sites in cities to useful purposes are exactly the kinds of investments that Canadians, their pension funds, and their governments should be encouraged to make. And as a 2003 David Suzuki Foundation report notes, brownfield redevelopment would help solve another problem that concerns Canadians: urban sprawl. It was heartening to encounter a reference to contaminated sites in the 2004 federal budget, which allocated funds for cleanup. Our diligence will be required to ensure that this will become a reality.

Even though many brownfield rehabilitation projects are worthy and successful, an important lesson remains: we must be far more careful about soil contamination before it happens. We need strict standards to regulate the use and discharge of pollutants because many contaminants remain in the soil for centuries. The legacy of contaminated industrial sites endures long after the corporations have moved on or died out, affecting the health of people and the environment. We also need strict enforcement of those standards—and in an era when governments have reduced government services, eliminated inspectors, and cut back enforcement, we must demand accountability. As conservative governments clamour for "less government" and "business-friendly" environments, the consequences will have to be paid, sooner or later. And should our lack of oversight, and foresight—let alone the reckless behaviour of governments and corporations—be dumped on future generations?

As Henry David Thoreau is often quoted, "What good is a house if you don't have a decent planet to put it on?"

Last time I checked, ours was the only planet we've got to live on. Relocation opportunities are limited. Imaginative people, working with far-sighted governments, both local and national, are creating ways to protect our planet and stimulate our economy. It's time Canada took a leadership role.

Asphalt is the land's last crop

Protecting what you've got is a lot easier than reclaiming what you've had. This is especially true of Canada's agricultural land.

Only about 7 per cent of Canada's land can be reasonably used for farming. Prime agricultural land (what we call Class 1) makes up less than one-half of 1 per cent of the total—and over half of that land is in Southern Ontario. On a clear day (and there are still a few!) from the top of the CN Tower in Toronto, a person can see about one-third of the best food-producing land in Canada—and this terrain is subject to the most rapidly rising population and prone to the worst kinds of urban sprawl.

We are losing our best agricultural land fast. Once it's gone, it's almost impossible to reclaim. As one wag put it, "Asphalt is the land's last crop." Ontario now loses about one square kilometre of prime agricultural land *every day*. In the past thirty years, urban uses across Canada have eaten up about 6,000 square kilometres of dependable agricultural land. Picture the whole of Prince Edward Island built on and paved over.

Not only is agricultural land being squandered, but the number of farms in Canada is declining as well. Since 1941, we have lost about two-thirds of our farms. Correspondingly, the average size of a farm has grown about 2.5 times. Traditional family farms are disappearing, and the number of larger farms is increasing.

In British Columbia, agriculture occupies less than 5 per cent of the province's territory, but it provides food for over half the province's people. Employment in B.C.'s farms and food processing industries tops 200,000, and the agricultural sector contributes $2.2 billion to the provincial economy. Realizing the importance of protecting its food-producing land, B.C.'s NDP government in the mid-1970s created what's known as the Agricultural Land Reserve, setting aside areas almost exclusively for agricultural purposes. (Land can be withdrawn from the ALR, but it's not an easy process.) Quebec's Commission de protection du territoire agricole du Québec has similar objectives enshrined in law. We need the federal government to support agriculture near cities. Agriculture Canada should have programs that help farmers adapt to markets on their doorstep.

In the 1990s, another NDP government in B.C. directed a portion of its gasoline tax revenue to Vancouver, with the stipulation that the city put restrictions on land use. This sensible solution provided funding and agricultural land protection at the same time.

Just as the provinces can do smart things to protect agricultural land, so could the federal government. For instance, Ottawa could work with provinces to tie infrastructure funding to the control of urban sprawl, assisting provinces to create ways of keeping farmland in farmers' hands. Smart federal funding for municipal infrastructure can help achieve national goals like preventing sprawl, thus preserving vital agricultural lands.

We're losing those lands and farmers, but there are remedies.

Food security

Like all elected politicians, I receive my share of politely indignant proposals telling me what to do. But a letter I received in 1985 kept nettling me.

It was addressed jointly to me and to my (then) new partner, Olivia Chow, who had just been elected to the Toronto School Board, representing the same downtown ward that I did on city council. It came from Dr. Cyril Greenland, a professor of sociology at the University of Toronto and a constituent to boot. The essence of his letter: too many thousands of children were going to school hungry, and we needed to address that issue.

"Mr. Layton," he said, "you are the new chair of Toronto's Board of Health. Ms. Chow, you are the school trustee for downtown, where there are many hungry kids. You two should propose a program to feed kids in schools, not just in Toronto but across Ontario."

Over lunch, Olivia and I had a long chat about the idea. What would it cost? How could it be delivered? Later, we turned on the computer and sketched a plan to provide every child in Ontario's school system with one hot nutritious meal every day. With funding of roughly $1 a day for each child plus some set-up costs, our plan totalled $180 million. Given the size of the provincial budget, and considering the health and educational benefits that would flow in the long term, this was not an impossible number.

On the day before Christmas, we had tea with Professor Greenland at his kitchen table. He helped us with the details of the concept, and he emphasized the importance of feeding every child every day. "Surely this is a responsibility of a well-functioning society," he said. He was right.

After checking our calculations and our facts, Olivia and I simultaneously presented the idea to the Toronto School Board and the Board of Health. A key to bringing the idea into reality was the mobilization of community groups in support, and they quickly lined up behind the plan. Both boards were energized by the idea—and they supported it. Of course, provincial funds would be required because local governments are chronically starved for cash, so we sent the proposal and our appeal to the Ontario Liberal government of the day. Sadly, they ignored it.

Despite that, the city initiated pilot projects with its own funding, and gradually they grew. Today, 65,000 Toronto kids benefit every day from nutritious snacks and meals. Governments, the private sector, and parents all provide funding for the program.

It's time Canada had a national school meal program like every other OECD country, including the U.S. School meal programs do a lot more than just feed kids:

- They provide a head start for kids from low-income families who might otherwise have their learning interrupted by hunger or be involved in misbehaviour.
- They cut health care costs, especially those associated with childhood obesity, by making sure all our kids, even those from middle-class families whose parents might be squeezed for time, get good food inside them.
- They support our farmers by providing a large local market for local foods.
- They educate our students about our agricultural system, how composting works, and how food preparation differs across cultures.
- They create local jobs for micro-processors and for short-order cooks.

Let's start helping our kids—and ourselves too!

The most fundamental of human rights

According to the United Nations Food and Agricultural Organization (FAO), more than 800 million people in the world go hungry every single day. Most of them are children. That's a daily tragedy, but the real disgrace is that the world already grows enough food to feed them.

FAO director general Jacques Diouf writes, "We do not have the excuse that we cannot grow enough or that we do not know enough about how to eliminate hunger. What remains to be proven is that we care enough, that our expressions of concern...are more than rhetoric, that we will no longer accept and ignore the suffering of 840 million hungry people in the world or the daily death toll of 25,000 victims of hunger and poverty." Diouf calls on us to ensure that people have "the most fundamental of human rights—the right to food that is essential to their very survival and existence."

- **Percentage of Ontario farms that were family owned in 1976: 91**
  In 1996: 57
- **Number of people in the world who suffer from malnutrition as a result of hunger: at least 1.2 billion**
- **Number who suffer from malnutrition as a result of overconsumption: at least 1.2 billion**

Many factors "explain" the world's failure to provide people with access to food. In the developing world, armed conflict, unequal land distribution, and natural disasters are among the most prevalent reasons. But so-called market forces are often the underlying cause.

A study released in the fall of 2003 showed that over three-quarters of a million Canadians use food banks in an average month. The 482 food banks that participated in the study (there are 639 food banks in Canada) distributed about 3.2 million kilograms of food and about 2.3 million meals a month. Children make up 39 per cent of the recipients.

In 1989, Ed Broadbent—on his final day in Parliament as leader of the NDP—called on the House of Commons to work toward the elimination of child poverty in Canada by 2000. (At the time of writing, let me share my hope that Ed will be back in the House of Commons very soon!) His resolution passed unanimously. Today, more children—almost 1.1 million—are living in poverty in Canada than were in 1989. More children are homeless. More children go hungry. More children are being denied a decent future.

The reasons for their poverty vary—and are almost always surmountable. However, the consequences are clear. Growing up in poverty puts children at risk—of physical, social, and psychological damage; of leaving them more susceptible to disease; of making them less resilient to stress and more prone to anxiety and aggression; of inhibiting their ability to learn at school and increasing the likelihood that they will drop out.

The interconnections between feeding people properly, improving health, reducing poverty—and economic growth—are direct. Right-wing politicians and economists have been telling us for years that the way to stimulate the economy is to cut taxes, when what we really should be doing is making sure that everybody has enough to eat.

But food security is not a worry only to those people who have to wonder where their next meal might come from. Food security is everybody's concern. If overfishing, changes to the environment, pollution, and habitat destruction deplete the world's supply of fish, that's everyone's problem. When the world's breadbaskets are affected, it's an issue for all of us. As more and more crops are being genetically modified by multinational corporations (which own and control these new life forms)—and we don't know how they will affect people—everyone's food security is at risk. Big cities usually have only about three days' supply of food. If, for some reason, food cannot be delivered every day, a city's residents will soon run out. When the power went out during August 2003 across much of eastern North America, refrigeration and freezers didn't work—and that became everyone's problem. So food security isn't only a poverty issue, it's a people issue.

War, however, constitutes the biggest threat to food security. War prevents people from growing food—and receiving it—and the dislocation of families and communities only makes a bad situation worse. Land mines—millions of them—make both farming and grazing animals either impossible or enormously dangerous, and minefields often cut people off from their access to water and food.

Now consider the impact of drought and flood, climate change, loss of habitat, soil erosion, depletion or chemical contamination of aquifers, or salt-water intrusion preventing irrigation, and so on. Environmental changes that affect our ability to grow food, catch fish, or raise livestock all directly affect our food security.

In case you thought that was all, there's one more main threat. Oddly enough, it's cheap food itself. The number of farmers in Canada is incredibly small, relative to our population—only 1 per cent of Canadians are classified as farm operators. Obviously, many more work in the food sector (it's one of our largest employers), but only one person in a hundred is a full-time farmer. And when farmers can't earn enough money growing the food we all eat, they get out of the business. Between 1996 and 2001, the already minuscule number of Canadian farmers dropped by over 10 per cent. Cheap food drives down the number of people who can afford to make a living by farming. (Our agricultural critic, NDP MP Dick Proctor, has told me of many farm families throughout rural Canada who have family members working off the farm, often in a nearby city, to earn enough money to keep the farm going. They're literally helping keep our food cheap with their off-farm work.)

Subsidies also constitute a major factor in keeping food prices artificially low. Developed countries use subsidies to support their export-oriented agricultural industry. In the European Union, for example, the average cow gets about a $3-a-day subsidy—which, incidentally, is about three times what a typical person in India is likely to earn. Farm subsidies in the developed world, including Canada, put great pressure on farmers in developing countries; agricultural subsidies are a serious bone of contention between first- and third-world nations.

Subsidies are a rich country's way to prop up their farmers' incomes (and others in the agricultural industry) while keeping prices low. Tariffs are a poor country's solution—they cost the taxpayer nothing and protect local markets for local producers. And so international trade is at an impasse: developed countries with their large subsidies argue for the elimination of tariffs; developing countries argue for the elimination of first-world subsidies so their farmers can compete.

But when it comes to playing the subsidy game, Canada knows it can't match U.S. subsidies. Which means that the price paid by Canadian consumers for U.S.-grown food is often cheaper than for food grown at home. Once again, this affects our own farmers' ability to earn an income, and it affects our food security.

Not only that, but it reduces Canadians' capacity to grow our own food. If Canadian farmers can't compete with crops grown in the U.S.—and dumped in the Canadian market (permitted under the trade deals we've already signed)—they may be forced out of the business of growing food for local consumers. Amazingly, most of the Grade A fruit grown in British Columbia's Okanagan Valley, for example, is sold in Europe, while B.C. consumers buy fruit grown in Washington, Oregon, and California. Needless to say, this makes no environmental sense—and it reduces our own food security.

Finally, there's the issue of our retail food industry. In this business area, Canada has the highest degree of corporate concentration of any country in the world. Two retailers drive this sector of the economy: Loblaws and Sobeys. These retailers squeeze the food processors, who, in turn, squeeze the farmers. It's a nasty chain. Food, which we all might agree is a fairly important national issue, has the least government intervention of any major sector of our economy. Is there a national program to produce food? No. A national program to distribute food? No. A national program to sell food? No. Though we understand the need for a public presence in making and selling electricity, for instance, we have no Food Canada to offset the power of corporations, no public ownership, and very little regulation. And, as we have seen in other sectors, when provincial governments cut back their own agricultural inspections, everyone's food security suffers further when we wind up with tainted meat or other products.

Our marketing boards (of eggs, milk, and wheat) control the supply or guarantee a price to the farmer. Yet we learn that these efficient, public, and accountable regulatory bodies are also on the trade chopping block, with the federal government sharpening the axe. The U.S. government keeps attacking the Canadian Wheat Board in international legal proceedings, even though it loses every time. Preserving our right to organize the sale of wheat through the co-operative mechanism of our Canadian Wheat Board is important not just for farmers and agricultural sustainability with subsidies required but also as a matter of Canadian sovereignty. Canada should be helping other countries develop similar mechanisms.

Healthy cities

Is there anything new we can do about the emerging food problem? Yes. However, I found out while chairing Toronto's Board of Health that the good model comes from England—not Canada.

In 1990, the board was implementing the concept of a "healthy city," talking with people from every kind of interest group in Toronto. It took no time for food to emerge as a common issue for people of all interests, in every community. We asked ourselves, Where in the world are people dealing with food issues in cities? The answer resided in the Greater London Council, where a Citizens' Food Council had been set up as a catalyst. A Ryerson social work professor, Marvyn Novik, had come back to Toronto from London, raving about how successful it was. In no time, we pulled together community groups, farmers, local grocers, and environmental and public health groups to learn about the idea. Soon afterwards, I had a proposal to take to city council.

Opponents of the idea slammed our plans, saying, "Food is not municipal business!" Or "Why should we have farmers telling us what to do?" Fortunately, the 1988 municipal election had produced a majority of council seats for our allies, and we were able to establish Canada's first urban Food Policy Council.

A key lesson I learned from my friend and right hand at City Hall, Dan Leckie, was this: "Always create a structure with a clear goal, made up of diverse constituencies who believe in that common goal." We put that lesson in place with the Food Policy Council. Finally, farmers from the Toronto environs were dealing directly with consumers. As a result, many ideas emerged that had economic, environmental, and social benefits. As I'll show below, two of the best were the "green box" organic foods delivered to homes directly from the farm by the farmer, with no giant retail middleman scraping off the biggest share of the revenue; and the community kitchen concept, where a large kitchen is built or commandeered and used by community members to prepare collective meals to cater community events, to share cooking knowledge across cultures, and to feed the neighbourhood kids.

The Toronto Food Policy Council (TFPC) has been the only organization of its kind in Canada for years, though other communities have adopted similar ideas lately. It's a municipal food initiative, with a small number of staff paid by the city's Department of Public Health but under citizen control—and with a big mandate. The city recognizes the importance of food to public health and pays its staff to be advocates on behalf of food security, and they bring together people concerned with all aspects of food questions. Participants include farmers, retailers (big and small), nutritionists, urban growers, environmentalists, schoolchildren, transportation industry members, churches, local food agencies and processors, specialists in community and economic development, composters, and others.

The TFPC lobbied to have access to food and other food security issues incorporated in Toronto's official Community Charter, and the city is now one of a select few across the country that has made this kind of commitment.

May they rust in peace

As leader of the NDP, I get to travel a lot, but not as much as the average American grape. It clocks more than 3,400 kilometres to get from vine to table. A tomato travels almost as far. Food travel tends to be costly, bad for the food value of the grape and the tomato, and no good at all for the environment. The fundamental requirements for food security include a Canada-wide food strategy, regional food programs, and local food initiatives. Those aren't contradictory objectives.

Local food initiatives are springing up all over the country—even in cities. In China's eighteen largest cities, for example, vegetables grown right there supply 90 per cent of the residents' needs. Fortunately, we're starting to do the same thing in Canada. People are realizing that they can grow their own food in community gardens and on the rooftops of apartment buildings. (Growing food on an urban roof has the side benefits of insulating the building from heat and cold, thus lowering energy costs, and of storing rainwater and keeping it out of the storm-water sewage system.) Backyard vegetable gardens—and why not in the front yard, too?—are becoming common, as people realize that they can replace grass with something they can eat, while letting their air-polluting lawn mowers rust in peace. Psychiatric patients at a mental health facility in Toronto are growing vegetables in a garden, and their caregivers call it the best therapy available.

Of course, the food grown in yards and community gardens doesn't have to be for personal use; it can supply an urban market hungry for fresh produce. Local markets are popping up like crocuses, providing revenue for growers and good food for consumers.

Brilliant regional programs linking urban dwellers with nearby farmers are also on the increase across Canada. Two of the best are Farm Folk/City Folk in B.C.'s Lower Mainland, and FoodShare in Toronto. These ventures bring together farmers and consumers with a range of services that put local food on the table, and they help keep the farmers farming.

In Quebec, Équiterre (from the French words for "equity" and "earth") is a not-for-profit organization dedicated to promoting ecological, socially just choices through action, education, and research from a standpoint that embraces social justice, economic solidarity, and the defence of the environment. As part of its program, Équiterre promotes local agriculture and about fifty farms across Quebec, helping new farmers to get started.

Through these programs, city dwellers can buy into community-supported agriculture programs, purchasing in advance a share of a farmer's crop. Farmers get the cash in the spring, when their costs are highest, and their customers get a weekly box of fresh local produce throughout the growing season. Or consumers can opt into buying clubs and other bulk-purchasing programs, pooling resources and paying wholesale prices for their fruit and vegetables. Urban communities are also finding more and more locations for farmers' markets, drawing the farmers directly into the cities' and towns' neighbourhoods.

Innovative strategies like these provide for more than just good nutrition. They reduce the environmental impact of long-distance transportation. They spur local economic growth—not only among farmers but also among local processors and retailers. These projects help ensure that agricultural land remains in active agricultural use, with the farmers assured an income and a market, so they're not obliged to sell out to suburb-hungry land developers. In other words, these strategies help preserve the family farm. They also make consumers more aware of where their food comes from and how it's grown. And, of course, they increase our food security and our food safety.

Organizations like Farm Folk/City Folk and FoodShare operate with very little government support or input. Municipal governments across the country ought to be facilitating programs like these, because good food makes good sense. The FCM Sustainable Communities project is moving in this direction, especially with its exchanges of best practices. More federal assistance and encouragement could move these solutions along more quickly.

In Finland not long ago, I picked a gorgeous tomato from a four-metre vine in a vast greenhouse. The farmer and her team proudly pointed to the pipes coming all the way to the greenhouse from a factory-like building on the horizon. That factory produced wood products; wood chips and sawdust were burned in a co-generation system that supplied electricity for both the factory and the neighbouring town; and the waste heat from that process was used to create hot water that was piped to the greenhouse. (In many similar factories in Canada, the heat goes up the stack.)

Finland went a step further. The relatively cool combustion gases from the co-generation plant contained lots of carbon dioxide. And guess what tomato plants need? Yes, that nasty greenhouse gas. So the factory in Finland pipes the CO_2 right into the greenhouse, creating a super-charged atmosphere for photosynthesis and tomato growth. Without this inventive approach, tomatoes would have to be trucked long distances from southern Europe. So the pollution from those heavy trucks is avoided. There is no wasted heat—it is used to create warmth at no cost. And the greenhouse gases become, instead, tomatoes for the Finns to eat.

For five years I tried to get such a co-generation plant and greenhouse onto Toronto's parklands—with Toronto Hydro in partnership with the Boralex cardboard recycling plant. But the provincial governments of Mike Harris and Ernie Eves so badly mauled Ontario's electricity system that, as of this writing, the project has been unable to proceed. Perhaps Premier Dalton McGuinty will see the light, and to give him an incentive, the federal government should begin redirecting some of the hundreds of millions of dollars it currently gives to subsidize fossil fuel production toward innovative businesses that want to improve energy efficiency through co-generation. Perhaps it's time for a national green energy greenhouse initiative: locally produced Canadian tomatoes in the winter without genetic modification or toxic chemicals, grown with the help of waste heat and CO_2. Get out the mayonnaise!

Playing Russian roulette

Have you ever met kids who didn't play with their food? Me neither. That's why all parents have to tell their children not to do it. Now, however, we aren't just saying that to our kids, we're telling it to big corporations: "Don't play with our food."

I don't really know the consequences of eating a tomato that's been modified with fish genes. I do know that the soybeans that go into my tofu are almost certain to have been genetically modified, but I don't know how that's likely to affect me. Or you. And that's precisely the problem. We just don't know—and neither does anyone else. Genetic modification is like playing global Russian roulette: fish genes in the tomato may be an empty chamber. Maybe they're not. I'd rather not find out the hard way.

We do know some things about genetic modification. Corporations want it so they can control a farmer's use of seeds. A corporation cannot patent a native seed, but it can patent a genetically modified seed—and corporations can (and have) sued farmers for planting seeds of GM crops they've saved from a previous season. Corporations can also deliberately use what they call "terminator technology" so the plant produces sterile seeds, thus making sure that new crops can't be grown from them. Corporations can also modify crops by building in compatibility with their own particular brand of chemical fertilizers, herbicides, and pesticides, compelling the farmer to buy them and no other. No wonder "designer genes" is the term du jour. And the long-distance shipping, already mentioned, is another motivational factor behind the genetic modification of food: corporations like Monsanto are looking for ways to get food to ripen after it's been harvested, so it won't spoil during shipment.

At the 1992 Rio Summit on the Environment, most of the

world's nations agreed to adopt what's become known as the Precautionary Principle about the environment. It applies on many fronts, but perhaps none more important than the genetic modification of food. Principle 15 of the Rio Declaration says, "In order to protect the environment, the precautionary approach shall be widely applied by States according to their capabilities. Where there are threats of serious or irreversible damage, lack of full scientific certainty shall not be used as a reason for postponing cost-effective measures to prevent environmental degradation."

"Lack of full scientific certainty" undoubtedly applies in the case of GM foods—and we should never go down that road until we learn where it leads us.

Labelling of all GM foods should be mandatory. Consumers must have the right to know what they're buying and eating. The corporate line—"It's too complicated to label products"—is pathetically self-serving. (Labelling food must be far easier than splicing genes.) Once more, Europe has led the way on the labelling and restricting of GM foods. However, the most dramatic illustration of resistance to GM crops can be found in Africa. There, in Zimbabwe, Mozambique, and Zambia, countries with many desperately hungry people, officials have refused shipments of genetically modified U.S. corn.

At the same time, and behind the closed doors of the World Bank and World Trade Organization, corporate moguls are working out the rights of investors to do whatever they want. The intent of these two powerful organizations is to fashion trade agreements that suit corporations and maximize profits, even at the expense of human health, the viability of the ecosystem, and every human being's right to decent food.

It's clear to me that the citizens of the world are increasingly saying no to GM crops and trade agreements designed to maximize profits at the expense of human health and ecosystem viability. The federal government must ban GM wheat. Farmers, environmentalists, and communities all agree on this one. How can Canada be the breadbasket of the world if our bread is dangerous? As well, the federal government should put a moratorium on all new genetically engineered crops, and it should change current regulations so that biotech corporations must prove new technology is environmentally safe before it is used. Not only would these measures protect Canadian markets oversees, but they would mean Canada could once again be a leader in environmental protection.

If ever we should err on the side of caution, it's with what we eat. Don't play with our food.

The web of life

Scientists call the complex, interconnected relationship among living things "the web of life." This very apt phrase symbolizes the way things are woven together to sustain one another. Through millions of years of history, human beings have worked their way to the top of the food chain, and now we seem intent on gobbling up our precious resources with the same insatiable appetite we have brought to our conquest of every other living thing on earth.

There is another way, a way that respects the other forms of life with which we share this planet—and that respects the planet itself. We can live and flourish without destroying our atmosphere, polluting our waters, and fouling our land. We can support each other—environmentally, economically, and ethically—in ways that are sustainable. Let's construct Canada's way forward by building according to these principles.

[CHAPTER 4]

A Caring Society

Every year since 1990, the United Nations has published a Human Development Report, assessing trends and measuring countries in a wide variety of categories. Part of that report is its Human Development Index, which compares societies for their citizens' life expectancy, educational attainment, and standard of living. The index serves as a kind of international report card.

For many years, Canada stood at the top of the list. Our "human development," though not without fault, was the best in the world as measured by these standards—and we were proud of that, particularly former prime minister Jean Chrétien, who endlessly boasted of our standing.

But we've begun to slip, and the Liberals have stopped talking about this index. In 2001, when Canada fell to third place, I gave a speech in which I said, "Mimic those below us and we'll end up there." I explained the point: "If we keep trying to copy the conservative policies of the U.S., which is in sixth spot, rather than copy the social democratic policies of Norway, which is above us, we will continue to fall." And that has been exactly the case. We hung on to third place in 2002, but in 2003 Canada fell to eighth, the lowest we have ever been. Since data inevitably lag behind reality, we are likely still declining.

Years of cuts in public services and community investment have started to unravel the fabric of our society. We need to reconsider that direction, review its consequences, and once again assess the value we place on what the UN calls human development. Sweden, which has moved from sixth place in 1999 to third in 2003, should be our model.

In Canada, our defining social program, the one most val-ued by its citizens, is public health care. Indeed, Canadians consider universal access to health care a right of citizenship, not a privilege only for those who can afford it. Public health care is one of our principal measures of a caring society—a system that is not supposed to be based on income, age, eth-nicity, or place of residence. At least that's the idea.

Olivia emigrated from Hong Kong with her parents. When asked why her family chose Canada rather than the U.S., she says, "We chose Canada because we wanted to be a part of a society that put the health of everyone ahead of everything else and made sure that everyone had equal access to taking care of their health needs." Frankly, like a lot of people, I had sort of taken our health system for granted until Olivia said that. You know, maybe we should listen more to recent immigrants to this country about what is good here.

> The real measure of a nation is the quality of its
> national life, what it does for the least fortunate of its
> citizens and the opportunities it provides for its youth
> to live useful and meaningful lives. —Tommy Douglas

Our country hasn't always stood for the principle that everyone should have equal access to care for their health needs. Older Saskatchewan farmers still grimly remember the desperation on the prairies caused by the Depression and the dust bowl of the mid-1930s. They know, too, that out of poverty and deprivation often come community will and cre-ativity. In my campaign for leadership of the NDP, I had a chance to talk with some Saskatchewan farmers in rural Legion halls.

"We weren't allowed to meet in halls like this back then," one of them told me. "No. We were branded revolutionaries and Communists and shut out. All we knew was that we had to co-operate with each other to make it through the hard times, and that we needed our government to respond to our basic needs."

"We needed health care for our families, and electricity, like they had in the cities," another man explained. Those farmers had to create financial institutions to lend them money fairly, instead of suffering under the brutal hand of the Eastern banks. If community halls were closed to them, they met in fields, standing in circles out in the cold—little cells that organized the Cooperative Commonwealth Federation (CCF). Their dream was a political party that would give expression to those needs.

"It was Tommy Douglas, the young preacher from Weyburn, who showed us how. He just wouldn't accept the reality of families with their sick children waiting on hospital steps, unable to afford care and being refused."

PUBLIC HEALTH CARE COMES TO NORTH AMERICA

Through sheer determination, the voters of Saskatchewan elected on June 15, 1944, the first social-democratic government in North America, the CCF, forerunner of the New Democratic Party. Tommy Douglas was the party's leader.

Douglas's government introduced free hospital care; free medical, hospital, and dental services for old-age pensioners; and free cancer, tuberculosis, and mental illness treatment. The government also lowered the voting age to eighteen, introduced the first public auto insurance plan in North America, began a government-operated air ambulance service, and issued a Bill of Rights. Saskatchewan's civil servants became the first in the country to receive bargaining rights, and the government created a provincial bus line, timber board, power corporation, and airline. And that was in just their first term of office.

On January 1, 1947, the Saskatchewan government launched its Hospital Insurance Plan, the first public hospital coverage in North America. Family premiums were $10 a year. The very first patient to benefit showed up at Regina General Hospital shortly after midnight on New Year's Day. She delivered a healthy baby.

For ten years, Saskatchewan funded its hospital coverage without a dime from the federal government, even though Ottawa had been promising a national program since 1919. Canadians had to wait until 1957 for a partial national health care plan, the Hospital Insurance and Diagnostic Services Act.

In 1961, the Saskatchewan government passed legislation that provided universal medical coverage in doctors' offices. The province's doctors and the Canadian Medical Association launched bitter opposition, but the people's support for public medicine was simply too great. In 1962, the doctors backed down. In 1966, the federal government finally passed the Medical Care Act, bringing health care coverage to all Canadians, thanks to the determination of the CCF/NDP and the people of Saskatchewan.

A wise person once said that you can accomplish much if you don't need to take credit for it. In politics, that's a tough pill to swallow. If the New Democratic Party, the successor to the CCF, shies away from trumpeting its role in creating Canada's medicare system, people who think it should be protected or expanded might not realize how it came about. Modesty is tough when you're trying to convince people to support your party because of what its team has been able to produce in response to real needs.

You'll even find other parties claiming the credit. Still, Paul Martin goes too far. In the fall of 2003, he compared himself to Tommy Douglas by suggesting that Douglas was a fiscal conservative with a social conscience. (Douglas would have succinctly dismissed such a self-congratulatory opinion.) The public health system that Tommy brought to life, Paul Martin critically wounded—by billions of dollars in cuts. The federal government used to pay 50 per cent of the hospital and physician costs of provincial health care. Under Martin, federal transfers were drastically chopped unilaterally without consultation.

To be sure, Tommy Douglas ran Saskatchewan finances with care. After all, the poor—as the Saskatchewan population was in those days—tend to husband their resources better than the rich. But rather than do what Paul Martin did as Liberal finance minister—slash programs in order to spend $100 billion on tax cuts—Douglas used a system of fair taxation to fund programs. Paying taxes is like buying insurance; they ensure that health, education, and electricity (among other services) are available to everyone. Tommy once said to a young Lorne Nystrom, the NDP's longest-serving MP, who used to drive with him on long, straight roads of rural Saskatchewan, "If they don't trust you at the till, they won't trust you at the ballot box." Unfortunately, we're fighting to save the services Tommy built.

Protecting Canada's health care system

During his ten-year tenure as prime minister, Jean Chrétien appointed a string of Liberal hacks, hangers-on, backroom boys, wealthy contributors, and corporate buddies to an array of agencies, boards, commissions—and the Senate.

Yet he had the courage, in April 2001, to appoint former Saskatchewan NDP premier Roy Romanow to head the commission on the future of Canada's health care system. The report of the Romanow Commission, appropriately titled *Building on Values*, could serve Canadians well for a long time to come. It is thoughtful, comprehensive, and visionary, on a par with the 1964 report of Mr. Justice Emmett Hall that helped create public health care in Canada. While key recommendations by Judge Hall were implemented, we're still waiting for substantive action to realize Romanow's recommendations.

Much has been written about the Romanow Report, so I won't go into great detail here. It's available on the Internet at www.healthcarecommission.ca. I do, however, want to make a few comments and summarize some of Romanow's conclusions and recommendations because they point the way to a more accessible, affordable, and workable health care system. He wrote:

> Early in my mandate, I challenged those advocating radical solutions for reforming health care—user fees, medical savings accounts, de-listing services, greater privatization, a parallel private system—to come forward with evidence that these approaches would improve and strengthen our health care system. *The evidence has not been forthcoming* [emphasis in original]. I have also carefully explored the experiences of other jurisdictions with co-payment models and with public-private partnerships, and have found these lacking. There is no evidence these solutions will deliver better or cheaper care, or improve access (except, perhaps, for those who can afford to pay for care out of their own pockets). More to the point, the principles on which these solutions rest cannot be

reconciled with the values at the heart of medicare or with the tenets of the Canada Health Act that Canadians overwhelmingly support.

Amen. Privatized services, parallel systems, user fees, co-payments and the like all have no place in a universal, public, accessible health care system. They betray the fundamental Canadian values that gave birth to this special national protection. In November 2003, a report called *Funding Hospital Infrastructure: Why P3s Don't Work, and What Will*, was issued by five well-respected and senior economists, including the former director of audit operations for the auditor general. Their report exposed the fact that the latest fad in hospital privatization—the so-called public-private partnership (P3) approach—is not only at least 10 per cent more expensive than the public system Canadians have valued but that it also lacks accountability. They concluded that Ontario would be ill-advised to proceed with plans by its former Conservative government to allow the privatization of two hospitals. That's good advice.

The Romanow Report also recognizes that our system is now seriously underfunded. Though some provincial governments can be faulted, the main culprit in the crisis is the federal government, which seriously cut its funding between 1977 and 2000. Is that because we can't afford our health care system? No. Public spending on health care increased by about one-third between 1985 and 2000, but that represents an increase of only 0.8 per cent of our gross domestic product. The major amputation in federal funding came during the period when Paul Martin, as minister of finance, declared that reductions in transfers (to the provinces) were essential to eliminate the deficit. However, when surplus funds built up in Ottawa's coffers, he and the prime minister chose to cut taxes of the well-to-do and corporations—rather than restore their investments in health care.

And let's not forget that when people talk about reducing spending on health care, they mean reducing *public* spending. That doesn't make health care any less expensive; it only shifts the burden to the bank accounts of individual Canadians, many of whom will be unable to pay. Many people cannot afford the medications that their physicians prescribe, so they increasingly go without. Again, that is a denial of the universality principle.

As well, projections of costs of health care into the future show that the financial demands will grow over time. These should be funded with a step-by-step strategy based on the actuarial analysis of the needs into the future. Right now, without these, Canadians are asked just to "trust the government." Such trust has not been well placed recently, that's for sure. We don't need more studies and waffling. We need clear and decisive action and the political will to ensure it.

Romanow recommended "the establishment of a minimum threshold for federal funding," and recommended $15.3 billion in new spending over the next three years. This requirement is only a fraction of the massive tax cuts instituted by Paul Martin. Canadians could have had both modest tax cuts and fully funded health care, but that choice has not been made. It should be.

It's worth quoting one more section of the report at length:

> We also need to renovate our concept of medicare and adapt it to today's realities. In the early days, medicare could be summarized in two words: hospitals and doctors. That was fine for the time, but it is not sufficient for the 21st century. Despite the tremendous changes over the past 40 years, medicare still is largely

organized around hospitals and doctors. Today, however, home care is an increasingly critical element of our health system, as day surgery has replaced the procedures that once took weeks of convalescence in hospital. Drugs, once a small portion of total health costs, are now escalating and among the highest costs in the system. The expense associated with some drug therapies or of providing extended home care for a seriously ill family member can be financially devastating. It can bankrupt a family. This is incompatible with the philosophy and values upon which medicare was built. It must be changed. I am therefore recommending that home care be recognized as a publicly insured service under medicare and that, as a priority, new funds be invested to establish a national platform for home care services. I am also recommending the creation of a national drug strategy, including a catastrophic drug insurance program to protect Canadian families.

Cuts by the federal government in health care funding over the past ten years have eroded the federal ability to enforce the Canada Health Act and display leadership in health care reform. This became abundantly clear when the federal government failed to prevent Alberta from establishing a private hospital, in violation of the Canada Health Act. Perhaps we shouldn't be surprised given that many of Paul Martin's staff were former corporate lobbyists employed by health privatizers.

Despite the federal cuts, overall government health care spending in Canada has averaged a 2.5 to 3 per cent per capita per annum increase since the 1970s. These increases had to be borne by the provinces and have created much of the "fiscal disequilibrium" often referred to, and rightly so, by our premiers. It is true, however, that key issues in health care have as much to do with new ideas as with money.

A national drug strategy and community health care delivery

Canadians now spend more on drugs than on doctors. The average family spends over $1,200 a year on prescription drugs, yet 27 per cent of Canadians have no drug coverage. Families that can't afford prescription drugs just go without them.

In the past ten years, drug companies in Canada had a phenomenal 41 per cent rate of return on average every year. Svend Robinson, MP and the Community Health Advocate in our federal caucus, has been citing this statistic from an in-depth academic study out of Quebec, by Léo-Paul Lauzon and Marc Hasbani, during his current campaign for pharmacare in Canada. During those ten years, drug costs to governments in Canada have gone up by 87 per cent.

Some also suggest that drug cost increases are at least in part driven by the propensity of doctors to prescribe expensive new drugs when old ones work as well or better.

Have you noticed all those drug company ads on TV telling you how much money they spend on research? I wish they would actually spend the money on research, because in the past decade drug companies spent three times more on marketing than on research. When I see the ads featuring the middle-aged guy having a heart attack and his family in a panic, urging people to get their blood cholesterol tested, I wonder about those people who can't afford the medication they might have to take if their cholesterol turns out to be high. If you're not on a medical plan, how do you afford the thousands of dollars a year for Lipitor or similar medications? I guess you just tough it out and hope your heart doesn't stop. And eat celery. But not laced with pesticides! (You don't want prostate cancer, because the drugs for that are even more expensive.)

It also burns me to know that some families that need puffers for their kids can't afford them. While my son was covered by my drug plan at work, the hundreds of dollars we spent every month on puffers so Mike could breathe were paid for. But what about the kids in his class whose parents don't have a drug plan and live on a modest income? Don't they have the same right to breathe as my son has? Or does the right to breathe now depend on income in Canada?

- **Number of drugs licensed for human use by Health Canada: 5,200**
  Number of "essential drugs" classified by the World Health Organization: 326
- **Amount Canadians spent on prescription drugs in 2002: $12 billion**
  Increase from 2001: $1.2 billion
- **Number of new nurses who could have been hired with the increase alone: 24,000**
- **Number of children who live in poverty in Canada: 1.1 million**

The Liberal government did nothing to reverse the Mulroney government's doubling of drug companies' patent protection (from ten to twenty years), while it slashed the budget for the Health Protection Branch by 50 per cent. Now called the Health Products and Food Branch, it allows the minister of health to enforce legislation and regulations that ensure our food, drugs, and health products are safe. The time has come to put in place a national pharmacare plan so that all Canadians have coverage for the prescription drugs they need. We need to roll back patent protection to ten years and introduce, as Romanow suggests, a national drug agency to make bulk purchases, keeping the price down by forcing the multinational manufacturers to compete for Canadians' business and ensuring availability to all Canadians. The NDP government in Saskatchewan purchases generic drugs in bulk for its drug plan. They estimate that it saved the province and consumers about $6 million in 2002–03.

And do we need all these high-tech drugs in the first place? After I started living in a Chinese family, I had a chance to discover the magic of 10,000 years of Chinese medical wisdom. Our drug companies may do double-blind tests on drugs for several years, but when herbs and plants have been studied for some 400 generations, you'd think we might accord these traditional medical approaches some level of credibility. It's true that the teas brewed by my mother-in-law taste terrible, but that's not reason enough to avoid them. We put the traditional Chinese medicine retail industry through every kind of hoop imaginable rather than facilitating the availability of traditional medicine. Some of the best medication ideas that work come to our country from immigrants who know all about them. Let's remove the barriers and start learning about what we have available right in our own communities.

Finally, Romanow demonstrates how much better it would be to shift health services out of hospitals and into smaller clinics, which would become models for a new delivery of a wide range of health care services. The network of clinics in Quebec (CLSCs—Centres locaux de services communautaires) and the Group Health Centre in Sault Ste. Marie, Ontario, are good examples.

Sault Ste. Marie's clinic houses about 350 health care professionals, including nurse practitioners, doctors, dieticians, physical therapists, speech pathologists, and others.

The nurse practitioners can provide 85 per cent of primary care. Patient records are computerized, and doctors can consult electronic records from their offices. The clinic provides day surgery, lab analysis, a women's health centre, cardiology, physiotherapy, vision and auditory care, diabetes prevention, and many other services. Patients and health care professionals benefit from the comprehensive services and team approach; the community benefits from health promotion and disease prevention. It's also less expensive for the government because fewer tests are repeated, and there is less overlap in care. Quebec's CLSCs provide similar services; many also provide social services.

Again, as the Romanow report suggests, "We must transform our health care 'system' from one in which a multitude of participants, working in silos [isolation], focus primarily on managing illness, to one in which they work collaboratively to deliver a seamless, integrated array of services to Canadians, from prevention and promotion to primary care, to hospital, community, mental health, home and end-of-life care."

Community clinics have other benefits. They provide faster access to care for small ailments and reduce reliance on expensive emergency rooms. They also build positive relationships and strengthen neighbourhoods in powerful ways. Having had a small hand in creating the new Regent Park Community Health Centre, I've seen the benefits up close. Here was a group of mothers, living in the lowest-income community of the whole city of Toronto, deciding that the health of their families needed better attention. They came from every continent, so services had to be available in many languages. Cultural traditions concerning health had to be infused into the daily operations, otherwise depressed and isolated women and their families suffered. The low income of the community produced predators—drug dealers and

pimps who looked for weakness to attack—giving the neighbourhood a bad reputation. Fighting back, mothers such as
Betty Hubbard, and young people like her daughter, Joy
Henderson, struck out to create a positive image and reality
for the community. Targeting an abandoned and polluted gas
station on the tough corner of Parliament and Dundas East,
their committee surmounted every conceivable hurdle to
realize their vision. As the local councillor, I witnessed their
tenacity and honesty as we canvassed the surrounding
houses to tackle the inevitable opposition that arose from a
few homeowners just next door who imagined the worst.
Even more difficult was securing the support of bureaucrats.
Thankfully, the NDP government in Ontario had brought the
financial commitments sufficiently far along that later the
Mike Harris Conservatives could not stop the momentum.
The building, designed by the award-winning architect Jack
Diamond and his team, has breathed new life into the community. This initiative became the epicentre of energy for the
complete redevelopment and revitalization of the entire
Regent Park housing project, now moving forward amid opti-
mism and hope.

Good ideas in health promotion, disease prevention, and
health care can be combined. When I chaired the Toronto
Board of Health in 1986, Dr. Jack Lee, the brilliant director
of the city's dental program, proposed that we cancel all the
dental nurse checkups being performed on every child, every
year, in the school system. "Why would we want to do that?"
I challenged. He had a better idea, he said, about how our
dental health funds could be used. As he began to outline the
plan, I could already imagine the hostile public meetings of
parents protesting the firing of their beloved school dental
nurse. Dr. Lee told me that our nurses found essentially two
kinds of children in the schools. First, there were those
whose teeth were in relatively good shape. Their parents had

dental insurance at their workplaces, so their kids' teeth were already being checked regularly in private dentists' offices, and needed dental work was done right away. Then there were the kids whose teeth were never checked except in the schools. Their parents had lower incomes and had no dental insurance. When the nurses detected problems and sent notes to the parents recommending dental work that needed to be done by a dentist, many of the families simply couldn't afford it. The children's teeth would then, sure enough, be worse when the dental nurse next visited the school.

Dr. Lee and I discussed his idea. Cancel all the nurses' dental visits. Then set up full dental clinics with nurses and dentists, and have all the work done free. Teach dental health in schools, and publicize the clinics in the schools so that all parents would know to get their kids' teeth checked regularly, and set up a tracking system to ensure this was done. Encourage those with insurance to go to their private dentists. Those without coverage would be urged to go to the clinics. All this, Lee demonstrated, could be accomplished within the same budget, but the overall level of dental health of Toronto's children would go up significantly because needless duplication of checkups would be eliminated, and kids who couldn't afford follow-up care would get it. This would also reduce more serious health care costs later. As well, kids with all their teeth are happier and have a better chance to succeed in all areas of life. I enlisted the support of Olivia, who happened to have been recently elected to the school board in Toronto. She was delighted about the way the plan addressed inequalities in our city, especially for lower-income immigrant families. After all, she had lived that experience herself.

Sure enough, the public meetings were tough. The idea was so persuasive, though, that by the end of the process, opposition was reduced, even though it had been unsuccessfully fanned by some city councillors looking to be local heroes. Both council and the school board approved the dramatic changes, adding the idea that poor seniors could also use the services of the clinics. A decade later, when the megacity of Toronto was created, the newly merged suburbs demanded the same services that the old inner city had had. Olivia, by then a city councillor, successfully pushed the plan to expand the service through the budget processes.

Smiles on more kids' faces! Low-income seniors with decent dental health, many delighted with their dentures! Who would have imagined that governments could produce that?

As the experience of such clinics suggests, many health care services can be provided by health care professionals other than doctors—in particular, Canada's well-trained nurses. Yet in the recent passion to reduce health care expenditures, we have eliminated hundreds of nursing positions, and overworked registered and licensed practical nurses are at the point of exhaustion and burnout.

Recent statistics show that Canada had 897 nurses for every 100,000 people. Finland had 2,162; Norway 1,840; and Ireland 1,593. Many other countries also had higher ratios than Canada's. But young, potential nurses here are well aware of the stressful, underpaid positions that our nurses are forced to endure, and enrolment in nursing schools is declining. (Between 1990 and 2000, admissions to basic-entry registered nursing programs dropped by 28 per cent.) The high number of anticipated retirements is another major factor—the number of nurses who provide long-term care, for example, is expected to decline by about 20 per cent by 2006. A 1997 study estimated a shortage of 69,000 nurses by 2011; other studies confirm these figures. To illustrate present shortages, the physician who heads one of the larger non-profit Chinese seniors' nursing homes in Canada told me that his biggest problem is finding experienced nurses to staff the new beds being opened.

Following the release of his film *Bowling for Columbine*, at the Toronto International Film Festival in 2002, the maverick filmmaker Michael Moore held a press conference. He said, "You Canadians actually think that everyone, no matter who you are or the size of your wallet, has the right to high-quality health care from the moment you're born until you die. Everyone! We don't have that idea in the USA!"

He's right, of course. Canadians do have that idea. And we're going to keep it. And we're going make sure we keep it real—with Roy Romanow's report.

Public health versus the medical model

In 1886, after having achieved justifiable and lasting fame in the Crimean War, Florence Nightingale was asked to open a children's hospital in London. The world's most famous nurse refused. She knew that the most important factors in improving children's health were not to be found in hospitals but in their communities. What hospital could adequately treat the young boys forced to crawl on their bellies into wet, airless coal seams and to work there for fourteen or sixteen hours a day? What doctor could repair their lungs? What nurse could restore their health?

The same coal dug by boys and men was used to heat people's homes, and the smoke that polluted their homes and their neighbourhoods caused innumerable respiratory diseases. Their diets were poor, their hours of work incredibly long, and the sanitation in their cities was a horror.

Florence Nightingale knew then—as we are finally catching on to now—that the most important factors in achieving a healthy population are not, strictly speaking, "medical." They are social, environmental, and economic. (The "medical model" is about the delivery of health care. The "public health model" is about improving overall health and preventing disease or injury.) Nutritionists know that a healthy society is not possible unless people have good food and a wholesome diet. Organized labour knows that a healthy society is not possible unless workers have clean and safe workplaces. Environmentalists know that healthy people need clean air to breathe and clean water to drink. And anti-poverty activists know that having a healthy society depends on reducing income inequality and bringing people out of poverty.

> I am standing by the shore of a swiftly flowing river and I hear the cry of a drowning man. So I jump into the river, put my arms around him, pull him to shore and apply artificial respiration, and then just as he begins to breathe, another cry for help. So back in the river again, reaching, pulling, applying, breathing, and then another yell. Again and again, without end, goes the sequence. You know, I am so busy jumping in, pulling them to shore, applying artificial respiration, that I have no time to see who the hell is pushing them all in. —Irving K. Zola, 1970

You'd think that Canadians would excel at promoting health and preventing disease. Not so. We spend over 95 per cent of our health dollars treating illness and less than 5 per cent on prevention. We have to get our spending priorities straight—helping to prevent illness rather than spending money to treat people after they've become sick.

Numerous studies show a clear connection between economic conditions and a person's health. A recent report by the Canadian Public Health Association says that "life expectancy depends more on the internal distribution of wealth than increases in income. The narrower the spread of income in a given society, the higher will be its overall health status." The *British Medical Journal* agrees: "The more equally wealth is distributed, the better the health of that society." A rich nation with an unequal distribution of wealth is not necessarily a healthy nation. Among the twenty-nine OECD nations, the richest is the United States, yet it ranks twenty-second in life expectancy for men and nineteenth for women—and the U.S. has the greatest gap between rich and poor. So policy that increases the gap between the well-to-do and the rest turns out to be literally lethal. Years of life are lost as a result.

The distribution of income in Canada is very unequal, too, and that disparity is increasing as we copy more and more American economic policies. In 2000, the wealthiest 10 per cent of families earned $18 for every $1 earned by the lowest 10 per cent. (In the richer provinces, the ratio is worse—it's 20:1 in Ontario and B.C.) And the gap is getting wider. Through the 1990s, families with the highest incomes had the biggest percentage of income gains (after adjusting for inflation): 14.6 per cent. The lowest-income families gained just 0.8 per cent.

The Canadian Public Health Association estimates that if the bottom half of income earners received just a 1 per cent increase in the share of income, the mortality rate would decline by 21 deaths per 100,000 people. That's equivalent to eliminating the deaths from all motor vehicle accidents and breast cancer among people of working age. If such a modest change in income distribution would save that many lives, imagine the impact it would have in reducing non-fatal illnesses, improving overall health, and reducing health care costs!

Infectious and communicable diseases are directly linked to living conditions. Poor nutrition, contaminated water, overcrowded and unsanitary environments, and similar factors result in tuberculosis, pneumonia, diarrhea, measles, and other common diseases. These days, medicine can treat them all, but *their causes are not medical*. And if we want to create healthy societies, the answer is not more or better health care but improved living conditions, a cleaner environment, and a more equal distribution of income.

In 1999, the U.S. Centers for Disease Control and Prevention listed the greatest public health achievements of the twentieth century. These included vaccines for children, safer and more healthful foods, control of infectious diseases, motor vehicle and workplace safety, healthier mothers and babies, and reduction of tobacco use. In Canada, for example, we've seen a 95 per cent reduction in preventable diseases among children and the total elimination of polio as a result of the use of vaccines. Promoting the use of bicycle helmets and seat belts is another successful public health measure. An estimated 22,000 fewer injuries and permanent disabilities per year result from the use of helmets and seat belts, with net savings of $500 million in health costs.

It's unfortunate that the links between public health and health care costs weren't made by Roy Romanow. Perhaps he saw public health as beyond his mandate. Nonetheless, it remains a serious shortcoming of the report. Almost nothing was said about strengthening public health. As the examples above suggest, federal investment in public health would create significant financial savings in the health care system, to say nothing about making us healthier! Romanow missed an opportunity to make this crucial point, and he missed the opportunity to note that the federal government should also make healthy public policy—that is, public policy in non-health sectors that is good for public health. For instance, designing our cities to encourage more walking and cycling not only helps us clean the air and combat climate change, it makes us more fit. Developing agricultural and food policies that support the production and consumption of non-GM and organic food not only helps our farmers and the natural environment, it means people eat more wholesome fare. And the healthier our natural environment is, the healthier we are and the fewer health care dollars must be spent on treating preventable illnesses.

In developed countries like Canada, the primary causes of death are no longer communicable or infectious diseases but chronic ones—cancers, heart disease, and strokes. And the main causes of these diseases are social, environmental, and economic—stress, addiction to tobacco and alcohol, toxic chemicals in our food and in our surroundings, unhealthy diets, and inactive lifestyles.

A shocking study released in November 2003 shows deteriorating health in Canada's kids. Toronto's Hospital for Sick Children studied a group of Boy Scouts and Girl Guides from age ten to eighteen and found that one-third of them were overweight. As a group, they were 5 per cent above normal weight, which is considered "dramatic" in a population, according to Dr. Brian McCrindle, head of the hospital's cholesterol clinic. Tests on the boys and girls showed their arteries already thickening and having trouble dilating—key markers of metabolic syndrome, the precursor to heart disease. McCrindle said, "We're getting to a point where 'normal' weight is associated with disease."

There's no question that many people's lifestyles are deteriorating, not just kids who are prone to sit in front of a television or computer. Obesity in Canadian society doubled between 1985 and 2001, from 6 to 16 per cent in men and from 7 to 14 per cent in women. "We live in a culture that promotes gluttony but glorifies thinness," says Heather Maclean, from the Centre for Research and Women's Health at the Sunnybrook and Women's College Health Sciences Centre in Toronto.

Needless to say, we must all take responsibility for our own health—getting regular exercise and avoiding junk food and fast foods. But as a result of industry supersizing our fast-food portions, we're beginning to "supersize" the population. So the food industry has a responsibility and a role to play here, just as it does with respect to the excessive amounts of dangerous transfats in our foods. But when governments cut funding for schools, and schools cut physical education programs as a result, or sign contracts with junk food companies to earn some money for their programs, that creates a social problem. Healthy lifestyles are a personal, a corporate, and a public responsibility. We have seen some corporate moves regarding soft drinks in schools in early 2004, but there is a long way to go.

Preventing disease is a central function of public health. It's also essential to promote healthy communities and healthy living. It's smarter, it's cheaper, and it's usually easier than treating disease.

Our national government should consider how some health care resources could be focused on healthy human physical development. Let's comb the world for best practices and adapt them to the Canadian context, working with provinces and communities: promoting and engaging Canadians with a focus on kids' health and physical fitness.

In 1985, just after being elected to my second term on Toronto City Council, I entered another contest—for the position of chair of the city's Board of Health. A new and mysterious disease had begun attacking gay men. My opponent for the board position was a councillor whose strategy for dealing with this issue was to close down the bathhouses frequented by gay men. (Deliberately, in the midst of the 1981 provincial election, Toronto police had raided four of these establishments, arresting nearly 300 men. I had joined with those who opposed the raids as they violated privacy rights. Tragically, several of those arrested committed suicide because police released their names to the press.) It was against this background that the vote for chair of the Board of Health was taken, and I was fortunate enough to win— and serve six years in that position.

Immediately, we set about the process of developing a strategy to address this new disease called AIDS. Instead of closing the bathhouses, we needed to turn them into centres for safe-sex education and provide condoms, health advice, and treatment.

In the midst of developing this plan, a bureaucrat from the blood diseases section of the city's Health Department came to see me in my office after hours. It was like talking to a spy acting contrary to orders.

"I shouldn't be meeting with you," he said quietly. "But the problem we're facing with HIV and AIDS is potentially so large that my conscience demands that I talk with you. There's a possibility that HIV is being carried in the blood of people who don't even know they're infected. They could be blood donors."

I began to get the picture.

"Their blood could contain the virus that is making people sick," he continued. "If this is happening, then blood products used in transfusions could be infected. Without knowing it, we could already be facing a disease that has spread well beyond those who are visibly ill." His voice was hushed. "My son is a hemophiliac," he said.

The gravity of what he had told me, the extent to which this disease might already be spreading, was terrifying.

"What do you think should be done?" I asked.

"I need a big increase in my education budget," he replied.

"How much is your budget?"

"It's $25,000 right now."

"How much of an increase do you need?"

"I think I need to double my budget!"

"You know that council has just finalized its budget discussions and set a 5 per cent cap on budgetary increases for all departments?"

"But we have to get the information out," he almost pleaded.

He was right, of course. And I also knew that another $25,000 wasn't going to do the job.

"I tell you what," I said. "Let's pull together the best minds we can find, people who know the most about this AIDS situation. Let's find out how large the problem is, according to the best information available. Let's invite the new groups that are forming to deal with AIDS and some of the doctors working with people with HIV."

We did. Through this, as on so many other issues, I worked with my executive assistant, Dan Leckie. We brought together, for the first time, a number of people who had been involved in the various aspects of this disease, all operating within their own silos, with little communication among them. The meeting produced a legion of ideas—and some of the most fascinating hours of my life. It was also horrifying.

HIV was moving through the community much faster than the "authorities" were saying—or admitting. This information wasn't being communicated to the public; it wasn't even being tracked.

We talked about how to control it, how to educate people, how to inform the public. We helped set up networks in the community and among the specialists. We began to lay out a plan. And over the next few weeks, Dan and I also figured out the costs. In the end, and instead of the $25,000 my friend from the Health Department asked for, we persuaded city council to give us $6 million for two and a half years.

Without a doubt, the public money we spent on the AIDS

Defence Plan was only a small fraction of what would have been spent treating countless more victims of HIV/AIDS, let alone the appalling toll in human suffering.

This was public health in action. I'm very proud of our AIDS strategy, and of all the people in the community, the medical profession, and the Health Department, who collaborated to make it work. I shudder to think what would have happened without it.

Unfortunately, the federal government appears not to have learned the valuable lessons we did at the local level. The government is currently two years into developing a new strategic plan for fighting HIV/AIDS. But as Ralph Jurgens, executive director of the Canadian HIV/AIDS Legal Network, noted in early 2004, "The federal government must show leadership and immediately develop a highly specific plan that clearly defines what its contribution will be....The plan should include a timetable, performance targets, and accounting mechanisms." We need action, not just consultation.

Jurgens also rightly points out that marginalized groups suffering from HIV/AIDS have been largely ignored by existing federal programs. There need to be specific plans for dealing with the epidemic in our federal prisons as well as among injection drug users. But as is usually the case, plans are not enough. There must also be a financial commitment to make these plans real. Since the early 1990s, the federal government has spent on average about $42 million a year fighting HIV/AIDS. This funding has not changed, even as inflation has eaten away at what this money can do and as the number of Canadians living with HIV has increased by 40 per cent since 1996. The government must invest more in dealing with HIV/AIDS. We cannot wait.

But federal involvement does not end here. We also have a moral responsibility to deal with HIV/AIDS at an international level. Stephen Lewis's passionate and seemingly endless work on behalf of AIDS victims in Africa is testament to the nightmare that happens when there is no strategy, no public health policy, and no money. For too long, the international community has stood by and done nothing while the HIV/AIDS pandemic has swept through Africa, killing millions and millions. In January 2004, Lewis gave a moving speech to my Rotary Club in Toronto. He laid out in stark detail the challenges and hopes facing the people in Africa ravaged by this disease. One of the most chilling points he made was the role played by the so-called developed nations: "At some point in the future, historians are going to look back at this period and ask, quite simply, how in God's name the world allowed this to happen. More than twenty million people have already perished, the vast majority in the developing world. It's of the same genre as General Romeo Dallaire's question, How did the world stand by and watch the genocide in Rwanda without lifting a finger? There seem to be these historical moments, these historical periods when moral resolve either freezes or evaporates. It's not just unconscionable; it's inexplicable."

Thankfully, as my friend Stephen suggested later in his speech, the world's moral resolve is beginning to awaken. In Canada, the NDP's Peace Advocacy Team (made up of MPs Alexa McDonough, Bill Blaikie, Svend Robinson, and Judy Wasylycia-Leis) spent much of 2003 demanding the federal government become proactive in dealing with the HIV/AIDS pandemic. The team has been campaigning for the federal government to contribute a fair share to the Global Fund, inspired by UN Secretary General Kofi Annan, and set up to deal with AIDS, TB, and malaria. And our MPs have worked tirelessly with NGOs and Canadians from coast to coast to push the federal government to introduce legislation that would make it easier to export generic drugs (in particular drugs that dramatically improve the life expectancy of people with HIV/AIDS) to countries that need them. The government finally responded in November 2003 and introduced Bill C-56, the Act to Amend the Patent Act and the Food and Drugs Act. At the time of writing, the bill contained fatal flaws favouring multinational drug companies, thus effectively and cynically undermining the achievement of its stated goal.

There is no doubt that dealing with the HIV/AIDS pandemic will cost money. But as Stephen Lewis reminded us in his speech, had the industrialized world put resources into dealing with the pandemic when it first began, "millions of people would still be alive today, and millions of others would have a fighting chance of prolonging life, and you wouldn't have between eleven and fourteen million orphans, no different in any way from your children and mine, from your grandchildren and mine, wandering the landscape of Africa, bewildered, forlorn, anguished, abandoned, exploited, hungry, despairing . . . cared for by grandmothers or older siblings or communities already reeling and further impoverished by the impact of AIDS."

I want to return to another important lesson I learned from my experiences with the Toronto AIDS Defence Plan. It's fine to have an expensive, ambitious new program to address important issues, but it's also crucial for those people responsible for the dollars—in this case, me, as chair of the Board of Health—to keep a very close eye on exactly how the money is spent. It is also essential that program leaders be able to shift direction if the problem alters or if solutions aren't working. Sometimes politicians come up with grand ideas, but they don't follow through to ensure that the ideas are indeed implemented in a timely and efficient way. The politicians who propose the ideas and put them in place need to be accountable.

Watching the federal government mismanage file after file through the late 1990s illustrates the importance of this basic lesson. A perfectly reasonable idea like gun registration mutated into a massively expensive program. Horrendous costs aside, it plunged the simple concept of registering firearms into disrepute and made further advances in real gun control, like prohibitions on more types of guns, more difficult. If accountability is ever to have any real meaning, a basic operating principle must be that each cabinet minister take responsibility for the monitoring of, and making adjustments and corrections to, each program that he or she initiates. Without this, government programs can never be effective or efficient. And without this, we will not do justice to the urgency of the HIV/AIDS pandemic.

Often it's nearly impossible to calculate money *not* spent. In health care, the pressure is always on to provide more money for treatment, because how can you possibly deny treating the injured, the ill, and the aging? As I mentioned earlier, spending on public health is less than 5 per cent of our health dollars. That's shameful. Because every dollar spent on public health—on education, nutrition, prenatal care, immunization, screening for disease, encouraging safe practices and healthier lifestyles, and so on—saves many, many more dollars down the road. More to the point, it keeps people and communities healthier. That's what a caring society does.

Aboriginal communities and public health

I can't leave this topic without raising one more critical problem we must face.

There is no more urgent need for public health than in Aboriginal communities. The appalling levels of poverty, disease, substance abuse, and suicide suffered by indigenous peoples living in Canada are a national disgrace. To witness, as I have on many occasions, the dignity and humanity so common on their reserves and elsewhere, in the midst of so much tragedy and poverty, is both powerful and astonishing.

In 1996, the Royal Commission on Aboriginal Peoples anxiously called for federal government action on many fronts to redress the disadvantages that so mark life in too many First Nations, Metis, and Inuit communities. Years have gone by while the government has disgracefully failed to act. No civilized nation should allow its first peoples to live the way they do in Canada.

In those communities, you can plainly see the direct social, environmental, and economic connections to the health of a population. The commission noted that infant mortality among registered Indians is twice as high as it is for the rest of the Canadian population—and it's three times higher among the Inuit. Tuberculosis is more than twenty times as common among so-called "registered" Aboriginals as it is among non-Aboriginal Canadians, and the prevalence of diabetes is at least three times higher. Suicides, alcohol-related motor vehicle fatalities, fatal fires, and other accidental deaths are also much more common among Aboriginal peoples. The high rates of poverty and unemployment, poor housing and sanitation, and lack of clean drinking water all create unhealthy and unsafe living conditions that contribute to appalling rates of infectious diseases and despair.

Bev Desjarlais, the NDP MP for Churchill riding, which comprises the entire northern half of Manitoba, took me to a remote First Nations reserve called Pauingassis in March 2003. The distinguishing feature of this community is its very high rate of youth suicide, perhaps the highest in Canada. No wonder the people there are struggling. I walked through the sole store in the community and couldn't believe my eyes. I wrote down some of the prices facing mothers shopping for their families. Apples: four for $7.79; oranges:

six for $6.37. A dozen eggs were $21. Three litres of milk were on sale for $8.99, down from the normal price of $11 when the winter road isn't in, but 1.5 litre plastic bottles of Pepsi were going for just $1.99! With a monthly stipend of $476 for a mother and one child, plus a housing allowance, residents have little hope of enough money left to provide a wholesome diet. No wonder Aboriginal people suffer from poor nutrition, too often leading to obesity or diabetes.

And yet, solutions abound.

Empowering Aboriginal communities by dealing with them all as First Nations rather than in the paternalistic way that has driven public policy for so many years is a key first step. Imposing stumbling governance models from above, as proposed by the Chrétien government in the closing days of its mandate, don't help, as our NDP MP Pat Martin and Bloc Québécois MP Yvan Loubier drove home during their marathon filibuster of Bill C-7, the dreadful First Nations Governance Act, in the House of Commons during 2003. Laws such as these fundamentally perpetuate dependence, not self-sufficiency. That's never a recipe for long-term community health.

The Royal Commission implicitly recognized this paternalism and explicitly called for all levels of government "to support the assumption of responsibility for planning health and social services *by regional Aboriginal agencies and councils* [my emphasis]." The commission also understood that Aboriginal peoples have a particular cultural approach to health care and healing, which we must respect, and called for the establishment of healing centres and healing lodges under Aboriginal control.

Sharing power and resources with indigenous peoples— who often willingly shared their own with waves of European immigrants, who then fenced off, mined, harvested, and polluted their lands, waters, and forests—would be a good start.

I've learned from my years in municipal government that healthy public policy should shift resources to communities themselves, empowering those who live there to implement their ideas rather than live under the dictates of others. In the case of Aboriginals and Metis in Canada, the principle of social justice demands it.

And, of course, we also need to be much more in tune with the needs of Aboriginal people living off reserve, often in cities, who are frequently victims of racism and violence in addition to the dislocation and loss of community they suffer.

I recall watching the birth and growth of the amazing Anishnawbe Health Centre in downtown Toronto. It seemed such a modest request when the centre's wise director asked if we could find a van so that soup and blankets, as well as respectful advice and transportation, could be offered to homeless First Nations men, women, and teenagers. Chairing the Board of Health allowed me to rummage around in the budgets, and we found an eight-year-old van that was being retired—sent off to auction where it would have fetched little more than pennies from an urban bargain hunter. The medical officer of health at the time, Dr. Sandy McPherson, pulled the van off the auction block, spent $1,000 on repairs, and gave it to the Anishnawbe group. They used it for years, with the help of hundreds of unpaid volunteers from urban First Nations and from the broader community. I know lives are still saved by the Street Patrol Service, and many a politician has driven in the van's late-night shift to learn about the faces of homelessness. That little van may actually have helped encourage political will to build affordable housing like the new First Nations housing we all worked to create on Coxwell Avenue, near the railroad tracks. From homelessness to housing, in a recycled van!

Seniors—and a personal comment about the people who really cared for my dad

The need for services for seniors really hits home when you actually have to start looking after your own parents. In my case, this experience started when our family had to go get nursing home care for my father. As my dad's Parkinson's developed, it became clear that my mom, Doris, wasn't going to be able to take care of him at home any longer, so we all set to work to try to find a place where he would be given dignified care, and where he could receive visitors, friends, and family in a way that would make everybody feel comfortable. We immediately ran up against the crisis in long-term care for seniors. My brother Dave, who was leading the effort, discovered that there were virtually no beds in the non-profit or public long-term-care facilities in the Toronto area. Waiting lists were long, and we didn't have much time. So, naturally, we turned to the list of private long-term-care providers. We visited one that was not far from my brother's home and was easily accessible to my mom.

Sure enough, the facilities for seniors who could mostly look after themselves seemed friendly enough, the common areas were nicely appointed, pretty plants grew here and there, and the cafeteria had the feel of a friendly restaurant. A quick visit to the secure floor, where seniors requiring care live, seemed to indicate that this might be suitable. The sales staff who led the tour seemed agreeable and competent. But what a difference a week can make.

When my father moved into the facility, we quickly realized that the service wasn't going to measure up to our hopes. There was a telltale odour of urine and other unpleasant smells, not enough to make you sick, but unpleasant. Maybe this was just the way it was in seniors' homes, we thought. How could we have known differently?

Our next experience was with the care levels. The workers were certainly earnest, and they tried their best to be friendly, but from the outset we could tell that they were overworked. Frankly, they looked exhausted much of the time. Their shifts seemed to be terribly designed as far as their personal lives were concerned, and there was no question that their wages would make it tough for them to support their own families. Most of the workers had many different functions, from cleaning up after seniors who had had accidents, to cleaning the rooms and hallways, and even performing some semi-medical functions.

But you could see in their eyes a real sense of unhappiness and strain. Naturally this was transferred to the seniors under their care. But it wasn't the workers' fault. The place just wasn't organized or designed for the caregivers to feel very positive about their work. We wondered if this was common in all seniors' homes.

And then there was the price we were paying—over $3,000 a month. How many families could even consider this? Fortunately, my father's pension, from a lifetime in business and political service, could cover it, but few working families today can afford such an expense without major hardship.

I watched my father's spirits deteriorate day by day. He had always been one of the most optimistic, upbeat people in any circle he travelled or worked in—his positive energy was his most distinguishing feature. I assumed at first that it was the Parkinson's disease, combined with the effects of the medication he was taking for prostate cancer, that was affecting his mood and making him unhappy.

Then he began to whisper the suggestion that maybe it wasn't worth carrying on. This is a very, very tough thing to hear from your father, someone who has always been the tower of strength in your life. It made me angry that he was having these feelings. I was angry at myself, I was angry at the situation, and I became increasingly angry at the treatment he was receiving. My dad had spent his whole life making other people happy, and for him not to be able to be happy in his last years seemed to me to be fundamentally unjust.

So we began to investigate other long-term-care options, and we tracked down a few possibilities, provided that we were willing to wait. One was very attractive. It was a non-profit, long-term-care facility that had been built with a lot of help from the Rotary Club of Toronto, and it was located right behind City Hall. This was going to be perfect—if there was any chance that my dad could move in.

I dropped in to visit, and from the very first moment the difference was absolutely clear. First, I smelled home cooking, not urine. A warm, welcoming receptionist, just inside the front door, greeted me—and a cat strolled by, getting a pat from some of the seniors in their wheelchairs. They were having conversations and keeping an eye on the comings and goings at the front door. My instant reaction was that this felt like home rather than "a home."

As I toured the kitchen and the residential areas with the director, I felt I was not being given a sales job. The underlying message was that this was a place that provided dignity and care for seniors. When I asked how long the workers had been there, I was told that the average length of tenure was many, many years. Obviously, this meant that the caregivers were treated with real respect. Frankly, you could see it in their eyes and in their smiles. And when I visited the floors where the care was being given, I could see it in the eyes and smiles of the seniors themselves.

At the end of the tour, I said to my tour guide, "It looks as if you give tender loving care here." And she said, "Well, of course we believe in TLC. It's our motto, and it's our name: The Laughlen Centre—TLC," and she laughed.

Naturally, I expected that the costs there would be at least equal to or greater than at the private operation where my dad was living; there were more staff here, and more attention was being given to the seniors. Wrong. The Laughlen Centre offered accommodation at a little over *half* the price a month that the private, corporate facility was charging.

So on one hand, we experienced a private, multinational corporation's long-term-care facility, with low wages for its workers, poor shift arrangements for its staff, and problematic care bordering on the denial of dignity to the seniors. On the other hand, we experienced a non-profit, long-term-care system that manages to provide everything that seniors need, from dignity to food to physical care, and all at a considerably lower price.

Eventually my father was able to move into The Laughlen Centre. And, if anything, the reality proved to be even better than the tour. My father was happy as he lived out his last months. Ultimately, pneumonia took him when a chest infection overpowered his immune system. Now I understand why pneumonia is sometimes called "the old man's friend"—it took him quietly and without pain. And he was surrounded by his family. By then, his "family" included many of the people at the Rotary's Laughlen Centre.

I'm grateful to everybody there, for what they did for my father. Mostly, I'd like to hope that we, as a nation, develop a plan that ensures that high-quality, non-profit, long-term care is available for our seniors, no matter what their incomes, no matter what their backgrounds, and no matter what circumstances have necessitated their families' need.

Seniors' health issues are wider ranging than just residential long-term care. Home care is another important issue. Home care refers to a wide range of services used to help people with health problems stay in their homes. Historically, most of these services were provided by non-profit charitable organizations like the Victorian Order of Nurses and the Red Cross. Their work included homemaking services and nursing services such as insulin injections, eye drops, dressing changes, and health assessment. In the past fifteen years, with the drive to close hospital and in-patient mental health beds, there has been a dramatic switch in home care services to meeting the needs of the acutely ill. Home care frees up hospital beds by allowing people who need IV antibiotics, dialysis, complex dressing changes, and palliative care to stay at home and get care. As the demand for acute care has increased, funding for services to allow the frail elderly to stay in their homes has taken second place.

In the 1970s, provincial governments started to take over the funding of some of these programs. Since home care falls outside the Canada Health Act, there is a disparity across the country in which services are funded through government programs and who delivers the services. Provinces like Manitoba provide their home care services though public agencies, while Ontario contracts out all its services, a majority delivered by for-profit companies. Services may include homemaking, personal support, social work, the full range of therapy services, nursing, and medical supplies.

It's time we had public or non-profit-based home care available in all parts of Canada. Every Canadian should have access to the same level of service: our elderly deserve it, and the women who disproportionately care for elderly relatives deserve it. And it will save us money, too. Care in hospitals is $9,000 to $16,000 more expensive per year per patient than community-based home care.

Canadians who are sixty-five or older now total about 3.5 million, and that number is growing. While most seniors feel that they receive good health care, provincial and national policies are not encouraging. In British Columbia, recent cuts to home care services resulted in a decline of seniors' health, increased hospitalization, higher admissions to residential care, and more deaths. These cuts didn't save money and, more to the point, they were cruel and counterproductive.

Seniors take more prescription drugs than other age groups, and the national pharmacare program I mentioned earlier would lessen the financial burden on them for medicines they need beyond the provincial plans that cover some costs now.

Better public health programs would encourage more physical activity in seniors and provide more opportunities to get together with other seniors. Such programs improve health and extend longevity and are major contributors to the quality of life.

Environmental programs that reduce smog, for example, would have a marked effect on seniors, who are especially vulnerable to respiratory diseases. Of the 5,000 people who die prematurely each year in Canada from the effects of smog, significant numbers are seniors and the young. These are probably the least responsible for smog, yet the most affected. Another of our world's nasty ironies.

Improvements in public pensions would help seniors, especially women, avoid the poverty trap that so many of them fall into.

What gets me is that seniors don't complain much. I remember the time we were petitioning against the cancellation of significant senior discounts on the transit system. As we knocked on doors in a seniors' apartment building looking for signatures, one kindly woman said to me, "Oh, it's not so bad, Jack. I do need to use to streetcar to get to my doctor. I'll just stay in touch by phone instead of taking those trips to have tea with my friends." It just about made me cry. Here's a woman who has made her contributions to our society for eighty years or more. Now we're going to make it impossible for her to have that little joy—tea with her friends. What sort of definition of "quality of life" or "prosperity" do we use that does not include a well-deserved cup of tea? The health of our seniors depends as much on that tea—and on that affordable streetcar ride—as any high-tech medical intervention.

A caring society would meet these needs. Surely ours is capable of doing so.

[CHAPTER 5]

Reawakening
Our Communities

A young friend of mine, Joy Henderson, once told me about her first time at a summer camp outside the city. Joy grew up in the low-income community of Regent Park in Toronto, and when she returned from her trip, she said to her mom, "You never told me about the stars!" She'd never seen the miracle of a night sky. Having grown up witnessing hundreds of star-filled nights in rural Hudson, Quebec, I was shocked to realize that big-city kids, especially poor ones with little access to the countryside, think the Milky Way is only a candy bar, and that they're denied the spectacle the heavens reveal on a clear night.

Country and small-town life are special. I grew up in a quiet little town, so there's a part of me that still nods secretly in agreement when friends in rural Canada tell me that they'd never want to live in a big city. Clean air, the smells of forests and flowers, and those countless stars.

But we are a nation of city dwellers. Statistics Canada says that 80 per cent of us live in cities, defining "urban" as any place larger than 10,000 people. Almost two-thirds of us live in fairly large cities—more than 100,000 people—and over half the Canadian population lives in one of the four urban regions of Toronto, Montreal, Vancouver, and the Calgary-Edmonton axis. For all our vast geography, we are one of the most urbanized countries in the world. And as is happening around the world, the population continues to gravitate toward cities—out of the countryside—including about 75 per cent of newcomers to Canada.

Towns and cities are now the heart of our country's life. Rural Canada is vital to our economy and our future—especially as resources are depleted and valuable non-urban ways of life are threatened by depopulation. However, it is time to recognize the social transformation that has taken place—and to take advantage of the opportunities that our cities provide.

Two elements of a new agenda are essential to keep the blood pulsing through healthy communities: reforming the basis on which cities are financed, and reforming the decision-making structures of all governments to achieve healthier democracy through community engagement.

A raw deal for cities

In Canada, cities have been considered "creatures" of the provinces. That, in a nutshell, is a big problem with the way we govern municipalities. The role, function, and structure of municipal governments in Canada derive from the Baldwin Act of 1849. At that time, fewer than 15 per cent of Canadians lived in urban areas, and local governments were concerned with problems like running cattle in public places, noisy disturbances, public drunkenness, profanity, and itinerant salesmen. (Some problems just won't go away.) The Constitution gives the provinces control over municipal institutions in their province. In fact, constitutional recognition of municipalities as a form of government doesn't exist. Cities are the poor cousins of the Canadian political family, the neglected relatives—except that our towns and cities are also the engines of the economy, the driving force of our society, and the centres of our culture.

Way back in 1901, towns and cities across Canada realized they needed to band together so they could speak to provincial and federal governments with one voice. They formed the Federation of Canadian Municipalities, an umbrella group now with a membership of more than 1,000 towns and cities. The FCM serves as a forum for mayors and other elected officials to share experiences, as a clearing house for ideas and innovation, and as a lobbying organization on behalf of municipalities. I was honoured to serve a term as FCM president recently.

My predecessor as president of the FCM, Kitimat Regional Councillor Joanne Monahan, used to say, "Somewhere between asylums and saloons, that's where you find municipal government in the Canadian Constitution." And it's true. Our cherished local democracies—the creation of which required rebellions, for heaven's sake—languish in a mundane list of the various responsibilities of the provinces!

Yet, as I've noted in many examples, true innovations come from municipal governments. So many of our best ideas first emerged locally, where creativity and experimentation can thrive. The idea that the most important public health measure is a secure roof over everyone's head produced the first affordable public housing through local medical officers of health and city councils. Infrastructure to create safer sewage treatment and drinking water first came from city governments. Public transit. Transport infrastructure for industry. Parks and playgrounds. Libraries. Concert halls. Health clinics. Bicycle lanes and recreational trails. Tree-planting programs. Food banks. Shelters for the homeless. The list of local policy innovations is long.

Now, more Canadians have come to recognize the importance of cities to Canada's future. In May 2002, the Toronto Dominion Bank issued a special report called *A Choice between Investing in Canada's Cities or Disinvesting in Canada's Future*. The title makes the option pretty clear. In their report, the bank writes, "The bottom line is that we are all stakeholders in our nation's future—consumers and businesses alike. Our cities are a vital part of that future, and we must work together to ensure their health and prosperity." I couldn't have said it better.

In January 2003, the Laidlaw Foundation issued a report that reminds us that "the social health of urban communities is essential to the economic future of Canada." A few months later, a group of prominent Torontonians, the Toronto City Summit Alliance, put out a report that stated the problem very starkly: "Quite simply, Canadian federalism is not working for our large city regions." The Calgary-based Canada West Foundation was among the first to make the same point.

What does all that mean?

The city of Winnipeg's gross domestic product accounts for two-thirds of Manitoba's economy; Calgary's and Edmonton's GDP is 64 per cent of Alberta's; Vancouver's GDP is 53 per cent of British Columbia's; Montreal's is half of Quebec's; and Toronto is responsible for 44 per cent of Ontario's GDP. The larger cities represent a considerable proportion of federal government revenues as well. The greater Toronto region (GTA) all by itself accounts for over one-fifth of Canada's entire GDP.

In Winnipeg in 2001, over 50 per cent of the taxes paid by residents went to the federal government, 43 per cent to the provincial government, and less than 7 per cent to the city government. In the GTA, residents' taxes resulted in a net contribution (that is, their tax revenue minus payments back to the city) of $17 billion to Ottawa and $3 billion to the province. The GTA municipal governments pay Ottawa about $100 million in GST, and they pay the province about $150 million in PST for the purchases they make.

These are a lot of numbers, but what they mean is this: Canada's cities generate enormous revenues for the federal and provincial governments. What they get in return is a pittance. Federal, provincial, and territorial governments control the spending of over 95 per cent of all tax dollars. Municipalities control less than 5 per cent. Across Canada, about half of all municipalities' revenue comes from property tax. (In the U.S., it averages about one-fifth.) So let's look again at Winnipeg, whose revenues and expenses are fairly typical of Canadian cities. In 2001, 54 per cent of Winnipeg's municipal revenue came from property tax. User fees, licences, fines, utility bills, and other miscellaneous local revenue amounted to 30 per cent of the city's income. Grants from the federal and provincial governments provided only 16 per cent of Winnipeg's revenue. And Winnipeg is lucky! Manitoba's NDP government has been transferring fixed percentage points of income taxes collected to municipalities on a per capita basis, essentially sharing a little income tax revenue directly with the city.

Yet, over the past decade in particular, as they sought to balance their budgets and reduce their deficits, federal and provincial governments have been steadily downloading costs and services to municipalities—the level of government whose hands are most tied when it comes to collecting revenue from the economic activity that they spawn. Because cities are creatures of the provinces, the provinces have traditionally limited the ways that municipalities can fund themselves. By law, with very rare exceptions, cities don't have the authority to collect income taxes, fuel taxes, sales taxes, or most other kinds of tax except property tax. So when the federal government wants to wrestle the deficit to the ground, it does so by passing on costs to provinces, which pass some of them on to municipalities, the level of government with the least capacity (by far) to pass them on to anyone else—or to raise money to backfill the fiscal excavations. The result? More potholes. As MP Brian Masse, our federal caucus Urban Advocate has been saying, higher property taxes bear no resemblance whatsoever to a citizen's ability to pay. It would be no exaggeration to state that the corporate tax cuts implemented by Paul Martin in recent years are paid for in part by property tax increases on everyone, including retired people. Bad policy and unfair to boot.

Speaking to a symposium we organized at the FCM in 2002, the former Ontario NDP premier Bob Rae said:

> The governments at the provincial and federal level
> have to be challenged: if you're not prepared to transfer
> the resources yourselves, then at least give us the finan-
> cial room to make those decisions and let the local
> governments really decide. Governments are much bet-
> ter at downloading than at transferring resources. The
> only way the senior levels of government have been
> able to balance their books is by sabotaging other levels
> of government. What do you do about the services that
> have been underfed and starved? If you really want to
> discipline all levels of government, you have to make
> sure that the level of government that is actually deliv-
> ering the service has the taxing authority and capacity
> to deliver that service.

The mayor of St. John's, Andy Wells, summed the problem up nicely: "We've got the responsibility, but we don't have the legislative authority and the fiscal tools." At FCM, we used to refer to the federal government's attitude toward cities as a "culture of non-recognition and neglect."

How has this downloading affected cities? Let me give some examples from my own city.

In the mid-1990s, the provincial government downloaded all the responsibility for affordable housing and 20 per cent of the Family Benefits and Ontario Disability Support programs to municipal governments. They did this, of course, because they had promised to "lower taxes," but all they did was shift the burden to towns and cities. The province also increased the municipal share of social-assistance administrative costs to 50 per cent. And how is the city supposed to pay for this increase? About its only lever is to increase property taxes. There was no money in the city's budget for new affordable housing, and very little for the maintenance of the existing social housing stock.

Through the 1990s, government funding support for the Toronto Transit Commission (TTC) was cut by $92 million, to under 20 cents for each dollar spent. Because of this, over 80 per cent of the TTC's funding comes from the public transit riders paying their fares. This is far below government support for public transit in any comparable urban centre in the world. As a result, the TTC was trapped in the bind of either increasing fares or reducing service—both of which inevitably result in lower ridership, exactly the *wrong* public policy.

In May 2003, in a speech to the FCM, backbench MP and at the time Liberal leadership frontrunner Paul Martin said he would give municipalities a share of the federal gasoline tax. Good news? Canadians have heard Martin on gas taxes before. In 1995, when he was finance minister, he increased the gas tax by 1.5 cents a litre. He said it was to help pay down the deficit. (Actually, it would help pay for the hefty corporate tax cuts.) He emphasized that this gas tax hike was temporary, and that as soon as the deficit was gone, the tax would come off. But even when the government began to run up huge surpluses, the increased gas tax stayed, and *none* of it has gone to municipalities. The surplus resulted in more tax cuts for the well-to-do—and swelled corporate bottom lines.

The Federation of Canadian Municipalities estimates that our towns and cities need about $60 billion for necessary repairs and maintenance on the existing urban infrastructure—our roads, public transit, waterworks and sewer systems, and housing. Under the current fiscal framework, it simply isn't possible for the cities to pay for all this. As the 2002 Toronto Dominion Bank report on cities pointed out, "Hit by the double-whammy of weak revenue growth and downloading of services, it is hardly surprising that municipal governments have had to run up debt, defer infrastructure projects, draw down reserves, sell assets and cut services in order to stay afloat."

Cities need a new deal. But it has to be the Real Deal. Communities of all sizes need more tools to build healthy, workable, productive communities. And they need some share of the financial resources they produce ploughed back into their productive processes.

We need a new urban vision, one that looks into the future with the benefit of hindsight. Let's consider just one key area of urban policy that we actually had right in Canada—then we watched it collapse before our eyes.

The shame of homelessness

Forgetting basic lessons about the need to invest in our communities can actually be fatal. The people who died in Walkerton from bad water are testimony. So is abandoning the idea of building some housing for those who cannot afford the rough-and-tumble world of free-enterprise home ownership. But that's exactly what our former national finance minister, now prime minister, did—thinking he could do so with impunity and perpetrating such short-sighted injustices. Why he's regarded as a "deficit-wrestling hero" escapes me.

Especially after Eugene Upper died.

One cold and snowy night—January 4, 1996, to be exact—Olivia and I were walking home around midnight from Metro

Hall, up Spadina Avenue. Along the way we passed two homeless men huddled in their sleeping bags in doorways, the snow drifting up around them. We checked quietly on them, not to disturb them, but to see if they showed any obvious signs of trouble. They seemed okay.

Across the street, another person had sought refuge from the cold and snow in a TTC shelter. We didn't see him. All night long, Spadina buses passed him by every half hour, never stopping. No one's proud of it, but a homeless person tucked into a Toronto bus shelter is not an unusual sight.

Trudging on home, we wondered aloud what we'd do if we did meet someone who seemed to be in difficulty. Here we were, two experienced city councillors, and even we didn't know whom to call—911? Police? A hospital? The Salvation Army? We just didn't know.

We got home, glad to be out of the cold, glad to be in comfortable surroundings. It's something most of us take for granted.

Early the next morning, over coffee and the newspapers, we were both stopped in mid-thought by the CBC radio news: "Overnight, a man was found frozen to death in a bus shelter on Spadina Avenue," the announcer said. We knew immediately that we had walked right by him.

His name soon became known: Eugene Upper. He had died from the killer cold in the winter-moon shadows of the bank towers in the richest city in Canada. I felt sick that I hadn't done enough to prevent it—not only that night but in my job at city council. I should have been working to make sure there were more emergency services, more shelters, more housing, a hotline people could call. It is a tragedy and a disgrace that Eugene Upper died. Yet within a short period of time, two other Toronto men, Mirsalah-Aldin Kompani and Irwin Anderson, also froze to death. And the city finally took notice.

A few years later, I wrote a book called *Homelessness*, and I dedicated it to Eugene Upper, both as a tribute to the man whose horrible death galvanized us into action, and as a reminder that we must do so much more as a society to provide affordable housing and services for homeless people. That book describes in detail the plight and extent of homelessness and suggests solutions for Canada's housing crisis.

Canada is the only G-8 country without a national housing program. We had one for a generation, forced into being in 1972 by NDP leader David Lewis on the minority government of Pierre Trudeau as a condition of his caucus's support for the Liberals. Hundreds of thousands of co-op and social housing units were built for families, seniors, students, people with various challenges, and the general public. At its height, in the years between 1989 and 1993, an average of 12,675 new social housing units were being built annually. I am one of the hundreds of thousands of Canadians who have lived in co-op housing. What makes co-op housing especially successful is that it brings together people who can afford to pay market rents, like me, with those who cannot. This ensures a vibrant mixed-income community that avoids the many problems created when low-income earners are "ghettoized." This mixed-income model was recognized globally as a "best practice" by the United Nations Habitat Program.

In 1993, when the Liberal government came into office again, Paul Martin became finance minister, and the number of social housing units being built dropped, even as he instituted his $100 billion tax cuts. That's because Martin simply axed the whole program. The Conservatives under Brian Mulroney had frozen it; Martin amputated it. In the years 1994–98, an annual average of only 4,450 units of new affordable housing were built, a drop of 65 per cent. Those that survived were projects where construction had already begun, and those were built by provinces, like Ontario, British Columbia, and Quebec (all with social democratic governments at the time).

In 1990, as a member of the opposition and when he was seeking votes, Martin wrote the following: "[A]ll Canadians have the right to decent housing, in decent surroundings, at affordable prices.... Only the national government has the financial resources to address the full dimensions of the needs of this country." Are Canadians being sold a similar bill of goods with the promises of deals for cities today?

Let's also recall Article 25 of the Universal Declaration of Human Rights, adopted by the United Nations in 1948 and ratified by Canada: "Everyone has the right to a standard of living adequate for the health and well-being of himself and of his family, including food, clothing, housing and medical care and necessary social services, and the right to security in the event of unemployment, sickness, disability, widow-hood, old age or other lack of livelihood in circumstances beyond his control." Are those, too, just nice words, or do they represent a commitment? For the thousands of home-less people across Canada, they ring hollow when governments won't build housing.

In 1998, prompted by the Toronto Disaster Relief Committee, the mayors of Canada's largest cities declared homelessness a national disaster. The heroic street nurse Cathy Crowe and dedicated outreach worker Beric German had pulled together an extraordinary group of homeless peo-ple, along with others who believed in their cause, and insisted that we use the concept of disaster relief to address homeless-ness. As Crowe told me and the city council committee charged with these issues, "I was getting ready to go help out during the ice storm in Quebec. They told me I'd be dealing with people in cramped quarters, on mats or cots, crammed in hostels, without their homes, coping with the effects of the cold. There will be hundreds of these people in many communities. I said, 'Wait a minute! This is what I do every day in Toronto, working with 5,000 homeless people in our shelters and on our streets.' How come we react to an ice storm with the Canadian army and army of volunteers, but we languish in the luxury of inaction and blame-the-victim rhetoric when faced with a similar situation arising from homelessness?"

These powerful sentiments and the effective pressure of grassroots organizations prompted me to work with a group of municipal representatives in the FCM to lay out a detailed national housing strategy. We said, "Let's put forward a plan designed to reduce homelessness by 50 per cent in ten years." (It also included a five-year plan to cut in half the number of households whose rent is more than half their income.) The essence of the plan was to supply 20,000 new affordable housing units and to rehabilitate 10,000 units every year for the next ten years. Thus 30,000 housing units a year, which would have housed 60,000 to 65,000 people—a total of 600,000 to 650,000 over the next decade.

We envisioned what I like to call "Lilliputianism" at work—thousands of small local projects, maybe averaging one hundred units, developed and managed right there in the communities where they were being built, which collectively would produce giant results. This program would have created tens of thousands of jobs in planning and construction, provided an enormous stimulus to the economy, built new energy-efficient units, retrofitted older homes for greater efficiency, increased population density and reduced urban sprawl, and revitalized urban neighbourhoods. It would also have brought people like Eugene Upper in from the cold.

Too many people think of social housing as a blight. On the contrary, it can be a real community builder. One of the best examples is right in my own backyard.

Remember those brownfields I wrote about earlier? The

St. Lawrence community sits on once-polluted land from abandoned factories near Toronto's waterfront. Using funds resulting from NDP leader David Lewis's efforts in the early seventies, non-profit and co-op housing organizations worked together, and with the city, to transform a dreary post-industrial neighbourhood into a wonderful blend of social, co-op, municipal non-profit (under the cozy-sounding moniker Cityhome), and market rental and condo housing. A whole neighbourhood was grown from nothing, creating a district not only of decent places to live but of arts and culture. Now, far from having driven down the value of land, the St. Lawrence community has increased property values and economic activity. It's a thriving neighbourhood, located so close to the inner city that most residents can easily walk to work. (Walking to work—what a brilliant idea!) Across Canada, similar communities have been built and are flourishing today. They were a big part of the reason why urbanologists from all over the world trooped to Canada to study cities that worked. Such pilgrimages have stopped because our cities no longer work as they should!

The St. Lawrence community is an example of "smart growth," with increased density, mixed housing, access to public transit, job creation, cultural enhancement, and community participation. Everywhere in urban Canada, huge swaths of federally owned land languishes—vacant, underused, often polluted, and tied up in skeins of red tape. Federal politicians occasionally float pet schemes with much fanfare, but that's usually where the story ends. Where is the sense of urgency? Where's the vision? You would think, especially with the housing crisis evident around us, that action would be the watchword.

With careful study of both the long-term demand and the immediate problem, the FCM estimated the federal costs for its proposed national housing program at $1.6 billion a year. To achieve the goals we set, these costs would ideally be matched by the provinces and the municipalities, each contributing $1.6 billion in land, old buildings, financial support, or other forms of assistance.

Spurred on by the national attention that homelessness was getting, Prime Minister Chrétien named his labour minister, Claudette Bradshaw, as the person responsible for the homelessness issue. Just before Christmas 1999, Bradshaw did indeed announce the National Homelessness Initiative, a three-year program that was "designed to support community efforts" against homelessness. About half the money went into the Residential Rehabilitation Assistance Program, some was directed specifically to worthy Aboriginal initiatives, and $305 million (over three years) went toward the new Supporting Community Partnership Initiative (SCPI). The federal government's $100 million a year wasn't much, but it was a start. That money could be put into emergency shelters (new and expanded), other support facilities, and food and furniture banks. What it did not do—what it explicitly could *not* be used for—was to build a single unit of housing.

In all, sixty-one communities designed programs that were funded in part by SCPI. (About 80 per cent of the funds went to the ten largest cities; the rest went to small programs in fifty-one other communities.) When the initial program ran out in 2003, the government extended it for another three years, with funding of $405 million.

In Halifax, which was one of the first cities to sign on to SCPI programs, sixteen agencies received funding in the first round. They included residential facilities, transitional houses for both men and women, a centre for immigrants and refugees, supportive housing for low-income people, and more. They even funded the Shining Lights Choir, made up of homeless people and service providers. (The choir gave people a real sense of pride, belonging, and self-confidence; it even appeared on national CBC radio.)

SCPI funding in Saskatoon helped the food bank purchase the building they're housed in, it paid for staff for a round-the-clock mobile crisis-intervention service, renovated the Salvation Army's men's hostel, supported programs for at-risk young people (including purchase of a ten-bed transitional house for youth), and helped furnish a housing facility for women survivors of childhood sexual abuse. That names just a few.

Dozens of other small and worthwhile programs like these—in many Canadian towns and cities—have received, or are still receiving, federal SCPI funding. I want to give credit where credit is due. Claudette Bradshaw personally stick-handled this through the Liberal cabinet and came up with money that has funded some imaginative and necessary community efforts to ease the effects of homelessness. As far as it goes, it's a good program that relies mostly on local organizations to design programs that best meet their needs. It's a bottom-up approach, not a top-down one, and that's the way it should be.

But it doesn't build any permanent housing.

Communities across Canada, housing activists, the FCM, property developers, and the housing industry continued to draw attention to this huge and growing gap in Canadian public policy. The pressure was on. Finally, the government cracked.

The spring 2001 budget included $680 million to be spent on housing over five years, subject to agreements with the provinces. The months that followed featured fierce negotiations between the federal and provincial governments. As president of FCM at the time, I had a chance to help achieve wording for a federal/provincial agreement that would allow enough flexibility to permit provinces to work on affordable housing in their own ways, while (we thought) being true to the common goal of affordability.

Despite the feeling that the federal government was "invading" provincial jurisdiction, Quebec, ironically, was the province that moved the most quickly. The Parti Québécois government, realizing that the funds were essential to continue building affordable housing, designed a made-in-Quebec plan that produced new housing within months. That government even asked if it could spend its share of the five-year program funds in two years instead! (Who says Quebec is the problem when it comes to federal-provincial relations?)

However, several ultra-conservative provincial governments, led by Ontario's Mike Harris, sabotaged the programs in their provinces. Ideologically opposed to any social housing programs at all, they dragged their feet, refusing to invest any funds. Two and a half years later, there is barely a single housing unit funded and built in Ontario. The same goes for several other provinces. Where is the accountability to the public for promises made? Why didn't the federal government bypass, override, or cajole the reluctant provinces? Why didn't the federal government deal directly with the municipalities that were chafing at the bit to get going on housing construction?

The answer to these questions lies in the lack of political will of our national government. When the will is there, as it was in 1972 when the government had to act in order to ensure its survival, affordable housing solutions can be put into place rapidly and effectively. We need to reconstruct that will to invest and build.

A final key idea: affordable housing is an investment, not just "an expense." Funds invested in the bricks and mortar of housing create an asset. The economy grows and the asset becomes a basis for further growth. The embedded value of public and social housing could be capitalized to create more housing. This is out-of-the-box thinking—at least for government. The private sector has been capitalizing its assets since capitalism began. Why not do this in the public portion of the economy as well? Wouldn't Canadians be happier knowing that their pensions were invested in providing housing for people in need, rather than gambled away on speculative stock schemes?

One example of a real estate company doing just this is Concert Properties in B.C. The company is entirely owned by twenty-one union and management pension funds, and their commitment is to work with communities to develop rental housing projects that are both good for people and good for the bottom line. In the past several years, they've contributed over $28 million back to their affiliated pension, health, and welfare plans. These pension funds are making money—and they're making a difference.

Housing investments also save taxpayers' money. The total cost of helping homeless people in our cities is at least four times more than providing affordable housing for them. Hostels, police costs, emergency rooms and their staff, and jails all cost money—lots of it. So let's save that money, create a more caring society, and make people happier and more productive all at the same time, by investing in housing. A good idea whose time has come again.

One day, I got a call from a woman living in a family homeless shelter. She told me, amid angry tears, that her daughter was on the bed they shared in the tiny room, studying for college. She told me she thought she had made a terrible mistake. Her rent had come due at the same time that her daughter's tuition had to be paid. She was so proud of her daughter, who had worked so hard to get the grades to qualify for college. As a single mom with little support, she had to make a terrible choice—the tuition for her daughter or the rent to the landlord. She couldn't afford both. Because she wanted a better future for her daughter, she chose to pay the tuition and hope that the landlord would give a few days' grace, that luck would somehow intervene. The landlord showed no mercy, and hence the call from the shelter. No Canadian should have to make a choice like that.

Transportation in our communities

Our cities need a cardiovascular workout. Witness our clogged arteries. Check out the traffic reports for varicose veins. Ever been a part of a metaphorical blood clot on a broken-down subway train?

The right fitness program would make our infrastructure healthy—and encourage sensible solutions to transportation challenges.

People sometimes ask me, "What exactly is municipal infrastructure?" In the metaphor of the human body, infrastructure is the system that moves the things we need to wherever we need them to be—oxygen and nutrients to where they are used, wastes from where they're produced to where they can be sent on their way. Let these systems atrophy, and the body will suffer. Ditto communities.

In recent years, we have taken these systems for granted. For example, we thought our transportation networks could get by as we loaded them up with more and more demands. Now look at rush-hour traffic in most urban areas. Public transit provides an efficient and effective way to avoid transportation blood clots. Yes, the solutions involve federal government reinvestment in mass transport, but this alone will not solve the problems we face. So let's look at other solutions.

Working with the B.C. provincial government when Mike Harcourt was premier, the Greater Vancouver Regional District put together the most advanced approach in Canada for tackling the long-term problems of congestion, sprawl control, and smog reduction. With the help of community consultations, all the municipalities in the area identified green space they wanted to make immune from suburban sprawl or other development. (Future generations will be very thankful!) The communities could spell out how much development they would permit on the remaining lands. If they chose to allow higher density development, rapid transit lines would be developed to serve them. If not, then only minimal improvements in transportation would be provided. This produced an incentive to create new community growth in a way that encouraged transit use and reduced automobile travel. Sensible and efficient, and good for the environment, too.

The links between development patterns, intensity of development, and appropriate infrastructure are key to sustainable community planning. Vancouver has set a high benchmark.

- **Number of G-8 countries other than Canada with no national housing program: 0**
  With no national transportation program: 0
- **Number of people killed a day in traffic accidents worldwide: 2,425**
  Number of fatal jumbo jet crashes a day it would take to reach that number: 10
- **Percentage of urban trips made by bike in the Netherlands: 30**
  In the U.S.: 1
  Number of bicycles in Copenhagen available for free public use: 2,300

Most often, new directions in urban public policy come from the grassroots. A terrific example is the burgeoning and immensely healthy phenomenon of bicycles in cities.

In Montreal, cyclists have lead a veritable "vélolution" over the past quarter century. Travelling by bicycle produces no greenhouse gas emissions, and bikes use far less of our scarce urban land for storage. When hundreds or thousands of daily car trips are replaced by bike rides, pollution is reduced and human health improves. Community bike advocates in Montreal have urged governments to mark off lanes on roads for bikes only. Gradually, a network has been created that allows people to move around many parts of the city, most of the year, by bike. Many other cities have since followed suit.

But the federal government has yet to come up with any substantial policy and funding to promote cycling. It's as though they think biking is a frill in the transportation matrix. It's time that attitude was reversed. Federal investments in cycling infrastructure could well be the least costly way to improve transportation. Why not reward people who use their bikes and who, by doing so, keep the air cleaner and the roads less congested? And cycling improves the urban cardiovascular systems and the human ones, too! Just as I will propose rebating the GST for advanced technology low-emission vehicles, I think we should consider all bikes advanced technology vehicles themselves and rebate GST on every bicycle sold in Canada. Let's start rewarding good behaviour.

We should also be preserving rail services and railway lines and putting bike paths beside them. The abandonment of rail lines and their wanton auction to the highest bidder—usually the neighbouring landowners or speculators looking to subdivide—is blind stupidity. Once a rail line has been chopped up and sold off, there is no likelihood that it will ever be replaced. That's why the federal government should ensure that all rail lines, abandoned or not, are preserved as corridors in perpetuity, with federal laws and with appropriate financial arrangements for those who own them. Don't governments remember that they gave the railways the land on which those companies made enormous profits? Holding rail corridors in the public trust would allow future generations to use them for all kinds of transportation needs. Recreational uses are obvious. But what if we do develop new technologies for easier and more environmentally advanced movement of people, goods, and services? They will likely need corridors. If we keep them for future use, generations to come will thank us.

When it comes to sustainable infrastructure funding, Europeans can teach us a lot. There, the European Regional Development Fund (ERDF) is the main source of infrastructure funding. They wisely plan for the long term, and the 2000–2006 ERDF budget is for 195 billion euros (approximately $300 billion Canadian). Half of the infrastructure budget in 2000 went for transportation—including both public transit and roads. About 30 per cent of the ERDF allocation is dedicated to environmental and water projects.

France has its own national Transport Contribution Tax (the Versement de Transport), which is levied on all employers with more than nine employees and fixed at 1.75 per cent of their payroll. The tax finances the investment and operation of urban public transportation in France's larger cities.

Even the United States has surpassed Canada by a long shot—through the Clinton administration's Transportation Equity Act, which put hundreds of billions of dollars into long-term sustainable transportation financing. Revolving federal funds in the U.S. provide capital investment for water and sewer systems, paid back out of the water rates. Our policies should, I hate to admit it, emulate theirs—although with one proviso. Let's keep our systems public and not turn them over to the private sector in the fashion of our southern neighbour.

How do we pay for all this? Steady, step-by-step investment with long-term plans is far better than one-shot pre-election announcements for politically sexy projects of the moment. Boring? Yes. But like the daily turn on the exercise bike, it keeps the cardio ticking more happily and longer. It turns out that's the "real deal" training program for cities, too.

A case of empowerment: Hudson, Quebec

Even advanced policies from the federal government backed up by enhanced resources are not sufficient to chart the path and achieve the most sustainable results for communities. People in our cities and towns need more democratic decision-making power to shape their future. Vibrant local democracies are the best course to follow to overcome democratic deficits.

A case in point. I am so proud of my little hometown of Hudson. When a small group of women in this little bedroom and farming community (between Montreal and Ottawa on the Ottawa River) came to the conclusion, in the early 1990s, that pesticides were one reason their kids were suffering from asthma, they decided to act locally. Their local actions have shaken up Canada's Constitution, rocked the massive chemical industry, and produced global implications—as well as fewer asthma attacks in Hudson. And hundreds of other communities are following this example.

After some Hudson residents collected signatures on a petition to ban pesticides in the town, the local council brought in a bylaw to do just that, except in situations where special permission was sought. The mighty global pesticide industry feared that should the Hudson precedent ever become popular across Canada, pesticide sales could drop dramatically. Corporate moguls decided that this clearly could not be permitted, so the industry weighed in behind two small local lawn-care companies and mounted a legal challenge to Hudson's right to adopt such a bylaw. They claimed it exceeded the authority of municipal governments, and off to court they went.

Round one went to the companies. The Quebec courts ruled that, yes indeed, the good burghers of Hudson had committed an act *ultra vires*: they had exceeded the authority granted to municipalities. The argument was—and it's been long-standing conventional wisdom in municipal government—that city and town councils can adopt only measures that they have been specifically authorized to adopt by the provincial governments that supervise their activities. This limit on democratically elected municipal councils has for years stood in the way of innovation at the local level, preventing Canadians' creativity from flourishing and holding citizens back. Hudson explored the idea of appealing this reversal of its pesticide law to the Supreme Court of Canada. At the time, I was incoming president of the FCM. On behalf of the 1,000 local governments that the FCM represents, we joined with Hudson to appeal. Environmental groups also came aboard.

Canada's Supreme Court heard the arguments and issued a historic ruling on behalf of local democracy and environmental sustainability. The learned justices concluded that not only did the town of Hudson, or any other municipal government, have the power to adopt such bylaws but that they had better be considering the future health and well-being of their residents and adopt measures accordingly. Essentially, the Supreme Court changed the ossified interpretation of the Canadian Constitution that had hamstrung local democracies for over a century—liberating them and their citizens to take action to secure and enhance the health and safety of their citizens.

It was a clear case of empowerment of Canadian communities. Indeed, municipalities by the legion were beginning to follow Hudson's lead. Halifax was one of the first big cities to severely limit the use of pesticides.

But the international headquarters of the pesticide manufacturers were determined that this ruling not be allowed to stand unchallenged. Corporate profits were at risk.

As a result, multinational pesticide manufacturers are now attacking the Hudson initiative through world trade agreements, suggesting that controlling pesticide use is a restraint of trade! It remains to be seen if they will succeed.

Because the challenge takes place under the undemocratic structures of trade deals, there won't be the same opportunity to present the public interest perspective as there was at the Canadian Supreme Court. No. By contrast, the global tribunals that will rule on the case will not have representations from Hudson, or other municipalities, or any other citizens' groups. They will hear from the corporations and from national governments, *behind closed doors*. They will make their decisions without accountability or democratic contexts. The considerations will be limited to the impact of the laws on the commercial interests of the firms involved.

This is the new global constitutional framework in action—a set of rules designed not to ensure people's rights but to protect investment rights against the decisions of democratically elected governments. If allowed to stand, this new world order will set back the struggles for democracy that have taken place over the past 300 years.

Sovereignty from the ground up

The Hudson case is about much more than pesticides. It's the story of people using the level of government closest to them to achieve their desired goals. I call it sovereignty from the ground up.

There's a saying that national governments are "too big to solve the small problems facing citizens and too small to solve the big ones alone." That sentiment recognizes that local governments are best positioned to deal with the "small problems" that become big issues in people's lives. It also reflects what's called "subsidiarity," the idea that, as an FCM report explains, "decisions should only be taken at a higher level of government when there are manifest reasons to do so." It recognizes that people get the best, and the cheapest, governance when services are delivered by the most local level of government that can afford to deliver them. Properly funded, either by revenues collected nationally or by their own authority, local governments are often the most imaginative and the best equipped to deal with social and economic issues. There is no one-size-fits-all solution because everything is a different size.

Here's an example. The federal government designs labour-market training programs intended to provide people with skills to enter the workforce. But they take no account of the lack of child care or the availability of public transit, which can prevent the very people the program is designed for from taking advantage of it. Provincial governments might support clean air initiatives, but if they fail to give municipalities the powers to control urban sprawl or provide the funding necessary to operate public transit programs, it will result in increased air pollution. This lack of coordination and consultation with local governments undermines the good intentions of initiatives like these. Your local government, with the people of your community actively engaged in the process, plays—or should play—a very important role in shaping what goes on right around you.

Without being "told" to do so by the federal or provincial governments, the city of Calgary decided to build a wind turbine to generate the electricity to power its light-rail transit. (Are you thinking that cities can't do much about clean air? Studies show that half of a city's air pollution comes from cars and trucks in its own community.) Without the federal or provincial governments guiding it, Halifax decided to become a leader in waste management. Elsewhere, rent controls started locally. Settlement houses and immigration policy happened in cities first. Public potable water networks and sewer systems are city creations. Municipal policies can support urban agriculture, promote green space, reduce sprawl, provide housing, put meals in schools, stimulate the arts, and yes, even eliminate pesticides—sovereignty from the ground up, or as they said when I was a young activist, power to the people.

To fulfill its responsibilities, cities urgently need a new fiscal framework. I've already pointed out the very considerable revenue that cities generate for the federal and provincial governments and the little that they get back. We cannot continue along this path or our cities will decay— they are *already* decaying—and if we allow that, the quality of people's lives will deteriorate along with them. Classrooms are overcrowded, local environments are suffering, public transit systems are being cut back, and sprawl is encouraging the Wal-Mart-ization of our communities, just to name a few outcomes.

Ironically, Canadian cities used to be the shining North American urban success stories. Americans marvelled at our clean, safe, functioning cities, where people still live downtown and walk the streets at all hours of the night. (They're still much safer than our neighbour's because we fortunately lack America's violent gun culture.) Yet these days, it's south of the border where urban investment and renewal are taking place. For example, Americans are putting public money into urban transportation at more than one hundred times the rate of Canadian governments. The waterfront in Baltimore, the area around the new Rock and Roll Hall of Fame in Cleveland, downtown Philadelphia and Minneapolis–St. Paul, and many other American cities have all undergone wonderful renewal with considerable state and federal contributions.

In Canada, many towns and cities have been working hard to renew their infrastructure, improve their schools, and protect their environment, but they've been doing so with inadequate resources. Under our current system, even when cities do things to stimulate local economic activity, Ottawa benefits from it and the cities end up with more costs. Here's one example.

Let's say you want to promote a successful tourist activity. I'll pick Caribana, one of the best and largest community festivals in Canada. Toronto has to give money to the event organizers to help make it happen. The city also has to hire extra police, put on more buses, hire the drivers, pay for extra fuel, and pay municipal workers to clean up after the fabulous, colourful parade. Okay. I support all that, because it's important to the community, and because it draws thousands of tourists to Toronto every summer. They eat in the city's restaurants, stay in the hotels, support local businesses, and stimulate the economy in countless other ways.

Economically, activities like Caribana are probably break-even operations for the city. For the federal and provincial governments, they're a bonus, as they collect tens of thousands of dollars in additional corporate tax, sales tax, and GST.

It's clear—not only to municipal governments and the FCM, but also to the chambers of commerce, the banks, and the social scientists and academics who study the situation— that cities need a new deal from the senior levels of government. They need a better division of existing revenue, and they need new opportunities to collect revenue.

Municipal governments are in a bind, as I've said, because they have very limited opportunities to collect revenue, apart from property tax. In Europe, transfers from senior governments account for 31 per cent of city revenues.

In the U.S., it's 27 per cent. In Canada, it's less than 19 per cent. In the U.S., cities may legally charge sales tax, income tax (on people and corporations), and business tax. In Canada, cities generally don't have this authority. American cities may also issue tax-exempt bonds, another major revenue source denied to Canadian cities. And as I've pointed out, municipal governments must also pay sales tax on their purchases to their provinces and GST on goods and services to the federal government.

Some provinces are beginning to earmark revenue to cities. In Alberta, the provincial government directs 1.2 cents a litre of the tax on gasoline sold in Edmonton and Calgary back to those cities. In British Columbia, the Greater Vancouver Transit Authority gets 11 cents a litre in gasoline tax for use in sustainable transportation. (Wisely, the province sets some laudable guidelines for how the funds can be used; it doesn't tell the city specifically how to use the money.) Manitoba gives a grant to municipalities equal to two percentage points of personal income tax and one percentage point of corporate income tax. Quebec also gives a portion of the gas or fuel tax to its cities. In a couple of other instances, cities have some other sources of tax revenue (in Quebec and Nova Scotia, they can levy a land transfer tax), but these exceptions are rare.

It's the federal government, which spends the greatest portion of Canadians' tax revenue, that should really be dedicating funds directly to municipalities. One incident sheds light on the issue.

As FCM president, I had the chance to introduce Finance Minister Paul Martin as a featured speaker at our convention on the fateful weekend when he lost his job in June 2002. A month earlier, and just by chance, I had met him on a plane. "The cities are tired and struggling, after being downloaded upon in federal budget after federal budget. You need to help fund municipalities of all sizes with a new deal," I urged. Martin replied, in a conspiratorial whisper—Alan Rock was sitting a couple of seats behind!—that "the budget cycle won't allow me to make an announcement in June, and besides, you have to convince Number One about this."

I found this "budget-cycle" excuse lame. He had told me and an entire assembly of big-city mayors a few months earlier that he did not agree with diverting the $4.5 billion gas tax toward sustainable urban transportation, as we had requested. "I don't agree with dedicated taxes" was the extent of his explanation at that time.

On the plane, I told him, "Well, I'll have the pen, so you'd best have the cheque."

A few weeks later, there we were at the FCM convention, me with my pen, and Paul without his cheque! On stage in front of hundreds of mayors and councillors from every town in Canada, I offered the pen. Martin laughed at what he considered a joke. Still, Finance Minister Martin let fly, for the first time, the revolutionary phrase "new deal." The place erupted like starving masses being thrown flyers with a promise of water and rice in the next truck. The reaction from "Number One" was swift. Martin was pulled out of our intimate post-speech lunch to be told, apparently, that he was about to lose his job. Number One had spoken!

Can a national focus on cities turn around these revenue inequities? Sure. With the proper funding, our towns and cities will blossom, our infrastructure will be restored, and our communities will thrive. Consider these initiatives:

The Okanagan Valley in B.C.'s southern interior is using its wineries and tourism as a departure point for building a knowledge-based high-tech sector. Saskatoon has developed an innovative community program linking its large First Nations population with jobs and training in an Employer Circles Program. This provides skills and employment for young Aboriginal men and women, as well as training in cultural understanding for business owners and managers. Saskatoon also put in place an exciting program linking social housing to community economic development. The region in the Beauce, Quebec, is organizing to turn itself from small, localized production into a new "techno-region." Hamilton is undertaking a Vision 2020 plan. The city of Ottawa held a Smart Growth Summit as part of its planning initiative. Winnipeg embraced principles of sustainable development in its Homegrown Economic Development Strategy for Winnipeg. Dozens of bright ideas are turning into bright futures, where cities are thinking smart.

Now Paul Martin has himself become Number One. No more passing the buck. Let's review his commitment to date. And let me also lay out my proposal for a new relationship between the federal government, Canadian communities, and provinces.

Watching Martin work his way through his first months as prime minister has been eerily similar to observing his nine years as finance minister. Before assuming the new office, he spent much of 2003 talking about his much-hyped new deal for cities. But the deal becomes less and less ambitious the longer he's on the job. In his first month, Prime Minister Martin's priorities were a freeze on public spending, ballistic missile defence (BMD) talks with the U.S., and more corporate tax cuts. Indeed, he flatly refused to follow Ontario Premier Dalton McGuinty's lead and cancel corporate tax cuts he can't afford; Martin proceeded with further corporate tax reductions. Joining the Americans' dangerous BMD (or Star Wars) program could cost Canada $10 billion if we were told to contribute only 1 per cent of the cost (based on a complete cost of $1 trillion, according to the Center for Arms Control and Non-Proliferation).

These are significant choices with large impacts on

government finances and our ability to help cities. These choices could be made in a month, but the most basic first step toward helping cities—sharing the gas tax—has gone from an inviolable commitment to something that may not occur at all, if we follow the direction of prime ministerial musings.

We're told instead that municipalities may get a bigger GST refund. This is good, but not great. It's actually just a promise not to collect as much money from cities as the federal government has done since the GST was imposed.

While returning the GST to cities would be a start, it would not even begin to address the infrastructure crisis, let alone get rid of the infrastructure deficit. For example, the city of Toronto alone has paid $500 million in GST since Martin became finance minister. A full refund would provide about $49 million a year to Toronto, which will mean that the infrastructure deficit will continue climbing by $1.5 billion a year instead of $2 billion while still leaving the city's transit authority underfunded and doing little to alleviate the housing crisis. Each Canadian city can tell its own tale of GST woe as its property taxes marched dutifully into Paul Martin's ministry's pockets. Celebrating a GST refund is akin to thanking a robber for no longer taking your cash after years of stealing from you, and not asking for the return of what he's already gotten.

If a GST rebate is all Martin gives to cities, our country is in deep trouble.

A Real Deal for Canadian Communities

After spending years in municipal government, at the Federation of Canadian Municipalities, and now as leader of the New Democratic Party, I know we can do better. I call it a Real Deal for Canadian Communities.

First, municipalities should stop paying any GST. Second,

the federal government should share half the federal gas tax as a dedicated transfer for sustainable transport such as public transit, cycling, pedestrian infrastructure, and rural roads. Sustainable transport is key to our economic health and central to fighting smog and climate change.

Let's dismiss the nonsense we've been hearing from the federal government that sharing the gas tax is somehow "complicated." It's not. Nothing prevents gas tax revenue from being transferred immediately. Funds could be forwarded for the first year with a simple letter of transmittal:

> To the Premiers:
> As promised, this portion of the gas tax is being returned to your provinces and territories for distribution to municipal governments for sustainable transportation improvements. Please forward the funds to the cities and towns ASAP. Next year's installment will be sent after we have worked out a plan together that accomplishes national objectives concerning climate change and transportation while assuring maximum local flexibility.
>
> Yours sincerely,
> Government of Canada

Immediately after this announcement, the government could then put together a high-level negotiating team to finalize a permanent arrangement with the provinces over the subsequent year. If Martin believes in cities, he must have faith in our mayors' ability to ensure that provincial governments extend the funding. I firmly believe that the way to a healthy federalism is to start with a little good faith, and flow the gas tax now.

It's not naive to believe that Mayor Bill Smith of Edmonton or Mayor Gérald Tremblay of Montreal would make their premiers pay a heavy political price if the received federal gas tax money was not passed on to municipalities. But it is naive to require provinces to match federal funds, since most provinces (unlike the federal government) are facing deficits. In fact, it would be unfair and bad public policy for the federal government to insist on this in these times. Demanding that cash-strapped provinces share the bill for cities is a delaying tactic that lets Martin take credit for trying while being able to blame the provinces for failing. It's also hypocritical, given that Martin refused long-term investment plans when he was fighting deficits federally in the mid-1990s.

Third, a national affordable housing plan is needed in Canada. We know this is a good idea and works in Canada because we've done it before. Some 2.2 million people live in houses built by the housing program that NDP leader David Lewis began with Pierre Trudeau in the 1970s, during a rare period of federal minority government. Martin abolished it in the 1990s and has repeatedly refused to announce a significant new program, despite housing crises in our biggest cities and smallest First Nations communities.

Affordable housing is key to fighting child poverty, increasing disposable income, creating jobs, and creating markets for our beleaguered softwood lumber industry. I propose that Canada launch a national project to reduce homelessness by building 200,000 new affordable homes and 100,000 renovated houses at reasonable rents over the next ten years. This would cut by half the affordable-housing-deficit number.

I have heard from countless Canadians that they want an end to homelessness and that we have a responsibility to provide decent, affordable housing to all our neighbours. It's time to allow Canadians to mobilize the construction of housing. The details of the plan have already been developed by the FCM. I know this because I was there, in charge of that project.

Fourth, municipalities need a permanent infrastructure program (instead of starving municipalities and forcing them to privatize public services such as water, noting that Martin is a proponent of deeply flawed P3s, which actually cost tax-payers more and are profoundly unaccountable). This program would help Canadians repair and upgrade their water and sewage systems, invest in green energy solutions, as well as improve their building infrastructure through energy conservation measures. And the program would create jobs, lots of jobs.

This plan costs money. But corporate tax cuts and weaponizing space cost money as well. I believe cities that work are more important to our economy than helping the banks make even more money; and that we should be building affordable homes to cover our heads before building missile shields to cover our skies. So far, Paul Martin has been clear that he doesn't agree. But after a decade of his choices, Canadians are ready to start disagreeing back. We're fed up with the smog, the traffic, and the housing crisis. We want a government prepared to make wiser choices that improve our cities, our economy, the natural environment, and our quality of life.

Revitalizing local democracy

There is a final and fundamental piece to this puzzle. We have to unleash our urban democracies from the bonds of archaic decision-making structures imposed long ago, when we were a rural country. We need to enhance local democracy by permitting flexibility and creativity so that communities can put our national financial resources to work to meet their local needs. They can do this while helping to achieve broad national goals—like a cleaner environment, more robust local economies, and greater equality for our citizens. The exciting community events and projects that bring people together and give them a chance to celebrate their collective achievements are often rooted in the processes of their local governments. It's time they were exalted, not demeaned.

Radical democratic reform really begins by engaging and involving people in the local governance of their communities. The stronger local democracies are, the more infused with democratic culture the population as a whole will be. Want to increase voter turnout in elections? Start with the local. Involve people directly, and in a meaningful way, through local democracies in their neighbourhoods and communities. This is more easily done if the resources are available to create, build, sustain, and nurture those communities. The healthiest communities are the ones with the greatest amount of local engagement.

Quebec City's stunning system of arrondissements, with community-based budgeting processes and real engagement of citizens, is the best of its class in Canada. Too bad so few in English-speaking Canada know anything about it. Other communities, like Banff, in Alberta, have truly exciting plans afoot to achieve community sustainability through local involvement. Instead of being afraid of their citizens, effective local democracies reach out and grab them, pulling them in to take responsibility and allowing their creativity and community spirit to flow.

There are countless examples of success stories when Canadians focus on the hard but rewarding work of making their communities better places to live—for everyone, not just a few. The FCM's Sustainable Communities program, accessible through its website at www.fcm.ca, provides a treasure trove of optimistic and successful stories from our municipal grassroots. It's very hard to find examples of successful federal policies and programs that engage people as directly and positively. So let's turn government on its head, and use our federal government to raise the funds that can be funnelled back into dynamic local community efforts.

A new national policy is needed, one that focuses on our economic and community roots and nurtures them. A spirit of co-operation and collaboration with provinces is essential. That's always been important. What I am proposing is a serious commitment to engaging local energy and enthusiasm through our local democracies, through our cities and towns, to achieve the dreams we have for our communities.

For Canada, this is how our sovereignty and our democracy can best be enhanced. I'm talking about a call to think nationally, act locally.

[CHAPTER 6]

Building the New Prosperity

It's time to put our hands on the tiller of our economy once again. After twenty years of both Conservative and Liberal governments telling us we should abandon the ship we call Canada to the winds of the global corporate marketplace, Canadians need to take charge. We have done this before with powerful and long-lasting results: over the years, Canadians have invented fiscal and social infrastructure for our own advancement. The National Dream became a railway that tied a countrywide economy together. The Bank of Canada provided a financial framework for building and rebuilding our country through measured and strategic investment in the public interest, allowing growth and fiscal prudence to be pursued simultaneously, especially during the reconstruction period following the Second World War. The Canadian Broadcasting Corporation/Radio-Canada—established so our voices, and subsequently our images, could be transmitted to one another across the land—has been central to our appreciation of both our unity and our diversity, and laid a foundation for the now vibrant communications industry. In its original format, the unemployment insurance system provided stable financial assistance for citizens between jobs. And finally, Canada's public health care system is perhaps our best example of Canadians taking action on behalf of all, to ensure our individual and collective physical well-being—the foundation of a flourishing economy, society, community.

Engaging in a proactive economic agenda again would mean a considerable shift away from Canadian policies of the past two decades. We have experienced almost a generation of economic policies calling for the reduction of public services, rampant privatization, and the removal of regulations and protections. As we look around, we have begun to see the consequences: homelessness, increased smog and pollution, record student and personal debt, provinces that can't balance their budgets, cities and towns forced to cut basic services, health care unable to keep up, and children in increasing need, despite the statistical affluence.

Simple laissez-faire economics does not serve the public good. Individual enterprise is essential, but dynamic economic development requires its complement—national goals—with strategies for achieving those goals clearly laid out. We need to create a working system within which enterprise can flourish sustainably, jobs can be created, and Canada's talents can be effectively focused to achieve their potential. Lately, the very idea of collective public effort has been rejected in favour of unbridled corporatism. The result is a vacuum, rather than the substantive support provided by a nation-building program.

Prime Minister Paul Martin is touted as having delivered, as finance minister, an economic recovery at the same time as ridding the nation of chronic deficits. What really happened during Martin's tenure at the till? First, revenue from the enormous cuts to health and education funding was subsequently given away in tax cuts to the corporate sector and the highest-income earners. But those cuts were not responsible for eliminating chronic deficits—what did the job was the Bank of Canada's decision to dramatically lower interest rates. This move unleashed a flow of economic growth that produced nearly $100 billion in surpluses from 1997 to 2003. But this helped few Canadians. Between 1993 and 2001–02, average weekly earnings grew by 16.8 per cent while the Consumer Price Index (CPI) rose by 16.9 per cent. Wages stagnated and income inequality increased greatly while corporate pre-tax profits tripled and the top 20 per cent of Canadians significantly increased their income.

Mr. Martin's policies did little for most Canadians and even less for creating a healthy economy. Let's look at some of the key indicators. In the absence of industrial strategies or policies, the productivity gap between Canadian and American industry is growing. Wages and salaries have increased only slightly, and there is an increasing discrepancy between high- and low-paid work. Job growth continues to be sluggish. Canada attracts less foreign investment per capita than the U.S., but most foreign direct investment goes to purchase existing firms, creating nothing new in the form of economic activity except to drive up the value of the dollar, throwing people out of work in export-focused sectors.

What would a nation-building economic policy look like? It would focus on the domestic economy first, creating the conditions for strong local and regional economies across the country—shifting from what has become an overly exclusive focus on international trade. It surprises most Canadians to learn that trade accounts for less than 20 per cent of our total economic output. Canadian policies of the past twenty years were designed to place trade considerations first, but they ended up benefiting a relatively small number of Canadian businesses. Only 4 per cent of all exporting firms accounted for 82 per cent of the total value of merchandise exports. Of course 20 per cent still represents millions of jobs and is vital to the economy. By incorporating trade into a broad, nation-building strategy, we will work to guarantee more value added to our resources before they are traded away—ultimately strengthening our position in the global economy.

Four out of five businesses in Canada do not sell outside the country. A nation-building policy would pay more attention to the needs of these enterprises, which tend to create most of the jobs. How do we strengthen the domestic economy? Invest in infrastructure throughout Canada. Recognize that cities are vital economic engines. Explore strategies to create higher-wage jobs, the very ones we are losing today. Those higher wages drive spending and generate tax revenues, fostering a new prosperity.

A nation-building concept would create and then invest in industrial strategies that target the technologies of the future—particularly, as I'll argue below, leading-edge renewable energy and energy conservation sectors, but also value-added strategies for our natural resources. Every time a truckload of raw British Columbia logs crosses the border to Washington State to be turned into two-by-four studs, jobs for Canadians go with it. It's time to restrict raw log exports and keep those jobs here.

Nation building needs minds, well developed and well trained. Education is a fundamental economic and social foundation. That's why investment in our public schools, universities, training centres, and Canadian cultural industries is crucial. Modern economic growth will flow from ideas, and they must be nurtured. Indeed, the ideas sectors of the economy such as the arts have been shown to have the highest impact on job creation.

The Bank of Canada's tight money policies, particularly in the early 1990s, have hurt job creation. They restrict the building process. Healthy economic growth can happen when the reins are loosened a little; current low interest rates are aimed to stimulate the economy. Compounding the difficulties facing the Canadian economy today is the U.S. deficit, which has been exacerbated by Bush administration economic policies and the Iraq War. That historic deficit, approaching $521 billion, devalues the American currency, thus driving up the Canadian dollar. The higher Canadian dollar makes our exports more expensive to Americans; they buy less, so our workers are laid off—a rather perverse example of how deficit spending and war can cause unemployment.

Paul Martin's new government is apparently to be guided by the same principles as the previous Liberal regime, when Martin held the purse strings. He was doggedly determined to pay down the national debt at the cost of many important social programs; this produced higher unemployment, reduced public services, increased poverty and homelessness, and created more pollution, among other consequences. Now he wants us to achieve, as a national goal, a debt-to-GDP ratio of 25 per cent. What harm can it do to have such a target?

To understand this concept, I always suggest that people consider the analogy of owning a house with a mortgage. It's great to be able to pay down a mortgage faster than the scheduled payment plan. But should it be the priority for a family under all circumstances? What if the roof leaked, Grandma was sick, or a teenager needed money for post-secondary tuition? I don't know any family that would say, Sorry, we can't afford to do anything about those problems because we're going to use our extra funds this month, and every month from now on, to pay down the mortgage.

Our country cannot build if we are so fixated on paying down the national debt. We should use any surpluses to invest, thereby stimulating the economy and creating jobs at the same time as providing essential services like health care, education, housing, and transportation. Such new activity strengthens the domestic economy as the wages and salaries of a more robust workforce are injected into local community businesses. And by strengthening the economy, GDP increases and the debt-to-GDP ratio falls as a result.

Imagine what a cross-country child care program could do—creating tens of thousands of jobs and contributing to the well-being of the workforce of the future. Surely this is more important than accelerating the payment of our national mortgage. In fact, such an investment in human potential improves our capacity to retire the already shrinking debt over the long term. This kind of economic thinking allows the building process to flourish. Although people are a country's constant resource, every new generation must be nurtured afresh, which is why a reliable continuum of funding for child care and education ensures ongoing stable productivity. Just paying down the debt faster than we have to, if it impoverishes such programs, is short-sighted; we can't afford *not* to continuously invest in the future.

Does this mean "tax and spend"? Does it mean a George W. Bush deficit? Not at all.

Having served two decades on Toronto City Council, I've learned to live comfortably with balanced budgets. Every time you propose an idea, you have to identify a source of funding. Sometimes you can find money by saving in other programs or by financing through efficiencies. Other times you have to argue that the policy you are advocating is a higher priority than an existing one, hoping to persuade a majority of your colleagues to support you. Usually, in the days before federal and provincial government downloading became an annual tradition, mopping up any surpluses, there would be some new funds each year as a result of growth in the property tax revenue because of new buildings. And the council would be prepared to enact a small tax increase to keep up with inflationary costs, for example, or to backfill where downloading had left an unacceptable hole. I learned in municipal government always to think about the tax dollar as something precious. When you consider the work that someone had to do to create that tax resource, it takes on real meaning. Knowing my constituents in Riverdale and the work they do daily, I think of them flipping burgers, teaching kids, making films, working a factory line, running a small business, with a piece of that paycheque each hour being shipped to the government. I always feel as if I'm holding someone's tax dollar in my hand and making choices that I should be able to explain if I'm asked. And in local government, you're asked, believe me! It comes up all the time on the street corner, in the coffee shop or pub. That's accountability. It's also one of the reasons I'm always on the lookout for municipal councillors to run for the federal Parliament. They get it. They have held that tax dollar in their hands and made the difficult choices. It's a lot like meeting a payroll—a similar sense of responsibility flows from the experience.

When governments run deficits, they are essentially deferring the inevitable. Banks and investors benefit because they will collect the interest. That's why it's always better to pay as you go rather than chalk up a shortfall. Not that you can always predict these things perfectly. Unusual events such as SARS, mad cow disease, forest fires, and international peacekeeping missions can hit, and simultaneously, as they did in 2003. Major recessions can take the economic wind out of all the sails at once. Combined blows to communities and the economy have left almost all provinces struggling to maintain a balanced budget. Most people understand that in emergencies you have no choice but to dig deep. But as an operating principle, the annual balancing of current budgets is very sound.

The huge surpluses that the government of Canada has posted in the past few years, and that are projected to be collected in years ahead, mean that we can initiate the nation-building project on many fronts without having to consider deficits. At the same time, we should stop giving away those surpluses—by reducing taxes to those who earn the most. While everyone would love a tax cut, most would not call for tax reductions if they felt confident that the money would be responsibly used to tackle pressing needs. Recent scandals have shaken any remaining trust that citizens might have had in governments to spend their hard-earned money wisely. That's one of the most tragic impacts of the recent sponsorship debacle.

Balancing budgets while investing in the future also requires that we stop the panic-stricken rush to pay down the debt faster than we need to when we have a range of threatened social, economic, and infrastructure programs that require our attention now. Because the federal debt is shrinking so rapidly as a share of the GDP, interest payments are shrinking just as rapidly as a share of federal revenues. This opens up new spending room each year without deficits or increased taxes. As finance minister, Paul Martin allocated most of the past surpluses to tax cuts and debt repayment (80 to 90 per cent, according to the economist Jim Stanford). Instead, new spending and investment could be accomplished without increasing overall taxes. Intelligent and well-crafted sustainable strategies for the economy, combined with smart policy levers, open the door for Canadians to build.

While I am not, in this short book, laying out an industrial strategy for Canada, I would like to give an example of how one could be constructed from my own experience dealing with a large power corporation, Ontario Hydro.

I love those eureka moments when a good idea crystallizes. This time, a light went off, not on. Suddenly, I could see a way to create jobs, reduce costs, improve economic efficiency, and cut smog—all at the same time. The setting was the office building of the largest electricity company in Canada, Ontario Hydro. It was over a decade ago, and I was one of a small group of sustainable-energy enthusiasts who had gathered to talk to senior engineers at the Ontario utility about saving energy.

The venue for the briefing was a big boardroom on a wonderful, bright, sunny afternoon, high up in the Hydro building, facing south toward Lake Ontario. The window blinds were closed against the natural light abundantly available outside. White fluorescent fixtures flooded the room. As we began the meeting, it was easy to see that the Hydro officials and engineers were more than just a little skeptical about our ideas for practical, grassroots energy reduction in Ontario. What could we know about the high-technology business of energy production and distribution? Why on earth would they want to reduce electricity consumption and therefore sell less energy, make less money? They were one tough crowd. Then it hit me.

I got up, flipped the fluorescents off, and opened the blinds. Sunlight filled the room. I said, "How about that? We're saving energy right now. At the same time we have prevented some coal from being burned to produce electricity, reduced pollution a little, and saved money for Ontario Hydro's ratepayers—us. Win-win. Imagine if we made it possible for millions of similar modest win-win situations to happen over and over again by retrofitting thousands of buildings with high-efficiency lights, motion detector light switches, more insulation, draft proofing, better control systems and motors, new windows that lost less heat, and more?" Thus was born Toronto's Better Buildings Partnership.

Years later, the Big Blackout of August 2003 focused our minds. The blackout demonstrated that the solution to daily energy needs was best met by conservation and self-sufficiency. We were reminded that massive energy production from a small number of plants on a single grid could not guarantee our power supply.

Around the world, people have no shortage of bright ideas that are good for the environment, good for the economy, and good for people. What we often lack is the will; what often holds us back are bureaucratic lethargy in government and private-sector organizations alike and, to put it bluntly, short-sighted greed. It's time to open the blinds.

Energy for a new prosperity

Everything we do requires energy: from the food we eat, to the electronic equipment we use, to the vehicles we drive, to the products we build and consume, to the buildings we live in. The types of energy we use, the ways in which we transport it (electrical grids, natural gas pipes, gas stations, and so on) and the levels of energy use drive our economy. For over a century we've been completely reliant on hydroelectric power and fossil fuel. Since the 1950s, Canada has also developed nuclear power. In all the industrialized countries, this type of power production has evolved into a highly centralized system in which multinational corporations wield enormous economic and political influence. Oil-producing regions, particularly in the Middle East, have become powder kegs; and nuclear power plants around the world are now potential targets for terrorists. In short, our current energy system is not only fundamentally undemocratic and environmentally unsustainable, it is an international security threat.

The solution to the biggest environmental problem facing our generation is also the guarantee of new prosperity for future generations of Canadians. We now have a historic opportunity to no longer be held hostage to this system, to replace it with a new system of renewable energy resources.

Imagine a Canada where we are the recognized world leader in developing the most innovative and sustainable economy in the world. Imagine a Canada where over three million new person years of jobs are have been created to build this new economy. Imagine a healthier Canada that practises conservation and energy efficiency and that has more livable buildings and factories powered by electricity generated without creating the smog that kills thousands prematurely every year. Imagine a Canada where there are no nuclear power stations or coal-fired generating stations that are easy targets for terrorists who want to paralyze our economy and country.

Impossible, you might say; it would cost too much money and create too many economic hardships for Canadians. The fact is this new prosperity is not only imaginable, the way to make it a reality has already been outlined by some of the most innovative minds in Canada. At a minimum, it wouldn't cost us any more money than we are spending now. It may even save us substantial funds in the long run as health care costs, pollution costs, and climate change remediation costs decline.

How do we get there? Let me outline key elements of a green energy plan that, if implemented, would usher in a new prosperity for Canada, the likes of which we have never seen. I am drawing on any number of sources, but in particular, the 2002 report for the Suzuki Foundation by Ralph Torrie, one of Canada's foremost energy consultants.

We all live and work in buildings. Bad insulation, leaky doors and windows, old and inefficient furnaces and air conditioners mean many of our buildings use much more energy than they need to. By increasing insulation and installing state-of-the-art windows, doors, furnaces, and air conditioners, building owners can cut energy use, save money, and help create a large amount of economic activity. To make this happen, we need a national energy retrofit program for residential, institutional, commercial, and industrial buildings. I know this will work because a smaller version of it has already proven to be a big success. In Chapter 2, I described the highly successful Better Buildings Partnership (BBP) in the City of Toronto. To date, the BBP has retrofitted 32 million square feet of space in 467 buildings, creating 3,800 person years of employment, with a local economic impact of $126 million. At the same time, the owners of those buildings (private and public) reduced their annual operating costs by $19 million and cut CO_2 emissions by 132,000 tonnes a year.

In June 2002, I asked one of the foremost energy retrofit entrepreneurs in Canada to outline the details of a national program for the industrial, commercial, and institutional (ICI) sector. Here are the details:

- **Number of m^3 covered by program: 631 million**
- **Average reduction in GHG emissions: 20 per cent**
- **Average annual energy savings from retrofits: $7 billion**
- **Average payback period for retrofit investment: 6 years**
- **Direct employment from program: 839,000 person years**
- **Indirect employment from program: 2,097,300 person years**
- **Overall investment in retrofit program: $41 billion**
- **Estimated tax revenues to provincial and federal governments from program: $4.1 billion**

This is a fairly conservative plan, based on data collected in the late 1990s that does not take full advantage of all the existing technology and savings. So the real numbers are probably better. But even so, a conservatively calculated national retrofit program for *just* the ICI sector would create just under 300,000 permanent jobs for ten years running, put over $7 billion per year in the pockets of building owners after six years of no price increases, reduce GHG emissions by 20 per cent, and generate $4 billion of tax revenue. And all of this could be financed through a revolving loan fund, just like we did in Toronto.

Once we begin bringing the residential sector into the picture, we get even more exciting results because there are around 14 million households in Canada that can be retrofitted. But a residential retrofit program does much more than create new jobs and reduce our energy costs. It also improves the livability of our homes with state-of-the-art, energy-efficient windows and high-efficiency furnaces. Winter draughts that plague many of our homes disappear.

We also need to make sure all new buildings meet the highest energy efficiency building code standards. As I outlined in Chapter 2, energy-efficient buildings can be cost competitive. As Greg Allen, one of the most innovative engineer/architects in Canada, has often said, building state-of-the-art, energy-efficient buildings won't raise construction costs. It's time that energy efficiency standards become the law for new building construction. This won't cost a penny and will save everyone money.

Next, we need to make sure that all the machines, appliances, electronics, and motors in Canadian buildings are energy efficient. Right now, when consumers go to buy appliances and electronics, only a handful of models have an Energy Star rating (which means models meet existing energy efficiency standards). It's time all appliances, electronics, machines, and motors meet efficiency standards.

And why not have these electronics and appliances built here in Canada? Canada used to have a much larger appliance manufacturing industry, which was decimated when we entered into free trade agreements with the U.S. I believe it's time the federal government shifted the tax structure and created a policy framework to assist appliance manufacturers to build energy-efficient appliances in Canada. Think about the number of new jobs that would be created.

We need to think innovatively in all sectors. While I was a city councillor, I learned first hand about some innovative ways to reduce traffic congestion on the busiest highway in Canada (the infamous 401), increase rail freight transportation in a way that helps truck companies, and reduce smog. The answer is to put truck trailers on trains and move the truck trailers on a train track instead of a highway. These systems are already in place and working. But they are at a competitive disadvantage because governments subsidize highway construction, thus bringing down the cost of trucks using highways.

While highways should remain public, continuously building more public highways is not the answer. As anyone who has travelled in the Vancouver area or southern Ontario recently knows, traffic congestion is getting worse and worse. It makes little sense to focus heavy spending on highway expansion for goods movement, except where that is the only practical option, where bottlenecks are problems, such as at key border crossings, or where safety considerations drive the agenda, such as the twinning of the Trans-Canada. Rather, let's invest in innovative freight transportation systems. Fewer trucks on the road means less congestion and greater safety for other vehicle users, less pollution, and cost savings for businesses of all sizes, including, of course, the agricultural sector. It's time the federal government invested in rail freight transportation. It's win-win-win.

Another element of a green energy strategy is improving the energy efficiency of the industrial sector. Like building owners, many industries could save substantially by switching to more energy-efficient equipment. The federal government should set robust targets for each energy subsector and provide incentives to companies that could be paid back over time from realized energy savings.

Another industrial strategy focuses on industries that burn fossil fuels as part of their production process. This often creates large amounts of so-called waste heat. Most companies just dump it into the atmosphere or a nearby body of water. They don't realize that waste heat can actually make them money and help Canada reduce greenhouse gas emissions. How? By using it to turn turbines that create electricity. Called "co-generation," this method turns industries into small-scale power producers. So instead of building more large fossil fuel electrical power generating stations, the federal government could provide incentives for industrial companies to become small-scale electrical generators. When I have helped lead "energy tours" of Scandinavia over the years, municipal leaders who joined me to see district energy in action have marvelled at the efficiency and the economic development that flows from these integrated energy strategies. We also saw how countries like Denmark and Germany fostered remarkable export industries in insulated pipe and co-generation technologies, just as they did in the wind turbine sector. As the vice chair of Canada's largest district energy system, Toronto Hydro, I helped develop strategies to expand this remarkably sensible approach to energy in cities, including the use of the cold water at the bottom of Lake Ontario to provide cooling to central city buildings. It was a proud moment when, in June 2002, Robert Kennedy Jr. and I stood together, near the huge John Street Water Pumping station, to proclaim the launch of this new wave of energy thinking and practice.

Just as the cold water in Lake Ontario can be harnessed to provide green power, the wind across Canada can be harnessed. This would not only bring significant environmental benefits, it would create a significant number of jobs as well as sustainable economic activity. The Canadian Wind Energy Association (CanWEA) has calculated that there is enough wind in Canada to supply 20 per cent of our electricity needs (about 36,000 megawatts), enough to power about 14 million typical households in Canada. Currently, Canadian wind turbines generate enough electricity to power 126,000 typical households. CanWEA has challenged Canadians to achieve what they call the 10 by 10 goal: install 10,000 megawatts of wind power by 2010. This would supply almost 4 million households with green power, contribute 5 per cent of all our electricity needs, create between 80,000 and 160,000 permanent jobs by 2010, and generate between $10 billion and $20 billion of economic activity. And it would reduce greenhouse gas (GHG) emissions by 15 to 25 million tonnes per year. Currently, we must rely on foreign companies to supply most of the components for building wind turbines. I think it's time Canadian workers start building these turbines in Canadian factories, not only to supply the Canadian market but to export to the rest of North America.

I want to be absolutely clear: my plan doesn't cost Canadian taxpayers one more penny. The beauty of sustainable energy is that it can be entirely funded by reallocating existing federal government and consumer spending to new priorities. Let me illustrate:

It may come as a surprise to most people that the federal government subsidizes the fossil fuel and nuclear industries by at least $250 million a year. These subsidies might have made sense before we knew about the environmental threats posed by climate change and nuclear waste; before we knew of the tens of billions of dollars in economic and health care costs associated with smog-related illnesses and deaths; and before the security concerns resulting from the tragic events of September 11, 2001. But the world has changed. It's time to re-examine how government tax dollars are spent. I propose fully phasing in over four years a tax-shifting regime to transform incentive, subsidy, and investment programs from supporting energy sources that contribute to climate change, such as fossil fuels, or that produce toxic residue, such as nuclear power, to those that focus on green energy sources including wind, solar, and tidal power, as well as on transitional technologies.

Doing this will obviously affect the national economy and regional economies. That's why implementation of this plan must be sensitive to, and include negotiated adjustments for, regional economic impacts, maturity of sectors, and establishment of compensating strategies. Let's also make sure we use the federal revenues from the tax-shifting plan to ensure the most affected regions are the first places where new green energy jobs are created.

An even bigger source of funding for the green energy strategy would come from revenues generated by a new market mechanism that has emerged as a crucial policy tool for countries interested in fighting climate change: a domestic emissions trading (DET) system. Essentially, emissions trading is a way for companies to trade permits that give them the right to release greenhouse gas emissions (one permit typically allows a company to release one tonne of CO_2 or equivalent other greenhouse gas). For example, let's say Company A releases thirty tonnes of GHG emissions every year making widgets. Under an emissions trading system, the company must have thirty permits, one for each tonne of CO_2 it releases. But let's assume the company decides to invest in energy efficiency measures that reduce the actual emissions to twenty-five tonnes. The company can now sell its extra five permits at an agreed-on price to another company that needs them. Meanwhile, Company B thought it needed only twenty permits but because of higher demand for its products needs an additional five, so it decides to buy the five permits from Company A.

Emissions trading systems can involve trades among companies in one country as well as among companies on opposite ends of the planet. While all emissions trading systems rest on the principle that allows a company to make investment decisions in energy efficiency and/or GHG permits based on market decisions, not all systems achieve the same positive environmental results. To date, the federal government is advocating a system that will effectively give away 85 per cent of the allowable permits that companies want. And there will be no cap on the number of available permits. This system has the potential of actually undermining the very goal of reducing emissions. Giving away most of the permits means there is almost no financial incentive for companies to reduce their emissions. And by not having caps on the number of permits that will be issued, it is difficult to understand how actual emissions will be reduced.

That's why I'm proposing what is called a "cap and trade" system, based on the auctioning of permits. Under this system, there is an absolute cap on the number of permits available to companies. Over time, the cap is reduced, resulting in a steady decline in emissions from all companies. Unlike the proposed federal government system, under cap and trade companies that emit CO_2 must purchase their permits from an auction held by the federal government. The proceeds of this auction are collected by the government.

Interestingly, in spring 2002, the government released a report called "A Discussion Paper on Canada's Contribution to Addressing Climate Change." The report offered four possible options for meeting the Kyoto commitment, and noted that an emissions trading system that auctioned all the permits would be the most economically beneficial option for Canada. According to the government's own report, auctioning permits would raise about $4.5 billion annually, which could then be reinvested in the economy! As the report indicated, electricity prices would rise by 6 per cent, and the price of gasoline and natural gas would go up by about 2 per cent (for gasoline at 70 cents a litre, that's about 1.5 cents, much less than the average weekly fluctuation at the pumps). But the report does not identify how the overall energy costs to consumers would likely fall because less energy is used. Overall, the report concludes that the most economically beneficial way for Canada to meet its Kyoto commitments is by implementing an emissions trading system where permits are auctioned. But, sadly, the government has not decided to pursue this option. It's hard to understand, except that the carbon cabal of combustion multinationals has blocked such a move politically every step of the way. This, even though such a system was proven to work two decades ago, when Canadian campaigners successfully convinced Canada and the U.S. to implement emissions trading for sulphur dioxide emissions as a way to combat acid rain. Fortunately, the government of Manitoba is developing a carbon emissions trading system, hoping to be ready when good sense befalls Canadian and American policy-makers, with leadership from the minister responsible, the fervent Tim Sale.

Canada also needs an integrated energy grid to connect the sources of the most efficient, clean, and green power to the places where power needs are greatest. The winds of Alberta, Saskatchewan, and Manitoba must be able to deliver power to southern Ontario, not only for sustainability but also for security. During the summer 2003 blackout, most Canadians noticed the bizarre news accounts of a darkened Parliament Hill illuminated by the bright lights of the city of Gatineau (formerly Hull) just across the river. Cars could cross the Ottawa River, but not electricity. This is absurd. A pan-Canadian energy grid would be a project for our economy today, akin to the great railway construction projects of the past century, a modern National Dream. It would be best accomplished as a partnership, the federal government working with the network of public energy companies in the provinces and cities. Indeed, the provincial ministers of energy proposed the creation of such a grid to the federal Liberal government in the mid-1990s. The idea went nowhere. It would be hard to find a more important element in an industrial strategy for Canada than a public green power grid. Quebeckers know this well. That's why under the leadership of a young René Lévesque, then Liberal energy minister, Hydro-Québec was created by nationalizing private energy companies. In this bold move, a product of the Quiet Revolution, Quebec was duplicating one made in Ontario two generations before, when Sir Adam Beck created Ontario Hydro, under a Conservative administration. A move by the Mike Harris Conservatives to privatize Hydro One (part of their reorganization of Ontario Hydro) was rejected soundly by voters after a brilliant campaign by the unions involved, environmentalists, consumer groups, and the Ontario NDP. The defeat of this privatization plan paves the way for the trans-Canada power grid as the next great sustainable industrial development project.

To recap: by phasing in a tax-shifting regime and auctioning permits, the federal government would have $4.75 billion each year available to finance the green energy plan outlined above. Over ten years, this would mean investing $47.5 billion in green economic activity that would

- potentially create more than three million new person years of work—that's 300,000 new jobs for ten years straight;
- develop a brand-new green power industry with possible sales of over $20 billion;
- dramatically cut Canada's greenhouse gas emissions and put us on the path to cutting emissions by 50 per cent by 2030;
- reduce smog emissions that currently cost Canadians billions of dollars a year in health care

costs and lost economic productivity;
- **reduce overall energy costs for all Canadians, including businesses, by providing incentives and programs to invest in energy efficiency;**
- **not require any tax increases.**

As we saw in the debate around Kyoto earlier this decade, the fossil fuel industry will likely claim that the plan outlined above will bring economic ruin to Canada. As many studies show, they are wrong. For example, the Canadian Wind Energy Association estimates that every $1 million invested in wind turbines creates eight permanent jobs. Compare this to international estimates that $1 million invested in oil exploration creates only 1.5 jobs. With the help of a just transition strategy for workers and communities, as outlined in Chapter 2, the federal government can ensure a smooth transition to sustainable jobs. And the federal government can target the establishment of new green power industries and activities in provinces that currently rely heavily on the fossil fuel industry.

An industrial strategy for green cars

Canadians have always been at their best when they provoke their governments to pursue bold and strategic plans to build for the future: building a national railway, creating public energy companies like Ontario Hydro and Hydro-Québec, or even massive social projects like public medicare. In the early twenty-first century, our plans should focus on key economic sectors and be rooted in the concept of sustainability. Let's take our massive automobile manufacturing sector as a starting point.

With some 150,000 Canadians directly employed assembling vehicles and making the parts for them, the automobile manufacturing sector is essential to our economy. Its extensive use of robotics and computerization also makes the auto sector one of the most high-tech industries in the country.

And for every auto assembly or in-house parts production job in Canada, there are approximately 6.5 more related jobs in manufacturing, transportation, and the after-market service industry. Canadian auto workers alone pay over $2 billion in income taxes, and the GST and PST on automobile sales generate $7 billion in government revenue. The steel and rubber industries, in particular, are very dependent on the vitality of the auto industry. On top of that, the auto industry is an important source of export earnings for Canada in the global economy.

So, as much as I'm interested in reducing the negative impacts of our "car culture," we need to do so in ways that continue to assure employment and economic growth in Canada. Having a healthy automotive industry is crucial to our economy; making it healthier for the environment is crucial to our well-being. That's why I was delighted when Buzz Hargrove, president of the Canadian Auto Workers (CAW) union, Peter Tabuns, executive director of Greenpeace, and Joe Comartin, MP from Windsor and lead Sustainability Advocate, joined with me in the summer of 2003 to announce our joint commitment to a new green car industrial strategy. It's a strategy that protects jobs and the environment.

At our press conference, Buzz Hargrove said, "If you think about the future of the industry, any automotive policy, any automotive strategy, must include vehicles that are going to be environmentally friendly. We believe that is going to be the wave of the future."

How different a view that is from the auto manufacturers themselves, who are looking to earn greater profits by selling larger vehicles that consume more fuel. With rare exceptions, instead of being innovators, they're turning back the clock toward more gas-guzzling machines. And despite our commitments under the Kyoto Protocol, Ottawa hasn't done anything significant to insist on fuel efficiency and lower sulphur levels from the manufacturers, or to make it easier for consumers to buy alternative-fuel vehicles that reduce greenhouse gas emissions.

The green car industrial strategy we have proposed is based on the idea that the national government should shape our economic development with proactive strategies. We should jump in with both feet to create jobs, improve the environment, and allow businesses to make money responsibly. Of course, this is directly contrary to the let-the-market-rule philosophy of the Liberals. I challenge the view that we should sit back and let industrialists decide our future—with no guidance, incentive, or requirements by society as a whole. If that had been the philosophy years ago, we would never have developed the national railway system, the national health care program, the St. Lawrence Seaway, and much more. So what sort of proactive industrial strategy would be best for the auto sector? After all, Canada wouldn't have an auto industry today were it not for similar efforts in the past—like the Auto Pact, which required companies to invest here in return for granting tariff-free access to our market. How can we use equally far-sighted policies to stimulate made-in-Canada investment and employment in crucial high-tech industries like auto manufacturing?

Doesn't it bug you that if you want to buy a car that produces less pollution, it will cost you more? That you'll pay the government more GST on that higher price? And that you won't create one job in your own country because none of the advanced cars are built in Canada?

Back in the mid-1970s, my dad and brother Rob, both engineers with an outside-the-box approach to innovation, worked with another specialist to develop what we now call a hybrid car years ahead of its time—one that uses both a gasoline engine and an electric engine to conserve gas and reduce emissions. It was energy efficient and sophisticated. They fell short of having the car produced in quantity, though, because there was no Canadian strategy to encourage innovation that benefited the environment, and the big auto companies had no interest in developing the concept into production, as the oil crisis faded and their interest evaporated. Today, the crisis of global climate change has created a new awakening, or at least a possibility.

Why shouldn't Canada be the epicentre of advanced-technology auto manufacturing in the Americas? This could help revitalize our auto sector and restore a sense of confidence in our capabilities to create work and clean the environment at the same time.

The federal government should insist that by 2010, auto manufacturers develop and build vehicles with a 25 per cent improvement in the average fuel efficiency compared with the vehicles sold now. (Automakers in Japan and Europe have already agreed to similar goals.) But Canada should find partners: our government could work with American and Mexican authorities to develop a continental approach. Massachusetts and New York have already begun to move in this regulatory direction. California's rules have helped create markets for LEV/ZEV vehicles (low or zero emissions vehicles). And if Canada joined forces with those states, we would create a market of more than eighty million people for environmentally advanced vehicles—a force that could shape the entire North American auto sector.

Canada should encourage consumers to buy new, cleaner cars. Combined with regulations that would make a greater number of cleaner cars available (and thus less expensive), incentives would let consumers pay less for fuel-efficient vehicles. The NDP, CAW, and Greenpeace are suggesting that the federal government offer Canadian buyers a GST rebate of between $2,500 and $5,000, depending on the technology used, when they purchase an alternative-fuel vehicle (AFV). These include vehicles that run on compressed natural gas, hybrid power systems, ethanol blends, or hydrogen fuel cells. If provincial governments offered similar sales tax rebates on these types of vehicles, production would really take off. In addition, smog would be reduced, with all the attendant health benefits and cost savings.

To make more of these alternative-fuel vehicles available, we think Ottawa should enact a market-share schedule that would grow over time, steadily increasing the proportion of AFVs in the total new-car market, beginning with 5 per cent in 2010.

Ottawa should use its own buying power to set an example and expand the market. Every year, the federal government spends about $80 million to buy roughly 3,000 new vehicles, only 3 per cent of which are now AFVs. Imagine if we set as our goal, again by 2010, that if appropriate models were available, all federal light-duty vehicle purchases would be AFVs. The federal government should establish an AFV procurement purchasing agency, and work with provincial, territorial, and municipal governments—and the broader public sector—to demonstrate its commitment to this goal. If we pooled purchasing decisions and telegraphed well in advance the new performance directions we wanted, we would send a strong signal to industry—and that would help ensure that we meet, even exceed, Kyoto targets. We have it in our power to move the industry toward the manufacture of cleaner cars, and assure automakers of a market for AFVs during a period when people would become more familiar and comfortable with these new technologies. This is how we could make the new prosperity a reality.

The catalytic approach to transforming markets works.

For many years, I was vice chair of the publicly owned energy company Toronto Hydro. We introduced ethanol-based fuels into the mix for a significant part of our vehicle fleet. The results exceeded all the projections. And the public liked knowing that their Hydro trucks were powered, in part, by soybeans! The move also helped this type of fuel take hold, encouraging markets to grow and stimulating production.

Think about it: our powerful auto sector grew dramatically during a time when we had a proactive national auto strategy—the Auto Pact, negotiated in 1965. What a terrific example of Canadian bargaining savvy and strategic intervention in the marketplace. Thousands of working families and whole communities benefited because our nation was proactive.

Yet the Auto Pact was killed in 2001 on a ruling by the unelected and unaccountable World Trade Organization. Since then, the federal government has abdicated any role it had in a national strategy for one of the most important sectors of the economy. These days, the bottom-line corporate interests of the auto manufacturers determine whether they will keep investing in Canada. If they decide they can make more profit elsewhere, they leave. In the past few years, more than 7,000 Canadian auto assembly jobs have disappeared—most of them migrating to Mexico and the southern United States. Now, these same multinationals are starting to shift production to China and India, where even lower wages and virtually no benefits like pensions for workers are in place.

Once again, we need a made-in-Canada strategy for the application of new technologies in the auto sector. Despite the expertise and ingenuity of our own scientists, and the demonstrated technical capacity of Canadians in these areas, virtually none of the manufacturing and production of these new systems takes place here, which poses a great risk to the

Canadian industry, especially at a time when we need to be shifting gears.

Existing federal policies could be expanded so that government participation can stimulate investment and production in new high-tech sectors. For example, the Technology Partnerships Canada program could be extended to include strategic investments in the development and production of AFVs, and the existing Research and Development Tax Credit could also be expanded to encourage innovation in this area. We should make sure that Canada's auto industry—and the men and women who make the vehicles—benefit from the development and production of new technology.

Assuring our economic independence

Building a sustainable economy, expanding community economic development, and assuring people an adequate income through living wages, unemployment insurance, and public pensions—all this depends on having the tools we need as a country to maintain our economic independence. We wouldn't willingly give away our democratic rights; we shouldn't willingly give away our economic rights, either. The extent of corporate takeovers in Canada, and the provisions we've signed in international trade agreements, do just that.

In *The Vanishing Country*, Mel Hurtig quotes Alberta's former premier Peter Lougheed, a Conservative free trade advocate, who said in 1999, "I know people will fall from their chairs to hear me say this, but maybe right now we need to return to the Foreign Investment Review Agency. We need to be more interventionist. The passive approach isn't working. If [the present trend] continues, we are going to look at our country in about three years and say: What have we got left?"

The three years are up, and the rate of takeovers has only increased. Hurtig points out that "in 2000 there was a new record of 509 Canadian firms taken over by foreign nonresidents. The value of these takeovers, according to [Industry Canada's] Investment Review Division, was a startling $81.8 billion. The previous record, set the year before, was $18.1 billion."

And, as Hurtig says, "No one has any idea as to how much of the takeover of Canada is being financed with our own money." That's because former industry minister John Manley did away with many of the requirements that foreign corporations once had to report on their financial activities in Canada.

Corporate takeovers export profits and well-paying executive jobs from Canada. They also remove key decision making, research and development, and strategic thinking from Canadian industry. Takeovers make jobs in Canada dependent on doing what's best for American shareholders—and that isn't always going to be in our national interest.

Canadians have a right to know when investment is or is not in our country's interest. We should also have the right to do something about those cases where the Canadian national interest is harmed by the actions of any corporation, especially a foreign-owned one. In the early 1980s, I studied efforts by the Canadian government, through the Foreign Investment Review Agency, to screen the takeovers that were threatening Canadian economic independence at the time. My research found that the Review Agency had relatively little impact, with the exception of protecting some cultural sectors from accelerating foreign takeover. I also showed that if trends were to continue, Canada would experience continuing de-industrialization and high unemployment levels. Actually, I hate it when predictions like this come true, but that's what happened, with the 1990s overall showing continued high unemployment levels relative to the United

States and causing hardship for too many families. I also predicted that lack of concrete action "will strip Canada's political independence beyond the point where Canadians can have any say whatsoever over the direction of their own affairs." We have now seen early signs of that very prediction coming to pass, with trade deals overriding our ability to make democratic decisions such as controlling which toxic substances can be sold in our country.

Of course, our concern over the takeover of Canadian industry is only one, albeit vital, piece of the economic sovereignty puzzle. The larger context is the international trade agreements we've already entered into, and those we're in the process of negotiating.

Canada's Free Trade Agreement (FTA) with the United States came into effect in 1989, and the North American Free Trade Agreement (NAFTA), which includes Mexico, in 1994. We are also party to the World Trade Organization (WTO), which was formed in 1995, replacing the General Agreement on Tariffs and Trade (GATT). The unelected and unaccountable WTO is the only international body dealing with the rules of trade among nations. The negotiations that led to the creation of the WTO are conveniently recorded on 22,000 pages in volumes weighing 385 pounds—a formidable obstacle to anyone who would seek to question the organization. The Canadian government is also in the process of negotiating other major international agreements like these, more initials in the alphabet soup of trade deals.

Despite the "free trade" guarantees of these deals, the United States has felt free to impose tariffs on the import of softwood lumber and certain other products. Such American import duties have seriously affected these industries, causing thousands of layoffs of Canadian workers.

Under the provisions of these treaties, the Canadian government has willingly signed away some of our rights, and we stand poised to give away more. Trade is obviously important to our economy, but not at the expense of trading off our rights to determine our economic and environmental future. Others have written extensively on the various effects of the trade deals that we have embarked on. Let's consider how our right to control the use of our water resources may be affected.

NAFTA defines water as a commercial "good." It defines its delivery to people as a "service," and a corporation's involvement as an "investment." This includes the water that flows from your tap. Goods, services, and investments are all subject to NAFTA restrictions. NAFTA says that no country can favour its own private sector over a corporation in another NAFTA country when it comes to the commercial use of water resources. As Maude Barlow explains, "If a Canadian company, for instance, gained the right to export Canadian water, American transnationals would have the right to help themselves to as much Canadian water as they wished."

NAFTA's infamous Chapter 11 gives a foreign corporation the right to sue the government of a NAFTA country if the corporation feels that a government has "expropriated" the corporation's future profit by denying it the opportunity to make money from providing a good or service, or engaging in an investment, where a Canadian firm, or even a Canadian government, provides it on a non-profit basis. (Domestic companies don't have this right—but foreign companies do.) And it's happened. In 1991, the NDP government of British Columbia thankfully and wisely banned the export of bulk water. In 1998, Sun Belt Water Inc. of Santa Barbara, California, sued the Canadian government for US$10 billion because the company lost a contract to export water. This is just one example, and the outcome is still pending, costing taxpayers thousands of dollars in legal fees, just to protect our right to pass our own laws.

When it comes to controlling our energy, the FTA and

NAFTA also tie our hands. For example, if Canada decides, down the road, that we are running out of oil or natural gas, we still have to sell a proportionate share of our resources to the U.S., and we don't have the right to charge higher prices in the U.S. than we charge at home.

About 90 per cent of the trade in energy between our two countries flows in one direction: south. Over half of all primary energy now produced in Canada goes to U.S. customers. We are America's largest supplier. Alberta recently agreed to new coal-fired power plants that will export electricity to the U.S.—pollution here, power there. Nova Scotia is exporting its offshore, clean-burning natural gas to the U.S. but has to import American and other foreign coal to burn for its own electricity. We pollute; they get cleaner energy. Canadians have every right to wonder what our governments are doing when they agree to trade provisions like these.

In the 1993 election campaign that followed the signing of NAFTA, Liberal leader Jean Chrétien promised to renegotiate the treaty. Needless to say, once he became prime minister, that never happened. But if we are to regain our sovereignty over the environment and have more control over our economy, it will have to be done. How? By supporting the world's new superpower.

Since the collapse of the Soviet Union, people are fond of saying that there remains only one world superpower—the United States. Well, that's not quite right. There's another superpower emerging. We can call it the power of the world's peoples. Awakening slowly, coalescing in new ways, as in the anti-globalization movement, it's another energy source we need to tap into more fully. It's a movement dedicated to building international solidarity while respecting the rights of independent nations to chart their own future.

The trade deals of the WTO are squarely in the sights of this newborn superpower. How is Canada to participate in this exciting process? Shall we oppose the growth of a movement for fair trade, human rights, peace, and the environment? Will we be a junior partner in the sale of our own destiny? For me, the choice is quite clear and very important. We should work with new social democratic governments in the Americas and with labour, environmental, and development organizations to create democratic trade agreements based on the principles of fair trade. These new treaties must ensure that environmental, social, and labour rights take precedence over the trade in goods and services. Canada's goal must be to promote fair trade based on a sustainable environment and economy, working hand in hand.

As Ed Broadbent said recently, "As we did years ago with democratic states, it's time to ensure that human rights have the same global reach as the rights of property. Until this happens, there can be no global democracy."

Insuring your employment

Sometimes good ideas wilt. Years ago, Canadians developed an idea that worked well—an insurance program to help you out if you lost your job. That's why we called it Unemployment Insurance (UI). Working people paid into the plan and had somewhere to turn in times of need. That good idea isn't working anymore.

About a year ago I was having a meal in a Toronto hotel restaurant and started talking with the server, a cheerful, middle-aged Filipino man.

"How's it going?" I asked him.

"Not bad," he said.

"But with rents as they are, going up all the time, it's got to be tough," I prompted.

"Oh, not really," he said, really quite pleased with the explanation he was about to offer. "My forty hours a week here pays for the *entire* rent for me and my family, and my other job covers most of the other costs!"

He was proud that he was providing for his family, and you can't blame him, but it turned out that he was working seventy-six hours a week!

Is this the prospect that we offer our working families? Is this the promise we hold out to immigrants to Canada? Holding down two full-time jobs, just to make ends meet? He hadn't had a significant raise in years. The hotel always said they couldn't afford it. For too many Canadians, this is the new reality.

Very shortly after we had this conversation, the ownership sold the hotel to the University of Toronto for use as a student residence. More than 200 employees were laid off, including that hard-working waiter. To make matters worse, in the aftermath of SARS and the downturn in Toronto's hospitality sector, there was little prospect of jobs elsewhere in the industry. With as many as 30,000 working people laid off in the hotel, restaurant, and entertainment business, it was tough competing for the few employment opportunities that did exist. And, to add insult to injury, many laid-off waiters and hotel workers were not able to collect what the Liberals renamed Employment Insurance (EI).

When the Liberal government came into office in 1993, about 74 per cent of Canadians who paid UI premiums later found themselves having to apply for UI and received benefits. Today, over 60 per cent *do not* qualify, and for those who do, the benefits have been lowered, and so has the length of time they can receive them. The number of unemployed Canadians who have paid into the EI plan but who aren't eligible now tops 800,000.

Because of the regulations and the nature of employment in sectors dominated by women (especially those with more part-time work), they are particularly discriminated against in qualifying for EI. Only about one-third of unemployed women receive EI benefits. What good is an insurance plan that you have to pay into but that refuses benefits to two-thirds of those who need them?

Paul Martin as finance minister led the dismantling of Canada's unemployment insurance system and hijacked the EI fund to eliminate the deficit. The EI fund is generated by contributions from workers and employers. The government doesn't pay in a dime. By cutting off unemployed workers and reducing the benefits it pays to those who are eligible, the government has built up a surplus in the EI account that now surpasses $45 billion. This represents the cumulative difference between the money Ottawa has collected from workers and their employers and what they've paid out in benefits to the unemployed since the Liberals took office. (Roughly speaking, the government now collects about $19 billion a year in premiums, and pays out only $10 to $11 billion in benefits.) Martin built his budget surplus and eliminated the deficit on the backs of unemployed Canadians.

NDP MP Yvon Godin has spent a great deal of time studying unemployment insurance ever since he was first elected in New Brunswick in 1997, and just last year introduced a comprehensive bill to bring justice to unemployed workers under the EI system. His bill would have eliminated the two-week waiting period, reduced the hours needed to qualify for EI, and increased the benefits paid to workers who lose their jobs. It would also have created a trust account where all EI funds would go, so the government of the day could not use the money to pay down the debt, as the Liberals have done. Yvon's bill was defeated by the Liberals and the Alliance.

Increasing numbers of people are self-employed and running small businesses, taking risks, and creating jobs. Yet though they pay into the EI plan on behalf of their workers, they cannot pay into the plan for themselves, and naturally aren't eligible to collect benefits if their business fails. And once more, women are especially discriminated against, because successful young women running their own businesses aren't eligible for paid maternity leave should they decide to have children. Is there some reason why we can't provide insurance for self-employed women—which they would undoubtedly be willing to pay into—so they can raise a child and still keep their businesses running?

Training should be another crucial element of an unemployment insurance program, especially in an era when new technologies are rapidly being introduced into our workplaces. Workers ought to be eligible for an EI training benefit by taking compensated education or training leave, with a right to return to their jobs. Across the country (but unfortunately primarily only in cities) community organizations and numerous schools offer English-as-a-second-language courses; community colleges run training, retraining, and apprenticeship programs; private companies provide various technical services. In some cases, costs for these programs are covered by EI, but many are not.

Ten years ago, people were concerned that the fragmentation of Canada's approach to training would put us at a competitive disadvantage in the new economy. The Liberals in power, with Paul Martin leading the charge, responded by taking the government of Canada out of the training business—making a problem into a crisis.

Sharing pensions in the new prosperity

In Canada, one of the wealthiest nations in the world, about half the single elderly women live in poverty. Search as I might, I can find no excuse for it. And it's not as if single, older men fare much better—about a third of them are poor, too. Their labour made us rich, and we cast them aside. That's nothing to be proud of.

Our public pension system was supposed to ensure that all elderly people have enough resources to live in dignity, regardless of their income during their working years. It was also designed to assure people that their living standard would not decline significantly at retirement. These guarantees have expired.

Public pensions in Canada take several forms. We have the Canada and Quebec Pension Plans (CPP and QPP), which are income related and paid to all former workers. Then there is Old Age Security (OAS) and the Guaranteed Income Supplement (GIS), which are paid to eligible residents of Canada sixty-five years of age or over. Most provinces and territories also have smaller supplemental programs. These plans are the bedrock of income security for retired Canadians. Women sixty-five and up receive, on average, about 60 per cent of their income from these public pensions and other government transfers.

For several reasons, CPP or QPP benefits paid to women are significantly lower than those paid to men. First, women in the paid labour force earn less than men—as much as 27 per cent less, on average, in spite of equal-pay legislation. Second, women are much more likely to work in sectors of the economy where part-time jobs are predominant—reducing their pension plan contributions and benefits. Also, women frequently leave the paid workforce temporarily to bear and raise children and there's no government contribution to their pension for this work. While CPP rules mean they don't pay a penalty for the time lost, nothing compensates for the lost opportunity to improve their incomes. In addition, women still do much more unpaid labour than men. The year-by-year impact of such subtle but real discrimination leaves women at retirement age receiving lower pension benefits than men do. The average monthly CPP retirement benefit for new retirees aged sixty-five in September 2003 was $597 for men and just $362 for women.

The Old Age Security program is available to most residents of Canada over sixty-five, whether or not they ever paid into the Canada or Quebec Pension Plans. The average monthly OAS payment at the end of 2003 was $441.43. The Guaranteed Income Supplement is needs based and is paid to eligible low-income seniors on application. (The average monthly payment for a single person at the end of 2003 was $371.17.)

In recent years, our public pensions have come under attack. In his 1995 budget speech, then finance minister Paul Martin raised the spectre of what critics called a "demo-graphic time bomb," suggesting that when the larger numbers of the baby boom generation reach retirement age, the CPP would be unable to support them. He warned then that with-out cuts, the cost of the CPP/QPP, OAS, and GIS would "jump" from 5.3 to 8 per cent of GDP by 2030. (Never mind that the average pension cost in all OECD countries was already over 9 per cent of their GDP in 1995.) The arguments behind this ticking "time bomb" scenario have since been defused, but Martin nevertheless instituted changes to the CPP that resulted in higher contributions and lower benefits.

Pressure also came from others on the right—the corpo-rate and financial establishment, the Reform/Alliance Party, and others—who argued that our system of pensions should be privatized, or that people should have the right to opt out of the CPP in favour of their own private pensions.

We have to understand that public pensions are more than just retirement plans; they are a broad-based, universal social insurance plan. The CPP provides disability benefits, survivor benefits, and benefits to dependent children. It pro-vides protection for people who can't contribute to the plan temporarily—because they leave the workforce to raise children or because they become disabled. And the CPP is always there when you retire, whether you've suffered unemployment or lengthy illness or enrolled in education or training programs and the like. Those people who want to privatize pensions don't seem to see the virtue in pooling risk, or in accepting collective social responsibility.

When Margaret Thatcher's government allowed people in Great Britain to opt out of the public pension plan, insurance companies rushed in and persuaded people to put their money into private plans, which actually provide lower benefits. The unscrupulous companies made enormous profits and were later fined an estimated £11 billion. On top of that, one study showed that fees and commissions from the private money managers consumed 40 to 45 per cent of the revenue. By comparison, administrative costs for the CPP are about 1.3 per cent.

No wonder the stockbrokers want as much of this pie as they can stuff into their investment portfolios. Why can't we have more confidence in our capacities to invest our collective savings ourselves, through public processes?

In a January 2002 speech, Monica Townson, a Canadian pension expert, described the pitfalls of privatizing public pensions like this: "It would do away with the collective responsibility for and to our older citizens, which has been the fundamental basis for Canada's social programs." She's right.

Now is the time for all Canadians to decide what a fair guaranteed annual income for senior citizens should be. It's clearly inadequate and not guaranteed in any way at the moment. A cross-country discussion would produce a basic consensus, I have no doubt, just as it has on the funding of health care. Then a step-by-step strategy to achieve that fair, sustainable pension level needs to be put in place. Making it successful will have a lot to do with how we manage our public pensions and how we invest both private and public pension funds.

While we need to protect the public pension system for all Canadians, private pensions can provide additional income security. But only about 30 per cent of private-sector workers have a private pension plan. (About 85 per cent of government workers, on the other hand, are members of private plans.) With people shifting employment more often, we need laws to guarantee better portability of pensions. As well, laws and backup insurance plans should be put in place to protect workers' pensions in the event of the bankruptcy or refinancing of their company. Since private pensions are a form of deferred wages, I've argued that workers should be the preferred creditors in the event that their company goes broke. We have to protect workers from the next Enron.

Pensions as community investments

One of most exciting, but controversial, ideas about pension funds involves putting them to work by investing in our communities and the infrastructure they need. The patient, relatively low but steady rates of return sought by pension funds are ideal for investing in long-term projects like affordable housing, water- and sewage-treatment plants, transit systems, or sustainable energy development projects.

What about the idea of giving Canadians the option to invest in their country, not just on the stock market? One consequence of turning Canadian debt and pensions over to the private sector—instead of holding it in public bonds or Bank of Canada instruments—is that the interest is paid to others, not the citizens of the country. Another is that the savings of Canadians are less available to invest in the future they want to see for their children. During the Second World War, we called on Canadians to invest their savings in their country, as war bonds. We paid them interest. It worked.

We've largely given up that economic toolbox. The relentless drive to reduce debt continues, causing us to limit investment needed in our cities, environment, new industries, education, training, health, and culture. This is false economy. It's like deciding not to invest in maintenance of a key piece of machinery—it will begin to fail eventually. Let's establish a massive campaign to mobilize our pensions and our personal savings in an invest-in-Canada's-future project. I'm not talking about spending but about investing, just as in any successful business venture. By bringing our savings back home, so to speak, we'll be able to build the affordable homes, successful industries, liveable communities, and the society that we dream about.

I know this is possible because I've seen it done. A British Columbia pension fund group is building affordable rental housing in that province, and some of us persuaded their team to join with the Ontario Municipal Employees' Retirement System (OMERS) to build in Ontario. OMERS has also invested in the project to cool Toronto's downtown office high-rises with cold water from Lake Ontario, rather than continue to use outdated and polluting air conditioners. This shows that pension funds can be invested—safely and profitably—in projects that improve our collective well-being as a community.

Canada needs a raise

In Canada, according to the latest available figures, the top 10 per cent of the population holds 53 per cent of the wealth. The bottom 50 per cent own less than 6 per cent. The bottom 10 per cent actually owes about $2,100 more than they own. And not only are the rich getting richer and the poor getting poorer, but immigrants and families raising children, in particular, are much worse off than they were twenty years ago.

Our distribution of income is similarly skewed in favour of the rich—and is only getting worse. Since 1995, we've seen the most rapid increase in the inequality of incomes among Canadians since we've kept track of these things, and this at a time when the economy has been growing significantly.

I've already mentioned how the unequal distribution of wealth adversely affects people's health. In terms of building a productive economy, and in terms of human decency, the degree to which wealth is fairly distributed in a society is a mark of its success. Bringing poor people out of poverty does more than improve their own living circumstances and their health; it improves the foundation of the entire economy.

On January 1, 1995, Ontario's minimum wage was $6.85 an hour. In their eight years in office, the Conservative governments of Mike Harris and Ernie Eves never raised it a dime. Inflation chewed away about 20 per cent of that wage, leaving the 300,000 Ontario workers who earn minimum wage even further below the poverty line. And, once more, it's women who have borne the brunt of this economic inequality—61 per cent of minimum wage earners in Ontario are women.

In Alberta, the minimum wage is just $5.90. That hasn't changed in over four years. In British Columbia, the former NDP government raised the minimum wage to $8.00 an hour, but when the Liberals came to office in 2000, they introduced a new entry-level wage of only $6.00 for people with no job experience. Compared with the rest of the industrialized world, our minimum wages are appallingly low.

And it's not as if minimum wage workers are high school teenagers working after school just to earn some pocket money. The majority of minimum wage workers in Canada are adults, and 40 per cent of them are working full time. Many of them work more than one job and still live in poverty.

But instead of giving poor people real assistance to break the poverty trap, governments across Canada have cut off their assistance and driven poor people further into despair. The federal government did this by cutting access to unemployment insurance, by reducing transfer payments to the provinces, and by eliminating the national standards that provinces used to follow in their income support programs. The provinces have done it by cutting social assistance, freezing shelter allowances, and downloading services to cash-strapped municipalities. Some provinces imposed limits on the length of time people can receive social assistance and then cut them off any aid (as in British Columbia), and some instituted punitive "workfare" programs (as in Ontario and Alberta) that compel people to find employment without providing them with the necessary social supports, such as child care or public transit passes, to make it possible for them to hold a job.

Yet, as governments have been failing Canadians, communities across the country are running innovative, visionary, and helpful programs that provide people with support; that give them training, skills, and confidence; and that bring them back into the economy. Many of these programs fall under the umbrella of community economic development (CED), which also stands for three words that aptly sum up their goal—community, economy, and development.

The broad range of CED projects fall into five main categories. The first is employment, trying to help (usually) marginalized people get into the job market, as well as helping those in dead-end jobs find more meaningful careers. These programs take a variety of forms, normally involving personal-development sessions in groups (such as interviewing techniques and personal skills) and often including some hands-on training in a particular field, sometimes in connection with a community college or private training institute.

The second category is geared to self-employment, helping people acquire skills and knowledge to assist them in opening their own small businesses. Thousands of people have become entrepreneurs, and countless small companies have started up with the help of CED training.

The third is access to credit, often providing small start-up loans to allow people to open up shop, purchase tools, pay for formal education—or providing the security deposit people need to rent an apartment. CED organizations frequently require recipients of loans to take some credit counselling and money-management sessions.

Neighbourhood revitalization programs are the fourth category, bringing people in a community together to work with each other, frequently on a volunteer basis, to improve the quality of their neighbourhoods. These might involve setting up a community garden or operating a community kitchen, working to revitalize a main street or develop a farmer's market, and, in general, creating a business incubator.

Broader capacity-building is the final big category—helping people build their confidence and self-esteem, and going beyond personal development to community action, by getting people involved, developing local leadership, creating directories of community assets and resources, and speaking out to government.

The oldest formal CED program in Canada is called New Dawn, in Cape Breton, Nova Scotia. It was inspired by the famous Antigonish movement led by Father Jimmy Tompkins, who founded the People's School at St. Francis Xavier University in 1921. The People's School brought in students to learn leadership skills and to inspire others to "become masters of their own destiny."

Today, the New Dawn program follows that tradition. Incorporated in 1976, it now employs more than 175 people from the Cape Breton community. Its wide variety of programs and services involve 600 Cape Bretoners every day. Their oldest venture is the Cape Breton Association for Housing Development, a real estate company that provides affordable housing. New Dawn also manages a host of other projects, including a home care company, a private career college that provides industrial and occupational education and training, a thirty-bed residential care facility, a seniors' home living centre, and a residential apartment building. New Dawn also coordinates a volunteer resource centre and publishes an island magazine.

In Calgary, the year-long Fair Gains program run by MCC Employment Development, a CED organization, helps people living in poverty save money toward an asset. Participants (most are working poor) come together twice a month in the evenings, learning how to save and manage their income. The money they bank is matched—three to one—by the CED organization, helping them build up their resources. "Working toward an asset transforms not only their situation," explains veteran CED coordinator Lisa Caton, "but it changes people's minds; it changes how they think about themselves." These assets may be for capitalizing a small business, for their own education, for opening an RESP for a child, or for other goals. If participants want to save toward home ownership, they can sign up for a second year, during which time they learn repair skills, about managing household finances, home insurance, and real estate. Though the program has been running for only a few years, several Fair Gains graduates have managed to buy their own homes.

In Winnipeg, experienced CED activists brought together community leaders to form the North End Community Renewal Corporation, which strives to promote locally owned businesses, better housing, and a safe, clean neighbourhood in Winnipeg's North End. The group, now with more than ninety participating organizations, got long-term operational financing from the provincial government, an experienced business development officer seconded for two years from Manitoba's labour-based Crocus Investment Fund, and space donated by the Mennonite Central Committee. In 2001, the North End Community Renewal Corporation had an annual budget of $500,000, with nine employees and 200 volunteers. They have successfully revitalized two commercial districts, established a training and employment centre that serves more than 500 people, and designed a program to renovate more than 400 houses over a five-year period. They have also put in place a school literacy program, provided Internet access for North End residents, and held summer festivals centred on community diversity.

Another bright idea was hatched by the Pakistan Canada Association of Edmonton, which formed a seniors' group in 1995 and brought together older women who loved to sew. They started producing ethnic dolls, clothing, and multi-purpose bags, and soon wanted to reach out to other cultural groups and with other products. Before long, after getting help from a CED project, they had opened a Handcraft Production Centre and were working with women from Bosnia, Cambodia, Vietnam, China, and Arab nations, producing marketable cloth bags for conferences. As well, the centre offers courses in sewing and cooking. In addition to producing their products, the group helps its participants overcome the isolation often experienced by older women living at home.

The non-profit Highbanks Society in Calgary bought a building that houses the nostalgic but trendy Dairy Lane Diner. Above the diner, Highbanks renovated four apartments and dedicated them for use by teenage moms, who gain work experience in the diner, along with mutual support.

A group of women in the Niagara district of Ontario

turned to a CED organization to help them organize and manage their network of micro-entrepreneurs, each of whom produce their own local specialty food products. Now they operate a commercial incubator kitchen, a retail showroom, and a marketing and distribution service.

CED organizations have stepped in to fill a real social and economic need. They recognize the importance of personal development, skills training, financial assistance, mutual support, and community relationships—and roll them all into one coherent package, designed to meet individual and local needs. They've been much more creative and responsive than most government programs in helping people find jobs and keep them.

Some critics point out that they're small, and that they don't reach enough people. Both of these are true, and neither is a problem.

About 97 per cent of businesses in Canada employ fewer than five people. Altogether, small business (understood as having fewer than fifty workers) employ over one-third of all Canadian workers. In fact, most new jobs are created by small businesses, so CED projects that involve relatively low numbers of participants are part of the mainstream of economic development. And they should reach more people. Their model ought to be made available more widely, opening up CED-sponsored programs to much greater numbers of people. They are a valuable tool in building the new prosperity from the ground up.

- Corporate tax revenues as a percentage of total federal government revenues in the 1960s: 19.0 In the 1990s: 10.8
- Personal income tax revenues as a percentage of total federal government revenues in the 1960s: 32.2 In the 1990s: 46.9
- Estimated number of jobs created by a tax cut of $1

billion: 9,000
Estimated number of jobs created by spending $1
billion on roads and hospitals: 25,000

Measuring the new prosperity

The way economists look at it, the 1998 ice storm, Nova
Scotia's encounter with hurricane Juan, and British
Columbia's forest fires and floods of 2003 were all good for
the economy.

How's that? Because they all caused hundreds of millions
of dollars of damage that needed to be repaired. They forced
both governments and the private sector to spend money creating direct jobs. Those events resulted in a building boom.
Stimulus! Spending! That has to be good.

Of course, they were horrible events for the people who
had their homes destroyed, who went without power for a
month or more, or who were forced into shelters until their
communities could pick up the pieces—to say nothing about
the people who died or the grieving families they left behind.
But on the economic ledger, they go down on the plus side.

That's because our method of measuring the economy is
nuts.

Automobile accidents stimulate the economy because
they result in consumer spending (on repairs or a new car,
and increased insurance premiums). Crime stimulates the
economy because we pay more salaries for police officers and
the criminal justice system. Divorce stimulates the economy
because people set up separate homes and buy more stuff.
Spraying more pesticides on lawns is good for the economy,
because people are buying and spending. If this produces
increased health costs later, so much the better, as far as our
economic measurements go. The absurdities go on and on.

Our common measure of economic activity is the gross

domestic product (GDP). It simply adds up the total market value of goods and services produced in Canada. It attaches no value whatsoever to whether we actually want to be spending that money in the ways that we do; it draws no distinction between money spent on things that improve our well-being and those that diminish it. And, since the GDP measures only economic activity, where money changes hands, it leaves out everything to which no dollar value is attached.

The time you spend raising your family? Not measured. The contribution you make volunteering in your community? No value. If you spend $30 on a junk-food dinner in a fast-food restaurant, it's worth $10 more to the GDP than the $20 you might spend cooking a healthy meal at home.

And then there are all the detrimental things the GDP doesn't count at all. Damage to the environment? Not counted. Depletion of our natural resources? Not included. The GDP has no measure for strategies that might save the earth's ozone layer and protect us from damaging ultraviolet radiation. In fact, if suntan lotion and hat sales go up as a result, the economists are smiling. And if you walk to work instead of taking the car, that goes on the negative side, because you are not spending money on fuel, or on the wear and tear on your vehicle. Help Canada's economy—don't walk when you could drive!

Using the GDP as our economic measure gives us a completely false impression of the real costs and benefits of economic and social activity. It leads us to think that the economy is doing well, when what we're really doing is perpetuating costly mistakes. We need a different measure, one that acknowledges quadruple bottom line thinking and that measures our progress towards achieving the new prosperity.

One exciting idea being developed, largely in Canada, attempts to change these calculations so that they make more sense. Some economists are starting to use what they call the Genuine Progress Indicator (GPI). The GPI takes account of both plus and minus costs, and includes factors for which we've never assigned an economic value. In addition to personal consumption, it takes into account income distribution in a society, unemployment rates, and net capital investment. It factors in social costs, like family breakdown, and the contributions made by unpaid housework and child care. It takes away value for time spent commuting to work, for loss of farmland, wetlands, and forests, and for loss of leisure time.

Let's bring in new measurement techniques so we can honestly measure the new prosperity. The GPI adds value for additions to things we value, and subtracts value for the loss of things we value. If we used the GPI instead of the GDP, we'd know better what was going on around us, and we could help shape our economy in ways that recognize the interconnections between the economy, the environment, and the people.

[CHAPTER 7]

Building a Just Society

Pierre Trudeau coined the phrase "the just society" in the late sixties. I was captivated—so much so that I organized an early version of Rock the Vote at the Fairview Mall on Montreal's west island, all a part of Trudeaumania. In my late teens, in the era of Woodstock, I was caught up, as so many young people were, by the purity and the idealism of his political rallying cry. Human rights, equality, justice for all!

These were values that Canadians, young and old alike, wanted their country to fully embrace. At the same time, multiculturalism—the great Canadian welcome for immigrants from around the world—was the watchword. So was another Trudeau phrase: "participatory democracy." Trudeau himself abandoned many of these principles as he governed. Whether it was the War Measures Act or imposing the patriation of the Canadian Constitution without the consent of Quebec, the policies of the Liberal governments he led betrayed his original idealism. Over the Mulroney–Chrétien–Martin decades that have followed, such ideals have faded even from national discourse. The focus became what's-in-it-for-me economics, tax and program cutting, scandals, and security above all else.

There was a time when Canada was known as a world leader in human rights. John Peters Humphrey, a native of New Brunswick, was the principal author of the Universal Declaration of Human Rights, proclaimed in 1948, which has arguably become one of the most important human rights document ever. This UN document and two others, the asso-

236

ciated Covenant on Civil and Political Rights and the Covenant on Economic, Social and Cultural Rights, establish a just framework for human affairs that goes well beyond narrow concepts of civil or property rights to embrace the full spectrum of human needs. Canadians have long recognized the importance of understanding the connection between rights, equality, social justice, and democracy itself. As Frank Scott, the distinguished McGill legal scholar, poet, social reformer, and CCF/NDP founder put it, "The trappings of democracy hang loosely on an emaciated body politic."

Canada now has its own Charter of Rights and Freedoms, and a body of legal reform is emerging through laws and court decisions that is slowly expanding human rights.

Canada has taken a leadership role in other ways too. We were a world leader in advancing gay and lesbian rights, evident as early as 1967 in Trudeau's vanguard legislation as justice minister and in his famous pronouncement that "the state has no place in the bedrooms of the nation." I was glad to play a modest role in continuing the Canadian human rights tradition with our NDP caucus in September 2003 when we played an instrumental role in defeating an Alliance Party motion (supported by 53 Liberal MPs) that would have denied same-sex marriage under Canadian law.

In this chapter, I will touch on some of the elements of the broad understanding of human rights, equality, and democracy—all of which could help to define a more just society. Many eminent scholars, legal experts, and passionate advocates have tackled these issues, and whole sections of libraries are devoted to them, so don't expect an encyclopedia here. When it comes to a just society, the truth is, we can achieve much more than we are currently achieving; we can reverse the backsliding and, once again, be an example to the world. Let's consider some ideas about how to do just that.

Democracy and civil society

The most profound transformation needed to create a vibrant democracy involves what is called "civil society." Civil society encompasses all the ways in which people can be engaged in shaping their world outside the formal political process. A broad understanding of civil society takes in the thousands of groupings of Canadians who work away, on a daily basis, trying to make one or another aspect of their community better. It could be environmentalists, volunteers at a local homeless shelter, peace symposium organizers, workers advocating for improved safety in the workplace—the list is endless. But our formal political system doesn't include mechanisms for local organizations and the movements behind them to actually shape and affect public policy.

Within the NDP, there is a strong consensus that we should open ourselves up to working with groups in civil society. It's not that the social movements should be absorbed by a political party or even encouraged to advocate on behalf of a political party. It's actually very important that these movements retain their independent voices and their capacity to be critical. But on the other hand, there are advantages to working with such groups on common projects more often. We should seek to benefit from their front-line experience and the depth of their knowledge, and we should try to coordinate some of their efforts to have a greater effect on the direction of public policy in Canada.

Ultimately, we have to find ways to connect the delicious turmoil of citizen engagement and activism more frequently and effectively with government processes in general. One of the best models is found in Brazil, where thousands of citizens are drawn into the process of setting the budget for the nation. Some Canadian cities are starting to try this kind of participatory democracy. As a very modest experiment, I held budget hearings in the winter of 2004 with MPs Libby Davies in Vancouver, Alexa McDonough in Halifax, and Judy Wasylycia-Leis in Toronto, as well as one in Montreal. We also had a special consultation with national women's organizations in Ottawa. We asked community members and organizational representatives how they would rather have spent the billions of dollars in tax breaks Paul Martin gave to corporations in January 2004. Of course, this is only a beginning—we have a long way to go.

The electoral system

To build a more democratic society, we need to change our electoral system. We need to ensure that all Canadians have a more equal voice at the ballot box, and that they are better represented, both geographically and ideologically. Just because all citizens of voting age have the right to vote doesn't mean that their voices are equally represented.

The ten federal elections we've had since 1968 have produced eight majority governments. But in only one of those elections (1984) did the governing party actually receive more than half of the votes. In every other instance, a minority of votes produced a majority of seats for one party.

Of nearly eighty democracies in the world, *only two* rely solely on the first-past-the-post, winner-take-all system— Canada and the U.S. All the others have some form of proportional representation (PR), which means that the parties receive a share of seats in Parliament more proportional to the number of votes that they get. (Many of our largest cities used to have systems of PR. In fact, Calgary and Winnipeg used the system into the 1950s and 1960s. Some twenty cities—including Edmonton, Vancouver, and Regina—once had elections based on PR.)

The details of the systems vary greatly from country to

country, but in every case their elected governments are much more representative of the voice of the people. In Canada, such a system would also ensure that Parliament would have members from all parties, from all regions of the country—improving representation and reducing geographic alienation. All views would be represented, as they should be. PR would create a more responsive government, better equipped to listen and meet the needs of the people. I like the look of the approach taken in New Zealand, which recently transformed its voting system from the type we have—known as the "single member plurality" as well as "first past the post"—to PR. Essentially, such a system for Canada would have voters choose their local member of Parliament for their riding just as they do now. Then there would be an increase in the number of seats in the House of Commons for each party whose percentage of MPs fell short of the party's percentage of the popular vote. These additional MPs would be selected from a pre-published list. Local representation would be maintained, and that's important in a diverse country like Canada. But a party receiving 25 per cent of the popular vote would find itself with 25 per cent of the seats in the House.

Depending on which variation of PR we choose, it could also significantly improve the number of women in elected office. This is vital because of the different sensitivities, priorities, vision, and way of operating that many women would bring to our legislatures.

Of course, in order to get more women elected to Parliament, you've got to have more women running for office. In the NDP, our first step toward achieving this goal has been to adopt policies that ensure that women are recruited and assisted to become candidates. Thanks to these policies, the NDP consistently has had a higher percentage of women MPs in the Parliamentary caucus than other parties. Many barriers confront women when they consider running for political office. In our party, we require riding associations to show that they have made significant outreach efforts to recruit women candidates before we will authorize a nomination meeting to choose a candidate. We may have to look at other processes to facilitate women's overcoming obstacles to candidacy, whether they be financial, cultural, or social. However, I think that real change in this area will come only with more women's voices in Parliament. PR is a key to that change.

Proportional representation would revitalize voting itself. People would know that even if their individual candidate lost in their local riding, their ballot would still count toward the strength of the party they supported. People would always have something to vote *for*, and voter turnout would almost certainly increase. That makes for a healthier, more inclusive democracy.

In our last federal election, just over 61 per cent of the people voted—the lowest turnout in our history. (Compare that with recent turnouts of 93 per cent in Belgium, or 86 per cent in Austria and Sweden.) Elections Canada estimates that less than 40 per cent of young voters (under the age of twenty-four) cast a ballot in the 2000 election.

In the fall of 2003, Lorne Nystrom, one of the NDP MPs from Saskatchewan, introduced a resolution in the House of Commons calling on the Canadian government to consult its citizens in a referendum about modernizing our democracy with a system of proportional representation. It was the first time Parliament had considered PR since 1923. The Liberals and the Alliance voted down the idea of even asking Canadians for their opinion.

In this chamber, sir, one's stature is measured from
the shoulders up. —Tommy Douglas, responding to
an MP's quip about his diminutive frame

Elections that are more democratic would also help address the arrogance that can, and has, set in as governments begin to see themselves as invincible. As a result of our archaic voting system, invented well before the telephone, our governments come to learn that they can win elections even when most Canadians oppose their policies. Majority governments can become high-handed and inattentive to the public good. Abuse of power can follow, making politics susceptible to scandal.

The media tend to treat scandals as one-off affairs, a few politicians getting too close to their corporate friends. This ignores the systemic nature of corporate scandals, which, sadly, are as old as Canada itself. Even our first prime minister, John A. Macdonald, was embroiled in scandal in the 1870s over railway contracts to his corporate friends. Prime Minister Paul Martin must realize that the root of this problem, exemplified by the sponsorship scandal that came to a head with the auditor general's report in early 2004, is not a few rogue Liberals or bureaucrats but rather too many Liberal MPs who have become so comfortable that they believe they can do what they like. The arrogance is ironic, given that all three Liberal "majorities" were rejected by a majority of voters. But under our current system, the winning party takes it all and then shares it with its friends. In countries with effective PR systems, governments are somewhat more humble and accountable.

A fundamental principle of a just and democratic society is empowering its people and engaging them as active players in their economy and society. Ensuring that all our citizens—native-born or new to Canada—are equipped to participate fully must be a cornerstone on which Canada is built. And revitalizing our democracy—through proportional representation and by encouraging people to participate directly in their own communities—must also be our goal.

The gender gap

What if a group of women had written the Canadian Constitution, instead of a group of men? What would they have done differently? What guarantees do you think they would have assured all men, women, children, and the elderly in our society?

Everyone knows that there's an enormous ideological gender gap. Every poll verifies that. Women are much more inclined than men to support programs of economic and social justice—and to support the redistribution of wealth. That stands to reason: these attitudes reflect the reality of most women's experience.

So the point is not really what a constitution written by women might look like. The important thing to acknowledge is that women, by and large, have different experiences, different priorities, and different visions than men do. And the social and economic structures we share have been designed almost exclusively by men. They reflect men's points of view.

We've already gone over some of the territory of women's inequality in Canada: they receive 73 cents for every dollar that men earn; too often they're destined for low-wage and minimum-wage, service-sector jobs; and they spend years raising their children or caring for elderly relatives, which results in inadequate pensions. And that only names a few inequities. Systemic and institutional discrimination can be addressed in law and with better social programs, but that requires a political vision different from the one that has dominated politics in Canada so far.

In our culture, women still assume the primary responsibility for raising families. They are the unpaid caregivers, the "shock absorbers" in the system, as one report puts it, who remain out of the paid workforce to raise their children (or stay home from work to look after a sick child) or who quit their jobs to care for an elderly parent. Often they juggle all these responsibilities while they continue to work. To show the extent of this, here is just one statistic: in Ontario, about 95 per cent of single parents who receive family benefits are women. Yet our governments design punitive social programs that fail to acknowledge this responsibility. Wholly inadequate social assistance condemns women and their children to lives of poverty when young, and miserly public pensions force them into poverty in their senior years. A society that truly values families and that recognizes the family responsibilities that women take on would reward these duties accordingly. Workplace laws, social assistance, and pension legislation designed by women—or at least with the real world of women in mind—would look very different.

We also need to acknowledge the special forms of discrimination confronted by women of colour, women with disabilities, and Aboriginal women. Their multiple barriers to equality are almost always extremely difficult to overcome.

However, the past few decades have been marked by a vibrant, energetic, and progressive women's movement in Canada. And, thanks to their activism, we know better what the real issues for women are and what will make a real difference in their lives. Change has happened slowly, but we can point to some improvements.

Not so long ago, we didn't even have a name for sexual harassment. Now even men are beginning to understand what it is and why it's wrong. Laws and workplace codes have begun to address that.

We know that affirmative action programs can address inequalities of race and gender, and we know these programs can work. It's no longer unthinkable to have a female judge, prime minister, pipefitter, firefighter, doctor, or CEO; attitudes toward women and their capabilities in the workplace are starting to change.

As recently as the 1970s, abortion was still a shocking or, at best, an impolite word—an operation, though common enough, then taking place in back rooms, at great risk to women's health and lives, and without public acknowledgement. Laws restricting the procedure were eventually abandoned and attitudes readjusted, all as a result of an arduous struggle by a determined, dynamic women's movement. Though access to reproductive choice remains a divisive issue, our legislation and courts have at least recognized a woman's right to choose—and publicly funded women's clinics, providing a full range of reproductive health services, are becoming a reality.

Pay-equity legislation and related court challenges are other breakthroughs. The most significant settlements were achieved after long battles by women employees, their unions, and pay-equity advocates. Although the issue has been technically "won" in legislatures and courts across the country, employers continue to drag their feet on implementation, forcing women to fight again and again for the pay they deserve. And still women receive only three-quarters of what men do. There are even indications of backsliding. Working for economic equality requires constant vigilance.

Nowhere do we see this backsliding more than in relation to child poverty. As we dig beneath the surface, we find the deeper phenomenon of women's poverty. Canada has piously expressed its hope for a new prosperity for Canada's children. Have we delivered? At the United Nations World Summit for Children in 1990, Canada, along with many other countries, signed a statement that read, "The growing minds and bodies of children should have a first call on our societies, and children should be able to depend upon that commitment in good times and bad." Just the year before, Parliament had approved federal NDP leader Ed Broadbent's resolution calling for an end to child poverty in Canada by 2000.

The year 2000 has come and gone—and Y2K got a lot more attention than the children. Nice words didn't feed children, house them, provide them with an education. The number of children living in poverty in Canada now totals more than 1.1 million—about one in every six children— with a substantial increase since that resolution. Do you know what that means? In an "average" elementary school classroom of thirty kids, five live in poverty. In Canada. That's appalling, and shameful. Meanwhile, social assistance benefits to poor families, most led by women, have declined by about 20 per cent, and the total number of visits to food banks has gone up about 90 per cent. Children make up about 40 per cent of food bank recipients.

This has come about at a time when the economy was growing steadily—perhaps to no surprise: even the federal Finance Department virtually brags about the fact that among all OECD countries, Canada has had the sharpest drop in program spending since 1997—and that spending is at its lowest level since the 1940s. Can this actually be a point of pride?

Ideologically conservative provincial governments—particularly in Ontario from 1995 to 2003 (the jury's out on the new Liberal government elected in 2003), Alberta, and British Columbia, which together are home to two-thirds of Canada's young people—are greatly to blame for the current plight of children and their families, particularly their mothers. But once again, the federal government must take responsibility for its failure to fund social programs adequately, for its failure to implement pan-Canadian programs (like child care), and for its failure to provide affordable housing for low-income families. The Liberal government eliminated the Canada Assistance Plan (CAP) in 1995. Who knew what the CAP was, anyway? Such was the attitude in Parliament, where stone-faced advisers to the minister of finance, Paul Martin, counselled their boss. With a mere "doff of the CAP," the national government could claim victory over deficits while silently and simultaneously abdicating its role in meeting the needs of Canada's children and their families. Then the other shoe dropped: Ottawa's financial mandarins reduced federal funding to the provinces by about $12 billion under the Canada Health and Social Transfer. Most provinces in turn reduced their financial and program supports for children and their families. Then many provinces downloaded services (and their costs) to municipalities, the governments least able to respond to such demands because of their limited abilities to collect taxes. So the downward spiral finally hit families, and more families went into poverty, and those already living in poverty found it even harder to climb out.

Harkening back to the UN's statement that children should have "first call" on our societies, Toronto launched a pilot project called First Duty. This was the title of the first report of the child advocate, a new position on city council developed by Olivia Chow with her dynamic advisory committee on Children and Youth. This positive notion of advocates (rather than critics) I am now using in our federal caucus.

Toronto's Children's Services worked together with the school board and the charitable Atkinson Foundation to design the program and identify five pilot project locations, which have guaranteed funding for three years. In the case of the pilot project locations, individual elementary schools have combined with community centres and local agencies to administer the program and provide the services to children and families. Inevitably, governments complain that they can't afford programs like these, but once again, initial investments save much more money later, and people receive valuable services and experience improved lifestyles.

Combining the recommendation in the Romanow Report (about health care delivery in community clinics) with a broad range of seamless, community-based child care services integrated into the school system makes sense. It would also help put into action the values we share as inhabitants of a country filled with communities that believe in caring for one another.

Advancements—on these and other issues—have been made, but there have been other instances of serious slippage. For the past hundred years, Canadian women have shown tremendous energy and commitment to build a more just and equitable society. Undoubtedly they will continue that struggle. For my part, I commit the New Democratic Party to working alongside progressive women in their efforts.

In speaking out about the environment, the economy, or our cities, I've mentioned many times that workable, practical solutions are available, and I've stressed that a key to imagining solutions is to understand the interconnectedness of the issues. The same thinking applies to efforts to overcome the systemic discrimination that creates women's inequality.

The struggle takes place on many fronts—in workplaces, in legislatures, in courts of law, and in the community. Without having to be forced by laws to take action, the private sector needs to address women's inequality by providing all their workers decent pay and benefits, and by recognizing and respecting talent in women as well as men. Much greater equality would also come about if employers and governments removed the obstacles they throw up to union organizing. It's a responsibility of government to be aware of the barriers that deny women access to choices and equality. And they must play a major role in providing programs designed to overcome those barriers.

One exciting idea that reflected an understanding of this interconnectedness was adopted by the former NDP provincial government in British Columbia, which established a Ministry of Women's Equality, designed to infuse the perspective of women into all aspects of government decision making. It acted like an internal audit system, to ensure that the prevalent tendencies to reproduce existing inequalities were challenged and checked. It was smart, and it worked. In fact, it was such a good idea that the subsequent Liberal premier, Gordon Campbell, eliminated the ministry at his earliest opportunity. (His government also quickly did away with the B.C. Human Rights Commission, which also worked to address equality for women and other equity-seeking groups.)

But instead of just one ministry dedicated to keeping an eye on issues of particular concern to women (which, frankly, could be rendered quite powerless), think of the impact women's perspectives would have if they were completely integrated into the decision making of all institutions, whether the House of Commons, government departments, or major corporations. Imagine what society would look like if the decisions about priority spending and program design, for example, all had to run through the filter of "How will this affect women?" Then the systemic discrimination that women face would begin to get the attention needed for real change to happen. That's why a Standing Committee of the House of Commons on women's issues is a key proposal that New Democrat MPs are raising. Such a focus for discussion of women's inequality and how to eliminate it could help tackle a real democratic deficit.

Men's violence against women would certainly rate a higher priority in our national government's agenda if this kind of attention to women's concerns were in place. I know that some people are uncomfortable calling this injustice "men's violence against women." I remember having to push hard, even at the Board of Health in Toronto, to have the term accepted rather than the more neutral "family violence."

For me, the penny dropped with the Montreal Massacre in 1989. The moment I learned of that horrific attack and the murder of fourteen women engineering students, I reacted the way many other men did—by assuming it was the expression of just one man's hatred, one man's difficulty with women. As the months passed, it was as though women in many corners of my life decided that I just didn't get it. And although it was often extremely painful for them, they took the time to tell me about their personal stories. I was one of those guys who didn't doubt the statistics about the high percentage of girls and women who had experienced men's violence. It's just that I didn't seem to know any of the women who had had such a horrible experience! (Actually, I did know one: Jane Doe, attacked by the balcony rapist in my ward. In 2003 her book, *The Story of Jane Doe: A Book about Rape*, was published, and it's now the subject of a Gemini Award–winning docudrama.) One by one, over a period of months, women told me their stories. Finally, as yet another woman in my life took me to that terrifying emotional place in her history, I said to myself, I don't think I know any woman who has *not* experienced some sort of violence by a man!

Most men are not violent. But I had to confess that most men, including me, were not speaking out about the issue. By remaining silent, we were in a very real sense complicit. Women's groups had been working for decades, creating shelters, sounding the alarm, calling for changes to the justice system, and much more. But where were the men's voices? That conclusion led me to work with a group of men to kick-start the White Ribbon Campaign. Wearing a white ribbon would be easy for men—we wouldn't even have to say anything, tongue-tied as we so often are.

After an awkward start where White Ribbon men drew attention away from women's voices in the media around the

December 6 commemoration, which rightly angered some women's groups, we invited a group of wise women to advise us. At that meeting, a long-time worker at the Rape Crisis Centre made a summary comment: "The way you guys started White Ribbon really made me angry. The only thing that would make me angrier is if you stopped. Just get it right next time."

Working with women's groups over the years, White Ribbon became a modest but useful expression of men's opposition to violence against women that now takes place in more than twenty-five countries, and it continues to grow. However, the sad reality is that violence against women is still increasing worldwide. So much more needs to be done.

If women's priorities are not reflected in every government in Canada, the funding of shelters and clinics, improvements to the justice system, policies to reduce women's poverty, and many other needed initiatives will continue to get short shrift. The backsliding of the past decade will continue, and that's not fair, healthy, or acceptable.

Education and equality

By any standard, we are a rich country. But Canada's greatest asset is our people, and we can do a much better job of seeing to it that they have equal opportunities to be equipped to participate more fully in our economy, our society, and our democracy. As I've pointed out, there is no shortage of good ideas, only a shortage of willingness to try them. We have to be prepared to think outside the box.

Two pivotal factors affect people's ability to use their talents. The first is to make sure that our citizens are well educated and trained. The second is to make sure that the people who arrive in Canada already skilled are encouraged to put their abilities to work.

Just about everyone agrees that the key to success—for each individual and for the country as a whole—is education. That begins with early childhood education and care, which sets the foundation for lifelong learning and healthy human development, and continues through post-secondary education and ongoing skills training. Like so many other issues, our education policies need to be better integrated, and we need to remove barriers to education at every level.

In the 1980s and 1990s, progressive governments around the world developed early childhood education and care systems. Canada was an exception, lagging behind other industrialized nations. In the 2003 Canadian budget, for example, the federal and provincial governments agreed to a Multilateral Framework on Early Learning and Care, but funds allocated to this program were very limited, and there were no targets or timetables for implementation. Today, in most of continental Europe (France, Italy, Spain, Belgium, Denmark), virtually all children start publicly funded programs sometime between their second and third birthdays, whether the mother is in the labour force or not. These services are largely free, with parents paying some fees for publicly funded infant/toddler programs and "top-up" portions of the day that accommodate parents' work hours.

Wendy Lill, our NDP MP and critic on disability issues, has frequently pointed to the broad agreement that early childhood programs should include all children—whether their families are poor, wealthy, or middle class, whether the mother is in the workforce or not, whether they're able or disabled, and whether they live in a big city or in a remote rural community—*that is, they should be universal*.

Quebec is the only province in Canada to adopt a universal child care program. In 1997 the province launched a $5-a-day program as part of a new family care policy. Phased in by 2000, the child care program was available to all children under five years old, regardless of whether the parent works. Through to 2001, the Quebec government steadily increased the child care budget, ensuring more spaces and better wages for staff. By 2003 more than 150,000 spaces had been created. But with the election of the Charest Liberals in April 2003, this unique program is threatened. By late 2003, the Charest government had announced it would cut $25 million in funding from publicly funded daycare centres and increase the fees to between $7 and $10 a day. Ignoring all protest, the Quebec Liberals plan to open new spaces to the private sector, further undermining the universality of the system. More backsliding, but Quebec citizens are rising up to prevent the move. Let's hope they succeed and are able to retain this shining example of progressive social policy for the rest of Canada to emulate.

When a low-income mother is provided with child care services, she is able to go to work, replacing social assistance costs and generating taxes. At the same time, her child receives the opportunity for social and educational development and preparation for the schooling to follow. Making sure that expectant mothers get nutritional advice and proper diets also saves the rest of us money: Health Canada estimates that the cost of neonatal intensive care for each premature infant ranges from $32,000 to $52,000. Low-birth-weight babies (under 2.5 kilograms) are at much greater risk of death, disease, and disability than infants of normal weight. Cerebral palsy, learning disabilities, and visual and respiratory problems can affect these babies for their entire lives. Though low-birth-weight babies are fortunately relatively uncommon, women living in poverty—and teenagers, with little or no prenatal care skills—are more likely to deliver them.

About three-quarters of mothers of young children in Canada are part of the paid workforce. Their children need child care—not just so their mothers can hold down jobs, but also so their mothers themselves can take part in training and lifelong education. Our schools need to provide children with nutritious meals (a healthy diet is a key to the ability to learn), and maintain good health in kids with regular physical education. Schools need to be able to reach young people of many different linguistic backgrounds, with English-as-a-second-language (ESL) training and other cultural programs. Schools also have to ensure that they are equipped to provide initial skills training to prepare students for today's world. And, let's not forget, schools must give students the opportunities to express themselves in a wide range of creative arts.

- **Percentage of Canadian families with children headed by sole-support mothers who were poor in 1967: 52**
  In 2001: 56
- **Percentage of cuts to Ontario's social assistance benefits in 1995: 21.6**
  Increase since then: 0
- **Percentage cost of living increase, 1995–2002: 12.8**
- **Chances that an unattached woman over 65 lived in poverty in 1967: 1 in 2**
  In 1997: 1 in 2
- **Average income of men with disabilities, aged 35–54: $31,000**
  Of women with disabilities, aged 35–54: $17,000

It's surprisingly difficult to measure the rate at which young people drop out of high school. (There are complex reasons for different grade requirements in different provinces, and the fact that many people return to school later.) However, between 15 and 20 per cent of young Canadians leave school without receiving a diploma. They drop out for many reasons—often because they are poor and need to find a job—but whatever the cause, high school dropouts are usually doomed to low-paying, low-skilled jobs. Since a lot of kids are living in poverty when they quit school to earn income, their leaving often unfortunately perpetuates the cycle of poverty. Better income-support programs would help them stay in school, get their diplomas, and be equipped to hold more meaningful, better-paying jobs later on. That's an investment well worth making.

Generally, we are a well-educated people. Nearly half of Canada's adult population has post-secondary education. But access to college and university is getting more difficult—and not because we've raised the requirements. We've raised the fees.

At the beginning of the 1990s, tuition and other student fees accounted for an average of 18 per cent of a college or university's operating budget. But through that decade, as governments cut back their funding of post-secondary institutions, revenue from students increased. It now amounts to about 32 per cent of a school's budget. Tuition itself went up by over 125 per cent through the 1990s—six times the rate of inflation. And while tuition and other fees were going up, scholarships and grants were being reduced or eliminated altogether, forcing more and more students to depend on loans. The Canadian Federation of Students estimates that by the time someone graduates from college or university, he or she is saddled with a debt of $25,000. Young Canadians graduate indentured with a mortgage—but they have no house!

Here's a twisted irony: Paul Martin wants to reduce the debt of the country, but he apparently sees no problem with students going further into debt. His first Throne Speech even offered permission for student debt limits to be increased! National borrowing happens at a low interest rate.

Students pay higher interest rates on their debts. Who benefits from this shift of debt from Canadians' shoulders to students'? The banks. They pick up the extra interest. No wonder that in 2003 the banks were making record profits and donating "liberally" to the governing party. (Few students could afford to donate.)

At the same time, Canada's affordable housing construction programs have been axed, so we haven't seen very many student residences built or co-ops where students could find low-rent housing.

Needless to say, for many students, these extra financial burdens make post-secondary education simply unaffordable. A study at the University of Western Ontario showed that the participation rate from low-income families has been reduced by half as tuition increased. When the tuition at UWO's medical school jumped from $4,844 in 1998 to $10,000 in 2000, the average income of the families of first-year medical students rose from $80,000 to $140,000.

Inequality with respect to education is growing. We're shutting the door to thousands of potential college and university students, despite the fact that *everyone*—from advocates for the poor, the chambers of commerce, the Conference Board of Canada to right-wing think-tanks—says that a competitive economy depends on a well-trained and well-educated workforce. By excluding tens of thousands of families from participating in post-secondary education, we are also shrinking the pool from which we will be drawing our "best" students. Natural systems decline when gene pools shrink. So do societies and economies.

A 1999 survey of Ontario college graduates showed that two years after graduation, 97 per cent were employed, and 81 per cent were in work directly related to their education. Employers are always on the hunt for well-trained applicants, and many businesses say that finding skilled employees is their biggest challenge and most important requirement.

So why are we slamming the door in the face of so many potential students? As a country, can't we afford to lower fees?

Sweden, Finland, Norway, Denmark, the Netherlands, Austria, and Greece have no tuition fees for students from their own countries. Most of these nations cover significant living costs too. In Germany, not only is there no tuition for German students, there's no tuition for international students. French students at public universities pay a registration fee of under $100. In England, families with incomes under £20,000 (approximately $45,000 Canadian) can send their children to university without tuition. For the most part, Canada is headed in the opposite direction.

Some provinces have recognized the importance of keeping fees low to ensure access for as many students as possible. Quebec froze university tuition for fifteen of the twenty years prior to 2001, and college admission is free. B.C.'s NDP government froze tuition for five years (and in 2000 cut tuition by 5 per cent). Manitoba froze tuition for two years and in 2000 gave a 10 per cent reduction. Memorial University in Newfoundland reduced its tuition in 2001 and promised a 25 per cent cut over three years.

But elsewhere, the story is very different. At the three universities where I have taught in Toronto, for example, average tuition since 1995 has gone up by almost 50 per cent, and now Ontario's funding is the lowest per student in the country. In 2002, Ontario's colleges were teaching 35,000 more full-time students than they were ten years previously, but with $79 million less in public funding. One result is that my students have to sit on windowsills or stairs to take notes. Alberta and Nova Scotia also increased tuition significantly.

The effects of this transformation have been evident in my own classes. Having taught for most of the past thirty years in Toronto's three universities, I have watched the physical facilities deteriorate, the classrooms become more crowded. When I began teaching, most students could be fully involved in the educational community. They had time after class for clubs, sports, student associations, and study groups. There was lots of time in the library and for enthusiastic discussions with professors and other students outside of class hours. In those early days, few of my students had significant employment outside school.

For today's students, those days are long gone. I see the fatigue in their faces as they struggle to keep their eyes open. And before someone else says it, it's not because my lectures are more boring now than thirty years ago! Students are tired because they are carrying twenty hours—or more—of work a week after their classes. Some work even longer hours. They have no choice. Tuition, books, supplies, food, and housing costs have escalated. It doesn't help that in most parts of Canada, the minimum wage has lagged, been frozen, or even reduced (as has happened in British Columbia). Some lucky ones have parents picking up all the costs and can still experience the diversity of university or college life, but most endure as best they can. Four-year degrees take five. Debt limits further study. Too many drop out, wasting their precious time and our collective investments. In the end, the educational system suffers from inefficiency and quality concerns.

Training, apprenticeship programs, and lifelong learning also need to be priorities. Skilled labour draws industry, provides better wages for workers, and reduces inequality all at the same time. Trained and employed Canadians pay taxes that help the whole system to be adequately financed—another form of investment that's key to our long-term economic sustainability and human well-being.

The steady decline of our commitment to post-secondary education and to training in general is one of those social phenomena whose effects are not immediately apparent. The process brings to mind the story of frogs placed in water that is slowly heated to the boiling point. They are unable to detect the slow changes in temperature, and even though they might jump out, they let themselves get boiled to death without realizing what is happening. The signs of deterioration in education are evident. Let's do something about it. We need to invest in our education system, steadily targeting the best practices of European countries rather than copying the income-segregated educational tendencies of our U.S. neighbours. At the same time, we need to insist that international trade agreements protect our public, and more egalitarian, approach to post-secondary and trades training from intrusion by corporate, profit-making models.

Welcome to Canada?

Our other great untapped energy source is the skills that immigrants bring to our shores. Members of the Toronto City Summit Alliance (among many other groups) recognized the importance of newcomers' talents. The Alliance group wrote: "The large number of immigrants in our region are an unparalleled competitive advantage in today's global economy." No kidding. Like our citizens, over half of the newcomers to Canada *also* have some form of post-secondary education. In 1999, for instance, 25 per cent of immigrants from South Asia had been professionals in their home country, but only half could find work in their field in Toronto. The Conference Board of Canada estimates that "if all immigrants were employed to the level of their qualifications, it would generate roughly an additional $4 billion of wages across the country."

Immigrants bring specific skills and trades that are greatly in demand in Canada. Yet we put up barriers: newcomers commonly find it hard to get Canadian work experience, employment-relevant language training, recognition of their credentials, or even information about employment in their own trades or professions. Our programs to aid immigrants are fragmented among levels of government and dozens of private and voluntary organizations.

The average age of skilled trades workers in Canada is about forty-eight. In the next seven to ten years, most of these people will retire. The community colleges (and CEGEPs in Quebec) have about 900,000 full-time and 1.5 million part-time students, and they are doing a great job of training them, but even these graduates will not fill the gap. We'll need the skills that immigrants bring to Canada. For the sake of these newcomers and our economic growth and competitiveness, we need to smooth the way for their entry into the Canadian labour force.

Our colleges are creating imaginative ways to do this, and rather than cut their funding, we need to be improving their ability to train both Canadian-born and foreign-born students. Since the federal government is responsible for having both an immigration policy and a labour market strategy, Ottawa can—and must—play a role in skills development through the college and CEGEP system.

Canadian colleges already run programs and facilities all over the world. As one example, Centennial College in Scarborough, Ontario, provides training in the Middle East, Kazakhstan, Brazil, Sri Lanka, India, and China. These international connections are typical among our national network of colleges, and they represent a fabulous resource and link to people all around the world.

A number of colleges have presented the federal government with a proposal to reach out to potential immigrants even before they leave their country. People who want to immigrate to Canada can go to a local Canadian embassy or consulate and get information about the services Canadian colleges offer. They'd get a prior assessment of their own credentials, which would be matched against Canadian requirements, and they'd be told what they need to work in their field in Canada. The colleges would develop the capacity to provide potential immigrants with a program (or part of a program) that they need to fill the gap—and could even link these newcomers with potential employers. As well, programs could be designed to provide immigrants with co-op work experience while they study in Canada, completing their application for immigrant status while they're here. Instead of being stuck for years driving cabs or waiting on tables, they'd get the right credentials to secure the right job and be able to contribute their skills in Canada. Plus, they'd be on a much faster track to earning the wages they're entitled to. The federal government is still studying the proposal. They should go for it. Both Canada and the people who could take advantage of it would be better off.

In fall of 2003, a commitment made by the Toronto City Summit Alliance came into being, when the new Toronto Region Immigrant Employment Council launched two pilot programs. One provides internships for immigrants in finance, manufacturing, technology, and other industries. The other is a program where professional employees of the city of Toronto (accountants, engineers, information technology specialists, and so on) act as mentors to new immigrants in those fields. This idea was promoted by Toronto's new mayor, David Miller, when he was chair of the city's Working Group on Immigration and Refugee Issues, and it has great potential.

On Canada Day, 2003, I was invited to a Muslim community celebration of our country's birthday. In a modest backyard, several dozen families had gathered. The mood was upbeat.

The host led us in singing "O Canada" with gusto. In the conversation afterwards, one of his friends told me that he had been encouraged to come to Canada because the immigration officer had assigned him high points (on a scale that measures professional training and experience) because he was an electrical engineer. In his country of origin, he told me, many of his professors and most of his engineering texts were British. "Obviously, Canada wanted people like me, with my skills and training," he said, "because they gave me many points specifically because of my background." He became angry as he went on: "But I found out the Canadian government was lying to me! Since I came here, I have been unable to find work in my field, even though they say there is a shortage. They won't accept my credentials. Why did they give me points if they wouldn't accept my credentials? I brought my family here for a better life. I have ended up driving a taxi for eighteen years, twelve hours a day, for six or seven days a week. I'm trapped. I've been cheated."

Then his friends started sharing their stories—a dentist, an accountant, a medical technician, a surgeon, all driving cabs or working in cleaning or security jobs. The most successful one had a small cleaning business with five employees, all of whom had professional backgrounds. "What a waste of talent," he said. "What kind of society lets perfectly good talent like that go unused?"

These stories hit close to home, right in my own family. Olivia's mother and father were both professionals in Hong Kong in 1970 when they decided to come to Canada "to make a better life for our daughter." Wai Sun Chow, her father, was a baritone in the Hong Kong opera, a biologist, and a school superintendent. Ho Sze Chow, her mother, was an elementary school teacher. On arriving in Toronto, they tried to find work in the educational system, which was expanding at the time. Qualification issues stood in their way, but they had to earn a living. Dad struggled through various jobs from heavy labour to service work and was unable to find a long-term fit despite repeated efforts. Mom landed a job cleaning rooms and working in the steamy basement laundry of a downtown hotel. She brought home the bacon that way for thirty years. Their combined talents were never able to benefit their adopted country as they could have done. But as they would point out, they did make a good life for their daughter—now perhaps the best-known elected voice of the Chinese community in Toronto. (They did use their considerable teaching skills to introduce me to speaking Cantonese.)

In 2003, the president of the Canadian Council on Social Development, Marcel Lauzière, wrote an article in *The Globe and Mail* that was called "Welcome to Canada. We lied about the opportunities." He showed how immigrants aren't getting ahead, despite their qualifications and willingness for hard work. Programs like those I've described would go a long way to making the opportunities we offer genuine.

September 11, 2001, took a terrible toll on human life immediately and in its long and continuing aftermath. But in Canada, 9/11 also added an insidious new dimension to the diverse communities we live in: the fear and the racism that flows from it. Arab, South Asian, and Muslim families have told me their stories. In the immediate aftermath, our NDP leader at the time, now foreign affairs critic, Alexa McDonough, told the story in the House of Commons about the children with names like Osama being attacked in Canadian schoolyards. These children would angrily ask their parents why they had been given such names! One parent told me of her child wanting to change the colour of his skin.

Discrimination raised its ugly head in many ways, showing how easily our comfortable veneer of tolerance can be pierced when we live in a culture of fear. At the border, Canadian citizenship lost its meaning as Maher Arar was stolen from his family and shipped to a Syrian prison for a year of horrifying torture. Many young Arabs have told me how this has affected them. A young journalism student at Ryerson, brimming with wide-eyed energy and enthusiasm, for sure on her way to a funky new-wave newsroom somewhere in Canada, told me that she felt she could not travel to the United States or even *through* the U.S. because of her fear of similar treatment to that experienced by Arar. She did at the same time share her pride in the strength exhibited by Arar's wife, Monia Mazigh, as she mounted a courageous and single-minded campaign, first to free her husband and then to ensure that such a fate never befalls another.

From the insidious and growing practice of racial profiling to racial discrimination in the workplace, inequality based on race, culture, and religion is severely tarnishing Canada's former reputation as an open society that celebrates diversity. That's why, in our caucus on Parliament Hill, we have created a Diversity Advocacy Team to work with groups across the country to break down barriers, to make racial profiling illegal, to broaden the possibilities for families to reunite here in Canada, and to support immigrant settlement services. As Canada becomes more and more diverse, we need to reform our laws, policies, practices, and programs to reflect and enhance this basic fact of Canadian life.

Let's realize the potential of all our people. It's not only a matter of justice and equality—it would also be good for our whole society, in every way.

A Call to Action

Canadian society is an immigrant one, made up of people who have come to these shores from all parts of the world, from all cultures and civilizations and linguistic origins. Aboriginal societies in Canada have roots that go back thousands of years before the modern waves of immigration. Thus, Aboriginal peoples have a unique place in this country and unique claims upon it.

I doubt I'd be here today had it not been for the hospitality of Aboriginal peoples. My family, on my mother's side, arrived on the distinctly inhospitable shores of what we now call New Brunswick in 1765, in a small sailing ship packed with several other homeless German families. They were looking for safe sanctuary, where their religious beliefs could be nurtured in freedom and where they could build a community. It had been a tough journey; their chances of surviving the oncoming Canadian winter were bleak. Thankfully for the family, there were already people on these shores who welcomed them and helped them recover their health after the disease and hunger of the journey—the people we now know as the Mi'kmaq. The Steif family, now known as the Steeves, based in Hillsborough, near Moncton, numbers in the hundreds of thousands across North America. I'm named after Jack Steeves, my grandfather, who grew up in Hillsborough.

The treatment of Aboriginal peoples in Canada has been nothing short of disgraceful. Denied respect, denied the benefits and riches of the resources that were theirs, denied even the provisions guaranteed under treaties signed by the

Queen, the First Nations have been driven into desperate living conditions on reserves, in remote communities, even in urban areas. International organizations have rightly condemned Canada for its treatment of the original inhabitants of these lands.

It is now time to treat Aboriginal peoples as full and respected partners in the evolution of Canada. The excellent 1996 report of the Royal Commission on Aboriginal Peoples continues to offer a guide. By forming partnerships with grassroots organizations, we can put the report's recommendations into action. Witness, for example, the collaboration between the NDP, particularly MP Pat Martin, and First Nations organizations in the summer of 2003 to filibuster and ultimately defeat the patronizing First Nations Governance legislation, Bill C-7.

In recent years, New Democratic governments have made great strides toward settling outstanding claims and finding new ways to work with First Nations. Recent land agreements, such as those reached with the Nisga'a and Sechelt peoples, are particularly significant, but there are many other achievements that should be acknowledged. Participants in the NDP's Yukon roundtable a few years back, for example, were proud of the partnerships that Aboriginal, municipal, and territorial governments have developed. Svend Robinson often reminds me that the 1982 Constitutional package recognized Aboriginal rights only because the federal NDP caucus, led by Ed Broadbent, succeeded in their fight to have Aboriginal rights included.

The true heroes, however, are First Nations leaders and communities. Like Barrière Lake Reserve Chief Harry Wawatie, whose community of four hundred people live in sixty decrepit houses in abject poverty while resource-extracting firms and tourism companies suck the enormous economic wealth out of the lands that should provide the community with sustenance. Courage and wise determination are what you see in the chief's eyes, along with deep sadness as he watches an affluent nation systematically deny basic human rights and security to the next generation of his community.

In most immigrant cultures, there is a convergence around one common language for public discourse. In the United States, this is English; in Argentina, it's Spanish. In Canada we find not one but two such languages of convergence: French and English. Essentially, there are two immigrant foundations in this country—two dominant, coexisting foundations that have been enriched and strengthened by several waves of immigration from all corners of the globe.

Aboriginal peoples are in an important sense part of this duality, in that their societies were forced by circumstance or coercion to choose English or French as the language used to interact with public institutions. The most brutal instance of imposed acculturation was the re-education of Aboriginal children in residential schools.

French and English each have their areas of geographic strength. Acadians in the Maritimes are a key francophone component, as are significant communities in Ontario and Manitoba, but the centre of Canada's French-speaking immigrant society is clearly the province of Quebec—dynamic, varied, multicultural. As the heart of Canada's francophone population—a diverse one comprising several Aboriginal groups and people from all parts of the world—Quebec has responsibilities and challenges unlike those of any other province.

Quebec is the vibrant, distinct society it is today primarily as the result of its policies since the Quiet Revolution, which began with the election of the Liberals under Jean Lesage in June 1960. I grew up in the midst of this transformation from hidebound conservative traditionalism to the inspired reform of economic, social, and cultural institutions. Debates were passionate, and there were deep disagreements and crises in Quebec at the time. Still, the policies that prevailed and allowed Quebec to flourish were frequently based on the values of social democracy. Indeed, the province's progressive agenda in the latter part of the century influenced policy-making in Canada as a whole.

I find it tragic that language and culture continue to divide Canada into two solitudes. One key reason I decided to seek the leadership of the NDP was to see if I could somehow assist in making a bridge between the social democratic impulses of Quebec and those found elsewhere in Canada. I believe that the NDP, a social democratic party, could be the ideal means to accomplish this, but we have a great distance to go. And we have had to revise our traditional, rather centrist, approach to a relationship with Quebec. We need to assist in the evolution of a flexible federalism that allows Quebec to achieve its goals within a Canadian nation-state.

I witnessed the possibilities for flexible federalism up close when I was involved in trying to bring the federal government and the provinces toward an agreement on a new affordable social housing construction program. As a vice president of the Federation of Canadian Municipalities at the time, I was charged with working with the federal minister of public works, the singularly unhelpful Alfonso Gagliano, and the provincial ministers responsible for housing. Fortunately, the lead ministers were Tim Sale of Manitoba and Louise Harel of Quebec. Flexibility in our approach ensured that Quebec could pursue its social housing program the way it wanted to—essentially elaborating on the excellent initiatives that it had under way. In fact, the Quebec approach was the best in the whole of Canada. It was beautifully ironic, I thought. Here was Quebec, the most likely to object to federal dollars being devoted to a policy field that was being actively pursued by the Quebec National Assembly, and yet Quebec was the most effective at achieving the affordable housing goals with dedicated federal dollars. It put other provinces to shame, particularly those like Ontario that refused to match the federal funds and thus left the homeless in that province out in the cold.

Prior to my becoming leader, the NDP began work on a framework for flexible, asymmetrical federalism structured around co-operative decision making, respectful of the jurisdictions that have been established in our Constitution, in order to achieve the goals that Canadians agree on. This practical concept of managing the relationships of Canadian federalism has a lot of appeal. Hard work? Yes. But worth the effort. In the process, I am extending my hand to today's Quebeckers with an invitation to help build a coast-to-coast-to-coast social democratic movement to serve as a real, viable, and exciting alternative to the corporate drift we see in the two old-line parties, the Liberals and the Conservatives.

Elsewhere, relationships in our Canadian federation are terribly strained. Years of neglect and even disdain at the hands of a remote and uninterested national government have left deep scars in Western Canada. And those wounds have been reopened with the inadequate response to drought, mad cow disease (BSE) and its impact on the cattle industry, killer U.S. agricultural subsidies, punishing softwood lumber tariffs, and federal fishery management ineptitude. The lists of grievances are long and detailed.

I've learned a lot about the realities faced by Western Canadian communities from my years building the national movement of communities of all sizes through the Federation of Canadian Municipalities.

I've also learned about the grievances in Eastern Canada. Population flows out to Central Canada like a hemorrhage.

Especially of young people. No wonder communities lose hope. As laissez-faire economics has taken hold, central Canadian corporate interests have shifted investment in ways that leave communities struggling. A clear case in point is the Saint John shipyards. Once a source of secure, well-paid jobs, these operations have been closed down following decisions by international firms to build ships where cheap labour is plentiful—firms like Canada Steamship Lines, which used to build ships in Canada and now uses low-paid workers in the shipyards of China. Or the coal mining community of Sydney on Cape Breton Island, where unemployed coal miners watch ships roll into the harbour to unload Venezuelan coal. The polluting coal dust floats over the community and into the lungs of the residents of Whitney Pier, while coal of equivalent quality lies in closed mines underneath their feet and Cape Breton families struggle to survive. No wonder the East feels left out of the so-called national equation. Where's the national strategy for the shipbuilding industry?

Canada's North raises similar concerns. Climate change will have the most dramatic effects in the North, yet Canada is not leading the way to respond to the crisis. Northern health needs tend to be forgotten. When the provincial premiers met in 2003 to hammer out some modest federal funding, for instance, the northern territories were completely forgotten. NDP Health Advocate Svend Robinson made a trip to the North to collect evidence, and only then was there a response from the governing Liberals. Ottawa loves to exploit the image of the exotic North but does not give a considered response to its needs.

Over the years, I've learned how diverse groups can pull together in support of one another to secure federal attention and support. At the FCM, I argued that the neglected needs of all our communities should be presented as one. That's why we created the Rural Caucus to represent northern and remote communities. Their voices were added to the Big-City Mayors' Caucus, and the unified message was irresistible. The call for federal investment of the gas tax in community transportation for cities, towns, and rural areas across all of Canada was an example of the approach I recommended. At first, Paul Martin completely rejected the idea. "I don't believe in dedicated taxes!" he told me. But once he began to hear from a thousand democratically elected community governments, all with the same message, he could not continue to resist the demand for action.

That's why we need to build united voices around the full range of community concerns in this country. There's only one way to cure alienation: we must control the situation through united action. Westerners, Easterners, Quebeckers, and Central Canadians with common values have to come together to support one another in the effort to meet essential needs.

The fact is, Canadians have a basic instinct to do just that. I remember discussing the reaction in drought-ridden Saskatchewan when Eastern Ontario farmers got together with big-city politicians like Clive Doucet in Ottawa and with me in Toronto and pushed bumper-crop surplus hay into Western Canada to feed starving animals. People simply couldn't believe it. They were surprised that anyone east of Kenora cared. Well, I know that Canadians do care about each other. It's the federal government that doesn't care. That's what has to change.

Our relationships with each other within Canada need some work, but we all know how important they are. And what ties us together in our astounding diversity is the idea that we share sufficient core values to allow us to work together, in our different ways, on our common project—building the country that captures our hopes for the future.

Is this an approach that should guide our relationships with those outside our own borders? I think so. Let's consider our history. Canada has long championed multilateralism—the idea that many ethnic groups should work together to achieve security and improve the well-being of the human family. It is a logical position for us, politically situated as we are between Europe and the United States. Canada has played an important role in building and supporting multilateral institutions such as the United Nations. In general, Canada has been a voice for peace over aggression.

We saw this most recently with the outburst of opposition by Canadians to the invasion of Iraq by George W. Bush, armed with his new unilateral doctrine of the pre-emptive strike. As the newly elected leader of our party in January 2003, I found myself at the centre of the debate in Canada about what we should do. The NDP took the position that Canada should not participate in the invasion and should instead support the work of the United Nations arms control inspectors who were slowly making their way through Iraq, searching for weapons of mass destruction. We urged our government to take a strong stand too. Our MPs and I spoke at rallies in the freezing cold all over Canada. We mounted petitions and websites. At first, things did not look good. Jean Chrétien ridiculed the NDP in the House, saying, "They think a good sing-song would solve all the problems."

But we formed alliances with the broadly based movements that were working for peace. This created a positive process of connecting with Canadians across the land who felt strongly about an issue and were organizing on the ground to make their views known. And it produced powerful results: the most memorable moment for me was when Prime Minister Chrétien rose in the House on the eve of the invasion to announce that Canada would not participate.

Then, much to my dismay, Liberal leadership candidate

Paul Martin was quoted on the front page of a national newspaper suggesting that the decision not to go to war might have compromised our relationship with the Bush administration, and that to set things back on track we should initiate talks with U.S. officials concerning Canadian participation in "National Missile Defence." At first, the Chrétien cabinet balked at this idea, but it did not take long for the Martin forces in the cabinet to prevail, and talks were initiated.

The whole concept of a missile shield is the antithesis of multilateral action to accomplish greater human security. The Bush government has laid out a plan ultimately to involve land-based, sea-based, and space-based interceptor missiles. The idea is to erect the equivalent of a fence of weapons around America to block incoming warheads. Not only has the system never been successfully tested, it is also monstrously expensive and will certainly provoke a new arms race around the entire planet. After all, the mere deployment of the first phase of the scheme involving land-based missiles required the U.S. government to tear up the Anti-Ballistic Missile Treaty with Russia. As though to underline the dangers of this strategy, the Russians publicized their successful test of a new rocket that could be guided away from missile interceptors as it manoeuvred toward its target. This development effectively makes obsolete Bush's Star Wars II before it has even been built. The Russians rightly fear that the American initiative will provoke powers like China to develop more sophisticated weapons in greater numbers. All in all, a new arms race is effectively under way.

So what should Canada do? We are told by Prime Minister Martin's government that we have to "be at the table" to influence the program. His officials even suggest that by being at the table we could help to convince the Pentagon not to put weapons in space. Piously, Martin rose in the House to say that the National Missile Defence system did not involve weapons in space and that the Canadian government would never support weapons in space. I was criticized by Liberal MPs for scaremongering.

There was only one thing to do. I went to Washington to meet with members of Congress, to get the facts. The congressmen and -women I met with were incredulous that a Canadian prime minister could be suggesting that the plan did not involve the weaponization of space. Everyone in Washington, they said, knows what this program is about. The land-based missiles are only the first step. They showed me Defense Department budget submissions, clearly indicating the funds that were being requested for the development of more than three hundred space-based interceptors by the latter part of this decade. A study by the American Physical Society—the physicists—showed that a land-based interceptor system could not, even in theory, be effective. I was told that more than one hundred members of Congress had voted against these appropriations because of their fears of a new arms race.

Where does this leave us? If Canada participates, even in talks, it sends out a message to the world. The message is that we believe this is an idea worth pursuing. Such a message would undermine any Canadian credibility resulting from our decision not to support the invasion of Iraq. We would not be seen as an effective, independent, sovereign voice on the world stage. Our historic role as advocate for peace would have been abandoned. We would have instead become a lapdog, a bit player in the Bush initiative.

Is the NDP stance anti-American? Absolutely not. In my first year as leader, I met with members of Congress on two trips to the U.S. capital. They included John Tierney from Massachusetts, Rush Holt from New Jersey, and Bernie Sanders from Vermont. I also encountered many Americans who, like me and my party, often disagree with President Bush's policies but who, like me and my party, have a deep respect and affinity for America.

Sometimes our countries agree—on fighting acid rain, on the Second World War, on Korea, and on Kosovo. And sometimes we disagree—on the Iraq and Vietnam wars, our relationship with Cuba, the International Criminal Court, or the Kyoto Protocol. Though our values are similar enough to be good friends, they are different enough for us to disagree. Though our Canadian system of universal medicare is not perfect, it is fundamentally more equitable and efficient than the system found in the United States, a health care system that many Canadians find offensive—one designed to exclude those who cannot buy their way in. So we may share a continent, but we do not always share values. When we do have common goals, we do not necessarily use the same means to achieve them.

Like Canada, Mexico is sometimes moved to disagree with American policy. We need to look no further than the chilling of relations between Mexican President Vicente Fox and President Bush after Mexico took a far more public stand against the Iraq War than did Canada, given that Mexico sat on the UN Security Council at that critical time.

It is time for a different view of Canada-U.S. relations that enables us to co-operate on the one hand and respectfully disagree if necessary on the other. Canada is not a neutral nation, nor are we a pacifist one. We have unequivocally taken sides in some of the world's great choices and fought for freedom. In fact, some argue, Canada became an international citizen through the world wars of the twentieth century. Those wars shaped the world, and in their aftermath, Canada and the United States joined to find ways to co-operate with other nations to prevent future wars, most notably through the creation of the United Nations.

Whatever its faults, and there are many, the UN represents a very Canadian world view.

For a country like ours, multilateralism allows us to play an effective role in solving global problems such as the environment, arms proliferation, AIDS in Africa, or grinding poverty in developing countries. It also allows us to effectively contribute military resources to crises, working with like-minded nations in peacekeeping or peacemaking.

Canadians are justifiably proud of our historic role in the world and justifiably proud of the successes of multilateralism—from the Montreal Protocol on the ozone layer to helping rid the world of the scourge of land mines to creating the treaties now used to dampen the nuclear escalation between India and Pakistan. This is not to say the model is perfect. Given recent atrocities in Rwanda, the world's failure to respond to the emerging crisis of climate change, or our complacent acceptance of trading models that cement fundamental global inequalities, we clearly have much work to do.

Prime Minister Martin quotes his rock star friend Bono, saying "the world needs more Canadas." And Bono is correct, even if Martin's policies are, by and large, not. The world does need more nations working together on common concerns—in other words, multilateralism. President Bush recognizes this, too, given that he was so anxious to portray the Iraq War as a coalition rather than a unilateral American war. I'm still not certain what the Solomon Islands or Micronesia contributed to the effort, but at least Bush recognized that despite being the world's last superpower, America cannot be seen to be acting alone.

What neither President Bush nor Prime Minister Martin recognizes is that their joint choice to pursue Star Wars missile defence undermines their rhetoric on security, co-operation, and fiscal responsibility. The world does not become safer because a superpower decides to launch a new weapons system, nor is Bush's growing deficit helped by spending upward of $1 trillion to weaponize space. Furthermore, the position of the United States in the world is not strengthened by being seen to undermine arms control agreements such as the Anti-Ballistic Missile Treaty or the comprehensive test ban treaty, nor is Canada's position helped in the world if and when we become involved in these U.S. policies.

Inevitably, the credibility of American foreign policy has suffered. As the symbol of Western values to much of the world, the White House, if it resolutely espouses unilateralism, does us all a disservice—the United States included. America needs allies with credibility, making insistence on Canada joining Star Wars doubly dangerous. Multilateral arms control and weapons reduction require rules that are made by all, applicable to all, and protective of all, America included.

Fortunately, many Americans are joining what I call a new superpower, one proposing just such a vision—that is, the gathering strength of citizens around the world. We saw it in the streets in Canada, in the United States, and, indeed, in most countries during the Iraq War. I believe fundamentally that citizens can create the political impetus that requires governments to respond. I know this because I've seen it in action. In Canada, as we were deciding our role in the war, the public voice for peace played a role in the decision not to join President Bush in Iraq.

Yet in Canada, the new prevailing view in our government is that questioning Bush's policies is dangerous while obeying them is safer; thus, we consign Canadian values and those of millions of Americans to irrelevance. I do not believe in the false choice between foreign policy obedience and economic success. We need to recognize that there are ways in which we can co-operate that reflect our values, respect our security, and reward our economy. History does not justify the fear-mongering theory that Canada must blindly go along with our biggest trading partner on foreign policy so that economic growth will flow automatically. During the Vietnam War, Lester Pearson stayed out of the conflict yet simultaneously negotiated the Auto Pact, perhaps Canada's best trade deal ever. In Afghanistan, Jean Chrétien joined the American effort but received no consideration or no assistance at all on correcting the unjust U.S. softwood lumber surcharges that have thrown thousands of Canadian workers onto unemployment lines.

In U.S.-Canadian relations, I would like to outline one area badly in need of improvement, and that's trade. Workers on both sides of our border are hurt by the current NAFTA model, as corporations move jobs to countries whose workers are paid lower wages. In addition, Americans and Canadians are disadvantaged by the Bush administration's punishing duties on softwood lumber, which eliminate employment opportunities in both places and notably affect American families who rely on our lumber for construction jobs and affordable homes. With an economy in trouble, the U.S. should build homes with our lumber, not walls against it.

Equally, America's refusal to reopen its borders to live cattle imports from Canada, despite fundamentally similar regulatory regimes, suggests that Canada would be justified in closing its border to imports of U.S. beef. Such a policy would, in effect, shift Western Canada's beef markets from north–south to east–west, essentially replacing American beef consumed in Eastern Canada with beef from our West.

The American Congress needs to understand it cannot selectively penalize Canadian resource industries, all the while benefiting from safe, affordable energy from Canada.

This means putting all issues on the table when we negotiate. If President Bush wishes to ignore NAFTA as it affects lumber, there is no reason Canada should not ignore NAFTA as it affects energy.

Canada and the United States can work toward common ends, even if the means differ. Certainly this is true on environmental issues, as we share the airspace and watersheds of a single continent. President John F. Kennedy once said, "The deepest common thing in us is that we live on the same small planet. We breathe the same air. We all care about the future of our children and we are all mortal beings." This is true now more than ever before. Canada, which nominally supports the Kyoto Protocol, receives smog from the U.S., which does not support Kyoto. And my son ends up in an emergency room with asthma. And American sons end up in emergency wards with asthma as a result of pollution from our coal-burning plants. No gasping child cares if their government supports Kyoto, but every parent who's stood by as a child struggles to breathe wants clean air.

And so, though I hope America joins the world's only climate change treaty and hope Canada finally honours it, I say let's work outside Kyoto for the benefit of both. Canada should join with progressive American states such as California, Massachusetts, and perhaps New York to create larger markets for cleaner cars, as I've suggested in Chapter 6. California and Canada alone represent a market of almost sixty-five million people, which gives manufacturers a powerful financial incentive to build cleaner cars in greater numbers. If treaties alone are unappealing, we can use market mechanisms as well. Because, make no mistake, no politician's legacy can match that of helping arrest climate change. If humanity's going to Mars, let's do it as explorers, not refugees.

I say to our American friends, let's share each other's

technologies and ideas—from our deep-lakewater cooling in Toronto to your massive wind farms in Texas, from our fuel cell technology to Iowa's program that gives farm families money in exchange for wind turbines on their fields. As inhabitants of the continent, we've all seen floods, forest fires, and droughts. Melting icecaps are yet to come. And despite the American president's background in oil, or my prime minister's in coal, I say it's time for North Americans of good faith to use our ideas and pocketbooks to shame our timid leaders and show the world how it's done.

Let's also recognize that our militaries should co-operate. NDP MP Peter Stoffer made arrangements for me to have tea in the home of Rear Adm. Glen Davidson, commander of the Canadian East Coast fleet. He told me of some of the rescue missions Canada has carried out at sea thanks to American satellite data from the air, thus saving distressed sailors from countries near and far in a spirit of true co-operation. Our militaries have worked together often in a troubled world. Our diplomats should collaborate, too, to create tools to improve conditions for the international popu-lace. Nobody can be proud of the way member nations of the United Nations have responded to crisis. From Kosovo to Rwanda to the Congo, we have watched as millions were slaughtered.

We must establish a United Nations rapid deployment capacity in order to intervene in a timely way during crises. Days of delay meant the loss of thousands of lives in Rwanda. Months of delay meant the wrath of ancient hatreds unleashed in Kosovo. And since no country is perfect and all have their prejudices, we need a neutral force ready and willing to react. Democracy doesn't develop during strife. Though American sensibilities may be bruised by fol-lowing the orders of a military with UN blue helmets, American self-interest dictates that a multilateral response force be ready and willing. It's a vision based on practical co-operation and multilateral response. To draw from Noam Chomsky, the choice between these two visions, multilateral versus unilateral responses, amounts to a choice between hegemony and survival.

To be clear, I do not wish for continental security perimeters or a joint Canada-U.S. command, or even a massive increase in defence spending. Nor do I support draconian anti-terrorism or security laws like those that have already ensnared hundreds in the American prison at Guantanamo Bay, detained without access to justice.

Canada's next federal election will determine whether we pursue integration with the United States on security, economic, and environmental issues. As with the last such debate, in the 1988 federal election, I believe the choices will be clear and the debate invigorating. Over the past century of Canadian politics, we have had three prime ministers who are fundamentally integrationist: Wilfrid Laurier, Brian Mulroney, and now Paul Martin. Laurier was defeated over integrationist policies in 1911. Mulroney was indeed re-elected on those policies in 1988, thanks to an out-of-date voting system, but as their impact became clear, his party suffered the worst possible defeat in the following election. History shows Martin is entering dangerous territory in aggressively pursuing integrationist policies immediately before an election—and immediately after several decisions by the Bush administration that are deeply unpopular in Canada, the Iraq War and the U.S. decision not to ratify the Kyoto Protocol being chief among them.

I've travelled to many parts of the United States and Canada over the course of my life, and I've never heard anyone say, "You know, I don't mind my son being in the emergency ward, choking on smog-related asthma, because I got a tax cut today." Or "I'm really happy we're investing billions in Star Wars because I'm worried about a rogue state launching an intercontinental ballistic missile attack tomorrow."

What I do hear is people saying they're concerned about being able to afford university tuition for their children, or they're anxious about health care for their families, or they're worried about the future of the family farm, or they're nervous about the security of their pension plan. Though Canadians and Americans do in fact differ on some values, on essential issues we agree. And so while relations between our two governments can chill, the bonds among citizens across the border are far from severed.

Canadians have a unique contribution to make to the neighbourhood of our continent, to the rest of the hemisphere, and to the wider world. The values on which we propose to build a better society in our own complex and extraordinary country are values that serve us well in our relations with the rest of world. They are the values on which Lloyd Axworthy draws when he speaks of "human security," the values that motivate Stephen Lewis when he urges us to adopt proposals to save millions of lives by eradicating AIDS and tackling poverty in Africa. We have the opportunity to reject policies of fear and to embrace initiatives of hope. At home and abroad, let's make that choice.

Index

Aboriginals, 265–67
  Employer Circles Program,
    179–80
  First Nations Governance
    Act, 142
  health care and, 140–43
  housing and, 143, 164
  language, education, and,
    267
  poverty and, 266
  Toronto's waste disposal
    and, 68, 69
accountability
  government and, 140, 193,
    194, 242
  private health care and,
    119
  trade agreements and, 174
agriculture. See also food
  farm size and ownership,
    96–97, 100, 102
  food security and, 97–112
  GM crops and, 101,
    110–12, 133
  land for, 96–97
  national policy on, 31, 97
  prairie drought and, 271
  subsidies, tariffs, and,
    102–4, 269
  water and, 76–77
AIDS, 34, 276, 282
  Defence Plan, 28, 135–40
Allen, Greg, 63, 199
Anderson, Irwin, 159
Anishnawbe Health Centre,
  143
Arar, Maher, 42, 264
Atkinson Foundation, 247
Atlantic-Pacific Forest
  Industries, 37
Auto Pact, 209, 211, 278
automobiles
  manufacture of, employ-
    ment in, 207
  manufacturing energy-
    efficient, 207–12, 279
  recycling of, 74–75
Axworthy, Lloyd, 282

Baldwin Act, 1849, 152
Banff, Alberta, 185
Bank of Canada, 187, 188, 190

Barlow, Maude, 30, 88, 89,
  216
Barrie, Ontario, 86
Beauce, Quebec, 180
Beck, Adam, 205
Better Buildings Partnership,
  54, 55, 195, 197
Blaikie, Bill, 31, 138
blind people, 19–20
Bombardier Co., 58
Bono, 276
Bradshaw, Claudette, 164,
  165
Broadbent, Ed, 100, 245
brownfields, 92–95, 162–63
Brudy, Norm, 26
Building on Values, 118–21
Bush, George, Jr.
  defence policy of, 273–74
  Iraq War and, 41, 190,
    272, 276, 277
Bush, George, Sr.
  Kyoto Protocol and, 42

Calgary
  Fair Gains program, 229–30
  Highbanks Society, 231
  wind power, public transit
    and, 46–47, 58, 175
Campbell, Gordon, 249
Canada Assistance Plan
  (CAP), 246–47
Canada Health Act, 121, 148
Canada Health and Social
  Transfer, 247
Canada Pension Plan, 221–24
Canada Steamship Lines, 270
Canada West Foundation, 154
Canadian Auto Workers'
  union, 58, 75, 208, 210
Canadian Broadcasting
  Corporation, 187
Canadian Council on Social
  Development, 263
Canadian Public Health
  Association, 130, 131
Canadian Wheat Board, 104
Cape Breton Association for
  Housing Development, 229
Caton, Lisa, 230
cattle industry, 269, 278
Charest, Jean, 253

Charter of Rights and
  Freedoms, 237
children
  child care and, 252–54
  dental checkups and,
    126–28
  health care and, 129, 133
  hunger, poverty, and,
    97–101, 245–46, 254
  obesity and, 133, 134
Chomsky, Noam, 281
Chong, Gordon, 27
Chow, Ho Sze, 262
Chow, Olivia, 15–16, 42,
  97–98, 114, 127–28,
  158–59, 247, 262–63
Chow, Wai Sun, 262
Chrétien, Jean, 113, 117
  Iraq War and, 41, 272
  NAFTA and, 217
  relations with U.S. and,
    278
Churley, Marilyn, 80
cities. See also government,
  municipal
  Canada's population and,
    151
  local democracy and,
    184–86
  problem-solving
    abilities/restraints and,
    174–86
  proportional representation
    voting in, 239
  provincial GDP and, 154
  safety and, 176
  "smart growth" and, 163
civil society, 238–39
Clarke, Tony, 30
climate change. See under
  environment; Kyoto Protocol
Comartin, Joe, 208
Communications Energy and
  Paperworkers union, 64
communities
  population distribution
    among, 151
  sustainability and, 184–86
  urban (see cities)
community economic devel-
  opment (CED), 228–32
composting. See under waste

Concert Properties, 167
Cooperative Commonwealth
Federation (CCF), 115. *See
also* NDP
corporations
contaminated industrial
sites and, 92–95
corruption in, 17–18
energy supply and, 196
foreign, Canadian inde-
pendence and, 24–25, 30,
32–34
foreign takeovers of
Canadian, 25, 30, 213,
214
GM crops and, 101,
110–12
pesticide use and, 172, 174
polluter pays principle and,
73, 75, 92
privatizing public-sector
services and, 15, 16, 18,
30
public-private partnerships
(P3s), 17, 30–31, 119,
184
trade deals and, 15
water exports and, 88–89
Council of Canadians, 88
Crocus Investment Fund, 230
Crombie, David, 26
Cross, James, 22
Crowe, Cathy, 161

Dallaire, Romeo, 16, 138
Dauphin, Manitoba, 78
Daviau, Thérèse, 21
David Suzuki Foundation, 93,
197
Davidson, Glen, 280
defence policy. *See* military
policy
Desjarlais, Bev, 141
Diamond, Jack, 126
Diouf, Jacques, 100
Doer, Gary, 91
Don River, 80–81
Doré, Jean, 21
Doucet, Clive, 271
Douglas, Tommy, 114, 241
health care policy and,
115–16
Paul Martin and, 117
War Measures Act and, 22
Drapeau, Jean, 21
drug companies, 123–24
Ducasse, Pierre, 47
Duplessis, Maurice, 20
Dupont Corporation, 74

economic policy
industrial strategies and,
190
key indicators of, 189
national debt, deficits, and,
190–94
privatization and, 188
economy
communities, development,
and, 228–32
distribution of wealth and,
226
Genuine Progress Indicator
as measure of, 234–35
Gross Domestic Product as
measure of, 233–34
investment from U.S. and,
24–25
Edmonton
Fuel Sense Program and, 53
Handcraft Production
Centre, 231
Pakistan Canada
Association, 231
education, 251–59
class size and, 257–58
community college enroll-
ment, 260
drop outs and, 254–55
early childhood, 252
ESL training and, 254
family income and, 256
immigrants, employment,
and, 259–61
investment in, 190
overseas programs, 260–61
student tuition, debt and,
255–56, 257, 258
election(s)
federal 1972, 25
federal 1988, 281
female candidates in,
240–41
Toronto 1972, 26
Toronto 1982, 27–28
Toronto 1988, 105
voter turnout for, 15, 41.
185, 241
electoral system, 239–42
electricity
delivery/supply of, 17
hydro, 64, 196
solar power and, 61–64
employment
automobiles and, 207
college graduates and,
256–57
green energy plan and,
196, 198, 199, 206–7
immigrants and, 259–61

lumber exports and, 215,
278
minimum wage and, 227
pay equity and, 245
small businesses and, 232
students and, 258
trade agreements and, 215
employment insurance (EI),
218–21
energy, 196–207. *See also*
electricity; solar power; wind
power
co-generation systems, 109
consumption, industries
and, 201
consumption statistics, 44
domestic emissions trading
(DET) and, 202–4
federal subsidies and, 202
fossil fuels and, 201, 202,
205, 206, 279
fuel efficiency and, 108–9
geothermal, 59–60, 64
integrated grid for, 204–5
lake-water cooling and,
56–57, 201–2, 226, 280
local generation of, 61, 201
nuclear, 35, 65, 66, 85,
196, 197, 199, 202, 205
renewable/sustainable, 62,
196–99, 201–7
standards for efficiency, 199
trade in, 216–17
Enron Corporation, 17
environment. *See also* Kyoto
Protocol
agriculture and, 102
air pollution and, 47–49,
72
Canada's North and, 270
Canadian attitudes about,
46
climate change and, 45,
49–52, 59, 66, 76, 77, 88,
102, 133, 182, 197, 202,
203, 209, 270, 276, 279
Precautionary Principle
and, 111
safe communities and,
34–36
water pollution and,
18–19, 44, 72, 78–84
Équiterre, 107
Eves, Ernie, 109, 227
Extended Product
Responsibility (EPR),
72–73, 75, 83

Farm Folk/City Folk, 107, 108
federalism, 268–71

Federation of Canadian Municipalities (FCM), 32–33, 88, 94, 108
  Big City Mayors' Caucus, 271
  formation of, 152–53
  municipal infrastructure and, 157–58
  national housing strategy and, 162, 163, 268
  pesticide laws and, 173
  Sustainable Communities program, 185–86
Federation of Metro Tenants' Associations, 26
fisheries
  environment, economy and, 35
  federal management of, 269
food. *See also* agriculture
  genetically modified (GM), 101, 110–12, 133
  land mines and, 102
  local growers. markets, and, 107–9
  marketing boards, 104
  national policy on, 104
  organic, 105
  retail industry, 103–4
  safety of, 18
  transportation and, 106–7
food banks, 100, 246
food councils, 105–6
food security, 97–112
FoodShare, 107, 108
Ford Corporation, 74
foreign policy
  multilateralism and, 272, 276
  relations with U.S. and, 273, 274–82
forest fires, 233
forestry
  logging practices, 44–45
  lumber exports and, 42, 183, 215, 269, 278, 279
Fox, Vincente, 275
Free Trade Agreement (FTA), 214, 216
Friends of the Don, 80
Front d'Action Politique (FRAP), 21, 23
Front de Libération du Québec (FLQ), 22

Gagliano, Alfonso, 268
Gardiner Expressway, 28
General Agreement on Tariffs and Trade, 215

General Agreement on Trade in Services (GATS), 33
German, Beric, 161
Gibbs, Lois Marie, 83
Gilbert, Richard, 57
globalization
  abandoning, 187
  accountability, trade agreements, and, 174
  anti- movement, 217
  multinational corporations and, 25, 29–30
Godin, Yvon, 18, 220
Goldrick, Michael, 25, 26
government, federal
  accountability and, 140, 193, 194
  census taking and, 31
  emissions trading and, 203
  Foreign Investment Review Agency (FIRA), 25, 213, 214
  Industry Canada's Investment Review Division, 30, 213
  Kyoto commitments and, 204, 208
  revenue surpluses and, 193–94
government, municipal, 152–58. *See also* cities
  constitutional recognition of, 152, 153. 155
  federal transfer of revenues to, 177–78
  infrastructure and, 157–58, 168–72, 184
  pesticide use and, 172–74
  provincial transfer of revenues, 178
  as source of solutions, 28–29, 153, 174–86
governments, provincial
  downloading and, 156–57, 247
  housing and, 165–66
Green Catalyst Group, 63, 90
Green Municipal Funds, 88
Greenland, Cyril, 97–98
Greenpeace
  energy-efficient cars and, 208, 210
  wind power and, 59
Guaranteed Income Supplement, 221–22
gun registration program, 140

Halifax
  pesticide use in, 173

waste management and, 71, 176
Hall, Barbara, 80
Hall, Emmett, 118
Hamilton, 180
Hancock, Trevor, 35
Harcourt, Mike, 168
Harel, Louise, 268
Hargrove, Buzz, 208
Harris, Mike, 63, 109, 126, 166, 227
Hasbani, Marc, 122
Hawkesworth, Bob, 76
health and health care, 113–50, 187
  Aboriginals and, 140–43
  Centres locaux de services communitaires, 124, 125
  children, hunger and, 97–99
  community services and, 124–29
  dental care and, 126–28
  drugs and, 122–24, 123, 139
  environment and, 34–36, 47–49
  federal funding of, 117–21, 121, 140
  hunger, poverty and, 100–101, 149, 245–46
  income distribution and, 131–32
  national policy on, 32, 114, 119, 132–33
  neonatal intensive care, 253
  nurses and, 128–29
  prevention and, 130, 132, 133, 134
  privatizing, 119, 121
  public health *vs.* medical model, 129–34
  as public service, 17, 19
  Romanow Report and, 118–21, 124, 125, 129, 132, 248
  SARS and, 15, 193, 219
  seniors and, 144–50
  in U.S., 275
Henderson, Joy, 151
Holmes, Oliver Wendell, 15
Holt, Rush, 274
Hospital Insurance and Diagnostic Services Act, 116
Hospital Insurance Plan (Saskatchewan), 116
housing, 158–68
  Aboriginals and, 143, 164
  energy efficiency and, 199
  government downloading and, 156–57

homelessness and, 101,
    158–68
  national programs for, 160,
    164–66, 183, 256,
    268–69
  rent controls and, 26–27
  retrofitting of, 28, 54–55,
    162, 197–99
  social, programs, 63
Hubbard, Betty, 126
Hudson, Quebec, 151
  pesticide use in, 46, 172–74
human rights, 236–37
Human Rights Commission
  (B.C.), 249
Humphrey, John Peters, 236
Hunter, Bill, 37
Hurtig, Mel, 30, 31, 213
Hydro-Québec, 205, 207

IBM, 74
immigrants, 259–64
  discrimination ad, 263–64
  employment and, 259–61
  qualifications of, 262–63
Imperial Oil Company, 92,
  93–94
International Panel on
  Climate Change, 49–50
investments
  foreign, federal government
    and, 25, 30, 213, 214
  foreign takeovers and,
    24–25, 30, 213, 214
  pension funds and, 225–26
Iraq War, 32, 41, 190, 272,
  274, 275, 276, 277, 281

Jacobs, Jane, 25
Jurgens, Ralph, 137
Just Transition strategy, 64–65

Kani, Mario, 63
Kennedy, John F., 279
Kennedy, Robert, Jr., 57, 202
Kirkland Lake, Ontario,
  67–69
Kompani, Mirsalah-Aldin, 159
Kyoto Protocol, 45, 49–53,
  64, 204, 279, 281

Laidlaw Foundation, 154
Laporte, Pierre, 22
Lastman, Mel, 27, 68, 69
The Laughlen Centre,
  146–47
Laurier, Wilfrid, 281
Lauzière, Marcel, 263
Lauzon Léo-Paul, 122
Laxer, James, 24

Layton, Alice (JL's great-
    grandmother), 19–20
Layton, Dave (JL's brother),
    60, 144
Layton, Doris (JL's mother),
    48, 60, 144
Layton, George (JL's great-
    uncle), 21
Layton, Gilbert (JL's grandfa-
    ther), 20–21
Layton, Jack (JL)
  elected chair of Toronto
    Board of Health, 134–35
  elected president of FCM,
    153
  first election to Toronto's
    city council, 26
  NDP and (*see under* NDP)
Layton, Mike (JL's son), 27,
    47–48, 123, 279, 281
Layton, Nancy (JL's sister), 21
Layton, Philip E. (JL's great-
    grandfather), 19–20
Layton, Rob (JL's brother), 60
Layton, Robert (JL's father),
    60, 144–47
Layton, Sally (JL's first wife),
    27
Layton, Sarah (JL's daughter),
    27
Leckie, Dan, 80, 105, 135
Lee, Jack, 126–27
Lesage, Jean, 267
Lévesque, René, 205
Lewis, David, 25, 160, 162
Lewis, Stephen, 27, 138, 139,
    282
Liberal Party. *See also* govern-
    ment, federal; Martin, Paul
  in Quebec, 20
Loblaws, 103
Loubier, Yvan, 142
Lougheed, Peter, 213
Lockheed-Martin
    Corporation, 31
Love Canal, 83
Lovins, Amory, 85
Lynnview Ridge, Calgary,
    93–94

Macdonald, John A., 242
Maclean, Heather, 133
Manley, John, 213
Marchand, Jean, 23
Martin, Pat, 142
Martin, Paul, 180–81, 281
  Canada Assistance Plan
    and, 247
  debt-to-GDP ratio goal of,
    191

employment insurance and,
    219. 220
  federal budgets, cities and,
    178–79, 180
  federal transfer reductions,
    117–21
  as finance minister,
    188–89
  gasoline tax and, 157, 179,
    181, 271
  housing programs and,
    160–61
  Kyoto Protocol and, 45–46
  military policy and, 273–74
  pension benefits and, 223
  sponsorship scandal and,
    242
  student debt and, 255–56
  tax cuts and, 41, 65, 120,
    156, 180
  training programs and, 221
Masse, Brain, 155
Mazigh, Monia, 264
McCrindle, Brian, 133
McDonough, Alexa, 18, 42,
    61, 138, 263
McGill University, 22, 24
McGuinty, Dalton, 109, 180
McPherson, Sandy, 143
McQuaig, Linda, 30
Medical Care Act, 116
Mexico
  auto assembly jobs in, 212
  clean water in, 78
  Iraq War and, 275
  NAFTA and, 215
military policy, 272–78, 281
  Iraq War and, 32, 41, 272,
    274, 275
  peacekeeping and, 32
Miller, David, 69, 261
mining
  coal, in Cape Breton, 270
  safety and, 18
Monahan, Joanne, 153
Moncton Shops Project, 93
Monsanto Corporation, 110
Montreal
  bicycling in, 169–70
  city council of, 21
  in 1880s, 19–20
Montreal Association for the
  Blind (MAB), 20, 21
Montreal Citizens' Movement,
    21
Montreal Massacre, 250
Moore, Michael, 129
Mulroney, Brian, 123, 160,
    281

NAFTA, 215–17, 278, 279
  gasoline additives and, 33
  power of foreign corpora-
    tions and, 31
  sovereign powers and, 29
  water exports and, 89,
    215–16
National Climate Change
  Process, 66
National Homelessness
  Initiative, 164
National Missile Defence,
  273–74
NDP
  Diversity Advocacy Team,
    264
  JL joins, 23
  leadership campaign and
    convention, 16, 114, 268
  Peace Advocacy Team,
    138
  peace movements and, 42
  Rural Caucus, 270
  Waffle movement and, 24
Netherlands
  polluter-pays principle and,
    73
  solar power and, 63
New Dawn program, 229
New Democratic Party. *See*
  NDP
9/11, 15, 202, 263
Nortel, 18
North Battleford, 78
Novik, Marvyn, 105
Nystrom, Lorne, 117, 241

Okanagan Valley, 179
Old Age Security, 221, 222,
  223
Ontario Hydro, 194–95, 205,
  207
Ontario Medical Association
Ontario Municipal
  Employees' Retirement
  System, 226

Parmalat, 17
Pearson, Lester, 278
Peel Non-Profit Housing
  Company, 63
pensions, 221–26
pesticides, 46, 172–74
polluter-pays principle, 73,
  75, 92
pollution
  brownfield cleanups and,
    92–95, 162–63
  coal dust as, 270
  of Don River, 80–81

energy-efficient cars and,
  208–11
  preventing, 82–83
  retrofitting and, 198
  smog and, 47, 48, 149,
    202, 206, 279
  transportation and, 175, 200
public transit, 13, 17, 35,
  153, 163, 168, 171, 176
  Calgary and, 46–47. 58
  government support for,
    157, 168, 182, 228
  seniors and, 149

Quadrangle Architects, 63
Quebec
  Aboriginal groups in, 267
  child care program, 252–53
  conscription crisis and, 21
  housing and, 165–66
  ice storm in, 161
  October Crisis and, 21–23
  Quiet Revolution and, 21,
    267
  social democracy in, 267–69
Quebec City, 185
Quebec Pension Plan, 221–23

Rae, Bob, 156
recycling, 45, 72–73
  of automobiles, 74–75
  co-generation and, 109
  of electronics, 73–74
  Halifax and, 71
  Netherlands and, 73
  Toronto's program for, 28,
    69–70
  of water, 90
Residential Rehabilitation
  Assistance Program, 164
Rio Summit on the
  Environment, 110–11
Robinson, Svend, 122, 138,
  270
Roblin, Manitoba, 90
Rock, Alan, 179
Romanow, Roy, 118–20
Rotary Club of Toronto, 81,
  146
Royal Commission on
  Aboriginal Peoples, 141,
  142, 266

Saint John shipyards, 270
Sale, Tim, 204, 268
Saskatoon, 179–80
Sault Ste. Marie, 124–25
Saunders, Bernie, 274
Scott, Frank, 237
Sequoia Energy, 58

Sewell, John, 26
Shining Lights Choir, 164
Smart Growth Summit, 180
Smith, Bill, 182
Sobeys, 103
solar power, 60–64
  California and, 62–63
  electricity and, 17, 61–64
  Japan and, 62
  Netherlands and, 63
  New York City and, 63
Spadina Expressway, 26
St. John's, Newfoundland,
  53–54
Stanford, Jim, 194
Star Wars defence program,
  14, 180, 273, 276–77, 282
Steeves, Jack (JL's grandfa-
  ther), 265
Stoffer, Peter, 280
Sudbury, 58
Sun Belt Water Inc., 216

Tabuns, Peter, 208
Tamblyn, Bob, 56, 57
tax cuts, 193–94
  corporations and, 15, 29,
    40, 41
  energy producers and, 65
taxes
  corporate and personal, as
    percentage of revenue, 232
  on gas to cities, 157
  on gas to municipalities,
    178–79, 182–83, 271
  goods and services (GST),
    154, 181
  government control of
    spending and, 155, 156
  governments' power to col-
    lect, 155, 177
  paid by municipalities to
    federal and provincial gov-
    ernments, 154
  provincial sales (PST), 154
  public services and, 15–16
Taylor, Charles, 24
Technology Partnerships
  Canada, 212
terrorism
  power plants and, 196, 197
  War Measures Act and, 23
Thatcher, Margaret, 223
Thoreau, Henry David, 95
Tierney, John, 274
Todd, John, 90–91
Tompkins, Jimmy, 229
Toronto
  Atmospheric Fund, 54, 58
  Better Buildings

Partnership, 54–55, 195–97
city council of, 28, 29, 42, 134, 192
City Summit Alliance, 259, 261
energy savings programs, 54
First Duty project, 247
GST paid by, 181
Regent Park Community Health Centre, 125–26
retrofitting programs and, 54–55, 197–99
St. Lawrence community, 162–63
waste disposal and, 67–70
water supply/treatment in, 87–88
waterfront of, 28
Women's Caucus, 42
Toronto Board of Health, 28, 98, 104, 126, 134–35, 249
Toronto City Summit Alliance, 154
Toronto Disaster Relief Committee, 161
Toronto Dominion Bank, 153, 158
Toronto Environmental Alliance, 69
Toronto Food Policy Council, 105–6
Toronto Hydro, 28, 201–2, 211
Toronto School Board, 97–98, 127–28
Toronto Transit Commission, 157
Torrie, Ralph, 197
Townson, Monica, 224
trade. *See also* NAFTA
agreements, manufacturing and, 199
agreements, pesticide use and, 174
agriculture and, 103, 104
Canadian businesses that, 189–90
domestic policies and, 31–34, 213–17
in energy, 216–17
fair, 217
GDP and, 189
GM foods and, 111–12
national policy, water treatment and, 33
with U.S., 278–79
transportation, 168–71. *See also* automobiles; public

transit
bicycles as, 169–70
highways, 200
low-emission vehicles and, 170
national policy on, 168, 169, 170, 182
pollution and, 175, 200
public, France and, 171
railways and rail lines, 170–71, 200–201
traffic congestion and, 200–201
Transportation Equity Act (U.S.), 171
trucking, 18, 200
urban, in U.S., 176–77
Tremblay, Gérald, 182
Trudeau, Pierre
1972 election and, 25, 160
"the just society" and, 235
War Measures Act and, 22, 236

Union Nationale, 20
United Nations, 275–76
Canada and, 272
Food and Agricultural Organization (FAO), 99–100
Human Development Index/Report, 113
rapid deployment capacity of, 280
Universal Declaration of Human Rights, 161, 236–37
World Summit for Children, 245
Upper, Eugene, 158, 159, 160, 162

Vancouver, 33, 92–93, 97, 168–69
Vanishing Country, 30, 213
Victoria, B.C., 58
Voisey's Bay, Newfoundland and Labrador, 93

Walkerton, Ontario, 18, 78, 158
War Measures Act, 22–23, 236
waste. *See also* recycling
composting and, 69–71
disposal of, 45, 67–75
heat emissions, cogeneration and, 201
living machines and, 89–91
nuclear, 202
packaging and, 73

producer responsibility and, 72–73, 75
sewage treatment of, 17
toxic, imports of, 35
Waste Management Corporation, 68, 69
Wasylycia-Leis, Judy, 138
water
agriculture and, 76–77
contamination/pollution of, 18–19, 44, 72, 78–84
Deep Lake Water Cooling initiative, 56–57, 201–2
exporting, 77, 88–89, 215–16
federal policy/standards on, 84, 91
fresh, Canada's supply of, 44, 76
glaciers and, 76
Great Lakes cleanup, 79–80, 82–83
NAFTA and, 215–16
national economy and, 76–77
shortages of, 86–87
solar heating of, 60–61
treatment and supply of safe, 17, 77–79
wetlands and, 89–91
Wawatie, Harry, 266
Wells, Andy, 156
Westray mine, 18
White Ribbon Campaign, 250–51
wind power, 28, 46–47, 58, 59, 175
wind turbines, 58, 60, 280
Windleigh Developments, 63
Winnipeg, 154–55, 180, 230
women
as caregivers, 148, 243–44
employment and, 219, 220, 222, 227, 231, 243–49, 253
health, health care and, 79, 125, 133, 245
in politics, 42, 240–43
poverty and, 149, 221
violence against, 165, 249–51
World Bank, 111
World Trade Organization, 29, 111, 215, 217
Auto Pact and, 211–12
WorldCom Corporation, 17

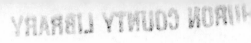

VOICES FROM
TIANANMEN
S Q U A R E

BEIJING SPRING AND
THE DEMOCRACY MOVEMENT

This book is dedicated to the memory of all those who lost their lives
in Tiananmen Square, Beijing
June 1989

How flourishing the grasses on the prairies are!
They grow and wither year after year.
The wildfire can only burn out some of them,
But they will come to life again when the Spring breeze blows.

Bai Juyi

edited by Mok Chiu Yu and J. Frank Harrison

VOICES FROM TIANANMEN SQUARE

BEIJING SPRING AND THE DEMOCRACY MOVEMENT

Introduction by George Woodcock

BLACK ROSE BOOKS

Montréal-New York

BLACK ROSE BOOKS No. S 142

Hardcover ISBN: 0-921689-59-4
Paperback ISBN: 0-921689-58-6

Canadian Cataloguing in Publication Data
Main entry under title:
  Voices from Tiananmen Square

Includes bibliographic references.
ISBN 0-921689-59-4 (bound).--
  ISBN 0-921689-58-6 (pbk.)
  1. China--History--Tiananmen Square Incident, 1989--Sources.
  2. Student movement--China--Interviews. I. Yu, Mok Chiu II.
  Harrison, J. Frank

DS779.32.V64 1990   951.05'8   C90-090136-5

Cover design: Marie-José Chagnon
Design and Layout: Nat Klym

BLACK ROSE BOOKS
Editorial Offices
3981 St-Laurent Boulevard, Suite 444
Montréal, Québec H2W 1Y5 Canada

U.S. Orders
BLACK ROSE BOOKS
340 Nagel Drive
Cheektowaga, New York, 14225 USA

BLACK ROSE BOOKS
Mailing Address
P.O. Box 1258
Succ. Place du Parc
Montréal, Québec H2W 2R3 Canada

TABLE OF CONTENTS

Preface by J. Frank Harrison   *xi*
Foreword by George Woodcock   *xix*
Introduction by Mok Chiu Yu   1

SECTION ONE:THE EVENTS—A CHRONOLOGY

The 1989 Democracy Movement   15

SECTION TWO:THEORETICAL ANALYSIS

I: Wang Dan, *The Star of Hope Rises in Eastern Europe*   37
II: Wang Dan, *On Freedom of Speech for the Opposition*   38
III: Ren Wanding, *Why Did the Rally in Memory of Hu Yaobang Turn Into a Democracy Movement*   42
IV: Ren Wanding, *Reflections on the Historical Character of the Democracy Movement*   47
V: *Our "April Student Movement" and the "April Fifth Movement"*   54
VI: *On One-Party Dictatorship*   56
VII: X.X. Yeung, *For a Socialist Multi-Party System in China*   57
VIII: *Some Thoughts on the Chinese Communist Party*   60
IX: Hue Yu, *Hoping For a Brighter Future*   63
X: Ma Siufang, *Statement of a Tiananmen Square Hunger Striker*   66
XI: Tian Chun, *A Critique of ASUBU*   69
XII: Su Shaozhi, *The Origin and Results of China's 1989 Democracy Movement*   74

SECTION THREE:CHINESE SOCIETY OPPOSES THE STATE

Student Comment

XIII: *The Shortcomings of the Stalinist Political System*   85
XIV: *An Outline of the Communist Party*   86
XV: *Who Causes the Turmoil?*   87
XVI: *Talking with Two Workers*   88
XVII: *A Short Commentary on the Slogan, "Down With the Communist Party"*   89
XVIII: *The Ten Differences Between the Patriotic Movement and the Cultural Revolution*   91
XIX: *The Patriotic-Democratic Movement Compared with the Turmoil of the Cultural Revolution*   92
XX: *For the Democracy Fighters*   94
XXI: *Statement of the May 13th Hunger Strikers*   95
XXII: *A Declaration of Emergency to all People of the Country from the People of the Capital*   97

XXIII: *A Statement for Citizens concerning the Army in Beijing*   99
XXIV: *A Statement for the Soldiers*   100
XXV: *The Most Dangerous Emergency*   101
XXVI: *An Open Letter to Our Brothers, the Soldiers*   101
XXVII: *An Open Letter to All Soldiers in the People's Liberation Army*   102
XXVIII: *A Statement to All Soldiers*   103
XXIX: *To the Workers' Picket Group*   103
XXX: *Who Created the Turmoils of the Last Forty Years?*   104
XXXI: *What do Factional Disputes Reveal?*   105

Response of the Workers

XXXII: *Letter to the People of Beijing*   107
XXXIII: *Ten Polite Questions for the CCP*   107
XXXIV: *Letter to Compatriots of the Nation*   108
XXXV: *Letter to the Students*   110
XXXVI: *An Open Letter to the Students*   112
XXXVII: *Letter to the Workers of the Capital*   113
XXXVIII: *Declaration of the Preparatory Committee of the
    Beijing Autonomous Workers' Federation (BWAF)*   113
XXXIX: *Public Notice "Number One" of the BWAF*   114
XL: *Public Notice "Number Two" of the BWAF*   114
XLI: *Declaration of the BWAF Preparatory Committee on
    Behalf of the Workers*   115
XLII: *The Initial Programme of BWAF*   115
XLIII: *The People in Command*   116
XLIV: *Aims of the Beijing Construction Workers' Autonomous Union*   118
XLV: *An Open Letter to the Standing Committee of the
    National People's Congress*   119
XLVI: *Declaration of the Guandong Workers' Autonomous Union*   119

Disillusionment in the Party

XLVII: *Our Suggestions*   120
XLVIII: *I Declare My Views*   121
XLIX: *The Choice Between Conscience and Party Spirit—
    An Open Letter to Party Members*   121
L: *Support the Actions of the Students!*   122
LI: *Quit the Young Communist League!*   123
LII: *Communist Party Members, Step Forward!*   123
LIII: *Urging Deng Xiaoping to Admit His Mistakes —
    An Open Letter to the CCP*   124
LIV: *Letter to the People*   125
LV: *Statement on Quitting the Party*   127
LVI: *Quit the CCP and Establish a Society for the
    Promotion of the Chinese Democracy Movement*   127

The Doubts of Soldiers

LVII: *From the Bottom of a Soldier's Heart* — 129
LVIII: *A Statement to All Soldiers in the PLA who have been Ordered to Enter Beijing* — 130
LIX: *A Letter to All Soldiers* — 131
LX: *An Open Letter to the Students* — 131
LXI: *A Letter to All Soldiers who are Ordered to Enter Beijing to Impose Martial Law* — 132

The Intellectuals Comment

LXII: *Declaration of May 17, 1989* — 134
LXIII: *An Extremely Urgent Appeal to the People of Beijing* — 135
LXIV: *To All Compatriots* — 136

A Chinese Solidarity in the Making

LXV: *Introducing the "Capital Union"* — 140

SECTION FOUR: INTERVIEWS WITH THREE LEADING PERSONALITIES

LXVI: *Two Interviews with Wuer Kaixi* — 147
LXVII: *An Interview with Chai Ling* — 158
LXVIII: *An Interview with Fang Lizhi* — 161

SECTION FIVE: WITNESSES TO THE MASSACRE

LXIX: *Chai Ling's Sense of Foreboding* — 173
LXX: *The Massacre in Tiananmen Square* — 176
LXXI: *Concerning June 3-4, 1989* — 180
LXXII: *Statement of ASUBU to Compatriots Everywhere* — 187
LXXIII: *This is How They Died* — 192
LXXIV: Chai Ling, *I Am Still Alive* — 194
LXXV: *After the Massacre* — 200

PREFACE

Tiananmen Square is no European Piazza. More than 100 acres in size, and capable of holding hundreds of thousands of people, it is the centre of a city of ten million people, which is the capital of the People's Republic of China (PRC), Beijing. It is the symbol of China and Chinese government in the same way that Red Square and the Kremlin symbolise the USSR, and Washington with its white monuments the USA. Around the periphery of Tiananmen Square, and in the streets and avenues leading away from it, are the buildings which house the personnel who lay claim to the governance of 1.1 billion people, about a fifth of the entire human race. Therefore, the Democracy Movement of April-June 1989, centred on the Square, can be said to have been of world historic proportions. That is certainly what the writers of documents given here thought, and they are probably right.

In this collection of writings, numerous Beijing place-names are mentioned. The reader will avoid confusion if s/he remembers that the events centred upon **Tiananmen Square**, in which is situated the huge **Monument to the People's Heroes** and the **Mausoleum** of Mao Zedong. On the west side of the Square is the **Great Hall of the People,** the meeting place for government bodies, including the National People's Congress. On the east side of the Square is the **Museum of Chinese History,** which is attached to the **Museum of the Revolution.** At the north end of the Square is the reviewing stand which stands over the entrance to the **Forbidden City**, now the Palace Museum. To the west of the Forbidden City is the **Zhongnanhai** compound for senior government and party personnel, the main entrance of which is called **Xinhuamen**. Running east-west (south of Zhongnanhai and the Palace Museum, through the north end of the Square) is the major thoroughfare, **Changan** Avenue. A mile to the east on Changan, past the **Beijing Hotel**, is the **Jianguomen** overpass. Just over a mile to the west is the **Xidan** intersection, then the **Fuxingmen** overpass after another mile or so, then **Muxidi** bridge, and then the **Military Museum** over four miles west of the Square. These were the killing grounds of Beijing in 1989.

The documents have no single ideological theme. However, many pieces directly reflect the immediate and passionate hatred for an entrenched regime indifferent to the thoughts, needs and desires of the larger population. Stimulated by the students, that population joined them in their millions, and the Student Movement of 1989 became a Popular Movement. One also catches sight of the divisiveness and distrust that develops between those who are allies in the struggle against authoritarianism, but who differ deeply on questions of tactics. We even see Chai Ling, a leader of the hunger strikers in Tiananmen Square, accusing fellow students of trying to kidnap herself and her husband. The situation was nothing if not complicated, with numerous elements and organizations involved.

Central to it all, however, was the assertion that civilised human beings must control their own lives, and that this will only happen if the *masses* (not just the students) make the power of the State subordinate to their practical needs. We see in response to this revolution in the making, reactionary and desperate military violence. The term, "fascist," was given renewed meaning as the communist party elite of a so-called socialist State used bloody domination with the single purpose of maintaining that State (and their associated privileges) against the challenge of the people.

The conservative and authoritarian element of the leadership of the People's Republic of China, led by President Yang Shangkun and Premier Li Peng, ordered dependable forces in the People's Liberation Army to kill the students and demonstrators of the capital of China, which they did on the night of June 3-4, 1989. We do not know how many they killed, but at least 3000, with some of the documents contained here suggesting figures of as high as 7000. The new reign of terror must horrify us, though it may not surprise us. Meanwhile, we should note that Mr. Gorbachev has distanced himself from the events in order to promote rapprochement with the Chinese State after the years of the Sino-Soviet dispute; and the American State Department continues its China policy of cozy compatibility. The modern State, be it represented by the opaque neo-conservatism of a disoriented George Bush, or the frantic scrambling of a Gorbachevian *perestroika*, consciously and deliberately ignores ethical principle for reasons of State. Therefore, we should remember that these voices of China are aligning themselves with neither East nor West, but presenting the need for a politics against the State, which is the only circumstance in which politics can have a truly human face.

There are numerous references to events in Chinese history in these writings, and in order to facilitate an easy understanding, the following brief summation of major events in modern Chinese history is provided for the reader.

1919: May Fourth Movement organised following a mass demonstration by students against the post-war delivery of Chinese territory to Japan, even though China had been a member of the anti-German alliance during World War I.

1921: Formation of the Chinese Communist Party (CCP). From now until 1949 the communists were either in an uneasy alliance with the Nationalist Party (Guomindang), or in open conflict with it.

1935-1945: War between the Chinese Republic and imperialist Japan.

1949: Foundation of the communist regime on mainland China: the People's Republic of China (PRC).

1950-1953: Korean War in which the army of the PRC was involved against the forces of the United Nations (principally the USA).

1956: The Hundred Flowers Movement. The short-lived freedom given to intellectuals to criticise the regime.

1958: The Great Leap Forward. The attempt, initiated by Mao Zedong, to establish the economic and organizational basis of communism through an enthusiastic commitment to collective goals by the masses. Of particular note was the creation of Communes for the 80% of the population which lived in rural China, which sought to integrate every factor of life within a single administrative framework. They were eventually dismantled in 1982.

1960: Withdrawal of Soviet technicians from China. For the next twenty-five years the relationship between the PRC and the USSR is summarised by the term, "Sino-Soviet Dispute."

1966-1976: The Great Proletarian Cultural Revolution. Mao Zedong initiated a massive purge of the Chinese hierarchy in order to guarantee his predominance in the Chinese Communist Party (CCP) and, thereby, the PRC. The youth of China were recruited by Mao as a vanguard force in his struggle, with stability imposed by the People's Liberation Army (PLA) after widespread social disorders developed in 1967.

1971: Lin Biao, Minister of Defence, and Mao Zedong's supposed heir apparent, was shot down whilst fleeing the country after an attempt to assassinate Mao and take power.

1976: Death of Premier Zhou Enlai. Prior to his death he had introduced the policy of the "Four Modernizations" (industry, agriculture, the military, science and technology), aimed at a calculated, technically-based economic modernization of the PRC by the year 2000. This became official policy, supported by economic reforms, when Deng Xiaoping became dominant two years later. At Zhou's funeral, on April 5th, a massive demonstration indicated opposition to the Cultural Revolution. During the days following further demonstrations were repressed by the authorities, and these events came to be known as the April Fifth Movement.

1976: Death of Mao Zedong, following which Deng Xiaoping became the dominant personality in Chinese politics. Famous for the phrase, "It doesn't matter what colour the cat is, as long as it catches mice," Deng typified an anti-Maoist, anti-egalitarian, economic pragmatism. The authoritarian egalitarianism of Maoism ended with the arrest of the so-called Gang of Four — Jiang Qing (Mao's widow), Wang Hongwen, Zhang Chunqiao and Yao Wenyuan — who were submitted to a huge show trial four years later.

1978: The 3rd plenum (i.e., meeting) of the Central Committee elected by the Eleventh Party Congress (of 1977), where an economic reform programme permitting a significant private sector was promoted.

1978: Xidan-Democracy Wall Movement. Through the winter of 1978-1979, many big character posters appeared, often criticising public officials and public policy. Brought to an end in March, 1979. The high profile dissident, Wei Jingsheng, was the chief victim of the crackdown.

1979: Deng Xiaoping's declaration of the Four Cardinal Rules, prohibiting all activities, i) against socialism, ii) against proletarian dictatorship, iii) against leadership by the party, and iv) against Marxism-Leninism and the Thought of Mao Zedong. This represented the dominant line in the ruling elite, which was a refusal to introduce socio-political reforms to supplement on-going economic reforms.

1982: The 12th Party Congress creates the Central Advisory Commission as an institutional "retirement home" for the senior party personnel. The body became a centre of reactionary intrigue against reform leaders of the CCP (such as Hu Yaobang and Zhao Ziyang) and social movements outside the party.

1983: The Chinese Communist Party (CCP) announced a crackdown on "spiritual pollution" and "bourgeois liberalization."

1984: Deng Xiaoping announced an "open-door" policy to encourage foreign investment in the PRC.

1987: Following student demonstrations in the final weeks of 1986, an "anti-bourgeois liberalization" campaign was promoted by the CCP through its newspaper, the *People's Daily*. The General Secretary of the CCP, Hu Yaobang, was forced to resign.

1988: The Central Committee of the CCP endorsed Premier Li Peng's policy of slowing down economic reform, and delaying price reforms for at least two years. This was a serious setback to the plans of General Secretary of the CCP, Zhao Ziyang.

1989: April 15 — death Hu Yaobang, which became the stimulus for the 1989 Democracy Movement, the details of which can be found in the first section of this volume.

The reader should refer to the following list of abbreviations and positions in the hierarchy of China. I have also provided notes for clarification at those points in the documents where it seemed useful. In this volume,

ASUBU refers to the Association of Students' Unions of Beijing Universities, which was the major spontaneous organization that developed during the period, uniting the activities of the seventy-plus institutions of higher education in the city.

CCP refers to the Chinese Communist Party, the ruling party of the PRC which is, effectively, a one-party State.

NPC refers to the National People's Congress, constitutionally the highest legislative authority, but effectively controlled by the CCP, as is its Standing Committee and the State Council, which it elects.

PLA refers to the People's Liberation Army, which includes the forces of the navy and the air force. It is controlled by the CCP through the Military Commission of the party, chaired at the time by Deng Xiaoping.

PRC refers to the People's Republic of China, which is mainland China, governed from Beijing.

It is the Standing Committee of the Political Bureau (Politburo) of the Central Committee of the CCP that decides the direction that China will take, supported by a party hierarchy which "benefits" from its power. The only opposition, the only alternative, was "in the Square." They crushed the alternative temporarily by persuading the PLA that the students and citizens of Beijing were criminals. However, as the central Europeans have shown, and we see clearly in these pages that Chinese eyes are on that part of the globe, even neo-fascist regimes have their military limits when the mass of citizens choose to disobey. In the PRC it is a question of whether or not the discontent of China's relatively sophisticated urban population will become the consciousness of the broader mass of citizens; and, as in all States, to what degree the military begins to identify with the people as opposed to the regime, thereby at least neutralising itself as a political force.

Finally, I would like to acknowledge those friends and comrades from Hong Kong who have participated in this project as gatherers of information and translators of the original documents: Dennis Lau, Amy Chow, Yuen Che Hung, Edna

Lam, Subrina Chow, C. Weng, Mary Chan, Winky Po, Evian Wong, Alice Ng, Helen Choi, May Yuen, Alice Chan, Olivia and Vincent, Jude Hui, and Susan Ho. Meanwhile, in Canada, the value of Ann-Marie Swarbrick's patient proof-reading was immeasurable.

J. Frank Harrison

FOREWORD

There are a number of things I now remember sadly and with a little incredulity about the China in whose northern regions, up to the Gobi desert, I travelled in 1987. One was the way in which people I encountered talked with a kind of reserved satisfaction about the freedoms that appeared to have entered in many directions into Chinese life during the 1980s. Surprisingly often they ended in a kind of undertone: "we only hope *it* will last."

I also remember the coded circumlocutions in which political matters that should not be discussed openly were presented. Classic Chinese figures had now — after the end of the Cultural Revolution — settled into their old niches, and Confucius once again represented authority, so that a remark in favour of Lao Tzu would be regarded — and often received with broad grins — as an oblique hit at the Party.

One piece of coding I found particularly directed towards me. Nowhere was I directly asked about my political attitudes, nor was it even openly said that they were known to the people I encountered. Instead what I found to be a standard coded circumlocution was applied to me. "You are the Canadian Ba Chin." Ba Chin, of course, is that marvellous survivor Li Pei-kan, the devoted anarchist I knew through correspondence in the mid-1940s, and who since then has gone through prison after prison and struggle session after struggle session as a dissident, and always emerged to resume his role as one of China's leading men of letters and a notable novelist. Half a century ago and more, he was already translating Kropotkin into Chinese, and then he adopted the pen name he still uses — Ba being the first syllable of Bakunin's name and Chin being a Chinese adaptation of the last syllable of Kropotkin's. In his eighties he had become a symbol of steadfastness among the younger writers. I was flattered by the identification, and pleased by the subtle way in which so many people seemed to be expressing their tolerance for anarchist ideas. Perhaps I should have paid more attention to the fact that even in 1987 such ideas were *evoked* but *never mentioned, never named.* Tolerance — or daring — had not yet gone so far.

The daring would emerge — and counter to it a return to open autocracy — in the China of 1989, when the students and many of the ordinary people of Beijing acted as most anarchists merely intend to act, by fighting magnificently and non-violently in their fifty days of demonstrations for freedom of speech, assembly, political life, while the authorities cancelled years of apparently increasing tolerance in a few hours on the night of the 3-4 June, when the cruel gerontocrats who had seized control of the Communist Party and the People's Liberation Army ordered the massacre of the students in Tiananmen Square and then tried by propaganda lies, like the rulers in *1984*, to wash their crimes into the memory holes of history.

So the "it" of 1987, the promise of freedom, did not endure, and old Ba Chin, who had predictably expressed his support and admiration for the students, was imprisoned once again, though like Malatesta in Mussolini's Italy and Tolstoy in Tsarist Russia, he was considered a figure whose moral stature made it impossible to be done away with, and he was finally released.

We need all the witnesses we can get to the events leading up to that June night in 1989 which may in the end be seen as one of the turning points of history. There have already been some useful eyewitness accounts by foreign writers, of which perhaps the most immediate is *Tiananmen Square*, 1989 by the Canadian journalists Scott Simmie and Bob Nixon. But such narratives, though they may be vivid in their evocation of what it all looked and sounded and even smelt like, and in their highly sympathethic accounts of people engaged in passionate, self-denying struggle for a future many of them did not live to see, are still the accounts of observers, not of participants. In *Voices from Tiananmen Square* you will hear of the

struggle in the echoing words of the Chinese people who were involved, workers as well as students.

I do not know whether one can think of the events in Beijing in
May and June 1989 as an actual revolution. They may have been
revolutionary in promise, but they never reached the boiling point
of a complete uprising of the people, and only the scared rulers saw
them as a movement setting out to destroy the government. The students who participated, and the workers and common people who
supported them were concerned primarily with relatively limited
aims — mainly establishing dialogue, as they termed it, on basic do-
mocratic rights.

In the long run, of course, the Party bosses may have been right
in their fears, as the parallel though later events in eastern Europe
suggest. Many famous revolutions have begun with limited aims —
taxes in English seventeenth and the American eighteenth centuries,
bread in France in 1789, war weariness in Russia in 1917. The real
revolutionary ideologues and intriguers, with their plans to recon-
stitute society and seize power, are usually a manipulative, late-com-
ing minority, though at times specific grievances are accompained,
as they were in 1848, by a widespread sense that it is time to sweep
away the rubbish of outdated institutions. The Chinese uprising
seems to have been rather of this kind, starting off on limited issues
of free speech, but sustained by an awareness that society has
become corrupt and can be healed only by a change in political relations.

Most movements of this kind have turned out great masses of
literature which by its very nature is fragmentary. The pamphlets of
the Levellers and the Diggers emerged in the English 1640s, and
there was a vast production of leaflets, manifestos and posters in the
French revolution of 1789, out of which Kropotkin largely wrote his
study of the movement from below, *The Great French Revolution.* 1848,
The Commune, 1917 in Russia, the Spanish Civil War, all produced
their popular literature tied to the events of the time, and student
protest movements in China have always been characterized by a
great activity in posters and wall newspapers, as well as leaflets
passed from hand to hand. Much of *Voices from Tiananmen Square*
consists of such manifestos, and most of them reveal one of the important aspects of the 1989 movement; that political ideologues were
not in control, though the protesters were not politically unsophisti-

cated; how could they have been after the years of indoctrination against which they were reacting?

You will not find much of the personal and intimate here; these people are not concerned with impressionistic evocation, but with calling a society to moral order. Three or four people from among the student leaders appear as recognizable individuals in the handful of interviews that are offered, but nobody writing here has really had the tranquillity to reflect on his or her feelings during the days of insurrection. You will learn a great deal about their ideas, about their motivations, about their comprehension of events, and you will get a sense of the idealism that prompted their extraordinary endurance and audacity. Here they are, urging, defending, and to hear them doing so brings their cause to life. One day, one hopes, some of their survivors will be able to tell the personal drama of it all, as I heard it in tones of exaltation and grief from one participant who spent two hours telling me what he had experienced and felt; I can neither name nor describe him, for that might endanger others.

Voices from Tiananmen Square is material for history rather than history itself. It is concentrated in Beijing, and makes passing references only to what went on in other centres. It gives little indication of what effect the news from the captial may have had on the peasants, who still make up three quarters of China's population. And inevitably there is nothing said about what was going on among China's ruling groups except in so far as it directly affected the students and their fellow protesters.

Yet in any final analysis of events in Tiananmen Square the struggle that went on simultaneously in the centres of power has to be considered, since the challenge of the students set it going. It was a struggle not merely within the party but also within the army, and between the party and the army, in which the former gained in power to such an extent that we may be looking at a Napoleonic phase in Chinese history. Very soon after the student demonstrations started, rumours began to circulate regarding differences within the PLA, with the Beijing command opposing violent action against the protesters. The Beijing command in fact was the last to formally approve Li Peng's declaration of martial law. Its commander received a sentence of eighteen years imprisonment for having booked himself into a hospital rather than direct an offensive in Tiananmen Square. There are even persistent reports that six or seven lesser generals in the same army were summarily executed. What appears to be certain is that the PLA was captured by the faction headed by Yang Shangkun, the President of China, a Great Marcher as aged as Deng, who emerged from ceremonial retirement to play a key role in the resolution of the crisis. Yang is not only the head of the Chinese State; he is also nepotistic leader of a clan of high officers — sons, sons-in-law and nephews. One of these kinsmen commanded the troops who perpetrated the massacre in Tiananmen Square. They were brought down from the isolation of North-easterly Shenyang province, where for weeks they had been isolated and indoctrinated with hardline propaganda. When they were released to do their work on the night of the 3rd June they had been heavily inoculated with amphetamines and were no longer responsible human beings.

By accepting the aid of the hardline faction which won control in the army, the Communist Party in China has entirely lost face, and it is now the generals with their allies in the security police who are in effective control of China. Deng has become the feeble figurehead of the military, and both the leading poltical figures in China today, Premier Li Peng and party General Secretary Jiang Ximen are men without power. Li cut away his own popular following (such as it was) and his base within the party when he obeyed Yang and proclaimed martial law; when his own fall comes he will have no friend. Jiang, the party boss of Shanghai, had no base elsewhere, and it was for his dispensibility that he was chosen. When Deng dies either or both can be pushed aside without fear of effective protest within the party or elsewhere. That, of course, brings us round to the fate of Xhao Xiyang, of whom we have recently heard so little. Since he is apparently not dead, and his party membership has not been withdrawn, he is almost certainly being kept as a high-grade recyclable, ready to assume the appropriate role when the People's Liberation Army decides, like its Rumanian counterpart, to re-emerge in the guise of the Army for Liberating the People. Such populist initiatives are entirely within the Napoleonic tradition that now rules China.

One thing is certain, as *Voices from Tiananmen Square* suggests: The people of Beijing have gone through a process of radical political education and they are unlikely to forgive or forget Li Ping and his kind. One day these people will act and speak again, and perhaps, as happened before in China — their voices will carry what we metaphorically term the Mandate of Heaven.

George Woodcock

INTRODUCTION

From the moment of its foundation in 1921, the CCP has always structured itself along hierarchical lines. It assimilated all the forms, techniques and mentality of a bureaucracy. Its membership was schooled in obedience, and taught to revere the leadership which, in its own turn, adopted habits of command, manipulation and egomania. On winning power in 1949, they became the new bosses, setting up a ruthlessly exploitative and repressive bureaucratic system.

The party also took power in a country that was economically backward, a semi-feudal and semi-colonial society that was ravaged by imperialism. The May Fourth Movement of 1919 had sought a path of salvation in "science and democracy." The Marxist-Leninist-Stalinist dogma was not seen to contradict that policy, its anti-colonial and dialectical interpretation of history being singularly appealing to impoverished victims of imperialism. A Marxist-Leninist revolution was expected to revolutionise the social structure, and unleash great productive forces, resolving thereby the problems of poverty and dependency in a proletarian democracy of "the toiling masses."

However, the 1949 revolution had nothing in common with a genuine socialist revolution. The CCP took control of the State through its command of a peasant army. Having gained that control of the State, the only conceivable policy for the Leninist bureaucracy was to impose a regime of ruthless exploitation and austerity over the working people. Economic development rested on the most primitive methods of extracting surplus value. In the countryside, millions of peasants and semi-proletarians were put to work on huge construction and irrigation projects, built almost with bare hands. In the cities, workers were forced to labour for long hours for extremely low wages, strikes were banned, and mobility between jobs limited. The Leninist bureaucracy became a new class, controlling a new mode of production — one in which capital was monopolistically-controlled by the bureaucrats.

Establishing this system took almost the first ten years of communist rule under the direction of Mao Zedong. It also occurred in an environment of internal party debate and power struggles, that have characterised communist rule since its very inception.

Faced with the task of "socialist construction" Mao and his supporters believed that they must bring about the monopolistic control of all capital as soon as possible. They also believed that they did not need technical experts to achieve and operate the system. The Maoist goal was for the dominance of a hierarchy of dedicated and obedient communists, not a "techno-bureaucracy."[1] Mao did not want to see intellectuals playing an increasingly important role, and was particularly adamant against scientists and professionals taking up managerial positions, and separating the party from the people. On the other hand, Liu Shaoqi felt that a certain degree of private capitalism should be allowed, at least for a period of time; and Zhou Enlai argued for the need of techno-bureaucrats in addition to party bureaucrats. Deng Xiaoping was also in the latter camp, which suffered a major setback during 1956 and 1957, when, following an invitation to criticise, hundreds of thousands of intellectuals were persecuted as "rightists" after responding to the invitation.

Generally speaking, Mao was in command from 1949 to 1958. However, his influence was reduced at the end of 1958 because of the massive confusion caused by the Great Leap Forward. At that point, Liu Xiaoqi and Deng Xiaoping introduced a series of policies creating an environment more favorable to the techno-bureaucrats. However, in 1966 Mao initiated the Great Proletarian Cultural Revolution, again reversing the trend; and Maoists were able to dominate policy-making in China until his death in 1976. China was led down the road of a "feudalist social-fascist dictatorship," in which an explicit and demonstrable total subordination to the ideas of Mao and the leadership of his supporters was the condition of life for every Chinese.

Maoist rhetoric, particularly during the days of the 1966-1976 Cultural Revolution, sounded libertarian, and many socialists throughout the world accepted it totally and uncritically, believing that Mao was successfully building a self-managed socialist paradise. It was claimed that Mao was eliminating the three main contradictions in society: between town and country, between workers and peasants, and between manual and mental labour. However, the people of China indicated their unequivocal rejection of Mao's way in April 1976, and how they celebrated when the Gang of Four were arrested! For the reality was that, in Mao's China, the mass of workers and peasants were but slaves of the Leninist bureaucracy, not permitted to run their own lives.

That bureaucracy was obviously privileged, the more so the higher up you looked. They had special stores, luxurious apartments, chauffeured cars, with their children getting educational preference, travel abroad, and access to the best jobs. As for the universities, political loyalty rather than ability became the basis of entrance to institutions where lecturers were not learned professors, but politically-reliable soldiers, workers and peasants. Expertise gave way to toadying, wisdom to political fanaticism. Anyone who complained or criticised was accused of being bourgeois—including the workers who had to suffer miserable wages and working conditions.

Maoist "libertarianism" was never more than rhetoric!

The internal party conflict could be seen developing again in 1973 when "the Number Two capitalist roader" (Liu had been Number One, until his death in 1969), Deng Xiaoping, was reinstated in the hierarchy, after being purged early on in the Cultural Revolution. He was closely associated with Premier Zhou Enlai, one of China's most efficient bureaucrats, who was never trusted by the Maoists. The "Four Modernizations" (of agriculture, industry, science and technology, and defence) was the Zhou-Deng line, not liked by the Maoists because of its promise to raise the authority of intellectual techno-bureaucracy. An "anti-Confucius" movement was begun by the Maoist faction, with Zhou as the prospective target. Zhou cleverly diverted it into an "anti-Lin Biao" campaign, and its energy was spent attacking a man who had been dead since 1971.

Then, in 1976, the people demonstrated in the April Fifth Movement. This led to the dismissal of Deng Xiaoping, reported in the *People's Daily* as follows:

> *Early in April a handful of class enemies, under the guise of commemorating the late Premier Zhou during the Ching Ming festival, engineered an organised, premeditated and planned counter-revolutionary political incident at Tiananmen Square in the Capital... Openly hoisting the ensign of supporting Deng Xiaoping, they frenziedly directed their spearhead at our great leader Chairman Mao... On the proposal of our great leader Chairman Mao, the Political Bureau unanimously agrees to dismiss Deng Xiaoping from all posts both inside and outside the party while allowing him to keep his party membership so as to see how he will behave in the future.*

This is how the Leninist bureaucracy dealt internally with the questions raised by a spontaneous demonstration of the people, which they had brutally repressed, killing at least 2000 people.

Acutely aware of the unpopularity and ambition of the Maoist Gang of Four, when Mao died in September, 1976, Hua Guofeng engineered a palace coup removing them, and bringing Deng back into the ruling circle. Deng's Four Modernizations policy had substantial support both inside and outside the party, as an alternative to the deprivations of the Cultural Revolution. Deng's supporters, Hu Yao Bang and Zhao Ziyang, replaced Hua at the head of the CCP. In addition, those purged during the Cultural Revolution were rehabilitated, including many intellectuals, scientists and artists, in order to better implement economic reforms required by the modernization programme. The intellectuals and scientists were assured that, as brain workers, they were also proletarians, and would not suffer further oppression for their intellectual independence from the CCP. The Academy of Sciences confirmed a reduction of party controls, and political education received less emphasis in the education system. Emphasis was now to be placed on technical expertise, with many students being sent overseas to acquire it.

In the area of industrial management, material incentives, work discipline, and professionalization were the order of the day. The distinction between workers and management was re-emphasised, with the role of political workers reduced and subordinated to that of the techno-bureaucrats. The adoption of capitalist methods of organization and financing was taken as a mark of progress.

We should remember, however, that Deng was as much a Leninist as any other member of the CCP. The leadership role of the party was never questioned. The State machinery, the PLA, the trade unions and other mass organizations all continued to be subjected to the party's absolute leadership. Rural communities and industrial enterprises, schools and research institutes, were all to be led by the party. The discipline of democratic centralism was to be enforced in the party itself, with the individual obeying the organization, the minority obeying the majority, the subordinate obeying the superior, and the whole party obeying the Central Committee.

It was a rigid hierarchy; yet one which was instructed not to interfere in the day to day operations of the economy, and thus was less domineering than under Mao. Moreover, with a broader array of books, films, art and literature of all kinds, traditional and modern, and with the introduction of a new penal code, the perpetual presence and domination of the party in all spheres of life seemed less evident, even though it was unquestioned.

In this situation, the intellectuals were placed in a situation where they did become a class of techno-bureaucrats, encroaching upon the power of the party bureaucrats. This techno-bureaucracy began to reap the rewards of its elite position, gaining superior access to goods and services.

The techno-bureaucrats were not the only new class to be generated by Deng's policies; for his strategy of modernization also involved a de-monopolization of the economy (i.e., introducing a private sector with market relations determining prices). China developed both rural and urban entrepreneurs, as well as an identifiable group of speculators.

In the agricultural sector the large communes introduced back in 1958 were at last entirely dismantled. The so-called "responsibility system" [2] appealed to the self-interest of the peasants. Former production teams divided up the land, farming equipment, and livestock. Then families scrambled after fertilizers and supplies to "go it alone." Indeed, communal fields became family plots, free markets returned and flourished, peasants decided what they would grow and sell, cash crops appeared and side-line rural industries grew up. Peasants, paying a fixed rent for their land, kept all of their income from the sale of products. Some peasants have grown relatively rich (although you can still find starvation in other regions) with marked inequalities obviously developing — and quite acceptable to the Leninists, headed by Deng.

In the cities, similar developments occurred. The market was given a larger role, with profit to be taken as the chief measure of success. Managers were given more independence for economic planning in their enterprises, with the number of State directives substantially reduced. Profits, after deduction of taxes, were to remain with the enterprise for distribution and/or reinvestment. While the State maintained control of major sectors, many State-owned enterprises were rented out to groups and individuals. There was also a growth of a separate private sector, with many privately-owned enterprises, as well as joint stock enterprises developed with the aid of foreign capital. In special economic zones, foreign capitalists were encouraged to invest in new industrial development with the offer of cheap labour, tax incentives, low-priced factory sites, and a docile labour force in a politically-stable situation. Ten years of such policies had created, by 1989, a new class of entrepreneurs, whose interest was the legal guarantee of the right to private property — coexisting with, if not replacing, the system monopolised by the bureaucrats.

The co-existence of market and bureaucratic economies was bound to create problems. Of particular importance was the development of a dual system of prices — the free market price and the price set by the State. The existence of different prices enabled bureaucrats vested with power and information to profit substantially through the simple process of diverting State supplies to the free market. Such activities accentuated already existing shortages and the inflation of prices. When it was decided that the prices of many staples had been set artificially low, the price reform led to a new round of profiteering. The price increases were felt particularly by urban dwellers, who proceeded to demand higher wages, contributing to an inflationary pressure acknowledged by all.

The Student Movement of 1989, therefore, took place within this context of rampant inflation, official profiteering, and authoritarian rule, as the documents in this volume will show. It was the latest form of the corruption and bureaucratic privilege that had been a constant condition of the so-called "socialist" regime for forty years. They had always made use of public funds, and practiced nepotism as a means of establishing a kind of *de facto* system of inheritance. As the economy opened up in the eighties, new opportunities arose. Foreign investors were plagued by large and small officials demanding kick-backs, "gifts," and trips abroad. Many bureaucrats, or their families, including the children of Deng Xiaoping and Zhao Ziyang, were involved in business and trading, using their power and information for personal profit.

They could not be touched, for they controlled the power of the State and the PLA. They put people in prison without trial, and the torture of prisoners was endemic and systematic. Controlling the mass media allowed them to hide the truth and generate false impressions, denying criticism and preventing opposition. There was marginal improvement, as modernization led to relaxed controls; but the power and ruthlessness of the bureaucracy was intrinsic.

Inside the PRC, intellectual opposition to the situation by dissident writers took on a threefold character. These criticisms became visible as the intense pressures towards political conformity were relaxed in the late seventies, but were primarily a response to the continued party dictatorship. They became the arguments of a developing Democracy Movement, which occurred spontaneously in the major cities of China. Underground publications, big character posters, discussion groups and demonstrations were the vehicles by means of which workers, students, and intellectuals reconsidered the condition of their society.

The *first* theoretical tendency was represented by Wei Jinsheng, who argued that the dictatorship of the proletariat has to be abolished and a "liberal democratic" system established.

The *second* tendency was a Marxist-reformist current represented by Wang Xizhe, who wrote four influential essays outlining his position. His "Strive Hard for the Class Dictatorship of the Proletariat" argued that an underdeveloped country could develop into *either* i) a "feudal-socialist" society, if it isolated itself (as China did under Mao), *or* ii) a society of self-managed cooperatives involved in a world market where capitalism was predominant. In the latter case, dictatorship of the party might develop into a dictatorship of the proletariat, with the advancement of the cultural level and managerial competence of the masses. He suggested that Yugoslavia was following the latter path, which the Chinese should seek to emulate, replacing the control of the party, which should limit itself to ideological questions.

In "The Direction of Democracy," Wang emphasised his rejection of bourgeois democracy, but insisted that democracy was an end in itself, not dependent upon specific modes of production, or to be abandoned for reasons of expedience. Arguing in favour of an association of "free human beings," Wang argued for a renaissance of Marxism grounded in a reconsideration of the theory of alienation. Thus, in his essay, "The Dictatorship of the Proletariat is a Humanist Dictatorship," he asserted that the rule of the proletariat would be harmonious, and grounded in mutual affection. Any exploitative society was regarded as contradicting the nature of humanity.

In 1980, "Mao Zedong and the Cultural Revolution" appeared, stating that Mao was a peasant leader, perhaps the greatest in Chinese history, but still peasant. Preoccupied with becoming an emperor, Mao maintained the agrarian nature of Chinese society, promoting an agro-socialism to mobilise the masses in support for him. In contrast, the reform group of Deng Xiaoping received Wang's support as a vehicle of democratization.

The *third* tendency is a radical one, represented by Chen Erjin in his essay, "On the Proletarian-Democratic Revolution." This identified the social systems of countries like the USSR as revisionist — where a bureaucratic-monopolistic class controls the means of production under the title of socialism. China is said to be "at the crossroads," not having yet degenerated to that level, and can move towards either revisionism or socialism. The hierarchy and autonomy of the State, controlled by the Communist Party, might lead to revisionism, against which socialism must wage a life and death struggle. Reformism is a dead end in this struggle, which requires a proletarian democratic revolution.

Neither Wang nor Chen managed to escape from the concepts and analytical orientation of Marxism. However, their presence in China, along with many others like them, reflects the emergence of the question, "Whither China?" The answer to that will necessarily depend upon the attitudes and actions of the major groups and/or classes in Chinese society — techno-bureaucrats, workers, students, intellectuals, party bureaucrats, peasants, urban entrepreneurs, peasant petty-bourgeoisie, etc. Let us consider the major actors.

Concerning the peasantry, who constitute a majority of the population, most of them did not participate in the Democracy Movements of the seventies and eighties. Most peasants also found their situation improved by the responsibility system, although there had been some discontent over rising taxes and the cost of farming materials such as fertilizer. It remains unclear what the future development of the Chinese countryside holds, whether or not it will become more capitalistic, and even merge with entrepreneurs in the urban areas to form a united class front against the State bureaucracy, and demand complete de-monopolization. The new class of independent private producers has good reason to oppose the continued monopoly of economic and political life; and a free enterprise capitalist economy is its goal. Bourgeois, democratic, liberal pluralism provides the model for this new class.

As we saw earlier, Deng's modernization strategy gave an important role to technical experts, who were transformed into techno-bureaucrats. Their goals were not necessarily in conflict with capitalist ideas — unlimited growth, domination of nature, insatiable consumption, etc. — although in capitalist countries their rise had been at the expense of the actual owners of capital. In countries like China, however, the techno-bureaucracy could *either* develop against the ruling party in an alliance with capital, *or* develop in alliance with the party. Mao had distrusted and persecuted the intellectuals, but his policies failed. During the eighties the techno-bureaucrats definitely could be seen as a class in ascendancy. For a while there seemed to be a good relationship between it and the old State hierarchy. To the degree that it was permitted entry into the hierarchy of the State, it finds authoritarianism acceptable; in which context we should note that Zhao Ziyang was surrounded by advisers who toyed with the idea of "neo-authoritarianism," such as is found in Singapore and South Korea, as a model for Chinese development. That champion of Friedmanite market forces, we should remember, was also the creator of a para-military police, specifically designed for coping with social disturbances.

Nevertheless, in 1989, the techno-bureaucrats of China stood for a relaxation of controls and a reduction of the role of the party — particularly in those areas where they have expertise. They supported the 1989 Movement; for the student demands, if met, would have benefitted them. Historically, the majority of Chinese intellectuals have been characterised by their submission to the State; but circumstances now placed them in opposition to the old men standing guard over the monopoly of power which they call "socialist." Deng originally supported them, seeing them as cats who would catch mice, political neutrals who would get the job done; only later coming to see them as devils who might capture the CCP — as was the case in Eastern Europe. So, the party's techno-bureaucrats, symbolised by Zhao Ziyang, had to be stripped of their power.

The Beijing Workers' Autonomous Federation was the major organization of proletarian power that sprang up in the course of the Democracy Movement. Similar workers' organizations also existed in other Chinese cities. The Beijing federation's membership came principally from workers in the steel industry, railroads, airlines, restaurants and service industries. Using their tent in Tiananmen Square as a base, they promoted their demand for a workers' organization that was autonomous of the State. They discussed their practical grievances, including the large wage discrepancies between workers and managers, lack of democracy in the work-place, lack of genuine representation in the policy-making process, poor safety measures and working conditions, and the deterioration of the workers' standard of living over the previous decade.

By the end of May, the Federation had attracted interest and support from other parts of the country, and the organization was hoping to be able "to realise workers' participation in political affairs," demanding the right "to monitor the Communist Party," and seeking workers' control in the assertion that workers "become the real masters of State and collective enterprises." The Beijing Workers' Autonomous Federation thus signalled the possibility of an independent workers' Movement in China, which sadly had too little time to develop. Members of the Federation were right at the front of the crowds when the shooting started; and many members of the organization were killed. The authorities, of course, condemned it as counter-revolutionary; and after the killings anyone associated with it was rounded up by the police. We must recognise, however, that all of this was the experience of an embryonic organization. In 1989, the working class of China was not mobilised as an entire class, and its power was not fully realised.

As for the students, they had been seen as the techno-bureaucrats of the next generation, with a rosy future promised to them. However, like the students in the West in the 1960's, the Chinese students recognised the appalling quality of everyday life in China. Further, Chinese students are themselves materially impoverished, as well as being psychologically, socially and sexually alienated.

There had been a Student Movement from December, 1986, to January, 1987, lasting for more than a month. The largest demonstrations then were in Shanghai, where Jiang Zemin treated the students like children, when he had deigned to speak with them as mayor of the city. Other demonstrations occurred in Beijing, Tientsin, Wuhan, Shenzhen, Kunming, Guangzhou and Nanjing, demanding better conditions for students, democracy and freedom, honest elections, freedom of the press, price controls, and solidarity with student protestors across the nation. Beijing's students were extremely dissatisfied with press reports that claimed that the demonstrations had been initiated by a handful of disruptive elements, and that the students were accused by the authorities of "raising a red flag to attack the red flag," destroying social stability and social unity. The first document issued by the CCP Central Committee for 1987, on January 6th, said that it was necessary to oppose "bourgeois liberalization," and that the struggle must continue for another twenty years.

The 1986-1987 Movement was, therefore, officially regarded as a result of bourgeois liberal ideas, and the lack of a resolute attitude by "certain leading comrades," particularly Hu Yaobang. Hu was soon forced to resign from his position as General Secretary of the CCP. Intellectuals like Fang Lizhi, Wang Ruowang and Liu Binyan were expelled from the CCP for being leading and influential examples of bourgeois liberalism. Party publications called them "capitalist roaders," and a campaign against all who dared voice opposition to the party was organised. Meanwhile, one Shanghai participant wrote,

Our Movement, a spontaneous Movement has ended. However, this is the end of just one phase of development. Our past efforts will not have been wasted if we continue our activities. The Movement has encouraged serious thoughts in every university student. In just a few days we came to understand our society more deeply, and recognise our own strengths and weaknesses... This national Movement of students will undoubtedly contribute to China's historical transformation, its character reflected in its contribution to the democratic consciousness of students, of a generation of Chinese, even of the whole people.

The consensus of the students was, first, that there had been a lot of empty slogans but no concrete demands and, second, that they had not been sufficiently well-organised.

Remembering the Tiananmen revolt ignited by the activities to commemorate Zhou Enlai in April 1976, one should not be surprised that, when Hu Yaobang died on April 15, 1989, the commemorative activities ignited a prairie fire of student revolts, and near revolution. Hu was seen to be one of the rare clean bureaucrats, and a General Secretary who had been open to student demands for democratization. Also, the students, in April, 1989, were already forming organizations and discussion groups. The mood was that something ought to be done in the year marking the seventieth anniversary of the May Fourth Movement, the bicentennial of the French Revolution, and the fortieth anniversary of the foundation of the People's Republic.

However, it would be wrong to over-emphasise the revolutionary intentions (as opposed to consequences) of most of the students. As the documents in this volume demonstrate, they stressed their patriotism. For the most part, they did not demand an overthrow of the bureaucracy, but the creation of a legal opposition. They were not particularly concerned with the plight of the workers, and tended to view their Movement as one which was restricted to students and intellectuals. Happy to be cheered along from the sidewalk during their demonstrations, pleased to be assisted in their attempts to break through police cordons, the students retained a sense of their distinctness, and viewed the rest of society merely as a support mechanism. Even when martial law was declared on May 19th, and the people of Beijing flocked to the streets to prevent the army from entering the city, the students gave little evidence of a desire to broaden their Movement, and unite with the workers. Not until May 25th did the students in Tiananmen Square come up with a strategic proposal to go all out for the support of the workers, and even then they were afterwards sidetracked by debates concerning the date of their departure from the Square.

In the last analysis, we must see the Beijing spring, and the Tiananmen massacre, as evidence of the necessity of a self-conscious unity of interest of the people, rural and urban, against the Leninist State. The students, who in every society are capable of forming the catalyst of social renewal, must inevitably join with other social forces if their actions are to be anything more than an irritant to established authority. The documents in this collection suggest that this was the direction in which the Movement was heading, and that this will be the pattern of future conflicts which must precede the demise of the bureaucratic Chinese State.

As this analysis has shown, the various forces in China do not make for easy predictions concerning the final character of the changes that the Democracy Movement showed to be necessary and inevitable. However, as anarchists, we can hope and struggle for the generation of multiple areas of autonomous self-management and self-government. Therefore, as ever, it is the responsibility of libertarians to remain active in support of a non-capitalist, egalitarian alternative to the historically-defunct Chinese "socialist" State.

Mok Chiu Yu

NOTES

1. This term is from the programme of the Italian Anarchists, who explain it as follows: " The techno-bureaucracy defines itself in the intellectual work corresponding to managerial functions in the hierarchical division of social labour. The 'new bosses' have these functions and from them derive their relative privileges and powers not on account of private ownership rights of the means of production but rather by virtue of a sort of intellectual ownership of the means of production."

2. At the time of writing, this still exists. However, restrictions are being introduced, and the "past tense" is used on the understanding that more changes are likely to occur.

┌─────────┐
│   │
│   I   │
│   │
└─────────┘

THE EVENTS: A CHRONOLOGY[1]

THE 1989 DEMOCRACY MOVEMENT

April 15 (Saturday)

Former General Secretary of the Chinese Communist Party, Hu Yaobang, died of a heart attack. The CCP Central Committee's obituary concluded, "The death of comrade Hu is a great loss to our Party and our people. We must convert our grief into strength, study his selfless and firm allegiance to the party, follow his unceasing dedication to the service of the people, so that under the leadership of the party, we will progress along the path of Chinese socialism."

April 16 (Sunday)

Students and teachers of the various Beijing Universities began putting up posters[2] in memory of Hu Yaobang. Slogans attacking the corruption of the government also began to appear on campuses.

The CCP Central Committee decided to hold Hu's funeral at the Great Hall of the People on April 22nd.

April 17 (Monday)

In the morning, the CCP Central Committee held a meeting in the Great Hall of the People. Wreaths placed by Beijing University students at the Monument of People's Heroes in Tiananmen Square had been removed, to protest which some 3000 Beijing University students marched to Tiananmen Square. Their delegation submitted a petition with seven requests: i) re-evaluation of Hu Yaobang's achievements, ii) rejection of the 1987 "anti-bourgeois liberalization" campaign, iii) freedom of the press, iv) increase of the education budget, v) freedom to protest and demonstrate, vi) publication of the financial holdings of senior government officials, and vii) abolition of the municipal regulations controlling demonstrations in Beijing.

In Shanghai students and citizens began public mourning for Hu Yaobang, also demanding democracy.

April 18 (Tuesday)

Some 5000 students, largely from Beijing University, marched on Tiananmen Square shouting slogans like, "Down with tyranny," "Long live democracy," "Down with official profiteering," and "Down with corruption." Qinghua University students also marched into the Square, breaking through a police cordon in front of the Great Hall to lay a wreath. Students began to sit down in the Square, their number increasing to more than 30,000 by the afternoon, watched over by armed police.

At 10:50 p.m. about 1000 students rushed towards Xinhuamen,[3] trying to present wreaths in honour of Hu Yaobang.

April 19 (Wednesday)

In the early morning about 1000 students went to Xinhuamen to present wreaths and the petition. Armed police formed a blockade, and the crowd tried three times to break through it. Soon there were some 10,000 people shouting, "Down with Li Peng." As the crowd tried to push forward, it clashed with the police. Later, many students reported that they had been beaten up by the police. The authorities stated that the clash had been initiated by people throwing bottles at the police.

Throughout the day students from the various universities came to Tiananmen Square with their slogans and portraits of Hu. By 8:00 p.m. there were over 100,000 people, but the students were well-disciplined, singing the *Internationale* or shouting slogans like, "Down with official profiteering." At night the Monument became a temporary platform and many students and teachers gave speeches on democracy and freedom.

In Shanghai some 3000 students from Fudan University held a rally calling on the Chinese people to unite in the struggle for democracy and freedom.

April 20 (Thursday)

At midnight there were about 20,000 people outside Xinhuamen, while 2000 armed security police formed a barrier. At 2:30 a.m. armed police started using batons to disperse the crowd, which countered with bottles. About 100 students were injured. New China News Agency reported simply that four policemen were injured.

In the absence of action by the official Student Union, Beijing University students called for the formation of an organization responsible for the leadership of all student movements in Beijing. "A letter to all Beijing Universities" declared that mourning for Hu had become a Movement struggling for Democracy, affirming seven points of the petition. Demonstrations and protests were also held in other cities (e.g., Shanghai, Wuhan and Tianjin).

The New China News Agency accused the crowd of shouting "Down with the Communist Party" during the "Xinhuamen Incident."

April 21 (Friday)

A strike declared by the Preparatory Committee of the Solidarity Students' Union of Beijing University students, called to protest the Xinhuamen incident, was followed by other universities. Students from various universities arrived at Tiananmen Square, and by noon there were about 100,000 people there. At 3:00 p.m. some tried to break into the Great Hall of the People, but failed. By the evening, there were over 200,000 people in the Square, including workers and peasants.

Forty-seven scholars (including Yan Jiaqi,[4] Bao Zunxin,[5] Dai Qing,[6]) presented a petition to Zhongnanhai, requesting the government to support the students' Democracy Movement, to stamp out corruption and to re-evaluate earlier democracy movements. The document was rejected, and even thrown to the ground.

In Tianjin hundreds of Nankai University students were prevented from going to Beijing by the university authorities who cancelled their train tickets. Impersonating workers, thirty-six of these became the first group of non-Beijing students to enter the capital.

April 22 (Saturday)

The *ad hoc* Action Committee, formed by nineteen Beijing universities, had organized a march to Tiananmen Square to take part in Hu's funeral. By the early hours of the 22nd, 200,000 students and citizens were collected together. The committee made three demands: the safety of the students, permission to attend the funeral, and a true report of the police violence on the 20th. After negotiations, the authorities agreed to the first request. At 10:00 a.m. the funeral service began, undisturbed. The funeral service was conducted by Yang Shangkun, and the eulogy was delivered by Zhao Ziyang. After the service three student representatives outside the east wing of the Great Hall tried to present a petition to Li Peng, but were refused. Two of them knelt down, but the other student, Wuer Kaixi, refused to do so.

Students in Xian demonstrated outside the municipal buildings. Some hooligans, mixed among the students, tried to break into the government building, and set fire to it. More than thirty students and a hundred security police were injured.

In Changsha hooligans began looting shops and wrecking cars. Security police arrested nearly a hundred people, none of whom were students.

April 23 (Sunday)

Students from cities around the country arrived continuously in the capital. Student Unions of the Beijing universities formed the Temporary Students' Union of Beijing Universities.

Zhao Ziyang left the country on an official visit to Pyongyang.

April 24 (Monday)

In protest against the attack on students by security officers and the censorship imposed by the government, thirty-five Beijing universities started a strike. Then, breaking forty years of news control, Beijing's *Technology Daily* gave a true report of the students' Movement.

Lists of the relatives of high-ranking officials of the Central Committee appeared on the campuses of Beijing and Qinghua Universities, with demands that the government publicize their financial status and investigate official profiteering and corruption.

April 25 (Tuesday)

A government attempt to communicate with the students through the official National Federation of Students (NFS) failed due to student protests. Over 100,000 students flooded the streets to publicize the goal of their Movement.

Shanghai's *World Economic Herald* published an article quoting speakers at a conference who stated that Hu Yaobang should not have been removed from his post in 1987. Its editor, Yin Banli, resisted orders from Jiang Zemin[7] not to publish. An open letter, signed by 159 teachers from People's University, accused the media of distorting the image of the students.

The Temporary Students' Union organised a "Ten letters per person campaign" to break through the news blockade and report the situation in Beijing to the country, and thereby gain mass support.

April 26 (Wednesday)

An editorial entitled, "The Banner against Turmoil must be raised," appeared in the *People's Daily*. It claimed that the Student Movement had been instigated by a handful of troublemakers in illegal university organizations, that it was a planned conspiracy, a riot and a severe political struggle.

The 38th battalion, 20,000-strong and regarded as the elite of the military, was ordered into the capital.

The Temporary Students' Union held its first press conference. It presented the three demands: (1) equal dialogue with the government, (2) the government should apologize for the Xinhuamen incident, and (3) the New China News Agency and other agencies should report the Student Movement truthfully. The Union stressed that its goals were simply democracy, freedom, science, human rights and the rule by law; and that the means of achieving them would be legal and non-violent. In protest of the April 26th editorial, a large march was to be held the next day.

Beijing's Public Security Office issued an order forbidding any unlicensed demonstrations or marches.

The student representatives of Qinghua University decided to withdraw from the Temporary Students' Union, suggesting the resumption of classes. It also decided not to take part in the next day's demonstration, claiming that "this would scare away the moderate factions" and lead to bloodshed. This decision led to a heated debate and some students accused the leaders of being too meek.

April 27 (Thursday)

The demonstration began at 8:00 a.m. Over 200,000 students took part, and they were cheered on their way by over a million citizens. The students managed to break through eighteen barricades formed by police, with both sides showing restraint, with students even shaking hands with some of the officers caught up in the crowd. Students acted as marshals to prevent trouble-makers from getting mixed among the students. The march lasted fourteen hours.

A spokesman for the State Council, Yuan Mu, made a speech in the afternoon saying that: (1) the government had always welcomed dialogue with the students, (2) students must resume their classes so that the dialogue could be carried out through normal procedures, in a rational and calm manner, (3) the State Council had entrusted the NFS and Beijing Federation of Students (BFS) with the task of arranging the dialogue.

In Hong Kong and Taiwan students declared their support for the Movement in China.

The editor of Shanghai's *World Economic Herald*, Yin Banli, was removed from his post, leading to protests from workers at the newspaper.

April 28 (Friday)

The Autonomous Students' Union of Beijing Universities (ASUBU) was formally established in place of the Temporary Union, with the Beijing Normal University student, Wuer Kaixi, elected as the chairperson and one of the seven Standing Committee members. Wuer Kaixi said that the ASUBU would co-exist with the official organization, the NFS, whose Secretary declared that the government had expressed its wish for a dialogue. On the other hand, the latter had labelled ASUBU as illegal, and the authorities accused some of the student representatives of crimes which might lead them to being arrested at any time.

Representing ASUBU, Wuer Kaixi demanded:
1) that any dialogue must be reported by official news agencies;
2) that there would be no reprisals against student leaders; and
3) that the Student Movement be fairly evaluated.

He also listed the seven purposes of discussion as:

1) to confirm the achievement of Hu Yaobang in the fields of democracy and freedom;
2) to reject the "anti-bourgeois liberalization campaign;"
3) to publicise the financial holdings of high-ranking officials and their families;
4) to create freedom of the press;
5) to increase the budget for education and improve the circumstances of intellectuals;
6) to relax its controls over travel; and
7) to give a true report on the current Student Movement.

In Tianjin a demonstration was held in which over 6000 students took part.

April 29 (Saturday)

Invited by the NFS and BFS, government officials, including Yuan Mu, held discussions with forty-five students from sixteen Beijing universities, which were broadcast live. Wuer Kaixi was invited, but had been instructed beforehand that he would not be allowed to speak. He therefore refused to attend. He told reporters that it was no "dialogue," only an imaginary harmony presented by the government to confuse the students.

Zhao Ziyang returned to China from Pyongyang. It was believed that his absence was the reason for the Politburo's delay in making the final decision with regard to the Student Movement.

April 30 (Sunday)

Because of the firm attitude of Yin Banli and the resistance of his newspaper, the Shanghai Municipal Committee decided to enforce "strict discipline" on the *World Economic Herald* and assign a "working group" to it. This led to heated protest from press and intellectual circles, and also the demand for a dialogue by 150 journalists of the *People's Daily*.

Twenty-nine students from Beijing universities were invited to a discussion with government officials, including the mayor of Beijing, Chen Xitong, on the issue of "official profiteering."

The Central Arts Academy held an exhibition of photographs on the Student Movement. There were over 250 photographs. Some showing the police beating up the students at Xinhuamen were withheld by the authorities.

As rumours of impending secret arrests spread, student leaders of ASUBU temporarily refrained from appearing in public.

May 1 (Monday)

A rally organised by ASUBU in celebration of the May 1st International Labour Day.

May 2 (Tuesday)

Over 10,000 Shanghai students march in protest of the authorities' oppression of the *World Economic Herald*, with order kept by the students' marshals.

May 3 (Wednesday)

At the Youth Rally to Commemorate the Seventieth Anniversary of the May Fourth Movement in Beijing, Zhao Ziyang stated that their demands for an end to corruption and development of education and science were also the wishes of the government. He said that the students must be protected, but stressed that there must be stability as well.

At a press conference, spokesman of the State Council, Yuan Mu, claimed that the Chinese Democracy Alliance in the USA was the "black hand" in control of the Student Movement. He also accused the dissident intellectual, Fang Lizhi, of interference for suggesting that human rights be made a condition of foreign investment.

May 4 (Thursday)

About 200,000 students marched towards Tiananmen Square from various starting points, cheered on by the people. Many of the slogans cried were directed against Yuan Mu's speech. Later, at the Tiananmen Square rally, representatives from ASUBU stressed that the Student Movement was patriotic and not anti-governmental. They also presented a "New May 4th Declaration," calling for democracy, first in universities, and then gradually in the political system.

Over 500 news reporters and editors participated in the students' march. Their slogans included, "We want to tell the truth," "Do not force us to create rumours," and "The people have the right to know the truth."

In Shanghai over 10,000 students held a march and demanded the lifting of the ban on the *World Economic Herald*; similar marches and demonstrations were held in Nanjing, Hangzhou, Guangzhou, Changsha, Wuhan and Xian.

For many days rallies had been held by Chinese students in the USA, UK, Canada and France.

In a meeting with representatives from the Asian Development Bank, Zhao Ziyang analyzed the internal situation in China, and stated that the students were in support of the CCP and they only hoped that the government would correct its mistakes and improve its work. Zhao also pointed to an inadequate legal system and insufficient openness as reasons why the masses were dissatisfied with the government. Zhao wished to hold discussions with workers, intellectuals, students and members of democratic factions, to exchange opinions and solve problems with which they were mutually concerned.

An editorial in the *People's Daily*, entitled "Upholding the May Fourth Spirit and promoting Reform and Modernization," made a milder criticism of the Student Movement, claiming that young people were the new blood during this historic moment of social change. This editorial presented a stark contrast with the ferocious one of April 26th.

May 5 (Friday)

Except for Beijing University and Beijing Normal University, universities in the capital resumed lessons.

ASUBU elected a representative group for the purpose of dialogue with the government.

May 6 (Saturday)

The five representatives from ASUBU's dialogue group submitted a petition to the Office of the Standing Committee of the NPC and the State Council, asking them to send representatives to prepare an open and public dialogue with them.

May 7 (Sunday)

The Central Committee of the CCP told the ASUBU dialogue group to wait one more day for an answer from the government.

May 8 (Monday)

The Government still could not decide on a dialogue with the students. Its Communications Department told the student representatives that the Government would reply before May 11th.

May 9 (Tuesday)

About 1000 editors and news reporters signed and submitted a petition to the Secretariat of the National Union of Journalists requesting a dialogue with the official responsible for monitoring the propaganda work.

May 10 (Wednesday)

Thousands of students marched in support of the fight for freedom of the press.

May 11 (Thursday)

The University students in Beijing decided on a large demonstration to coincide with the visit of Soviet leader, Mikhail Gorbachev, to Beijing on May 15th. They made this decision in protest against the delay in the government's response to their demand for dialogue.

May 12 (Friday)

An editorial in the *People's Daily* by State Council representative, Yuan Mu, emphasised the importance of maintaining a stable environment in China.

May 13 (Saturday)

Some 3000 students started a hunger strike in Tiananmen Square. They demanded the Government start discussions with the students, and that the process be broadcast live on television.

May 14 (Sunday)

The hunger strike entered its second day. Chairman of the Education Commission, Li Tieying, and Beijing Mayor, Chen Xitong, came to visit the students in Tiananmen Square and promised to have a dialogue with them. Secretary of the Central Committee, Yan Mingfu, and Chairman of the Education Commission, Li Tieyin (both Politburo members) spoke with about 30 representatives from ASUBU, including Wuer Kaixi and Wang Dan. However, no agreement was reached.

May 15 (Monday)

More than 130 hunger strikers had been hospitalized, and 800,000 visited the Square to support the students. (In Hong Kong, some twenty students started a hunger strike outside the building of the New China News Agency.)

The talks with Li Tieying and Yan Mingfu continued. Gorbachev was welcomed at Beijing airport by President Yang Shangkun.

May 16 (Tuesday)

The hunger strike entered its fourth day. Over 600 of the 3000 students taking part had been sent to casualty centres. Ten students from the Central Drama Academy decided to stop taking liquids also. University teachers, secondary school students and teachers, editors, journalists and workers marched to support the students in the Square.

Yan Mingfu went to the Square alone and told the students that he had already submitted their requests to the highest level of the government. He asked them to give the government time and to re-gain their own health.

Zhao Ziyang, while meeting Gorbachev, disclosed that it had been decided at the First Plenary Session of the 13th Central Committee of the CCP that, on most important issues, Deng Xiaoping's guidance was needed.

Student Movements in cities across China demonstrated in support of the Beijing students.

May 17 (Wednesday)

At 2:00 a.m. Zhao Ziyang, representing the Politburo's Standing Committee, presented a written statement to the students acknowledging their patriotism and promising that there would be no reprisals. He hoped that the students would remain calm, rational, restrained, orderly and considerate, and that they would call off the hunger strike.

Over two million people marched to voice their support for the students. Among them were workers, farmers, intellectuals, members of the press, party workers and over 1000 soldiers of the People's Liberation Army.

May 18 (Thursday)

Four Politburo Standing Committee members, Zhao Ziyang, Li Peng, Qiao Shi and Hu Qili, visited some hunger strikers in hospital. These students stated that they were not trying to overthrow the government, that they only wanted to speed up political reforms and revive the people's confidence.

From 11:00 a.m. to noon Premier Li Peng, together with Yan Mingfu and Li Tieying, met with the representatives of ASUBU, including Wuer Kaixi and Wang Dan. Li Peng made it clear that the issue at hand was how to aid the students who were on hunger strike. Wuer Kaixi interrupted Li's speech and asked for more practical discussions. Wang Dan reiterated the demands of the students: (1) that the government reject the April 26th editorial and confirm that the Student Movement is patriotic and not riotous, and (2) broadcast the dialogue.

Li Peng pointed out that the Movement had caused confusion and disorder which had spread throughout the country. He did not answer the students' questions and the meeting ended inconclusively.

This was the sixth day of the hunger strike. Over 2000 people had been hospitalized. About two million people from different occupations had marched in support of the students. Some officers from the PLA sent an open letter to the Central Military Commission in support of the students, and the letter was broadcast to the students in the Square.

May 19 (Friday)

Zhao Ziyang and Li Peng went to Tiananmen Square for the first time to visit the students. With trembling hands and tears in his eyes, Zhao apologised to the students, asking them to call off the hunger strike, saying that such complex issues needed to be solved systematically. Li Peng did not make any speech. At 9:00 p.m. the students ended their hunger strike, replacing it with a sit-in.

Reports stated that, in a Politburo meeting, Zhao proposed a rejection of the April 26th editorial and a concerted attempt at stamping out official profiteering, starting with Deng and his son. Deng was said to be infuriated and said that whoever opposed the editorial destroyed party unity. Later, when the question was put to the vote, sixteen voted for labelling the Movement a riot, with only two voting against. Zhao is said to have handed in his resignation later that night.

Workers in Beijing formed the Beijing Workers' Autonomous Federation (BWAF) in support of the students.

May 20 (Saturday)

A meeting was called by the CCP Central Committee for leading party, military, and government personnel. Li Peng labelled the Student Movement a "riot," and claimed that a handful of people were using it to achieve their political goals. National leader and vice-chairman of the CCP Central Military Commission, Yang Shangkun, spoke immediately after, expressing support for Li's speech and announcing the arrival of the PLA into Beijing to restore order. He stressed that the PLA would not be used against the students. Zhao Ziyang was not seen.

In Tiananmen Square, after listening to a report of Li Peng's speech, students who had called off their hunger strike decided to resume it, and to call on the 200,000 students in the Square to join in. Li Peng declared that from 10:00 a.m. martial law was to be imposed on parts of Beijing. No marches, petitions or strikes were allowed, and censorship of the news was also imposed. Large numbers of troops, along with armoured cars and tanks, marched towards Tiananmen Square. Great numbers of people crowded in the streets and used their own bodies, buses and lorries to barricade the roads, trying to stop the trucks of the PLA from entering the city. It was reported that the soldiers ordered into the city did not know their mission, that for the past week they had not been allowed to read a newspaper, watch television or listen to the radio, and were made to read the April 26th editorial. The TV and radio stations were taken over by troops.

The hunger strike had reached its seventh day. When they learned of the PLA entering the city, student leaders called off the hunger strike. The BWAF called a general strike until the troops were ordered out. ASUBU's dialogue group sent a telegram to Chairman of the NPC, Wan Li, who was on an official visit to Canada, asking him to return and call a meeting of the Standing Committee of the NPC. They said that they would appeal to the law, through the Procurator's Office, against anyone who used violence against the unarmed students; and would also appeal to international human rights groups.

The Beijing masses from all walks of life marched towards Tiananmen Square, disregarding the martial law.

May 21 (Sunday)

Seven senior members of the military[8] sent a letter to the PLA's command centre in the capital and to the Chairman of the CCP Central Military Commission, Deng Xiaoping, requesting that the soldiers not be sent into Beijing. Before dawn, over one million had gathered at the Tiananmen Square. They set up barricades on all the important routes. In addition, more than 20,000 non-Beijing students and workers organized themselves into suicide squads to protect the students in the Square.

Satellite broadcasting from Beijing by foreign television stations was cut at 11:00 a.m. Twelve cities in China saw demonstrations, including Beijing, Xian, Nanjing, Shanghai, Guangzhou and Chengdu. At the same time Chinese and non-Chinese demonstrated in the U.S.A., Canada, Australia, Denmark, Sweden, France, the U.S.S.R. and Japan. About a million students and citizens went on a march along the main roads of Hong Kong Island in support of the Democratic Movement.

May 22 (Monday)

Each province was required to make clear its support for Li Peng's speech before noon. At 10:30 p.m. a clash between the army and the students was reported. Soldiers hit students with belts and bricks. The government denied rumours that it was using force to crackdown.

Wuer Kaixi was removed from ASUBU's Standing Committee after he had urged all the students to retreat from the Square. He fainted after his statement, which was condemned by many students. He believed that the PLA would soon come, and to avoid injuries and death students should leave the Square. At 6:00 p.m. 200,000 students and teachers swore that they would stay there even under the threat of death.

May 23 (Tuesday)

Three persons who had defaced the portrait of Mao Zedong which hangs over the Tiananmen reviewing stand were caught by students and handed over to the police. They identified themselves as a reporter, a teacher and a worker — from Hunan, as their dialect clearly showed. Some forty members of the NPC's Standing Committee had signed a demand for a special meeting of that body — leaving some thirty more required to enforce the request.

May 24 (Wednesday)

The non-Beijing members of the CCP Central Committee appeared in Beijing for a plenum of the Committee. Wan Li cut short his trip to the U.S.A. to return to China.

Large numbers of soldiers arrived in Beijing. Those armies which had earlier retreated from Beijing were stationed in the countryside near the city. Six (of seven) military regions had given support for Li

Peng, as had the PLA's national headquarters. The Beijing Military Region was the only one which had not come out in support.

The satellite link, which had been resumed on 23rd May, 1989, was cut again at 5:00 p.m.

600,000 joined in the Guangzhou-Hong Kong-Macau March that took place in Guangzhou.

May 25 (Thursday)

The students' Main Command Centre for Defending the Tiananmen Square called more than 300 representatives of all the universities in the Square to a meeting. The meeting continued from the afternoon through to the morning of the 26th.

Wan Li's plane landed in Shanghai instead of Beijing.

Li Peng appeared for the first time since his May 20th speech when he met the new ambassadors from Nigeria, Mexico and Burma. He remarked that the present disorders in China would be handled by the Government. He also claimed that Deng Xiaoping was the one who would lead China to the road of reformation and openness, and him alone.

The intellectuals and the BWAF march was joined by students and the press. There were about a million marchers.

Demonstrations and marches in support of the Beijing students were held in cities across China.

May 26 (Friday)

After a democratic vote, the meeting of university representatives adopted the policy that students should stay in the Square, at the same time proposing marches and a hunger strike on an even larger scale, and calling upon the workers to go on strike.

Peng Zhen, former Chairman of the NPC, invited the leaders of democratic parties to a talk in which he emphasized that the government's actions were lawful and constitutional. He also affirmed that what was happening in Beijing was a riot.

The Standing Committee of the CCP Advisory Commission expressed their firm support for Li Peng and Yang Shangkun's speeches of May 20th.

The Beijing Military Region finally gave its support to Li Peng.

May 27 (Saturday)

After a meeting between representatives of student organizations, the BWAF and the Autonomous Union of Citizens, it was decided that a retreat from the Square would take place on May 30th. Meanwhile Wan Li made a statement of support for the May 20th speeches of Li Peng and Yang Shangkun, calling a meeting of the NPC Standing Committee for June 20th. The Chairman of the CPPCC,[9] Li Xiannian, expressed support of Li and Yang.

A twelve-hour concert in Hong Kong raised $12 millions for the students in Beijing.

May 28 (Sunday)

About 1,500,000 people participated in a pro-Movement demonstration in Hong Kong, including members of trade unions and newspapers that usually supported the PRC.

May 29 (Monday)

As there were differences in opinion between the association of Beijing students and those of students from outside Beijing, the work of the Chief Command Centre became difficult. The commander, Chai Ling, and four other Standing Committee members, including Wang Dan, offered their resignation.

The students decided to delay their retreat until June 20th, when the meeting of NPC's Standing Committee was to begin.

The Autonomous Union of Shanghai Universities called on the Shanghai students to "empty the schools" until the beginning of the next school year in September.

May 30 (Tuesday)

The sculpture, Goddess of Democracy, reached Tiananmen Square before dawn and attracted thousands of citizens to the Square.

Leaders of the BWAF were arrested by the public security police. Eleven members of the motorcycle team who had brought news and information to the students were taken into custody.

May 31 (Wednesday)

The *People's Daily* condemned the Goddess of Democracy. At about 10:00 a.m. a man tried to push down the sculpture but was stopped by the students. In the face of increasing disorder, the Chief Command Centre appointed Gua Haifang to be the commander responsible for restoring order.

To the south of Beijing ordinary people marched shouting slogans in support of the government, and burned a facsimile of Fang Lizhi. Their demonstrations were promoted by the government and the CCP.

In the evening about 3000 students demonstrated in Tiananmen Square against the arrest of the workers' leaders. Nearly 10,000 students and workers then marched to the Public Security Office and demanded to know the reasons for the arrests. Later, the union reported that they had been released earlier.

June 1 (Thursday)

Student leaders Chai Ling and Fang Chunde told reporters that a kidnap attempt had been made against them. They struggled and shouted, causing the kidnappers to run off. Chai Ling claimed that a member of the Standing Committee of the Autonomous Students' Union of non-Beijing Universities, Lien Xiende, was one of the four persons responsible.

The *People's Daily* had a long article on Hu Yaobang. It gave credit to Hu for rehabilitating thousands of officials and intellectuals persecuted during the Cultural Revolution.

Several big hotels in Beijing hung slogans on their exteriors supporting the Government.

ASUBU reorganized its Standing Committee. Wuer Kaixi and Wang Dan were no longer members.

June 2 (Friday)

More than 200,000 soldiers had already been stationed around Beijing. The military had taken over control of all the communications. Before dawn about 10,000 soldiers were given orders to march toward the Tiananmen Square along Changan Avenue. However, they were blocked by thousands of citizens and students near the Beijing Hotel, and the army retreated.

As the day began, a police car with no plates raced through the Fuxingmen intersection, mounted the sidewalk and knocked down four people — two of whom died instantly. An eye-witness remarked that before this incident several jeeps had already driven through at high speed. The two policemen responsible were taken away after a few minutes by another police car. The injured were raced to hospital by nearby citizens. Several thousand people were angered by this irresponsibility and marched spontaneously towards Tiananmen Square.

The Beijing Municipal Government again organized peasants into marches. They shouted slogans in support of the government. One of the marchers said that each of them were given money, a straw hat and a two-day holiday.

About a thousand Beijing students demonstrated shouting sarcastic slogans like, "Support authoritarianism," "Support dictatorial rule," "Support Li Peng." When they marched along Changan Avenue, a large number of citizens watched, and when they realized that the students were being satirical, they cheered and applauded.

Popular songwriter, Hou Dejian, Beijing University lecturer, Liu Xiao, head of the planning department of Stone Computer Corporation, Zhou Duo, and the CCP member, Gao Xin, started their 72-hour hunger strike in Tiananmen Square at 4:00 p.m.

June 3-4 (Saturday-Sunday)

In the early hours of June 3rd, crowds blocked military trucks at Jianguomen and Xidan. Inside the trucks they found machine guns, rifles, gas masks, etc., which they took to exhibit at Xinhuamen, attracting 10,000 onlookers.

During the course of the day (as in the previous few days), military-looking people, dressed in civilian clothes, were seen in the city familiarising themselves with the layout.

At noon about 2000 soldiers and military police with iron helmets and clubs, came out from the west gate of the Zhongnanhai Compound trying to disperse the crowds in Xidan Avenue and at Xinhuamen. The police broadcast warnings, fired tear-gas, and dispersed the crowd with violence. Meanwhile, about 300 soldiers suddenly dashed out of Xinhuamen, waving their clubs and cattle prods, beating up whoever they laid their eyes on. Students of the Political-Legal University who had been sitting-in there for two weeks were forced to leave. At Xidan soldiers dispersed the crowd with rubber bullets, wounding many.

At about 2:00 p.m. over 10,000 military police rushed out from the west gate of the Great Hall of the People to form a blockade; but the crowd blocked them with two buses. After futile discussions between students and soldiers, with casualties on both sides, all of the troops withdrew. Over 100,000 people were gathered on Changan Avenue. They angrily overturned a jeep that was parked on the road side and smashed the windshields of two military vehicles. From the early hours to the evening of June 3rd, numerous clashes broke out between civilians and military, both sides increasingly emotional.

After 6:00 p.m. the government broadcast three warnings in the media, indicating that violent suppression was imminent. The first one was issued at 6:00 p.m., saying that "martial law troops, public security officers and military police have the right to deal forcefully with anyone who does not take heed of the warning and violates the martial law." The second warning was at 8:30 p.m., repeating that the troops were to use all necessary means to remove opposition. Meanwhile there were tens of thousands of people in the Square, including students, workers and civilians. The third warning was issued at 10:00 p.m., cautioning people to stay indoors or risk danger. In the meantime, the atmosphere was tense in the Square.

At 11:00 p.m. gunshots were heard at Muxidi, signifying that troops were advancing onto the Square. Shortly after midnight two armoured cars moved along Changan from the west, driving aside all obstacles, clearly making way for military vehicles to follow.

At 1:25 a.m. about 600 soldiers advanced towards the Great Hall of the People shooting into the air. They were about 100 metres away from the crowd.

At 1:40 a.m. the soldiers arrived at the Great Hall of the People. At 2:00 a.m. Changan was alive with gunshots, and soldiers of the 27th Group Army surrounded the Square. At 4:00 a.m. the "clean-up" started. The lights in the Square flashed on and off. The noise of gunfire mingled with the cries of the victims, the hysterical laughter of the slaughterers, and the rumble of tanks. After a short time ambulance sirens were added to the noise. At daybreak there was a pile of bodies covered by canvas in the Square.

For the next few days tanks lined the Square, the soldiers busied themselves cleaning the ground and burning lifeless objects, and afterwards helicopters took the remains away in sacks.

The 27th Army continued its mission of suppressing the "counter-revolutionary riot." Rifle shots were heard wherever they went. Among the "counter-revolutionary hooligans" were a nine year-old boy and a three year-old girl. One hospital reported that the oldest victim was over seventy, while the youngest was thirteen.

Aftermath

By June 5th, over 5000 had died, and 30,000 had been injured. On June 6th, the suggestion that of 7000 were killed was being heard, not to mention the "missing." The bodies of those who had died in the early hours of June 4th would never be recovered. On June 7th, Yuan Mu, spokesman for the State Council, stated that, in the oppression of the anti-revolutionary riot, 5000 soldiers of the People's Liberation Army and 2000 civilians were injured, while the death toll amounted to less than 400, including only twenty-three students. The government declared ASUBU and BWAF to be illegal organizations, and ordered their leaders to give themselves up or be regarded as criminals. A hotline was also set up for informers to call and turn in those who had been active in the Movement.

On June 9th, Deng Xiaoping appeared on television for the first time since May 16th, congratulating the martial law troops. Accompanying Deng were Li Peng, Yang Shangkun, Peng Zhen, Wan Li, Li Xiannian, Qiao Shi and Yao Yilin; but Zhao Ziyang and Hu Qili were not seen. He said of those taking part in the Movement, "Their aim was to topple the Communist Party, socialism and the entire People's Republic of China, and set up a capitalist republic." About the army, he said, "They are truly the people's army, China's Great Wall of steel. They have stood and passed this test." He did not mention the civilians and students who were killed, ending with, "The direction established by the party at the 3rd Plenum [1978] was correct, as was the adoption of the Four Cardinal Principles — both are correct!"

NOTES

1. This chronology was provided by Mok Chiu Yu and the "Hong Kong Group" organized to promote the true story of events in the Square through publication of underground documents from the PRC.
2. Pasting up a "character poster" in a public place is an established mode of political comment in Chinese society, especially where that comment is critical of the regime which controls all other media forms.
3. Xinhuamen is the main gate to the walled compound for senior government officials (called Zhongnanhai) to the northwest of Tiananmen Square.
4. Born in 1942, Yan was director of the Political Studies Institute of the Chinese Academy of Social Sciences, and a government adviser. He is now in exile in France.
5. Born in 1937, Bao was research fellow at the Institute of Chinese History of the Chinese Academy of Social Sciences.
6. A reporter on the newspaper, *Guangming Daily*.
7. Politburo member and Shanghai party boss who was later to replace Zhao Ziyang after the latter had been purged.
8. These were PLA navy commander Ye Fei, former Minister of Defence Zhang Aiping, former deputy Minister of Defence Xiao Ke, former chief of the PLA general staff Yang Dezhi, Korean War hero and former President of the PLA military academy Song Shilun, former PLA commander Chen Zaidao, and former politcal commissar of the PLA logistics department Li Jukui.
9. The Chinese People's Political Consultative Conference, established in 1949, legitimised the creation of the PRC. Later eclipsed by the National People's Congress, it remains operative as an organ for the organization and administration of various non-communist parties and groups, whose activities complement, and are guided by, CCP policy.

THEORETICAL ANALYSIS

I: *Wang Dan,[1] The Star of Hope Rises in Eastern Europe*

More than thirty years ago, Khrushchev's secret report to the CPSU,[2] the Polish and Hungarian events,[3] and our own Hundred Flowers Movement, provided moments of scintillating possibility for an international communist movement hovering on the edge of irrelevance. The saddest thing was that each was followed by a long period of military-autocratic rule in those countries. Today, however, eastern Europe is again reminding us of the spirit of 1956.

In February, 1989, the Hungarian Socialist Workers' Party [the ruling communist party] recognised the 1956 events as a "genuine people's uprising." The Hungarian party congress affirmed a multi-party system and pluralism, with the formation even of a "non-party faction."

Face-to-face meetings in Poland have produced concrete results, with opposition organizations like Solidarity and the Writers' Union, having been legalised, organising massive demonstrations. On February 10th, Premier Jaruzelski declared that the Polish United Workers' Party would be "giving up its monopoly of power."

· In Czechoslovakia, in spite of the caution and indecisiveness of the regime, there have been frequent and decisive actions by the masses. Recently, over one thousand cultural workers petitioned Premier Strougal to demand the release of students arrested in the Prague demonstrations in January.

What is happening in eastern Europe should teach us two things. First, we see that the dictatorship of one party (or some similar system known by a different name) should be abandoned, the introduction of democratic politics being a major trend in socialist development. It is now obvious that a refusal to reform the political system is an attempt to protect vested interests, and is against the tide of change. Second, the promising developments in those countries must be attributed to the ceaseless efforts of the opposition inside both the party and the general population. Their prolonged and untiring efforts in pursuit of freedom of speech and the protection of human rights is responsible for the creation of a healthy political atmosphere. It also reaffirms that democracy is not a gift, but the product of struggle from below by the people themselves. In this struggle, the educated elite must play a leading role by acting as a vanguard.

We think that the path taken by Poland, Hungary and Czechoslovakia is the only way to save socialist countries from their internal crises. Political developments in China must learn from these countries. Let us bluntly state: Only when China follows in the footsteps of these eastern European countries, and only then, will full democracy and full development be successfully accomplished.

March 4, 1989

II: Wang Dan, *On Freedom of Speech for the Opposition*

Although freedom of speech is proclaimed as an important principle in the Chinese Constitution, it has clearly been violated in an authoritarian manner. This is shown by the illegal and violent suppression of opposition voices by the political authorities. That suppression is based upon the formula that, Truth equals the World View of the Proletariat, which is equated with Marxism, which is equated with the World View of the CCP, which is equated with the proclamations of the Party Organs, which is equated with the views of the Leadership. There is no need even to comment further upon such poor logic.

Possible reasons for restricting freedom of speech are,

1) the ruling party knows the truth and properly represents the interests of the people,
2) the party has a responsibility to protect the people from the erroneous and practically dangerous views of an opposition, and
3) the growth of the opposition will disturb the prosperity, unity, and normal path of development of society.

To counter the first argument we can argue as follows:

a) There is no absolute truth, and truth is not held by a monopoly. Certainly the proletariat may grasp it, as may capitalists, as may a minority. Hence the statement, "everyone is equal before the truth." Even if the opposition's views are obviously flawed, it cannot be said with certainty that there is no element of truth in their ideas. Truth ought not be suffocated and weakened by its monopolization.

b) Those who know truth will not suppress opposition. On the contrary, fallacious argument leads to the promotion of truth through unfavorable comparison with the latter. Without this confrontation, that which is true loses its strength. Therefore, the suppression of opposition is a sign of weakness and lack of confidence, obstructing the promotion of that which is true.

c) People are diverse, and every stratum in society has its own special interest. The ruling party cannot represent everyone, at best representing the majority; and even then the legitimate interest of any individual citizen ought not be dismissed, but promoted through legitimate channels. Who can be so certain that the views of an opposition do not represent the legitimate interests of some small group of people? However, in such a situation, it might also be the case that the demands of the majority are being suppressed.

d) Political parties are made up of a whole range of individuals, including those who want to use power to satisfy their greed and ambition, and do so by distorting truth and fooling the masses. Without critical voices those consumed by ambition could fearlessly pursue their ends by distortion of the truth. Even if the party had a supervisory mechanism, it would be ineffective if it came under the control of such people. Moreover, China is in fact a political system monopolised by one party, and no effective mechanism of control can develop within it. Therefore, suppression of the views of the opposition encourages the corrupt elements who have infiltrated the party, which become the greatest danger to the party's ability to govern. Such is particularly true of our autocracy, where we see the suppression of opposition linked with the distortion of truth.

e) It should be permissible to criticise that which is true. We should remember that truth does not merely concern grand theories of human development. Truth involves such simple and self-evident statements as, "a sated person cannot be hungry." If I rushed around saying that we can eat our fill and still be hungry, I would not be punished, although I might be treated as a fool. Why not? Because this kind of opposition to truth is absurd. Therefore, if the views of the opposition generate intellectual confusion, it must be because some elements therein are correct. This must mean, first, that a minority can possess truth; and, second, that, whilst the absurd goes unpunished, the merely erroneous (but which contains *some* truth) is restricted. This is unjust. If communism also has truth, but cannot be criticised, it must be a function of the possession of arbitrary power. And how can things that must depend on arbitrary power be regarded as true?

The following can be used to counter the second argument (i.e., that the CCP must protect the people from erroneous views):

a) By recognising that the government and CCP must prevent deviance under the aegis of "political leadership," you encourage the secret perpetration of such views. The result is that the criticism is hidden, cannot be punished, and continues to influence the people. The suppression of free speech becomes responsible for the perpetration of such errors as may exist in opposition views.

b) As government should represent the will of the citizenry, so should there be mutual trust between the two. Fear of the opposition shows that the government holds the citizens in contempt. Only a government that rejects the slogan that, "the people's eyes are clear and bright," would attempt to suppress criticism.

c) However fallacious the opposition's views they should be permitted; for it is only the censorship authorities who call them erroneous. Now value judgments differ, and censors can never represent the majority of the people. Only when ideas are allowed to circulate freely will it be possible to judge on the question of their truth.

d) Freedom, like personal property,[4] is an inviolable human right. Marx himself likened the freedom of speech, association and assembly to "soil, air, light, and space." This is a very apt analogy; for, if thieves, fools and the insane should enjoy this privilege, even the views of an opposition might be allowed to circulate freely.

e) If opposition views create extremely undesirable consequences, the government can easily and legally punish it. However, there is no logic to the policy of prior restraint.

Finally, the third argument (i.e, that an opposition will create instability) can be rejected as follows:

Political activity generates many contradictions in practice, and these must be seen as balancing each other. If one side possesses a domineering coercive capacity, then imbalance will occur, creating social turmoil. For forty years we have suppressed opposition views, and still there is no unity and stability. On the contrary, we had ten years of turmoil [during the Great Proletarian Cultural Revolution, 1966-1976]. We must conclude that democratic politics will only occur when opposition views can circulate and opposition parties are permitted. Only then will the normal order of political life in society be properly maintained. Suppression of free speech will, by contrast, generate turmoil.

Please note that we do not support total freedom of speech. There must always be self-control; and absolute freedom is impossible. However, we do object to external restraints, especially those imposed upon us by violent means.

In this new Chinese enlightenment the intellectuals must make freedom of speech the priority. They must have the courage to criticise injustice, including the decisions of party and government officials. As intellectuals, we can influence others only with ideas and words. If freedom of speech is lost, intellectuals will not be able to promote the democratization process, we will lose our independent position, and we will become adjuncts of the party and government — as we have been for the past forty years!

[undated]

III: *Ren Wanding,[5] Why Did the Rally In Memory of Hu Yaobang Turn Into a Democracy Movement?*

Since April 15th, Beijing has seen the emergence of a huge Democracy Movement, with participants as numerous as those involved in the April Fifth Movement of 1976.

In fact, the death of the former General Secretary of the CCP should not have been commemorated in such an excessive manner. Like the April Fifth incident [in 1976], people took the opportunity to commemorate a dead man in order to wage an anti-feudal, anti-authoritarian, pro-socialist struggle. However, we must also remember that, at the time of the Democracy Wall Movement of 1979, when Hu Yaobang advised that, "people should not be arrested," the main leaders were arrested and prosecuted. At the present time the people's emotions, thoughts and ideas have been directed towards a criticism of the entire structure of the socio-political system of China. How should one respond to this?

There has never been any simple way of interpreting history; nor can any power define the character of historical truth. The CCP co-opted the slogans of the Democracy Wall Movement, and conditions improved for the people. Nevertheless, the evil suffered by forty years of monolithic party rule gave rise to numerous complaints.

Inevitably there appeared such shocking demands as, "Overthrow the Autocracy," and "Down with Dictatorship," in Tiananmen Square. The New China News Agency stated in its April 26th editorial that people were shouting the slogan, "Down with the Communist Party!" Slogans like, "Long Live Democracy, Human Rights, and Freedom," became loud and frequent in the protest Movement. The *Internationale* was sung again and again, with new meaning and significance.

No reasonable observer would attribute these developments to the ulterior motives of a small number of disruptive agitators. Those who use this interpretation are trying to protect their privileges, and the people will not accept such lies. In 1986 people were wrongly sent to jail for initiating student and worker demonstrations. I would like the legal authorities to open up their files.

Meanwhile, if the party cannot handle this Movement of the people, then the party must soon disappear. The workers will develop consciousness and link hands with the students.

Chinese politics is a huge reflection of the "eight-in-one" principle: party and power as one, party and government as one, party and legal system as one, party and State as one, party and the armed forces as one, party and people as one, party and the economy as one, and party and culture as one.

The Constitution merely defines the territory within which civil rights can be exercised, with specific limits. The rights of the government prevail over those of private individuals. The law is clearly restrictive and repressive, not open and expansive, on matters of civil rights.[6]

The existing and proposed regulations concerning demonstrations will, in a country where there is no rule of law, like China, necessarily become the chains that increase control and reduce the actuality of civil rights.

The Communist Party has in the past initiated a Cultural Revolution and many other ideological campaigns in violation of constitutional norms. The civil rights of more than a billion people have been denied for a long time. Several million people who were in social reform movements, party and non-party members, were persecuted and/or executed. That is the CCP's unforgivable crime against the Chinese people.

That the Chinese communists have ignored the loud call, from here and from beyond the borders of China, for the amnesty and release of those imprisoned for participation in the Democracy Wall Movement, again reveals the painful fact that, in a totalitarian one-party system, where there can be no rule of law, the law itself can be used as a brutal instrument for the repression of political opposition. The party remains above the law and can ignore the Constitution.

Public opinion at home and abroad calls for the release of certain political prisoners. How could this affect the stability of the country?

Examine the turmoils in modern China. Which one has not been caused by internal conflicts in the CCP? If there were no conflicts in the party, the country would have been saved from disruption.

The appearance here of harmony, stability and unity is grounded in the bloody repression of the masses, and in the bloody incarceration and execution of millions of the finest people in our country. We do not need that kind of false harmony and solidarity, brought on not by the wishes of the people, but brought on by the selfish goals of the one party and its eight subordinate systems of control.

To be sorry after having hit your children, the people; and to ask us to forgive the ugliness of our mother, the party; such are the excuses of those with the mentality of gangsters. No matter what the Constitution says, it will be necessary for us to continue to fight for our rights. Many members of both the CCP and democratic movements have lost their lives; but we must still try to ensure that the Constitution is untainted by those cliques of selfish profiteers, with their decadence, corruption and coercion.

Human rights are the rights of the people, and can exist only in a democracy, as an intrinsic part of democracy. The Enlightenment and social progress in Europe had their revolutionary beginnings in the respect for human rights and the individual.

We must strongly object to the accusation that we are using legal arguments as a basis for illegal actions, and to the suppression of our legal activities. Actions cannot be legal and illegal at the same time. If our actions are permitted in law, then they are legal.

On the other hand, constitutional reform is required, and the people's Movement is appealing to legal experts. In the Constitution we see defined the rights possessed by the people of China. However, these articles are only high-sounding, abstract and empty words. If the Four Cardinal Principles [7] do not disappear, they will always take priority over human rights, and the statement that "power belongs to the people" will be a fraud. If the monolithic socio-political structure is not eliminated, and replaced with a pluralist society and culture, then the "open door" policy and reform will be like a picture of food hanging on a wall — not satisfying. To reform the country's social system was the chief goal of the Democracy Wall Movement ten years ago, and remains so for the Popular Movement now and into the future.

Students! If the monolithic and imperial structure cannot be fundamentally changed, how can education save the country? Does the unity and well-being of the nation depend upon mobilization by a party, or does it depend on the voluntary coming together of individuals who are truly free and vested with rights? The slogan of the May Fourth Movement, necessary at that time [1919], was, "Save the country and struggle to survive." The Democracy Wall Movement performed a similar task, identifying the illusory condition and interests of the country, as defined by our rulers, and stating the real interests. The Democracy Wall Movement also met the needs of the time, represented the essential feelings of the masses, and raised the revolutionary standard of human rights and democracy; and it is that which gave historical significance to it.

However, although the demands for human rights of the Democracy Wall Movement were similar to those of the May Fourth Movement, their significance was different, for they were demands made of a communist government which had been in power since 1949. Thus, democracy and human rights are eternal themes, and we will be demanding them still on the centennial anniversary of the May Fourth Movement, the mantle of the latter inherited by a revolutionary Popular Movement, establishing not a politics of power, but a politics of people's democracy.

The Chinese have arrived at a crucial juncture for popular rights, people's democracy, and social reform. Earlier movements were cruelly repressed, and many of their participants are still in prison. Even those who have been released suffer from discrimination. However, the contradictions remain, with demands for reform threatening the "eight-in-one" system, and the profiteering of party and government officials.

What is the situation? We have greed and corruption, legal distortions, political degeneration, party regulations and discipline ignored, rampant inflation, increasing theft, people furious, people suffering, no firm laws and systemic crisis. In this situation, the earlier reforms look like being abandoned.

In modern China the Democracy Movement has had various forms. Again and again, huge protests and demonstrations informed the communist rulers and forced them to correct their mistakes by charting a new course. At times it looked like turmoil, but what was the alternative for the country and the governing party? What good did simple petitions ever do? So today, the wreaths at the Monument, the masses in Tiananmen Square, the marches along

Changan, and the demonstration outside Xinhuamen, are all appropriate ways of educating the party.

If the Democracy Movement has made a mistake over time, it has been its failure to form its own political parties, not developing beyond a series of popular Movements. It is true that the basis of the PRC is not to be found in the degenerate field of politics and party style, but in the heroism of a series of people's Movements. The people are the true radicals, the truly wise, the least corrupt and most powerful. The increasing incidence of their popular Movements, in this age of communications, indicates that our contemporary, monolithic, imperial order can not last — unless it closes the door on the world.

However, a freely-formed association is a common means for the transformation of society. The full development of the people's Democracy Movement, and its growing sophistication, will inevitably lead to the union of social organizations and leadership into political parties. Recent popular Movements here and in Taiwan have shown the persistence of democratic forces, which in their variety cannot be contained in a single political party.

The Democracy Wall Movement produced a simple programme, the Chinese Declaration of Human Rights, and a loose political organization, the Human Rights League. Various organizations arranged for joint meetings and common declarations for joint activities. The Student Movement in 1986 had only vague slogans for democracy, human rights, and freedom. There was no concrete programme or long term goals, and it did not voice the feelings of the masses concerning economic matters. In both cases, members of the working class associated with the movement were arrested and jailed. The lesson is that our organizations were too small. Students should join with the workers, who in their turn should fight for independent trade unions. Only when several million production workers understand that their democratic rights are not handed down to them, but are something that must be fought for, and take command of the situation, will democracy be realised.

In your dialogue with the government, amnesty for those arrested during the earlier movements must be an important part of the discussion. Further, we must fight for 1) higher wages and oppose inflation; 2) basic housing at low prices; 3) democracy in the universities, and opposition to administrative hierarchy; and 4) freedom of the press to oppose counter-revolutionary thought.

Workers! Brothers! Organise; but legally! Long live the coalition of students and workers!

Speech of April 21, 1989, in Tiananmen Square.

IV: Ren Wanding, Reflections on the Historical Character of the Democracy Movement [8]

Look at Tiananmen Square, the symbol of the rich land of the People's Republic of China! Look at the battlefield of the Xidan Democracy Wall Movement! Look at the Square from which the storm of the May Fourth Movement first began to blow!

The Importance of the Democracy Movement

This is a confrontation between masses of students and thousands of armed policemen and soldiers; but it is also a confrontation between the citizens of Beijing and the government, a political challenge and power struggle by people from all levels of society against the party. The massive demonstration, which began on April 27th, is another masterpiece of the people's Democracy Movement. To combat the authorities' irrational accusation that it created "turmoil," on April 27th the students of Beijing's institutions of higher education, and several hundred thousand ordinary citizens, marched through the city's streets in columns that stretched for miles. They broke through the police and military barriers many times, and gathered successfully in Tiananmen Square in the afternoon. Wherever the marchers went they were welcomed by the people, and given food and money. It became the greatest and most wonderful demonstration in the history of China. Not simply a student movement, it is a great Democracy Movement led by the students and joined by all levels of society.

During the last forty years, when has the people's democratic power been so well demonstrated? When has the authority of the ruling CCP dropped to such a low level? The party finds it impossible to restore its control over the situation and the confidence of the people. The people are not opposed to the CCP's rule, but it has performed so badly that it has lost the sympathy, support and understanding of the people. The party has suppressed democracy. Although it has many extraordinary members, they cannot change its fundamentally flawed political basis, nor its anti-democratic character. I repeat, people are not moving against socialism, but a socialist system led by a party that has performed badly. It has not created greater wealth and democracy, but has placed the burden of inflation on the people in a perpetual exploitation of them.

Over the past ten years of economic reform and an "open door" policy, in spite of some socio-economic progress, there has continued extensive corruption in the economy and the perpetuation of evil features of the political system. The party condemns those who criticise it, when they should be asking themselves why the criticism is there. To criticise the Popular Movement as the "conspiracy of a few people" is to cheat the people, and probably cheat themselves into even bigger political mistakes. The Chinese Communist Party has created a socio-political structure which is monolithic, the "eight-in-one," and which must now leave the historical scene.

The Movement's Historical Position

During the past forty years, beginning in the fifties when the democratic parties[9] tried to obtain equal status with the Communist Party, through the April Fifth revolution of 1976, through the Democracy Wall Movement from '79 to '81, through the student Movements in '85 and '86, through the intellectuals' petition for the release of victims from the Democracy Wall Movement in 1989, up to this Democracy Movement led by the students, we have developed maturity. If we cannot now show that this Movement represents everyone, then we cannot take on responsibility for the future of China.

The truth is that democracy is growing rapidly, developing theories and principles, but pays a high price for the experience it gains. The Democracy Wall Movement made political demands that were more mature than those of the May Fourth Movement, demanding a popular basis for democracy, Marxism and socialism. Moreover, the Democracy Wall Movement was the first to demand a reform of our current monolithic socio-political structure. Its specific arguments replaced the ambiguous poetry of May Fourth, principles replaced slogans, analysis replaced noise, and free societies replaced disorganised groups. Furthermore, this Democracy Movement, initiated by the institutions of higher education, has reached a new level. Its features are: autonomous organizations in each institution, a joint committee for these, joint action, and the full exercise of our rights as defined in the PRC Constitution. The movement has slogans and short-term tactics and goals; but no long-term objectives, fixed rules, firm organization, or support system.

Can the Communist Party be Replaced?

People should realise that the operation of the Popular Movement shows that society requires a new party organization and leadership. The historical circumstances and the will of the people necessitate it. The 1989 Democracy Movement is the embryo of the new party, a new societal organization. Perhaps this infant will die in the cradle, but it will surely be reborn in the next upheaval. My view is that the long-term goal of the movement is to reform, peacefully, the Communist Party's monolithic socio-political structure, and to replace it with a diversified democratic, cultural, national framework. This is the proposed ideal of the young scholars in the social sciences, and this is the right moment to make it happen. If we must get bloodied in the process, let it be so. Force must be met with force. The monolithic feudal structure is the product of a long period of feudalism and low economic output. With economic development and social development, it must now disappear from China. Do the Chinese like and accept totalitarianism and monolithic dictatorship? The current democratic wave denies that. However, if they are disliked by the people, why does the Communist Party force us to accept them? Why does the party think that only it can represent the people, that only it can consolidate the benefits of development? And can the party be replaced? Are we not only already beaten, but also immature weak and stupid, if we are opposing something that we think cannot be replaced? Have millions of brilliant Chinese been killed or imprisoned since 1949 for no reason at all?

Students! The historic burden is now on your shoulders. It is now time to organise a legal party and associations, formally to participate in the reform of the social system of China. The truth is that, though one may have a family and private interests, those who are the intellectual elite of society, whatever their age, must make the effort. Walking out of our institutions, steeled by the heat of the situation, we shall succeed. China does not lack the capacity for democratic politics, but it is suppressed. Countering this suppression, as when we ignored the decree banning demonstrations, we shall succeed.

The CCP Responds to Good Will with Hatred

The short-run objectives of the Movement should be the effective protection of the people's rights as defined by the Constitution, and dispensing with all of the irrational accusation that ours is an "illegal social formation." The legal rights to demonstrate and to strike must prevail over the accusation that we are creating "turmoil." The legal right to freedom of speech must overcome the irrational accusation that we are behaving unconstitutionally and going against CCP leadership. Only if we can counteract these accusations can our Movement continue, and the legality of our actions be recognised.

To destroy the CCP, or to oppose the CCP, are two different things. The first is a criminal act. The latter concerns the conflict between the Four Cardinal Principles and the Constitution of the PRC, which provides the right of free speech. Officials interpret this in any way they want. If the one party cannot be opposed, where is freedom of speech, where is socialist democracy?

Today, the fairest measure of freedom of speech is whether or not the ruling party can be opposed, without which it is only false and abstract propaganda. The monolithic structure of the party is the political and theoretical question. Even if the Movement is not opposed to the party, the intellectuals will be. Wisdom and politics cannot be separated. If the party cannot be opposed, then at times it will be dominated by destructive elements like the Gang of Four, who *are* the party for a time. Further, unopposed, the party can initiate random campaigns, directed against anybody, hurting people, party and country at random, without any understanding of what is being done. There are other so-called democratic parties, but what power do they have? So what value is the "long term co-existence of parties"? The ideological and cruel class struggles of the CCP continue without sign of remorse, which is the consequence of the impossibility of opposing the party. How many have suffered for the maintenance of the party's dictatorship? Only a minority of the population; but the legal and political institutions thereby repress everybody.

How can the party oppose its critics? The popular democracy opposes the *mistakes* of the party, which must benefit the nation and the rights of the people. Where's the problem? The Popular Movement awakens the party, preventing corruption there and in the society. To this good will they respond with hatred? With incarceration and dishonest rectification, the vicious relationship between ruler and ruled is continued in China, with so much suffering.

Since the current social system cannot be opposed, the stagnant economic system persists, threatening the national economy; for, since the social system cannot be opposed, the restrictive economic system, and the serfdom of the rural economy, continues. If the party and the socialist system had accepted opposition ideas, how many evil incidents could have been avoided in the past? And now, by correcting its mistakes, the socialist system could demonstrate its future superiority.

The Evil that Remains

Over the last decade, although there has been a widespread reform of our economic system, and some movement towards an "open-door" policy in international relations, the basic structure of the "eight-in-one" system has not been touched, and some possibilities have not been considered. False prosperity and hidden crises occur; and for the past ten years the party's policy has come to be based on three things:

1) The death of Mao Zedong, and the opportunity thereby for the party to reject his idealistic socialist policies.

2) The gradual policy change following the power struggle of October 1976, consequent upon the April Fifth Movement, without which there could not have been an "October Incident." [10]

3) The Xidan "Democracy Wall Movement," which exploded in 1978, placed a priority on political and economic reform, with particular reference to the ending of life-tenure for those in party and bureaucratic positions. Without Democracy Wall there would not have been the freedom of speech and the new lifestyle that you see around you today.

The party and government should be instruments of the people's will. The Third Plenum of the Eleventh Central Committee [in 1978] produced nothing to that end. Consequently, people associated with the Democracy Wall Movement remain illegally incarcerated to this day. Students, you should show some interest in this shady judicial question, and request their release and rehabilitation. The decade of [economic] reform, and the "open door policy" [in foreign relations and foreign investment] is a case of the government granting some concessions to the people, but maintaining the repression of the intellectual elite.

The method of oppression remains the same. The fact that Hu Yaobang twice spoke against the arbitrary arrest of Democracy Wall activists at a seminar in 1979, proves only that a party leader cannot rescue people, however virtuous and brave he may be. The monolithic "eight-in-one" principle can represent only the will of the party, and never the will of the people. Nor does the State Council, as the popular Movements during the past thirteen years demonstrate. Why do people express their ideas thus? Obviously because the ruling party, the government, the People's Congress, and the State Council do not represent them. The whole charade can be seen in the control of the electorate during elections. The corruption of the party, the politicians, the bureaucrats and the legal system is a tragic fact! Lies cannot cover up the promotion of the Four Cardinal Principles and the "eight-in-one" principle against the welfare of the people. Unless this is changed, when the party goes wrong, everything goes wrong.

How Can the Situation be Changed?

Because the Constitution protects the "eight-in-one" position, we can begin with the amendment of the Constitution. If that document and the State Council are unrepresentative, the way to do this must be through the institutions of higher education. It is necessary to organise People's Committees, based upon the grassroots organization of professors, intellectuals, and people from all levels, which will begin to exercise governmental functions, including the formation of new parties. Through them the theory of democratic politics can be transformed into practice; and they are necessary for this.

Such a change has been envisaged for many years by intellectuals representing the people — unlike in Poland where the same process was led by the trade unions. Such committees were suggested on the Democracy Wall ten years ago. In Poland the Solidarity union held a dialogue with, and worked with, the ruling party, providing us with a precedent. If we do not follow it, a corrupt politics will persist, an unstable China will achieve neither solidarity nor stability, and improved government policy will be impossible.

Our goals become: the creation of political parties, and government by people's committees, each of which have a popular basis. It has been said that, "Politics is the elimination of selfishness, without which justice will perish." China belongs to the Chinese, not to one or more political parties. If the CCP recognises the reality of the situation, it will not be surprised by popular dissatisfaction, and will not make irrational claims and criticisms concerning the relationship of the party to the people.

Viewed from a distance, China reminds us of the seventeenth century. The real foundations of the country should be democracy and liberty, not so many cardinal principles. Divisions within China in recent years were not created by the people. As in every other era when conflicts occurred, it was the evil result of a centralised and feudalistic monopoly of political power. It is now hindering our historical development, and the people must dispense with such false unity. The coercive unity of China, achieved in 1949, should give way to the popular franchise and people's committees. The intellectuals should inspire the people, demanding the return of power to the people. Opposition, hesitation, pessimism, or new authoritarianism are futile. Only the great power of democracy, and a people's organization created by it, can stabilise China and further stimulate its population.

The present and the future belong to the people!

Students, you are the pride of the nation, and I love you for it!

April 27-May 4, 1989

V: Our "April Student Movement" and the "April Fifth Movement" [11]

There are some startling similarities between the April Patriotic-Democratic Student Movement and the April Fifth Movement. We can look at these from many angles, including that of the *People's Daily*, which accuses the two movements of possessing the following similarities:

The April Fifth Movement [of 1976], according to the authorities,

1) was a counter-revolutionary incident;
2) utilised big and small character posters, poetry, essays and cartoons viciously to attack the leadership of the country and the party;
3) was essentially an attempt to overthrow the leadership of the CCP and the dictatorship of the proletariat;
4) tricked the masses into invading the Great Hall of the People, attacking security officers, burning police cars and fire engines, and setting buildings ablaze;
5) was a small minority with ulterior motives, using the pretext of honouring Zhou Enlai to attack the party Central Committee headed by Mao Zedong; and
6) caused turmoil which, had it not been resolutely repressed by the iron fist of the proletarian dictatorship, would have allowed a small gang of anti-party, anti-socialist, bad elements to restore capitalism in China; and the whole country would have had to suffer that again.
7) Therefore, the people had to stand fast in solidarity with the party centre headed by Mao Zedong and struggle resolutely against counter-revolutionary turmoil.

Our present *April Student Movement* is said to be,

1) a planned conspiracy, an anti-party, anti-socialist turmoil;
2) slanderously attacking the leaders of party and State;
3) essentially contradicting the leadership of the CCP and the socialist system;
4) tricking the masses into attacking and injuring policemen;
5) a small minority with ulterior motives, using the opportunity to honour Hu Yaobang as a pretext for undermining the confidence of the people and stirring up trouble in the country; and

6) causing turmoil which, if allowed to run its course, will cause serious confusion and destroy China's radiant future; so it must be repressed in the cause of peace.

7) Therefore, people must quickly distinguish right from wrong and act resolutely to stop the turmoil.

Three years after the April Fifth Movement, comrade Deng Xiaoping said, "Many of the people died in the Tiananmen incident. We cannot very well say that it was counter-revolutionary." Today, and in a similar vein, we seriously say to the nation and to the world,

"So many youth and students have joined the April Student Movement, and it has the support of so many of the people, how can it be an anti-party, anti-socialist turmoil?"

Each Movement can be seen as both Patriotic and Democratic, representing the awakening and growth of the self-consciousness of the Chinese people. They are both great historical events that propel China forwards in the process of modernization. Yet the present Movement is greater, deeper, more rational and more constructive than the April Fifth Movement. This is demonstrated by the fact that Beijing's students and citizens have not angrily set fire to vehicles, nor have they beaten up any of the running dogs suppressing the masses. They have risen above that mediocre mentality of simply wanting a good bureaucrat to replace the bad one — which was the demand of the April Fifth Movement. This time the banner clearly upholds the supremacy of the Constitution, and criticises all activities that contravene it and the law. They rightly go beyond the limitations illegally imposed by local authorities, exercise their rights to freedom of speech and association, and demand reforms in the economic and political system. They demand structural reforms and the right for an effective supervision of government officials, with whom they want an equal and frank dialogue.

If this precious awakening of the self-consciousness of the youth, the intellectuals, and the people of China is suppressed as a riot, there will be no peace in the country. China will be excluded from the world community yet again, left alone to face the most dangerous of crises.

May 1, 1989

VI: On One-Party Dictatorship [12]

It is truly said that China is practicing capitalism under the name of socialism. A handful of people have usurped the central authority and now exercise a one party dictatorship. What is commonly called "state ownership" is actually the ownership of this small group, who profit themselves by abusing their power in business transactions, exploiting the people in the name of the State. To sustain their rule they trample on law, distort public opinion, appoint their children and grand-children to important positions, and deceive the public through direct control of the media. They share power with those who will support them, mouthpieces who "voluntarily wear chains, and put chains upon others." They force people to subscribe to the Four Cardinal Principles, including the insistence upon the "leadership of the Party," which by itself has generated a deep alienation and indifference amongst the population.

If the people will "do whatever the party asks," then they merely demonstrate the degree to which they have been fooled. The party's so-called "unified consciousness" and "unified leadership" of the "whole people" is nothing but lies. An independent person does not blindly submit his/her opinion to that of another. Therefore, I will support the CCP only when it is correct, according to the revised principle of "supporting the party leadership *when it is correct.*"

According to the party, the future will be complex. In literature, the blossoming of "a hundred flowers" will be the norm. In the economy, different systems will co-exist. [13] Yet, in spite of this, the political system is to remain under monopolistic control, nicely justified by the CCP as "unity with diversity." No matter what you call it, it is totally unconvincing, giving us only a supposedly-free person dancing on the end of a chain. The only route to democracy is the end of the one party dictatorship, and the establishment of genuinely democratic institutions — such as unofficial "unions." For democracy and freedom, the power to make laws must belong to the people; and that is the only way to guarantee freedom of speech and freedom of the press.

The shortcomings of a one-party dictatorship are:

1) It cannot police itself, which means that internal corruption grows into widespread crisis.

2) Inefficiency.

3) It has a poor analytical viewpoint and cannot appreciate the complexity of things. Therefore, its reforms are always piecemeal and inadequate. Lacking competing parties, it lauds itself for its petty achievements, and cannot recognise its mistakes.

Nixon was forced to resign over the Watergate incident in the USA. In Japan, Takeshita met the same fate in a bribery scandal. In China, however, collective responsibility is the principle of government; which leads one to ask: Why did not Li Peng resign along with Hu Yaobang [in 1987] as a demonstration of sincerity?

I think that the only way to change the present system is to struggle diligently for democracy, to which end we must insist that all are equal before the law, and that nobody is above the law. This means that laws should not be the product of the will of a few, but should be the genuine manifestation of the will of the people, in whose hands must lie the legislative power.

The main aim of law is to achieve freedom and equality. Freedom can be realised only when all submit to a law which reflects the common will of the people. Democratic politics will replace the evils of this neo-feudalistic society only when we replace its legal system. Government should execute the will of the people, from whom its power is drawn. If the National People's Congress is to perform this task, then the one-party electoral system must be changed.

Without genuine supervision by the people, government is inevitably corrupt. So let us fight for a new beginning of genuine democracy and freedom.

May 2, 1989

VII: X.X. Yeung,[14] For a Socialist Multi-Party System in China

Received opinion presents the multi-party system as a monopoly of capitalism, and has nothing to do with socialism. There are democratic socialist countries like Sweden, but then we are told that they are not really practicing socialism — with arguments that are not persuasive. Hungary now has a multi-party system as part of its political agenda, and Poland is talking about diversification. The East Germans accuse them of being revisionist. And in other communist-ruled countries, including the USSR and the PRC, the rationale of a multi-party system is rejected.

Chinese leaders argue that the multi-party system contradicts the Chinese reality. I recognise that the position of the CCP is all-powerful, but that is not very convincing as a reason for rejecting the existence of other political parties in China — truly independent organizations and democratic parties. My preliminary thoughts on the question are as follows:

1) If capitalism can have a multi-party system, why not socialism? I can see many reasons for having one. Party politics is, in the first place, the common political form of modern civilised society. So long as there are different interests in society, different political parties will naturally come into existence. A multi-party system is based on this.

The CCP has long insisted that under socialism people have common interests, and use this to justify a one-party dictatorship. However, the fact is that the interests of people in a socialist country are not always the same. There are different interest groups. In China there are at least four distinct interests: workers, peasants, merchants, and intellectuals. This is a "class" basis for different political parties. The CCP claim to represent everybody is not true. It simply cannot do it. Moreover, it has developed into a party alienated from the people, practicing bureaucratic rule. In modern China there is not a single representative institution.

The CCP is the only political party in China (excluding Taiwan), with the so-called democratic parties being branches of the CCP. Without competition, the communists' rule will never be at risk, will be able to do anything they want, and become totally corrupted. Putting its own interests before those of the people, the CCP enjoys unlimited privileges which it is frightened of losing. Hence its opposition to a multi-party system, and reference to the "Chinese reality," is an unconvincing argument.

However, history is always progressing, and attempts to reverse history are futile. A multi-party system with various checks and balances will develop in response to the variety of interests in China.

2) Some people worry that a multi-party system will alter the nature of the socialist state. This kind of worry is unfounded. Hasn't the nature of the capitalist state remained unchanged in spite of the multi-party system? This is because diverse interests can share a common ideology. That is, different parties may represent different interests, but share a fundamental belief in capitalism. Could the same logic not be applicable to socialism?

In theory a socialist society is the most humane, democratic, prosperous and rational society, forsaking all corrupt and decadent elements of the past. At this stage socialism is far from perfect, but as a developing system, improving itself, the people will naturally be attracted towards it. A multi-party system would protect socialism against those who would destroy it. So a socialist multi-party system has a pragmatic value, and we should regard its implementation as an obvious necessity.

3) More than seventy years after the establishment of the first socialist country by the Great October Revolution of 1917, we are faced with the unpleasant fact that all of the socialist countries lag behind the capitalist countries. Socialist countries are, generally speaking, poor and undemocratic. It is not surprising, therefore, that some people say that socialism is feudalism, and is regressive.

The ruling parties of most socialist countries are now beginning to wake up to the situation. Reform sweeps through the USSR, Europe, China and Vietnam. The reforms themselves are a declaration of past failures. Some achievements were certainly made, but new problems have arisen, creating difficulties everywhere. Faith in socialism has been shattered, and people everywhere turn blindly towards western capitalism.

Why are so many problems arising even when these countries undertake reform? Probably because the reforms are not sufficiently comprehensive. Almost without exception they focus on reform of the economic realm whilst their political structure remains the same. Inevitably a stagnant politics hampers the development of the economic sector. Only political reform can ease the difficulties and crisis facing the socialist countries.

The most critical feature of political reform must be the implementation of democracy. Without democracy, corruption will remain, and economic development will be inhibited. Under a one-party dictatorship, democracy must be bestowed on the people by those in power, who also have the power to withdraw it. Therefore, genuine democracy can only be realised through political diversification, the superior form of which is a socialist multi-party system.

4) The superiority of a socialist multi-party system is obvious, although there is doubt concerning its applicability to China. That reservation is certainly justified under the present determination of the CCP not to share power. However, the people will not be content with the *status quo;* but neither can the party itself. Corruption is causing serious trouble, and growing popular discontent threatens the party's legitimacy. The current Student Movement causes great alarm because it threatens to create a multi-party system.

It is certain that the CCP will not allow a new party even if it proclaims itself socialist, for it would be competitive. Accused of being counter-revolutionary, it would be made illegal and disbanded. Does that mean that we are helpless? Certainly not. We could win over the existing "democratic parties," and it would be embarrassing for the CCP to deny them their independence. The worst they could do would be to refuse financial support, which would be replaced by the people and overseas compatriots if they were genuinely independent.

Comrades in the democratic parties are believers in socialism. Their independence is a precondition for a multi-party system in China, and that is where her future modernization and democratization lies.

May 12, 1989

VIII: Some Thoughts on the Chinese Communist Party [15]

At present China is in serious trouble and faces many difficulties. This has made it necessary for us to analyze carefully the monopoly rule of the CCP over recent decades. The conclusion of this examination is that most of the mistakes made in China can be traced back to the basic principles of the Party. The details are as follows:

Ideologically, the CCP upholds the Four Cardinal Principles as some predetermined truth upon which all theoretical considerations are based. As an organization with a common conviction, some commonly embraced principles are to be expected in the Party. But it is absurd to force the people of the whole country to accept and defend these principles. Take for example the statement, "insist on the leadership of the Communist Party." Every political party hopes, by implementing its political programme, to win the support of the people. But it has to be realised through the common will of the people (through a general election). It is ridiculous to force upon the people some subjective and self-fulfilling wish as an eternal truth, and to demand that the whole country either toe the line, or face the "big stick" and the "tall hat" (i.e., repression). The dozens of mistakes made in the ideological conflict, and the loss of an independent personality among the intellectuals, are proof of this absurdity. The creativity of the Chinese is seriously hampered by this heavy burden. They are held back because they must follow the views of a small number of people.

In terms of organizational principle and form, the Communist Party has become an excellent breeding ground of dictatorial rule and bureaucratic politics, the latter being a standard result and natural extension of the former. The secretive and military methods of the war years linger on. "The individual submits to the organization, the junior submits to the senior, the party submits to the party central, and the party central submits to one person (or a few)." In short, "to obey orders is the highest duty." How can such a rigid organization not become a breeding ground of dictatorship, patriarchy, and the personality cult. Absence of democracy, and dictatorship by an individual, is realised through mass terror, as in the Cultural Revolution and the downfall of Hu Yaobang. This dictatorship always begins inside the party, and in a one-party State like ours it is only natural that it become a permanent phenomenon. There are today people who rest their hopes on one or two benevolent personages in the party. Such a thought is terrifying. Have we not had enough of the time when we place the lives of one billion people into the hands of one or two individuals.

"Our great party will always redress all wrongs in the end." On the basis of this oft-quoted statement, one billion people have lost decades of their lives, tens of millions have been killed, and civilization was thrown backward hundreds of years — as occurred during the Cultural Revolution, and in Stalin's purges. If a party has spent the greater part of its existence committing inexcusable errors, what kind of gamble is it to place in its hands the destiny of one billion people?

The CCP also has the practice of picking out for punishment "a handful" of bad elements; so why doesn't it select a large handful from the party? If 80% of the party members are good (measured against the average moral standard of a common citizen), what shall we do about the 20%, which is about ten millions? Are they not a large "handful" who should be punished?

The Communist Party's position within the country's political structure is also ambiguous. Theoretically, all power has belonged to the people and their representatives in the National People's Congress since October 1, 1949, with everyday administration exercised by the Government. In practice, however, the whole country has always been under a one-party leadership. The political programme of the CCP is not supported by a nation-wide general election, nor is the party's will produced by the National People's Congress. Rather, it controls what the Constitution calls the "highest institutional power" (i.e., the National People's Congress) and the "highest executive organ" (i.e., the State Council). If both the Congress and the Council are merely vehicles of power for the CCP, what does the word "highest" mean here? If the elected People's Congress is merely for the convenience of the party, why bother to say, "All power to the people"? It is more appropriate to speak of power to the party, or the party's army. A party member who does not hold any governmental office [i.e., Deng Xiaoping] can decide, in a few statements, the country's policy in the coming years, which means that this one man's view is equal to those of one billion people. Isn't this shocking and sickening?

We keep hearing that party norms have been transgressed. Is this not because party members are given all kinds of priority and privileges? If they were just like ordinary citizens there would be no problem. Those who have joined the party in recent years, however, are living proof of the replacement of political commitment by pursuit of privilege. Why should they have more than ordinary citizens? And why should the public treasury support the party, rather than its members' contributions? Without that, would we still have a budget deficit? The dark side of our economy is "officials abusing power in return for bribes," whilst the old men who are our political leaders suck the blood of the nation.

Our country needs leadership, but it should be chosen by the people. A party ought to win the support of the people before it forms the government and implements a programme. In short, everything should be decided by the people.

If a citizen does not have the right to express her/his opinion, then s/he does not have an obligation to obey the government. Following this logic, when a political party appoints itself as the representative of the people, is not elected by the people, and has lost all its confidence, the people do not have a duty to support or even to pay any attention to it.

The order of our priorities should be: the People, the State and Government, and finally the Party. It should not be the other way round, where the Party is everything, and represents nothing.

May 17, 1989

IX: *Hue Yu,* [16] *Hoping for a Brighter Future*

Since the establishment of the Republic by the CCP in 1949 we have always thought that the main contradiction in society was that between the backwardness of our productive forces and the growing material and cultural needs of the people. However, this belief is based upon the deception of propaganda. The main contradiction at this time is the conflict between democracy and autocracy, between the rule of law and the rule of man; and therein lies the reason mainland China has not been able to catch up to the rest of the world.

Never resolved in any meaningful way, that contradiction must generate turmoil in our society whenever it deepens. It is the reason for all of the disruptions in the past, in spite of attempts to lay the blame at the door of "counter-revolutionary cliques." Turmoil, in fact, is a means of preventing the contradiction getting worse; and that too can be said of the Democracy Movement. When we hear the same old song and dance about class struggle and that the Patriotic-Democratic Movement is disruptive, it all sounds very familiar. However, if this leads merely to a defusing of the situation, then the spirit of the Movement will have been betrayed.

How are we best to understand the Democracy Movement?

First, note that the students who constitute the main force of the Democracy Movement have generated some false notions. Remember the comment in the *People's Daily*, that some students promoted the slogan, "Down with the Communist Party!" The newspaper seized upon that as the basis of its April 26th editorial. In order to clarify the situation, on April 27th students held up banners unanimously stating, "Support the Communist Party!" Such a response implied, however, that the students support the one-party hierarchy of the CCP. In reality, one of the elements in democracy is to allow dissent. In terms of politics, it means the existence of many parties who might form the government. You cannot, as the students were doing, ask for freedom and democracy through a compromise with autocracy; and such false thinking leads nowhere. Therefore, in the discussions between government officials and student representatives, the persistent deadlock should be explained by that, not by the insincerity of government officials.

The harboring of erroneous ideas that run counter to the spirit of democracy, freedom, science and the rule of law, as manifested by the students themselves, should be seriously considered. It is a weakness that can be fatal. Student organization is loose, and their representatives are not always dependable. The appearance of certain bureaucratic phenomena has been disappointing, and has led to the disillusionment of some overseas Chinese. That such problems exist is amply demonstrated by the withdrawal of Wang Dan and Wuer Kaixi from the leadership of ASUBU.

Even worse is the fact that some students have adopted feudalistic policies to fight for democracy. Before the Chairman of the National People's Congress, Wan Li, returned from his trip outside China, there were many people placing their hopes in him as the "incorruptible magistrate." Once again, we are looking for a master, a single individual to whom we can link our fate. Mao Zedong once said that Deng Xiaoping was useful, but that he should not be given power. "He is a wolf in the high mountains and, once he is given power, he runs wild." However, since there are no legal checks, nobody is able to escape from the ability to run wild when in power. Our experiences under Mao and Deng should serve as a constant reminder of that. A leader who acts properly may be permitted to continue as a leader, but life-long leadership can never be allowed. In the latter event, the poison of feudalism floods over modern society.

We can all see that in China the people who are under the iron fist of arbitrary rule and slavery are not the students, but the workers, peasants and other strata of society. In the Democracy Movement the students, who have had greater freedom than others, are making the loudest demands for democracy and freedom. This should change, and the people who should speak are not students, but the people.

We know that the tradition of China is, "The victors become kings, and the vanquished become bandits." That is because, throughout Chinese history, there was no rule of law. In modern society there is no necessity for politics to be a life or death struggle. The progress of history is in fact the transformation from individualism to contract. Contract is law; and its key feature is the enabling of a political struggle in which opponents check each other. The checks come from the exercise of democratic political rights; and the guarantee of personal security is the precondition of those rights.

Students are not independent personalities, being economically dependent on others; and their role in society is temporary. Therefore, their voice is never very strong. At best they can form a vanguard, a herald, speaking on behalf of social development. The fact that the government treats them with such indifference demonstrates the point.

Some have argued that the students can rely on overseas financial backing to carry on the struggle. However, democracy is both a means and an end. It is doubtful whether a countervailing force could be developed whilst depending on other people's help for economic security. Foreign help is a factor, but the decisive ones must be internal. Sun Yatsen sought overseas help in his struggle for democracy, and failed. Mao, on the other hand, was victorious.

[undated]

X: *Ma Siufang,[17] Statement of a Tiananmen Hunger Striker*

The students' Patriotic-Democratic Movement asserted in April that its main tasks were, i) the initiation of political reforms in China; ii) protecting the civil rights and liberty defined in the Constitution; and iii) ensuring the smooth implementation of economic reforms. With these in mind, tens of thousands of students have been staying in Beijing for a month-long public demonstration, hunger-strike and sit-in, in order to persuade the government, through these peaceful activities, to undertake a critical review of the ten-year old [economic] reform programme. They urge the government to investigate the mistakes and drawbacks of the reforms and to take legal action against corrupt leaders in the government. At the same time, the students demand that the government take immediate action against serious corruption among bureaucrats and others. However, the "feudalistic absolutism" of the government, faced with the students' reasonable demands and peaceful expression of discontent, chooses to take a fraudulent and high-handed attitude — ignoring the dignity of the country. In government statements, such as the April 26th editorial and the speeches of May 20th, and by constantly delaying a "dialogue," again and again, the government suffocates and scorns the Patriotic-Democratic Movement. It makes use of news censorship and an incredibly large amount of news distortion to blur the real picture of the Movement. All those righteous, responsible compatriots concerned with Chinese democratization become doubtful, and ask, What are the students trying to do?

However, their dishonesty will not last long. Ultimately, the corrupt government will not be able to hide its ugly face and distorted mouth from the people. At this time the people in Beijing are bravely surging to the streets, and shouting, "Down With Li Peng." Clearly, the previously silent and serene Chinese are awakening. This signifies the imminent advance of Chinese democracy.

The recent series of events plainly show the deep despair of the Chinese people over the feudalistic absolutism. The tragic fact of the hunger strike totally destroys any remnant of faith in the good intentions of the government. At last, the people rise up. April's Student-Patriotic-Democratic Movement has now become May's Popular-Patriotic-Democratic Movement. No matter what the outcome, this Movement is certainly a new page in Chinese history, a milestone in Chinese progress.

At the present stage of the Movement, what are the tasks ahead? Are they just the ending of martial law and downfall of Li Peng? We want these things, to clear away obstacles to democratization, which is our ultimate goal. Moreover, the call for the downfall of Li Peng is a concrete move against corruption in the bureaucracy, not just a pure slogan.

The first important task of the people is to exterminate corruption in the government. The cause of this deterioration in the government is "feudalistic absolutism." Therefore, breaking absolutism is an essential goal of the Movement. Only if all-round political reform can be effectively and urgently implemented can corruption be removed and our nation made strong. To hand this task over to corrupted bureaucrats would be a historical farce, and this splendid Popular Democratic Movement would fail and fade out.

To overthrow absolutism and to strive for democracy we must do following:

First, we should activate our civil capacity in the State through the promotion of a strong sense of our civil and political rights. The present absolutism deprives the people of their electoral rights, to vote and to be elected. The citizens cannot freely choose the candidates and, thereby, the right to be elected is lost. This leads to the situation of where the National People's Congress (NPC) is a rubber stamp, and the government is corrupt. Our citizens should no longer accept the corruption and oppression of our government. We must rise up and strive for our civil rights as they are defined in the Constitution.

Second, citizens should have the right to check the operations of the government; i.e., the right of political participation. After ten years of [economic] reform, we now should not be silent. We need real political reforms, not slogans. As long as the CCP does not introduce a fundamental political reform, we should not cease our struggle. As long as our constitutionally-guaranteed civil rights are not guaranteed, we cannot rest. Our nation should no longer be silenced by political machinations.

Third, we should strive for a democratic administration and the end of patriarchal feudal methods. If we are proud of our ancient culture, then we should now recognise that the existing, brutal patriarchal system is most destructive of it. The Chinese myth of the good ruler has been broken since the death of Mao Zedong. Whoever desires to establish it again opposes the will of the people. We have no reason to retain this patriarchal system, and 1.1 billion people no longer must put the fate of our country in the hands of a senile 85-year-old. Gerontocratic politics must be ended by this Popular Democratic Movement; and the life-long tenure of office for cadres must end. Otherwise, democracy will never take root in our country, and we will fester in feudalistic absolutism, with only the corrupt bureaucrats standing to benefit.

Fourth, we should abolish the rule of man and establish a rule of law. For thousands of years human rights and freedom of speech have not existed in China. The most distinctive characteristic of the [Confucian] "rule of good men" was a poor legal system. Powerful bureaucrats could not be punished. This is still the situation in China. Huge errors and losses have been produced during the last ten years of reform. The Li Peng group should be held legally responsible. But Li's group boldly requires the people to suffer whilst they deny all responsibility. This is the miserable outcome of the rule of man, which must be totally rejected if our country is to avoid the unacceptable consequences.

Fifth, we should abolish press censorship. Freedom of the press is the first step towards democracy. If this is not there, we can only have a pseudo-democracy. The voices of the people, the sincere criticism of the corrupt government, cannot be heard. Today, we should have a check on the government, to fight against the monster; and that check is a free press. The press should express truth and the will of the people.

Sixth, we must get rid of elitist politics and set up people's justice. The first priority of the current ruling group is the preservation of its authority without reference to the will of the people. Only a popular politics can place the people's welfare to the fore. And the homespun argument that, "someone must be rich first," is a mere excuse for the privileged classes in authority.

In a nutshell, the hope of our national State lies on the path of democratization. Without it, we have nothing. All those government and party personnel who oppose this principle will be opposed by the people, and must eventually be buried under the surging tides of the Popular Democratic Movement.

Our people unite together in this Patriotic-Democratic Movement. We must build the basis for the nation-State; and the task of nation-building is ours. Let us join together to take up the burden.

May 24, 1989

XI: Tian Chun,[18] A Critique of ASUBU

Many people have come to realise that the main problem with the current Movement is a lack of cohesive organization, as shown in a confusing movement of staff, ineffective command, disorderly assignment of tasks, and a low level of efficiency. A further drawback is the rather undemocratic nature of the organization, with power concentrated in the hands of a few people who are isolated from the public. In the early days of the Movement many valuable opinions were prevented from being communicated to the decision-makers. This has led to faulty decision-making and considerably weakened the general public's confidence in the Movement and in the students.

Organizational defects show themselves in the absence of necessary departments (such as an Overseas Liaison Department), and the lack of cooperation between decision-making and the execution of policies. The student leaders get buried in details and cannot concentrate on strategic decisions that should be made by them. For example, the question whether or not the students should withdraw from the Square affected the entire Movement. Therefore, after the decision had been made not to retreat, discipline in the Square should have been maintained by various means. The implementation of the decision should have been arranged.

Moreover, the organizers tend to forget the public because of an over-concentration on events in the Square. For example, a few days after the [May 13th] beginning of the hunger strike, support for the students from the populace reached a peak. However, we kept our attention directed at the Square and the hunger strikers, ignoring the need to make propaganda in the factories and on the streets, organising the masses — with some of us innocently disapproving of the workers going on strike. With so many people out on the streets, we failed to inspire and guide them. We were so involved in the mobilization of the masses, that we made that an end in itself. This was an emotional indulgence. In addition to that emotion, there was fear, expressed in the underestimation of the power and consciousness of the crowd, and our ability to control the situation. So when the crowd appeared, ironically, we became afraid and confused, and failed to look to the next stage of our Movement; that is, we were not daring enough and hesitated to join hands with the crowd.

Another important strategic mistake that we made was to call upon the students and citizens to block the army trucks. Even if the citizens went out to block the trucks on their own initiative, we should have dispersed them. Since the government had made the mistake itself in ordering the army into Beijing, we should have let it go farther down this wrong path. The farther it went, the more advantageous to us. (The fact is, the army would not dare to stage a bloody crackdown against the students and citizens. The main purpose of their coming into Beijing is rather to prevent the activity of the Zhao Ziyang's supporters in the party). Concentrating upon establishing a blockade against the trucks, we have neglected the education and mobilization of the masses. Therefore, once the troops retreated, we became inactive in anti-climactic response.

Therefore, we can recognise a lack of general policy and organizational purpose in the Movement, which is to be seen as both blind and passive. On the other hand, the problem can be solved by establishing a democratic and efficient leading organization, uniting the various elements in the Movement. This is the problem that we are now working to solve.

The Movement is reduced. The enthusiasm of the people and the students has lessened, deceived by the government's manipulation, and the public's failure to give a strong response to the students' demonstration. This regression is caused by ourselves, however, and may also be ended by putting in more of our effort.

An analysis of this situation can be made from three analytical perspectives: the government, the general public and the students.

1) The government is now regarded as one which is controlled by our opponents. Yang Shangkun's and Li Peng's May 20th

speeches were full of hostility, but these statements isolated them. The reason why they can gain the upper hand is that they are in control of the military and the propaganda machinery. They have two main opponents. The first are the so-called Reformists led by Zhao Ziyang, with supporters in the party, government and the military. They are not to be dismissed lightly. The second, as we know so well, is the group composed of the students and the general public.

Using the propaganda machinery the government tries to downplay the power struggle within the party, but it remains. The government is very weak, very scared. This can be illustrated by the meager support reported by the mass media every day. On the other hand, they are preparing themselves, getting themselves ready for "war." As Yang Shangkun said, they cannot retreat. Retreat means, "Down with the Communist Party." Here, the party refers to a handful of people. So — either the fish die or the net breaks. If we do not get free, what little we have achieved out of this Movement, along with the future of China, will be crushed.

2) As for the people in Beijing, their enthusiasm has decreased. There are people who need our support and inspiration, waiting for our renewed efforts. When the time comes, they will stand on our side. A small group of citizens and workers has already joined us. We must actively strengthen this kind of bond. Whenever danger appears, we have to help them. This is the best policy for promoting our goals. The tactic of the government is to separate people and workers from the students, and to deal with them separately; and that must not be permitted to succeed.

In addition, there are the intellectuals and the support from overseas. The intellectuals are still carrying out their struggle with a hunger strike to be launched tomorrow. Those who are prominent will not easily give up their fight, and those who have been less prominent almost all support the students, and are simply awaiting new opportunities. On the other hand, overseas support has always been very concerned over the students' ability to organise themselves effectively and stand firm. Demonstrable organizational ability will strengthen overseas support and produce a continuation of material aid.

Moreover, the Movement is nation-wide, with Beijing as the pioneer. The whole nation is watching Beijing. Therefore, we must quickly end this anti-climactic depression and let the burning fires of Beijing spread through the whole country.

3) Students are perhaps the most important aspect of the Movement, and a display of low morale is always disappointing. Due to insufficient organization and promotion, many students are scattered. This condition must not continue. On the one hand, promotion must be carried out more vigorously and, on the other, the students' own organization must also be strengthened. At the moment, the link between the student organizers and the ordinary students seems to be broken. Beijing University had a division-of-responsibility committee, which must have been dissolved. It relied mainly on broadcasting, but that medium is limited, and liaison units must be immediately established, or a mass meeting of students held in the near future. Generally speaking, the students' present situation is as follows: Although there may be some pessimistic elements among our organizers, we must present a united front and a determination to see things through to the end. We must make this decision for ourselves, recognising that success or failure depends upon the moves that we make.

This attempt to analyze different aspects of the situation, in general, notes that the situation at this time is relatively quiet. This is a very crucial moment, for we still have the opportunity to reorganize ourselves and renew our strength. Also, we should realise that if we persist, unyielding, faced also with the pressure of world-wide commentary, even this foolish government will be forced to compromise. The contraction of foreign investment and the public's withdrawal of bank deposits, are aspects of an economic ultimatum that will directly influence government interests and make them reconsider. We must not relax!

Basically, our goal is to promote the process of democratization in China, and to lead her onto the road of prosperity. Specific demands which will realise this main purpose are seen in the call for a free press and the punishment of corrupt officials. As the movement develops, specific demands will change continuously as well. For example, we began with a request for an audience with the government; and then demands for the resignation of Li Peng, the recall of the National People's Congress

(NPC) and the termination of martial law took predominance. Through it all, however, we must not lose sight of the chief task, whatever might have been achieved. And what have we achieved? Apart from awakening the masses, not much; which is one good reason for keeping going!

Having clearly defined our general goal, it becomes more possible and appropriate to talk about the immediate tasks of our Movement. What we most urgently need to do is form a better organization, with ASUBU taking the lead and presenting itself as a model. At the same time, the following concrete measures should be given due attention by the Movement's organizers:

1) Launch an information programme to combat government propaganda.
2) Try to help the workers who have been arrested.
3) Improve discipline in the Square.
4) Begin preparations for the NPC, including meetings with members of the NPC, and drafting a general report on the Movement. We must not place much hope in the NPC, but it will be an opportunity to renew the strength of our struggle.

It is most important also to realise that we have two kinds of tactical actions to follow. One is active, with planning, preparation and execution. The other is passive, which involves taking advantage of events over which we have no control; for example, announcing support of a hunger strike by intellectuals, or using the government's attempt to manipulate the workers into an anti-student movement as an opportunity for renewed struggle.

Now there is a question to be answered: Is ASUBU the leader of the Universities in Beijing or of the whole nation? For now, its duties centre on Beijing. However, in terms of direction and spirit, it bears the responsibility of directing the Movement of the whole nation, and is waiting for the right time to set up an Autonomous Students' Union of China to take over its duties. What we can be sure of at this moment is that the ASUBU should have the whole nation in mind and should not adopt any policies based on localism and parochialism.

For the Movement to have reached its present state, we have already paid a painful price, and yet the fruits are few. To make our past tears and sweat worthwhile and to save China from the black hand of a few schemers, to live up to our conscience and to history, we should persevere, persevere until a new dawn arrives.

June 1, 1989

XII: Su Shaozhi,[20] The Origin and Results of China's 1989 Democracy Movement

"Truth will inevitably defeat sheer power. Righteousness will eventually eradicate evil." This is the opening sentence of an essay that I wrote in 1988 in memory of Bukharin's execution fifty years earlier.

Today the USSR has rehabilitated the victims of the Great Terror of the thirties; Hungary has done the same with Imre Nagy, the victim of events there in 1956; and in Poland Solidarity has been made legal, with its members being elected to the national assembly. While these socialist countries advanced gradually along the road of democracy, humanism and rationalism, the sound of gunfire and the rumble of tanks were the harsh sounds echoing through Beijing on the night of June 3-4, 1989. The so-called People's Liberation Army suppressed the students' and citizens' peaceful Democracy Movement with armed force, with a massacre followed by mass arrests and executions, producing shocked criticism around the world.

Characteristics

The 1989 Democracy Movement was a dynamic and peaceful mass movement unprecedented in Chinese history; and its repression by the *people's* government and the *people's* army was just as unique.

Today the world is so integrated by systems of mass communication that it is impossible to isolate people from the news. Consequently, falsehoods and lies are increasingly fabricated to create doubts concerning the deaths in Tiananmen Square. The number of deaths is, of course, important; but even more important is the fact that the government and PLA fired on their own people. Deng Xiaoping said on June 9th that, "If tanks have rolled through the

Square, then the difference between right and wrong is confused in this country." The fact remains, however, that guns and tanks were to be found in the square, and their presence declared the government's loss of legitimacy.

Debate is no longer necessary, and we must now make an objective analysis of the Democracy Movement and its military repression. Its main characteristics were:

1) *Endurance.* During the fifty day period between Hu's death on April 15th to the armed repression of June 3rd-4th, in spite of ups and downs, the scope of the Movement never decreased.

2) *Massive size.* Initiated by the Beijing students as a Student Movement, people joined from all strata of society, developing it into a massive, peaceful Democracy Movement. From Beijing it spread to universities in other cities (e.g., Guangzhou, Shanghai, Xian); from the universities to the larger intellectual community (educational, technological-scientific, literary and journalistic circles); and from there to the whole society, involving mass organizations like the Student Federation, the National Women's Federation, the democratic factions, even the Central Party School and segments of the party hierarchy. The street demonstrations that were first organised by the student organizations, were supported by the citizens, and later joined by the citizens. Marches involved hundreds of thousands, even millions, of people. When the PLA first began to move into the city, they were blocked by those same citizens, including old people, women and children. Their spontaneous actions could not have been instigated by a "handful" of conspirators.

3) *Spontaneity.* Initially a spontaneous outburst, organizations gradually began to emerge, but too late to be effective. The government repeatedly asserted that it was an organised conspiracy; but the facts indicate that it was spontaneous and gradual development of an organization similar to Poland's Solidarity — embryonic in the examples of the Autonomous Students' Union of Beijing Universities, the Autonomous Students' Union of Foreign Universities, the Beijing Workers' Autonomous Federation, and the Autonomous Union of Beijing Intellectuals. Their formation alerted the authorities, who immediately declared them to be illegal. They were largely ineffective because they were organised too late, developed little strategy and tactics, and were often torn apart by internal disagreements.

4) *Non-violent.* Both students and citizens embraced peaceful means, with the students advising the citizens against destructive activities. For example, on May 23rd, when three people defaced Mao Zedong's portrait in Tiananmen Square, they were immediately taken to the police by the students. In early June, when there were clashes between citizens and soldiers, students protected the soldiers. There was an improved civility between citizens and students, as the overseas edition of the *People's Daily* indicated on May 23rd, in an article entitled "The current civic mentality of the Beijing people." Instead of taking advantage of this situation the government labelled the Movement "an organised conspiracy, a riot," in the April 26th editorial, initiating political pressures that eventually led to armed suppression. Bloodshed being the last resort of politicians, when the government resorted to violence it was demonstrating its frailty.

5) *Inner-party conflict.* In dealing with the Democracy Movement the highest levels of the party and government have been involved in a power struggle, and this immensely complicates the analysis. Ultimate decision-making power undoubtedly lies with Deng, who favoured economic reform, but is conservative in politics and ideology. Therefore, he must confront and make compromises with both reformers and hard-liners. Hard-liners used the Movement to put pressure on Deng, and reformers tried to use it to protect themselves. Faced with this conflict, the government was unable to work out a strategy, which is one of the reasons that the 1989 Movement was able to last so long in spite of its ups and downs. Since Deng labelled the Movement a "riot" from the very start, he had to compromise with the hard-liners, and move towards the use of force. Both the students and Deng became victims of forces beyond their control. Deng's image as a reformer, which had led former Chancellor Schmidt of West Germany to call him one of the greatest contemporary politicians, disappeared in an instant, as have his reforms.

6) *Military presence.* The government moved some 200,000 troops to Beijing, even whilst declaring that the troops were not meant for use against the students. It was not necessary to use soldiers and tanks against the unarmed and peaceful masses; and is linked rather to the power struggle in the party — establishing the unfortunate precedent of using the army to resolve such conflicts.

Because of these six features, in spite of opportunities for mitigating the situation, neither side behaved rationally, and compromise was impossible. However, the authorities were primarily responsible by declaring the Student Movement to be an organised conspiracy, a riot that had to be put down by military force, intimidating the masses by insisting upon the need to eradicate "liberalism",— and thereby making bloodshed and a national disaster inevitable.

The past is the teacher of the future. We must, therefore, remember these events and seek out a theoretical explanation.

Origins

Although initiated by the Student Movement, triggered by the event of Hu's death, the 1989 Democracy Movement has its origins further in the past.

Since it was established in 1949 the People's Republic of China has undeniably had many achievements; but numerous problems have also emerged. Movements and policies initiated by the party and government devastated the economy and produced popular dissatisfaction. These mistakes were not investigated or corrected until the extremes of the Cultural Revolution utterly destroyed the people's confidence and led them to press for democracy and reform. Since the Third Plenum of the Eleventh Central Committee of the CCP, ideological liberalization, an open door policy, and reforms have been widely advocated, and China has thereby had an opportunity to strengthen herself. However, because of the limitations of the old ideology and organization, they developed in a distorted manner. Nonetheless, changes were in the air and the demand for democracy could not be thwarted.

Deng Xiaoping understands this. In his June 9th speech he said, "International and domestic circumstances made this storm inevitable, independent of any human will." A proper analysis of the situation, and correct policies, could have produced a favorable conclusion. Unfortunately, an erroneous path was taken.

When considering the international situation we must take into account the whirlwind of events raised by the USSR and the East European countries, including the development of pluralism in a one-party system in the USSR and Hungary, the victory of Solidarity in the Polish elections, and the power demonstrated by the people in Asian countries like the Philippines, South Korea and Pakistan.

When considering the domestic situation in China herself, the important factors are as follows:

1) *The economic background.* Reforms moved away from the single unified system of nationalization and collectivization towards the creation of various modes of ownership. We now also have joint-stock enterprises (of Chinese and foreign firms), a private sector based on household enterprises, and cooperatives operating according to the [profit-based] "responsibility system." This has produced various interest groups in society in addition to the workers, peasants and intellectuals. Demands for political pluralism inevitably follow, as people want delegates in the National People's Congress who will represent their interests. Conceding to this demand is the first step towards democracy.

At the same time, the market economy produced demands for the elimination of monopolies and economic privileges, which were also expressed in a demand for democracy as the vehicle to this end. A new middle class is, therefore, the basis of the new Democracy Movement — the weakness of which is due to the fact that this class is not yet fully formed.[21] Nevertheless, economic reform will lead inevitably to political reform.

2) *Ideological developments.* Since 1987 the doctrinal monopoly of Marxism has been broken, and people are beginning to re-evaluate socialism and communism from the perspective of western ideas that are an inevitable product of the open door policy. The appearance of ideological pluralism has, however, led to a toughening of resistance to it. So, in 1981 we see the official criticism of the film, *Bitter Love;* in 1983 there was the "anti-spiritual pollution campaign;" and in 1987 the "anti-bourgeois liberalization" campaign. However, after each repression and brief period of silence, there was a reaction; and the 1989 Democracy Movement has emerged with tremendous force.

3) *Corruption.* Because of a failure to reform the political system, the ruling group has been able to use its privileges to make money, resulting in a concentration of power and wealth. Official profiteering, corruption and decadence increasingly characterise the CCP, government, and PLA organizations. As people's lives are made more difficult by inflation, so is this inequality felt more keenly by the people. Moreover, the development of unemployment, and the associated social contradictions, leads to a loss of confidence in the party and government and a desire to change the *status quo.* The immediate cause of the present political crisis was the students' strong

sense of corruption in the government, which was then supported by the masses, as it developed into a demand for democracy.

Economic, ideological and social forces all made the demand for democracy inevitable in the Chinese domestic situation.

Now the CCP is Marxist, and therefore supposedly concerned with the liberation of the individual. China is known as a *people's re-public*, and its Constitution and government are said to be dedicated to the service of the people — granting freedom of speech and assembly. The students and the masses believed this, up to the point that they were so bloodily repressed. How could an act which so contradicts the principles of the legal system occur?

1) China's system is a mixture of Stalinism and feudal despotism. One of its characteristics is the unity of party-government-economy-military-culture-ideology into an indivisible hierarchy. This includes not only political machinery, but factories, schools, and all social organizations. Every government employee is absolutely subordinate to his/her superiors, not to the masses, at the peak of which pyramid is a single person around whom there must develop a personality cult. His power decides everything, without room for different opinions. Collegial leadership is a myth, not to mention democracy and legalism. Such a leadership cannot tolerate demonstrations and Movements of democracy and the citizens. Such a political system inevitably produces a powerful bureaucracy which, after forty years, cannot be easily overturned. The bureaucrats will oppose any measures that threaten them, justifying themselves with a Stalinist ideology.

2) Under this political system, economic reforms and the open door policy did bring economic improvements; but those with special privileges in the government distort those reforms, taking advantage of their power, and resisting political change — "economically anti-left, politically anti-right." It is worth noting that the privileged children of officials, who opposed the 1983 and 1987 campaigns, supported the hard-line policies of their parents in 1989.

3) Internal struggles at the highest levels of the CCP played a part in the political response to the Democracy Movement. The struggle between hardliners and moderates was resolved by the victory of the former, who regarded any compromise as a sign of weakness.

So, from the political perspective also the repression of the 1989 Democracy Movement was inevitable. That it was so bloody can be ascribed to tactical errors on both sides, the impotence of Li Peng's government, and the power struggle within the party.

Consequences

In history a similar situation to that which developed in China in the summer of 1989 is the Hungarian Revolution of 1956. Matyas Rakosi's government was bureaucratic and despotic, opposing the masses until the latter rose up against the small ruling group. Russian tanks suppressed that rebellion. The difference between the two situations is that in Hungary the main force was the working class, and the oppressors were foreign soldiers. At the time Mao Zedong stated that "part of the [Hungarian] masses had been deceived by counter-revolutionary forces inside and outside the country." Thirty years later we see the rehabilitation of the Hungarian uprising, the rehabilitation of the executed leader, Imre Nagy, who is now called a "martyr for democracy and a national hero." In this example we see that truth will be victorious.

Military force has temporarily crushed the 1989 Movement. Yet it stimulated the political awakening and democratic thoughts of every Chinese, making us aware that we can no longer remain in the worsening circumstances of totalitarian government. Spreading like wildfire, this underground ideology is sowing the seeds of an even greater future Movement. The bloodshed also destroyed the authority of the CCP, of the government, of Marxist socialism, all of which have lost their future credibility.

In the short term:

1) Suppression, arrests and executions lead to a loss of popular support; while all the propaganda justifying it leads to popular alienation. Apathy and non-cooperation surface, and confidence in the authorities can not be renewed.

2) The victory of the hardliners produces an economic re-centralization, taking the country backwards ten to twenty years, reintroducing methods that have already proven themselves to be bankrupt.

3) The 1989 Movement demonstrated the necessity of punishing corruption severely. This is a positive consequence. In July, 1989, the Politburo announced the need to further de-Stalinize and pro-

hibit the children of officials entering commercial ventures. Whether this can be implemented, however, is doubtful.

4) Suffering from inflation, a decline in foreign tourism and foreign loans consequent upon the repression, agricultural shortages and production slowdown, all indicate an intensification of the economic crisis in China.

5) Economic crisis will intensify the power struggle within the party, starting with a new round of struggles between Deng and the economic hardliners. Once Deng dies this struggle will be intensified.

6) Military suppression cannot but influence the policy of "one country, two systems," referring to the Sino-British agreement whereby the administration of Hong Kong will be turned over to the PRC in 1997. The agreement cannot be cancelled, but the middle and upper classes will drain the colony of capital, jeopardizing future prosperity. The possibility for a future agreement with Taiwan has been reduced to a minimum.

As for the long run implications, the very existence of Marxist theory and practice in the PRC is threatened. The official leadership has failed to solve the main problems facing the PRC, and obviously distorts reality with inappropriate concepts. Unable to break with a disreputable past, they are incapable of analyzing the problems with which they are now faced. They called the Movement a counterrevolutionary riot, which is obviously mistaken.

Meanwhile, the masses and the healthy elements in the CCP are helpless, for China lacks the fundamental prerequisite for productive analysis — which is free and independent exploration by means of various complicated theories, which in their scientific independence need not bow to the official ideology. By contrast, to have no frank opinion, to be dominated by the official media, to have ideological leaders interfering constantly, to be permitted only to praise those leaders, whilst severely punishing dissidents — such is the present situation.

The 1989 Democracy Movement and its suppression is a world-historical event. If China is to develop towards democracy, then she must modernize by reform and openness. It is, therefore, essential that the Movement be properly understood by the CCP, the Chinese masses, Marxists, socialists, and all progressive people who seek democracy and justice.

[undated]

NOTES

1. Born in 1965, Wang Dan was a first year History student at Beijing University. A high profile figure in Tiananmen Square during the April-June events of 1989, he was top of the post-massacre wanted list put out by the government, and was arrested in Beijing in July, 1989, having failed to escape the country.

2. Wang is referring to the denunciation of Stalin and Stalinism at the 20th Congress of the Communist Party of the Soviet Union (CPSU) in 1956.

3. The Polish "event" refers to the necessity of the Soviet leadership accepting Gomulka as Polish leader in 1956. The Hungarian "event" is the Nagy regime in Hungary prior to its repression by Soviet tanks in 1956.

4. There is an important distinction between "private property" and "personal property" for anyone living in a socialist State. The former is bourgeois property, which can be used to employ the labour of others for the generation of a surplus; it is the fields, the factories, the workshops. Personal property is, by contrast, that which is possessed as a result of one's own non-exploitative work, be it a bicycle, an automobile, or a house.

5. Born in 1945, Ren Wanding is a graduate of the Beijing Agricultural and Engineering College. Imprisoned for four years (1979-1983) for his participation in the Democracy Wall Movement, he was working for the Beijing Equipment and Fixture Company when this pamphlet was written. Following the massacre of June 3-4 he was arrested.

6. The reader should note that Article 51 of the 1982 Chinese Constitution states, "The exercise by citizens of the People's Republic of China of their freedoms and rights may not infringe upon the interests of the state..."

7. These principles were first formulated in a speech by Deng Xiaoping at a party conference on theoretical work on March 30, 1979. The speech defined the four limits of opposition in the statement, "Activities against socialism, against proletarian dictatorship, against the leadership of the Party, against Marxism-Leninism and the Thought of

Mao Zedong...are prohibited according to the law and will be prosecuted."

8. The full title of this statement is, "The Historical Functions and Objective Goals of the People's Democracy Movement — Edited Speeches delivered at Five Institutions of Higher Education in Beijing, April 27-May 4, 1989."

9. Totally under the control of the CCP there are eight "democratic parties" in China, which are expected to promote official policy in society and through public statements in the Chinese People's Political Consultative Conference, which is convened simultaneously with the NPC. The parties are i) the Revolutionary Committee of the Guomindang (i.e., Nationalist Party), ii) the Democratic League, iii) the Democratic Construction Society, iv) the Promotion of Democracy Society, v) the Democratic Party of Workers and Peasants, vi) The Zigong Party, vii) the September 3rd Society, and viii) the League for Democratic Self-Government of Taiwan.

10. The "October Incident" was the arrest of the Maoist "Gang of Four," and the beginning of Deng Xiaoping's domination of the body politic and introduction of economic reforms.

11. Written by a "Ph.D. candidate at the Chinese People's University," and dated May 1, 1989, the complete title of this piece ends with, "a comparative analysis that the authorities try desperately to avoid."

12. Produced by an anonymous author from Beijing Normal University.

13. We should remember here that during the previous ten years economic reforms had permitted a significant private sector to develop within the Chinese system of state socialism.

14. The name is probably a pseudonym. At the beginning of the document was the statement, "The author is a student in the Chinese Department, lacking in theoretical sophistication, and would be grateful to hear the views of others in response to his own."

15. This piece appeared on the Beijing University campus, May 17, 1989.

16. A student, writing before the massacre.

17. Ma, aged 25 at the time of the May 13th-20th hunger strike, had left school eight years earlier. He had followed various professions, including those of editor, free-lance writer, reporter, employee in a cultural bureau, and accountant. In 1986 he had been admitted to the Beijing Cinema College, taking the Literature Editing programme.

18. Prominent figure in the Student Movement.

19. This is an interesting play upon an old theme. Mao Zedong had said that the revolutionary guerrilla fighters are fish, and the people are the water in which they swim, and which they need to survive. Now, the people are seen as the fish, but the communist party is presented as a net restraining and destroying them.

20. Former director of the Institute of Marxism-Leninism-Mao Zedong Thought of the Chinese Academy of Social Sciences, dismissed during the "anti-bourgeois liberalization" campaign of 1987, and today a political exile in the U.S.A.

21. In an otherwise coherent analysis of the economic variables involved in the 1989 events, this view, that the Movement was linked with an emerging bourgeoisie, is unpersuasive. The reader will note that students and workers were the core of the Movement, and the documents in this volume are representative of that fact. Furthermore, the demands are most obviously egalitarian and communitarian. Analytical speculations of the kind that Su Shaozhi gives here, unwarranted by any facts, are the sort of thing that made Wuer Kaixi, a leading spokesman of the students, reject the intellectuals (see Section Four of this volume). Such views also imply that revolutions in "socialist States" have a single option, which is capitalism — a denial of alternatives which strips the Movement of its entire radical character.

CHINESE SOCIETY OPPOSES THE STATE
Pamphlets and Wall Posters [1]

STUDENT COMMENT

XIII: *The Shortcomings of the Stalinist Political System*

The fundamental shortcoming of all socialist countries is a political system that replaces the people with bureaucrats as the masters of society. The leader enjoys life-long tenure of office with enough power even to appoint his own successor. Such a practice runs counter to the principles of a republic, and carries rather the characteristics of a monarchical autocracy. That is why socialist countries are republics in name only, and monarchies in reality. China is no exception. Our socialism has been a feudalistic socialism, which is the socialism of the Stalinist Model. Stalin was a typical tyrant whose regime was a proletarian or socialist monarchy; and that of Mao Zedong was of the same kind.

The shortcomings of this political structure are,

1) concentration of the power of the leadership,
2) life-long tenure of office,
3) leadership choice of the successor,
4) the unity of party and government, and
5) high-ranking cadres are concerned only with gaining privileges.

With this in mind, I think that our most immediate task is to carry through a political reform with speed and determination.

April 25, 1989

XIV: An Outline of the Communist Party

The party leader: The party chief, lionized, and treated like a god in a movement tied to traditional Chinese culture, is alienated from the people. Egocentricity and the autocracy in turn make him into a dictator.

The party cadres: Humble servants of the patriarchal party chief and the arrogant *nouveaux riches*. They demand the subservience of the people, abuse their privileges and power for personal gain, and corrupt the legal system.

The party organization: A hierarchy of gangsters, riddled with factional struggles, whilst eradicating any non-party opposition.

The quality of the party: 75% of this 47,000,000-strong "vanguard" have received only a primary school education.

Party membership: A pragmatic act for the acquisition of a party card. Presenting the image of progressiveness, but being the means of extortion for personal gain, party membership creates a bunch of schizophrenic hypocrites, whatever their original characters. This seriously influences the consciousness of the people, inhibiting their development.

The behaviour of the party: Irrefutable sacred order and empty dogmas allow the leader to initiate "cultural revolutions" and "rectification campaigns" that threaten the survival of the nation, whilst causing widespread suffering and death. Under cover of these orders and dogmas, the cadres deceive the people, making dirty deals in the shadow of their sacred banner.

The Party's Four Modernizations:

1) idolization of the party's image,
2) unending justification of the party's role,
3) intensification of its power and privileges, and
4) the corruption of the party cadres.

The CCP: Omnipotent Leviathan, God Almighty, to whom the people must bow. The party leader gives orders to start the machine, the cadres and party members[2] act as cogs. So many of the best of our race have been strangled by this machine.

The greatness of the party: "She can correct her mistakes."

Blood might cleanse the shame of the autocracy, and breed a generation of genuine communists; but it can also be the breeding ground for a new sect of the rich and the powerful, as well as a new dictator.

[undated]

XV: Who Causes the Turmoil?

The great Student Movement has been called a "turmoil" deliberately manufactured by the students. However, any thinking person can see that this is an attempt at distortion and deception. Who does not know that the corrupt and incompetent government is the creator of the widespread, patriotic "turmoil"?

A peaceful Movement which organises a petition is no bad thing for an enlightened government. From the very start, however, the government adopted an indifferent attitude to the students, responding only after it became too large to ignore. And their response was to use their control of the media to point an accusing finger and shout, "Turmoil." Thus did turmoil begin.

We were all small children during the Great Cultural Revolution, and we do not know much about it. The voices of officialdom remember it, however, and use the language of that time. They speak of "a small minority," with "ulterior motives," in "a conspiracy long concocted." It sounds so frightening, and so silly, as they try to take China back to the days of the Cultural Revolution. Let us, the students and masses, respond by accusing *them* of being the real "small minority, with ulterior motives," and tell them that we will not allow *their* "long-concocted conspiracy" to succeed!

It is true that stability and solidarity are conducive to development. However, remember that a docile population provides huge opportunities for those who would exploit the masses. Therefore, we must not continue to be passive. We must eliminate the termites of reforms and the parasites of development. Only then will China be able to develop in healthy stability and solidarity.

Of course, a country's leaders cannot be ever available "on demand." However, could they please let us know under what circumstances they will meet with the people. More than one hundred thousand are asking for a meeting with the leaders on matters of life and death for the nation. Is that not enough?

China's democratization must proceed. History has seen nothing like what is happening today, and as history the experience is important. All righteous compatriots, including open-minded officials in high positions, think seriously about it with us!

April 28, 1989

XVI: *Talking with Two Workers*[3]

I did not have much understanding of the Student Movement, and did not join in the demonstrations of April 20th and April 22nd. What has happened since then, however, has left me very disturbed, and I have decided to join the organization of patriotic students and be more than a spectator of revolution.

I was one of the participants in the demonstration of April 27th, the character of which requires no further description. Here I would like to describe a conversation that I had with two workers at noon today, showing thereby the views and hopes of the citizens in relation to our movement.

The two workers were from different enterprises, and both were university graduates. One of them had resigned from his government position and had opened two cafes. The other was a worker in a research unit. Our main topic of discussion is summarised in the following statement by the latter: "The Student Movement has gained the support of the citizens and the workers." To prove this he told me how the workers of his unit responded to the editorial in the *People's Daily*. The workers asked a lot of awkward questions, and complained about unequal rewards, long working hours, poor social welfare, and lack of protection of workers' right to an education, etc. A low ranking party official, listening to them, replied sarcastically that everyone has problems.

One of the workers told me that he went to the meat store to buy some ribs, and was told, "the ribs are reserved for the university students." The customers supported this. He also said that if students went to enterprises for donations, they would get anything they needed. The workers are waiting for our requests.

Fellow students, your actions are recognised by society, people support you and want you to carry on. The government has already lost the support of the people. If the students lose a single drop of blood in the fight, the workers in the city will unite in a protest strike against the government.

Finally, the workers repeatedly asked me to pass on the good will of the workers to the active students. They want to hear more of our theories, and to be made aware of the government's deviousness.

When we said goodbye they made the "V" sign, and also clenched their fists and shouted, "The people appreciate you, and history will remember you. Struggle on obstinately. Victory belongs to you and to the people."

April 29, 1989

XVII: A Short Commentary on the Slogan, "Down with the Communist Party" [4]

The state radio has been saying that the slogan, "Down with the Communist Party," was heard during the April 20th demonstration.

If it were shouted, and by whom, is not my concern here. What does the slogan itself reflect? That is more to the point.

When Sun Yatsen founded the Nationalist Party [Guomintang] at the time of the national revolution [1911], that party was undoubtedly the vanguard of its time and, therefore, well received by the people. Even founder members of the CCP, like Li Dazhou, Mao Zedong and Zhou Enlai, were members of the Nationalist Party for a time. The slogan, "Down with the Nationalist Party," was surely counter-revolutionary then. With the passing of time, however, and the degeneration of the Nationalist Party, things changed. During the Great Revolutionary and Anti-Japanese War [1936-1945] and the Liberation War [1945-1949] period, the Nationalist Party was opposed to the historical trend. It wanted a one-party, one-man dictatorship in China. The people responded with the slogan, "Down with the Nationalist reactionaries" and, "Overthrow the feudalistic regime of Chiang Kaishek." Such slogans were undoubtedly the general will of the progressive forces and historically correct.

The process through which the Nationalist Party moved from a progressive to a reactionary position illustrates a general Marxist truth: when a party (or its leaders) cease to represent the people as a whole, it will be forsaken by history.

In the late eighties of the twentieth century the People's Republic of China is in its middle years. We are confused when we awake to find ourselves a member of the international community, and ask, "What has the CCP achieved during the past forty years?" Living standards have certainly improved, but there is reason for concern. Information in student pamphlets, and the violent response of the government, must lead us to the conclusion that we are building on foundations of sand.

What does the slogan, "Down with the CCP," imply?

If the CCP still represents the people, let me suggest the following:

1) If the slogan was shouted ask, "By whom?"
2) If it was shouted by the "enemy," ignore it. Our one billion people will scotch the rumour, no matter how vicious it is.
3) If it is the people who are shouting, we should take it as an alarm signal.
4) Fear is a sign of a lack of courage, which produces a lack of confidence.

I believe in the communist blueprint outlined by Marx. I will firmly support a CCP that represents the interests of the people.

April 30, 1989

XVIII: *The Ten Differences Between the Patriotic Movement and the Cultural Revolution*[5]

	THE PRESENT MOVEMENT	THE CULTURAL REVOLUTION
Nature	Opposed to remnants of feudalism, anti-bureaucratic; for science, democracy and freedom.	Strengthened the personality cult and placed one billion people in intellectual bondage.
Basic Character	Awakening the people.	Serious turmoil.
Goal	To quicken the pace for democratic form.	To protect the bureaucracy and the party.
Results	Ideas of democracy have been embedded in the minds of the people. Support for reform.	No progressive results. Major historical retrogression.
Initiation	Spontaneous organization of students.	Chairman Mao alone.
Methods	Non-violent petitions, constitutional.	Violence, arson, robbery and lawlessness.
Means	Strikes, demonstrations and requests for dialogue.	The more confusion the better, the whole country paralysed.
Attitude towards CCP	Supporting correct leadership and opposing corruption therein.	Making revolution by destroying party committees, autocratic rule by the head of a sect.
Response of the masses	Respect for the masses produces widespread support and sympathy.	The hoodwinked masses groan.
Its place in history	Of equal importance to May Fourth Movement.	Eternally despised!

April 30, 1989

XIX: *The Patriotic-Democratic Movement Compared with the Turmoil of the Cultural Revolution*[6]

The *People's Daily* editorial of April 26, 1989, described the current Democratic-Patriotic Movement as an anti-party cause of turmoil. It attempted to liken it to the turmoil experienced during the decade of the Cultural Revolution. Moreover, when students and government officials met on April 29th, Yuan Mu stated that the two were similar. From the perspective of this writer, however, there are great differences, as the present analysis will show to the reader.

Considering the background of the two disruptions:

1) The ten years of turmoil were initiated, wrongly, by a faction of the party to promote its interest in factional struggles by upholding the personality cult. The present Movement is the consummation of the whole complex of social contradictions. It is the spontaneous product of a society in a state of crisis, and has the purpose of accelerating the democratization of China, promoting political reform, fighting official corruption, and eliminating decadence, so that intellectuals, workers and peasants can benefit from reforms in a richer and stronger nation. Nobody with "ulterior motives" is making use of the movement!

2) The Cultural Revolution remained under the influence of the personality cult, with the main force of the rebellion, the masses and the Red Guards, ignorant and easily misled. This made its manipulation inevitable. The current Movement, on the other hand, came into being after China had experienced ten years of reform. The mass of young students and intellectuals have studied and learned from western liberal-democratic ideas, have made a special analysis of the Chinese situation, and have suggested a series of political and economic reforms. Formulating ideas on democracy and freedom, intellectuals, students, workers and ordinary citizens from the different economic strata, have clearly organised their thoughts in order to fight for democracy, freedom, prosperity and the future strength of China. They are certainly not used by anyone with "ulterior motives." They have brains, and their IQs are certainly no lower than those of the bureaucrats!

3) During the ten years of turmoil sects and factions flourished. The present Movement, however, goes to the people not to form factions but to arouse them as a whole, and to enlighten them with democratic ideas for the early implementation of a democratic system. One must go to the people to achieve the realization of freedom of speech.

Concerning contradictions in the CCP, we may also note:

4) During the Cultural Revolution some people made revolution simply to get rid of the local party committee and satisfy their own greed for power in their schools, departments, factories, mines, etc. The present Movement, however, stands for the correct leadership of the CCP. We are demanding that the party not abuse its power in society, and desist from intervention in normal administrative matters. We are definitely not opposed to the proper leadership of the CCP, and are trying to promote that through a separation of party and government. Those who attack us for being anti-party have ulterior motives. We must not permit anyone, using the excuse of the Four Cardinal Principles, to muddy the issue.

Concerning the consequences of the two situations:

5) The ten years of turmoil brought great disasters to the nation, involving the persecution of intellectuals, damage to democracy and the legal system, taking the economy to the verge of collapse, and disrupting the education system. The present Democratic-Patriotic Movement will lead eventually to the strengthening of the democratic system and rule of law. The masses will have greater democracy and freedom. Government officials will be honest. Education will benefit. The Chinese nation will prosper!

In sum, and taking into consideration the participants in the two movements, the present one differs greatly from the ten years of turmoil. One hopes that people can see the difference between right and wrong. We must not let government officials make false linkages and accusations, and destroy the solidarity of the students, intellectuals, workers and peasants. We must not allow the government bureaucrats to use this pretext to suppress the students' Democratic-Patriotic Movement. We must unite and fight for our common democratic goals!

May 3, 1989

XX: For the Democracy Fighters [7]

Nearly three years ago I experienced the end of the Shanghai Movement with a sense of hopelessness. However, as a person with that experience, and as a sympathizer, there is much that I can say to you.

This movement surpasses the earlier one in both its size and the range of its activities. However, the response of the authorities is exactly the same. One cannot help thinking that the end will be the same.

In Shanghai the students first marched, then organised a sit-in strike. The authorities resorted to the guerrilla tactic of "hitting when the enemy is tired," using the military and police to disperse the students when they were at their weakest. The basic move of the authorities is the human wall tactic, sending a mass of soldiers and police to confront the students face to face. How could under-nourished students compete? So, regretfully, they had to back down, and the armed forces were victorious. Then, as now, we thought that we held an advantage; but look what happened.

In 1986 in Shanghai, after a week of marches, demonstrations and sit-ins, we began a general strike in the institutions of higher education on December 24th. We held theoretical discussions, seeking to give direction to the movement. We were optimistic. On the evening of December 31st, at an open forum at the university, the mood was jubilant and victory was proclaimed. Nobody anticipated that on the following morning, the first document of the new year totally reversed the situation. Serious matters became small matters, which then became irrelevant. That is the entire story. The revolution was aborted.

Here in Beijing the participants in the current Movement realise the need for theoretical direction. A leadership has been organised, think-tanks are in operation. I am encouraged by this, and hope that the lessons of 1986 will enable us to formulate a victorious policy for the Democracy Movement. In so doing, I recommend the following:

The success or failure of the Movement will hinge on a resolute leadership and the willingness of some members of the Movement to sacrifice themselves. Students have mixed feelings. Some see the Movement as the opportunity of a lifetime; and to be involved is, of course, more exciting than the boredom of lectures and academic work. Others regard the struggle for democracy as a holy task. Yet, compared with the May Fourth Movement our modern activists are faced with many more difficulties. Success or failure, as in 1986, will depend upon a willingness to face the authorities, "not shying away from bloody incidents." That should be our greatest concern.

[undated]

XXI: *Statement of the May 13th Hunger Strikers*

We commence our hunger strike in the lovely May sunshine. In the full bloom of youth, however, we leave beautiful things behind, but with great reluctance.

Yet the condition of our country is one of rampant inflation, economic speculation by officials, extreme authoritarian rule, serious bureaucratic corruption, a drain of products and people to other countries, social confusion and an increase in the number of criminal acts. It is a crucial moment for the country and its people. All compatriots with a conscience, please heed our call:

The country is our country.
The people are our people.
The government is our government.
If we do not cry out, who will?
If we do not take action, who will?

Our bodies are still tender and not full grown, and the prospect of dying frightens us all; but history calls us and we must go.

Our purest and patriotic love, and our most generous sentiments, have been called a "turmoil" with "ulterior motives," which is "manipulated by a handful of people."

We ask every Chinese citizen with a sense of justice, every worker, peasant, soldier, intellectual, celebrity, government official, policeman and even our accusers, to look into their hearts and ask what crime has been committed. Is it a "rebellion" to strike, to demonstrate, and to go on a hunger strike? Why must we hide ourselves away? Our feelings have been treated too lightly. We live in miserable conditions as we search for truth, and then are beaten up by the police. Student representatives kneel to request democracy, and are ignored. Our request for an equal dialogue is repeatedly ignored, and the student leaders are put in a very dangerous position.

What shall we do?

Democracy is a desire intrinsic to the human condition. Freedom is an inherent human right. We now must sacrifice our lives for them. Is this something that the Chinese race should be proud of?

The hunger strike was forced upon us as a last resort. We face death resolutely, although we are fighting for life. We are still very young. China, our mother! Look closely at your sons and daughters. Hunger is ravaging their youth and death is near. Can you stand unmoved?

We do not want to die. We have a passionate desire to live on in the prime of our lives. We want to live and to learn. Our motherland is poor, and we do not want to leave her so. No, we are not seeking death; but if death could lead to improved conditions and prosperity for our country, then we ought not shun it.

Though we are starving, dear parents, do not despair. When we bid farewell to life, dear uncles and aunts, do not be unhappy. We hope only that you will live better. Remember always that we were not looking for death, and that democracy is not the product of a few, nor the accomplishment of a single generation.

Death awaits. Farewell. To our colleagues who share our loyalties. To our loved ones, whom we would rather not leave, but whom we must. To our mothers and fathers, for whom we cannot be both patriotic and filial at the same time. To the people of our country, from whom we ask permission to pursue this final act of loyalty.

We make a commitment with our lives, to make the sky of the republic clear and bright.

Reasons for the Hunger Strike:

First, to protest against the casual attitude of the government towards the demonstration of the Beijing students. Second, to protest the government's continued refusal to engage in a dialogue with the representatives of Beijing's institutions of higher education. Third, to protest against the government's condemnation of the patriotic movement as "turmoil," and the distortions of the media.

Demands of the Hunger Strikers:

First, that the government quickly enter into equal, concrete discussion with the Dialogue Group of the Beijing institutions of higher education. Second, that the government retract its statements concerning the nature of the Student Movement, and evaluate it fairly and honestly as a patriotic and democratic Movement.

May 13, 1989

XXII: A Declaration of Emergency to all the People of the Country from the People of the Capital

The capital is in danger! China is in danger! The nation is in danger! The People's Republic is in fatal danger.

Faced with the recent struggle for democracy by thousands of patriotic students and citizens, the ruling group destabilized the situation by declaring martial law, and defining the widely supported and great Patriotic Movement as "turmoil." This is an outright denial of the republic's Constitution. They go totally against the people, becoming their oppressors, and are therefore traitors and enemies of the republic. They cannot be representing the party and the country.

Now is the darkest, bloodiest, most inhuman and disappointing moment of the republic's history. The republic faces a most difficult task as a "Tiananmen Incident" again occurs. The situation becomes totalitarian, cruel, dictatorial and bloody.

In this serious situation, we call upon the several hundred thousand students, and ten million citizens, are urgently called upon to make a general strike. Vast quantities of propaganda are also directed at the People's Liberation Army, asking them to stand alongside the people, and refuse to become the weapons of a bloody crackdown by the governing group.

That group is prepared to kill. In this emergency they have openly trampled on the Constitution, openly become an enemy of the republic, and openly betrayed their responsibilities as members of the Standing Committee of the National People's Congress. Therefore, we must struggle to enforce the collective resignation of the ruling group. They must openly confess their crimes, and their political actions must be investigated. This is the only acceptable choice.

The population of the capital opposes bloody repression and terror, and is mentally prepared to fight to the end. Now that it is mobilised and prepared for conflict, we say to the whole country:

1) Start a "national non-cooperation movement" against the government. The ruling group does not represent the country, and its instructions can be ignored.

2) Begin countrywide support activities, especially in relation to the provision of medical and first-aid supplies.

3) Start a petition for all elected People's Representatives [to the National People's Congress] demanding the resignation of [President] Yang Shangkun, [Vice-President] Wang Zhen, [Premier] Li peng, and [Vice-Premier] Yao Yilin, who must be removed to avoid widespread bloodshed and save the republic.

4) Urgently demand the various armies [of the PLA] to stand by the people, protect the people, and punish the political criminals.

5) Demand of the governments in the provinces, cities, autonomous areas and military areas, that they support the people of the capital, condemn the ruling group, protect administrative stability, object to the use of military force, and openly state that militarism is the character of the central government.

6) Urgently appeal for the support of all governments and peoples of the world.

7) Urgently appeal to all people for an unyielding struggle with the anti-democratic and anti-revolutionary group of Yang, Wang, Li and Yao. It is they who have become the main representatives of power corruption, and who, by means of an anti-revolutionary military coup, have stolen the supreme power of the party and the country, betraying the National People's Congress and its Standing Committee.

8) Everyone must rescue China from this danger. We must begin to develop a new republican order, following the example of the new generation. To do this great thing, victory must go to the people.

9) The current military government must be held responsible for the bloodshed and repression that is about to occur. The united strength of the people must punish them for these crimes through the highest legal channels.

10) The population of the capital and all patriotic students have determined to protect the republic, and the dignity of the Constitution, with their freedom, their blood and their lives, risking all in the fight.

Everyone must unite! The people must win! Long live the people's Democracy Movement!

May 20, 1989

XXIII: A Statement for Citizens Concerning the Army Entering the Capital

To all citizens and comrades:

The Patriotic-Democracy Movement has lasted for more than one month, during which time you have actively participated and contributed to the national well-being. Of late, people in the central government have destroyed the honour of both the party and the government. They have lied to the soldiers of the PLA as they seek to suppress the people with bloody violence. In these circumstances we appeal to everyone to stop the army from entering the city, doing so with reference to the following points:

1) The soldiers are not our real enemies, but our brothers. They are lied to, and do not know the real situation. Some of them are not now permitted to read newspapers or watch television. Therefore, tell them the true story, inform them of our intentions, using persuasion rather than force, and thereby gaining their understanding and respect.

2) An irresponsible and dishonest government, which has lied to the soldiers, is also providing inadequate rations for them, in order to increase the tension between them and the people. Consequently, we must care for the soldiers, and help them to solve their food problems.

3) We must recognise that soldiers must obey orders, but we must let them know that they can refuse orders which go against the people. We must block them, but avoid conflict with them; and remain aware that policemen in civilian clothes and others with bad intentions might attack soldiers in order to increase tensions.

4) If the army wish to retreat, permit them to do so.

May 20, 1989

XXIV: A Statement for the Soldiers[8]

Greetings to all soldiers in the People's Liberation Army!

Before everything else, please remember that you are the army of the people and the country, responsible for the protection of their welfare. Know also that the real reason for your entering the capital is to repress the people. However, the people here believe in you, and ask you to look at the real nature of things.

You will see clearly that people are suffering, that the future of our nation lies in your support for the university students, some of whom have been on hunger strike for seven days. Everyone is worried about them, trying to help them. The police have disappeared, and volunteer pickets are spontaneously organising the movement of traffic. So why does the government continue to ignore our two minimum requests (i.e., withdraw the April 26th *People's Daily* editorial and hold a dialogue with the students, to be broadcast live)? Several thousand students, 3000 of whom have already fainted, are on hunger strike in support of these two demands. They are met with weapons.

We speak with the voice of the people, and want to replace economic manipulation and corruption by the bureaucracy with democracy and legality. What is wrong with that? The demonstration by a million people in Beijing, and the petitioning of the students, are systematically organised with cool-headed and rational restraint. There has been no disastrous incident. So the government delay is contradictory. Instead of saying, "There is no government," we should be asking, "Where is the government?"

Then out comes the government at last, after a struggle within the hierarchy. There is no turmoil here. They are using you, soldiers and brothers, to suppress the people in the interests of those few people.

Soldiers! We love you, and your hands must not be stained with the people's blood. Facing you there are starving students supported by millions of people. On this day dictators have attempted to cheat the people, and as such will their names live in history!

In the last analysis, history is written by the people!

Soldiers and brothers, please think again, and do not violate the hopes of the people. Think carefully about your own families!

May 21, 1989

XXV: *The Most Dangerous Emergency*

The current situation gives cause for widespread concern. Martial law has been declared, and soldiers summoned to Beijing. These soldiers are sons and brothers of the people, nurtured by them. The army and the country rise and fall together. When the country is in danger, it is there to protect the people. With the people in jeopardy, the soldiers will protect them, not harm them. We believe that they will make a reasonable choice on the matter of martial law. The people's wishes cannot be countermanded by a small group with special powers. Denied information for a month, our soldiers must now be told the truth, that they may unite with us in the promotion of the Patriotic-Democracy Movement, for total victory.

XXVI: *An Open Letter to our Brothers, the Soldiers*[9]

For six days the patriotic students have been on a hunger strike; and what has been the result? Their petition and actions have been described as turmoil, and in need of repression. How rational is that? And why should we agree with those in power?

When the students began their hunger strike on May 13th, the government was unsympathetic, and resorted to removing the police who control the traffic [in the square], and refusing to meet with them. These are cunning and underhand tactics.

Soldiers of the People's Liberation Army, sons and brothers of the people, remember that the people are not slaves, and that they love the soldiers. Join with the people to defeat totalitarianism and promote democracy in China!

The sleeping lion has wakened! There is hope for China!

Dated, "one morning in May."

XXVII: *An Open Letter to all Soldiers in the People's Liberation Army*

To all soldiers in the Liberation Army:

From mid-April, in Beijing and throughout the country, thousands of students have held rallies, written big character posters, held study strikes and hunger strikes. They have urged the government to get rid of corruption, abuse of power, black-marketeering bureaucrats, inflation and other problems. In the last few days newspapers, radio, and television have been reporting these facts. Why have you not been allowed to know it? Is the government afraid to let you know the truth, and that workers and farmers generally support the students, providing food and drink for them. In the last few days the people of the capital have gone onto the streets in support of the hunger strikers, including many people from central government organizations, the *People's Daily*, Central Party School, the central radio, departments of the State Council, and even policemen and soldiers.

Soldiers of the army, you are brothers of workers, farmers, and citizens from all strata of society. The Patriotic-Democratic Movement, begun by the students, demands rights for the people. The students have made great sacrifices for all of the people. For eight days thousands of them have been on hunger strike, two thousand have lost consciousness, many might die. All generous people think that the government is conscientious, but is ignoring the people, rejecting the two reasonable requests of the students: i) to admit that the Student Movement is a Movement, and ii) to meet the students for equal dialogue. On the contrary, it sends you to suppress them, treating you as a mindless tool, pursuing its ends by having the people kill each other.

Soldiers! The people understand your situation. Our common goals, however, are destroying corruption and fighting for democracy. The 38th Army has refused the order to suppress the students, and have retreated from Beijing. What would you do?

The whole country is watching you! We hope that you will not do anything to break our fraternal hearts!

May 21, 1989

XXVIII: A Statement to All Soldiers [10]

Dear Soldiers of the Liberation Army,
The PLA is made up of the sons and brothers of the people. You guard and protect the republic, not just a small minority. In a life or death situation you should look closely at the wishes of the people, and not become the tool of their repression at the orders of one or a few.

In the development of the Patriotic-Democracy Movement you have supported the people in your own way. The soldiers of the 38th Army have refused to obey the illegal order to suppress the people, and are thereby the brilliant representatives of the people, who welcome them.[11]

Stand with the people! Protect the Constitution! Maintain democracy and reform!

May 21, 1989

XXIX: To the Workers' Picket Group [12]

All workers, citizens, and comrades,
Thank you for your hard work. For more than a month you have given your support to this great Patriotic Movement, both materially and spiritually. The patriotic students have spoken for you, and we have strong linkages. When we marched through the streets, you clapped and cheered for us, gave us food and water, and unselfishly supported us. When we protested against the government's shameful actions, you gave us passionate support, without which we could never have lasted. Honest people, you are usually quite ordinary; but you gave tremendous strength at a critical time. Before you, all other powers are comparatively small and pitiful.

The pitiful and pathetic Li Peng, whose hypocritical government did not respond to the legitimate demands of the students, even falsely accused the Student Movement of fomenting a riot, using this as an excuse to order troops into Beijing. They said that the troops are needed to keep the peace, when in fact they are for a brutal crackdown. The Patriotic Movement is about to be destroyed, and you have stood by our side, bravely preventing the troops from entering Beijing. Today is the eighth day of martial law, and this hypocritical government has vulgarly and treacherously organised something called the workers' picket group, helping the troops enter Beijing. But don't think that workers and students are going to fight each other for the benefit of the government. There is a rumour that plainclothes police have infiltrated the workers' picket group as agitators with evil designs. Workers, citizens, and compatriots, keep your eyes open. We believe, however, that, even if there are police among you, as Chinese with a conscience they will not help Li Peng clear the streets in opposition to democracy and the people.

If the government acted honestly they would get more support. The Li Peng government, however, in its final struggles, dishonest, cannot last much longer.

Workers, farmers, soldiers, students and businessmen, unite to fight for democracy in the People's Republic of China.

May 28, 1989

XXX: Who Created the Turmoils of the Last Forty Years?

In 1957 Mao Zedong waged an anti-rightist struggle in which millions of intellectuals were condemned. Many were imprisoned and exiled, whilst countless others were forced into suicide.

From 1958 to 1962 Mao promoted the Great Leap Forward, which produced an unprecedented decline in the national economy. Countless numbers died of starvation. Everywhere people suffered from illness and malnutrition.

From 1966 to 1976 Mao Zedong pursued the Great Cultural Revolution, which brought disaster to the whole nation.

During 1983 and 1984 Deng Xiaoping promoted the national campaign to eliminate criminal elements. Many people were falsely accused, and a widespread criticism of the campaign developed.

In 1987 Deng Xiaoping initiated the campaign against bourgeois liberalism. This generated serious confusion in ideas and ideology, and led to the resignation of Hu Yaobang and the exile of many intellectuals. It was also a barrier to scientific and cultural progress.

From July to October, 1988, serious inflation was produced by poor central economic decisions. Panic buying occurred as people emptied their bank accounts.

On May 20, 1989, Deng Xiaoping, Li Peng, and Yang Shangkun assaulted public opinion and established military law in Beijing. Hundreds of thousands of armed soldiers were sent to suppress the masses. Huge opposition to this move came from the students and people of Beijing, who sought to keep out the troops. They were supported by the people of all of China, of the whole world.

Experience demonstrates that none of the turmoil since the beginning of the people's republic [1949] has been created by democratic parties — nor by the people, nor by the USA, nor Taiwan, nor the USSR. It has been caused by a small group of people in the Political Bureau of the CCP, who have usurped power over the party, the government, and the armed forces.

[undated]

XXXI: What do Factional Disputes Reveal? [13]

The abnormal phenomena occurring in the contemporary political scene lead us to think that there are factional disputes occurring within the government. What these disputes reveal is of some concern.

Our party's history is riddled with factional disputes. From Chen Duxiu,[14] Zhang Guodao,[15] Wang Ming[16] to Liu, Deng and Zhou,[17] and the Jiang Qing — Lin Biao clique;[18] and it continues today, the scars of the past being no guarantee against new wounds today. These scars are a record of the great price paid by the people and the party, being evidence in particular of a lack of democracy in the CCP.

The supposed infallibility of Mao Zedong in the revolutionary struggle created in the people a psychological dependence, incapable of defending one's position, of surviving, without the powerful leader. Under a spell like that, people lose their ability to think critically and independently. All they can do is swear allegiance to whoever is in power, whilst allowing those who possess authority to consolidate power; and that is the source of factions.

Factional struggles can only be avoided if people in power respect democratic procedures. Without democratic structures no party organization can develop a common goal. Rules and regulations which are supposed to generate unity must be a sham, and crises are inevitable. This is particularly true in the context of the traditional culture of our bureaucracy, whereby the sole end of knowledge is to pass the official examination for the recruitment of government officials. Officials tend to desire power in this environment. Coups are almost inevitable, as the experience of our party painfully demonstrates. Some of them may be necessary, but the political circumstances generating them are not healthy. Genuine democracy in the party is the only way to eliminate the problem.

Without democracy, factional disputes are inevitable, and one-man rule will remain. The serious consequences will be exhaustion and chaos everywhere, as can be seen in our country. The struggle for genuine democracy is, therefore, a struggle against factions, and a commitment by the people to the strengthening of the whole of China.

Long live democracy! Long live the people!

May 25, 1989

RESPONSE OF THE WORKERS

XXXII: *Letter to the People of Beijing (BWU)* [19]

The entire population of China must now face up to an intolerable situation. Long accustomed to bureaucratic-dictatorial forms of control, they must now live with uncontrolled inflation and declining living standards. To recover from their extravagant behaviour, the ruling elite have issued various government and treasury bonds, squeezing the people for every penny of their cash. In this situation, people from all walks of life must join together to reveal the truth and protect the future of China.

Those of us who are policemen and soldiers must stand by the people, for truth, not serve as tools of the people's enemies. You are also being oppressed. As for the murderers in the April Fifth Incident and the April Twentieth Bloodshed [of 1976], the people will never forget your crimes.

We earnestly demand the following: a wage increase, price stabilization, and a publication of the incomes and possessions of government officials and their families. We, the workers of Beijing, and citizens from all walks of life, support the university students and their fight for honesty and justice.

April 20, 1989.

XXXIII: *Ten Polite Questions for the CCP (BWU):*

1) How much did Deng's son bet on a horse race in Hong Kong, and where did he get the money to place the bet?
2) Mr. and Mrs. Zhao Ziyang play golf every week. Who pays the green fees, and other expenses?
3) How does the Central Committee [of the CCP] judge the ongoing reforms. In his New Year Address Premier Li Peng said that there have been mistakes. What are they? What exactly is the situation now?

4) The Central Committee has proposed a reform for the control of prices, yet inflation continues, with the people's living standard declining. Can they explain this?

5) China must begin the repayment of foreign loans in 1990. How much must each citizen contribute to this? Will it affect basic living standards? Please answer us.

6) Deng Xiaoping has suggested raising the status of intellectuals from "stinking ninth" to "top rank." [20] What is a top ranking person? Would that be a landlord? Or a landlord's father?

7) How many residences and retreats do top party officials have spread around the country? What do they cost? Can this be made public? Please answer us.

8) Make public the personal incomes and possessions of top party officials.

9) How is the party going to respond to approaches from the government of Taiwan for peace talks?

10) Would the party be so kind as to explain the meaning and implications of the following terms: i) Party, ii) Revolution, and iii) Reactionary.

Would the party please publish their responses to the above ten questions as soon as possible?

April 20, 1989,

XXXIV: *Letter to Compatriots of the Nation (BWU)*

The illegal behaviour of the corrupt officials has reached the extreme! The brutality of officials reaches the extreme! In a vast country like China, there is no place for truth! No repression can stop the people's anger; no longer will people believe the lies of the government; and the words on our standard are: science, democracy, freedom, human rights, laws and institutions!

The Beijing Workers' Union was established on April 20th to protect the rights of workers; and we published our "Letter" to the people of the city and "Ten Questions." The April 26th editorial falsely stated that these documents were counter-revolutionary. We must request that, in the absence of any answers to our ten questions, that you publish the two documents in your newspaper. Or are you too much afraid, even after parading the slogan, "Believe in the People," for the past forty years? We demand a retraction of the April 26th editorial comment, and the punishment of its author and party sponsors.

We have carefully considered the exploitation of the workers. Marx's *Capital* provided us with a method for understanding the character of our oppression. We deducted from the total value of output the workers wages, welfare, medical welfare, the necessary social fund, equipment depreciation and reinvestment expenses. Surprisingly, we discovered that "civil servants" swallow all the remaining value produced by the people's blood and sweat! The total taken by them is really vast! How cruel! How typically Chinese! These bureaucrats use the people's hard earned money to build luxury villas all over the country (guarded by soldiers in so-called military areas), to buy luxury cars, to travel to foreign countries on so-called study tours (with their families, and even baby sitters)! Their immoral and shameful deeds and crimes are too numerous to mention here.

Concerning the general welfare, Comrade Fang Lizhi's views on the subject of off-shore investment is true. Foreign investment eventually becomes the legal property of top officials, through *Guandao* (i.e., bureaucratic corruption). The victim is the country, the beneficiaries are a small minority, and the people pay for it.

We strongly protest the savage action of forcing the people to buy treasury bonds. We demand that the government provide a report on income and expenditure in this trade, return the money with interest to the bond holders, and close the bond markets which are a main source of income for *Guandao*. We demand an increase in wages, the stabilization of inflation, an end to the refusal to adjust wages according to age and experience. We demand the investigation of the top party officials of the CCP Central Committee's Central Advisory Commission, the Central Committee itself, the Politburo, the Central Military Commission of the CCP. The first to be investigated should be those who have luxury villas; like Deng Xiaoping, Zhao Ziyang, Li Peng, Chen Yun, Li Xiannian, Yang Shangkun, Peng Zhen, and Jiang Zemin,[21] and their families. This should be done by a "national investigation committee," elected by the people, and reporting to them.

The students are now responsible, the good discipline of their several millions in Tiananmen Square being ample proof. The people have awakened! They understand that, whatever the society, whatever the moment in history, there are only two classes, those who rule and those who are ruled. Viewing the history of the party, the society, and the individual, we see revolutionary progress starting with the overthrow of the Qing dynasty [1910]. However, it has to this point been change which is "ruled by man." That is why the Chinese still love, need, praise and remember the "honest official." The political movement in these past forty years, however, has been a political suppression of the people. History is showing that they are good at an "appraisal after autumn" [i.e., seeing their mistakes when it is too late to correct them]; and they cannot change history.

Those politicians who are using the Democracy Movement of the students should take heed. Deng made use of the April Fifth Movement to become leader of the party, and has demonstrated the awful consequences. The economic reforms which followed are both superficial and fake. The standard of living has declined for most people, and heavy debts remain to be paid by the people.

Workers. Comrades. Keep closely united to the Beijing Workers' Union. Under its direction the democratic movement should be pushed to a new climax. Our union is going to hold a workers' march to Tiananmen Square on May 22nd at 2:00 p.m., to demonstrate peacefully and support the university students. The slogan is, "In a vast country like China, there is not even a place for truth!"

May 17, 1989

XXXV: Letter to the Students [22]

Dear Students,

As you continue your struggle over the following days you must try to gain the broad support of workers, peasants, soldiers and businessmen. How can you do this? First, do not emphasize the treatment of intellectuals and the budget for higher education, and do not demand impractical democratic change; for this will alienate the workers and farmers.

The propaganda aimed at the workers, farmers and soldiers must emphasise the fact that the words "owned by the people" actually mean "owned by a small group of bourgeoisie." That group calls us the "masters of the country," yet we live in overcrowded conditions from generation to generation. On the other hand, those "civil servants" build villas, and have police escorts for their luxury cars — while we "masters" travel on crowded buses. Hoisting the flag of stability and unity, they accuse us; when they are the real cause of instability. Can we turn a blind eye to their draining of the national treasury? For where does that money come from? From our sweat and blood. They don't care about the welfare of the nation, in their luxury cars, or playing golf. What is their salary, and how much do they spend? The national output is the income of this small group, who are no different than feudal rulers.

We cannot depend on enlightened rulers, but only on a perfectly democratic system, a free press, an independent judiciary, and people's representatives who are really chosen by the people.

A small group makes use of the press, cheating and tricking the people. The scandal of their existence cannot be exposed, and the people's views cannot be expressed.

The people's representatives are appointed by this bureaucratic bourgeoisie, so how can they represent the people and reflect their concerns?

Dear students, remember the Student Movement of two years ago, when a small group made use of the press to lie to the people, and sow dissension between students on the one hand, and workers and peasants on the other. They said, "To train a university student means spending 10,000 yuan, which is earned by hundreds of workers and peasants; but the students have no respect for that." The real truth is that property is built on the blood and sweat of millions of our comrades, and spent by the small group, who are the biggest of capitalists, and disastrous for the people.

The interests of the workers, peasants and students are the same, and you can have their support.

April 28, 1989

XXXVI: *An Open Letter to the Students* [23]

Your honorable actions have raised the sympathy of our workers and of the whole society. Speaking from the heart, your worries and concern for China are the same as our own. The rise and fall of a nation is the responsibility of each individual within it.

For various reasons we, the workers, cannot act like the students, coming out on the streets in demonstrations, carrying out a general strike. However, our hearts are as one. We firmly support the seven reasonable requests which you have made. If this is a fight for truth, then death holds nothing to fear.

Although we cannot join your march, we can support you both spiritually and materially; so you do not have to fight alone. If you need money, we can raise it. If you need equipment, we can provide it. The working class will give you its generous support for your self-sacrificing action in the cause of the nation.

I also offer the following advice:

1) Because the official news agency has distorted the facts to keep people ignorant, I suggest that you promote widespread publicity, printing pamphlets, organising information groups, and ensuring that everyone hears the truth.

2) Following the strike, other activities must be promoted, including marches, demonstrations, and petitions, all of which create pressure.

3) Allow more institutions of higher education to join your processions, invite celebrities and important people to make speeches in support, so as to broaden your influence.

4) Hold on to the end in a spirit of self-sacrifice.

Finally, let me thank you again for your righteous action. The future is bright, but the road is winding. The first streak of light is breaking through. Struggle, now, comrades! Let us shout: "Long live democracy, equality and freedom."

[undated]

XXXVII: *Letter to the Workers of the Capital* [24]

Honorable Comrades,

Democracy and dictatorship are in a life or death struggle. The Li Peng government has become isolated and counter-revolutionary, publicly raising the banner of opposition to both democracy and the people. As it moves large numbers of troops towards the city, we see that this wonderful Democracy Movement is going to be swept away. This morning, 3,000 university students went on a hunger strike, but most of the students face a brutal repression. Only the capital's working class can save the Democracy Movement by taking immediate action:

1) Make use of all non-violent means to prevent the troops entering the city, inform the troops about the real nature of the Patriotic-Democratic Movement, its great historical significance, and persuade the troops to support the people.

2) Organise a workers' picket group, maintain order in the capital, prevent illegal behaviour, such as arson, theft and destructive violence, and thereby ensure that the struggle of the student hunger strikers can proceed.

May 13, 1989

XXXVIII: *Declaration of the Preparatory Committee of The Beijing Workers' Autonomous Federation (BWAF)*

It is our understanding that the students' democratic and patriotic Movement, which began in April, has become a national movement which directly influences the interests of the workers.

We understand that, in the national interest, the students have given their all, and that the lives of the hunger strikers are now in danger.

In the interest of those thousands of students, of workers, and of the welfare of the entire nation, we formally declare that the Politburo must unconditionally accept the two student demands within twenty-four hours. Otherwise, beginning on May 20th at noon, there will be a one day general strike, after which we will decide on further steps.

Further, let the workers of the whole nation know that the workers of Beijing are now organised.

May 19, 1989

XXXIX: Public Notice "Number One" of the BWAF

The BWAF is a spontaneous and temporary organization formed by the workers of Beijing in response to the unusual current situation. Its objectives are to fight for democracy, bring down dictatorship, support and protect the student hunger strikers, promote democratization in alliance with the students and citizens from all walks of life. We call for:

1) A general strike in Beijing (with the exception of electricity, water, gas, mail and communications), beginning at noon on May 20th, and lasting until the military withdraw from the city.

2) Opposition to the entry of troops into the city, defence of the Democracy Movement, the maintenance of discipline in Tiananmen Square, the blockage of all main roads into the city and subway exits with vehicles, the maintenance of the normal operation of radio and television broadcasting.

3) The cooperation of all citizens in informing the troops in Beijing concerning the true situation.

May 20, 1989

XL: Public Notice "Number Two" of the BWAF

This afternoon, the Standing Committee of the BWAF called an emergency meeting on our special role in the present situation. As the leading group they a set up secretariat, a public relations section, and a liaison and support section.

1) The BWAF is a Beijing workers' autonomous organization with the objective, democratically and legally, of promoting a Patriotic-Democratic Movement. It invites all workers in the capital to participate actively in our union.

2) Given the present situation, the meeting decided specifically, i) that the present task of the workers' picket group is to maintain a close cooperation with the Students' Autonomous Union, and to guarantee the safety of the students and the stability of Beijing society; and, ii) that the workers' picket group also ensure the movement of the city's resources and daily needs of the citizens, such as transportation and food.

May 21, 1989

XLI: *Declaration of the BWAF Preparatory Committee on Behalf of the Workers*

The working class is the most advanced class and we, in the Democratic Movement, should be prepared to demonstrate its great power.

The People's Republic of China is supposedly led by the working class, and we have every right to drive out the dictators.

The workers know best how to use knowledge and technology in the production process, so we will not permit the destruction of the students, who are of the people.

To bring down dictatorship and totalitarianism and promote democracy in China is our undeniable responsibility.

In the Democracy Movement, "we have nothing to lose but our chains, and a world to win." [25]

May 21, 1989

XLII: *The Initial Programme of BWAF* [26]

Since April 20th the national Patriotic-Democratic Movement, with the students as the vanguard, has enabled the bulk of the working class to demonstrate their desire to discuss and to participate in political matters. At the same time they realised that there was no specifically working class organization to represent them. Under these circumstances, we think that it is necessary to establish an autonomous organization to speak for the workers, to which end we organise BWAF and propose the following initial programme:

1) BWAF allows workers to join on a voluntary basis, is a totally independent organization, has a democratic foundation, and should be regarded as an equal of other people's organizations.

2) The fundamental aim of BWAF is to express the political and economic views of the workers, not just to pursue material ends.

3) BWAF should operate as a supervisor of the activities of the Communist Party.

4) BWAF has the legal right to protect workers in all public organizations and work-places.

5) Under the Constitution BWAF will protect its members from all incursions upon their legal rights.

May 21, 1989.

XLIII: The People in Command [27]

For many years this country, with its population of 1.1 billion, has been under the dictatorship of a handful of bureaucrats who raise the banner of socialism, but who in practice adopt policies that stultify the people and oppress the intellectuals. They are at the peak of the hierarchy, and wield absolute power, beyond any constitutional or party controls. They have an entourage of relatives and associates, and the worst of them is a modern-day Empress Dowager [i.e., Deng Xiaoping]. He manipulates politics from behind a curtain, cares about nothing but his game of bridge, closes his eyes to public suffering, and alienates himself from the masses. The country is trapped in an internal and external debt crisis, and the people's standard of living is reduced by heavy taxes and uncontrollable inflation. It is well known that China is one of the most backward countries in the world, yet he still tries to fool us through manipulation of the media into believing that China has a high GNP.

Does our country still have a place in the international community of nations? Why are we so poor and backward? If the excuse is that our population is too big, how is it that Japan, with its higher population density, fares so well? If the excuse is that other countries have had a longer time to develop, what about Taiwan and South Korea? Why are all these better than us?

In recent years the bureaucrats have become increasingly corrupt, and the leadership more incompetent. Why? People want answers.

Li Peng, you stated that your three children have not been abusing their position for economic advantage. That is not enough, however. As Premier, you must stop all abuses. If, as Premier, you have not been able to root out the most corrupt of the bureaucrats, the most abusive of their power, what are you doing in the job? You people have made a mess of China, a country rich in human and natural resources. It is too easy to say that China lacks experience building socialism, and that you are leading the people across a river, locating each stepping stone as you go. In what direction are you taking us? And what about those who find no stepping stone, and drown? Is the life of the people so worthless that it can be handled like a gambling chip by the bureaucrats?

We have had ten years of reform, and we still don't know where we are going. Who can tell us? Of course you can say, "It doesn't matter what colour the cat, as long as it catches the mouse." But if both cats start fighting over the mouse, only confusion and contradiction follow. Or, put another way, the bureaucratic cat will continue to get fat, and the people will starve. Is that the proper way to run a country?

Premier Zhou Enlai once said, "Who wins the students wins the future." Chairman Mao said, "Whoever represses the student movement will find himself at a dead end." Dust collects if you don't sweep it away. It is the same with reactionaries. We must struggle to bring them down, in the knowledge that, [in Mao's words] political power comes out of the barrel of a gun. We must be prepared to make sacrifices in a fight for democracy. The ruling class will not leave the stage of its own accord, handing democratic rights to us. We must take those rights ourselves. Without democracy, power abuses will remain; and for genuine democracy, the system of permanent officials must be abandoned.

Where there is a one-man dictatorship, democracy is an empty word. Without democracy there are no human rights; and without human rights we are simply slaves. We must not accept this; for we want to be master of the world. Not letting this opportunity slip, we must keep the fire of democracy burning. The evidence shows that the current Democratic Movement is primarily concerned with the question of political power. Only by overthrowing the dictators is there hope for the Movement. In the words of the song of the [wartime] Yenan Anti-Japanese University: "Workers, students, and national bourgeoisie, hasten to the battlefront of our patriotic movement. Listen to the voice of democracy calling. Look, the banner of liberty is flying. We, workers, students, and national bourgeoisie, move together through the torrential storm waves to receive the dawn. Workers, peasants, and national bourgeoisie, rise up, and hasten to the battlefront of our patriotic movement."

Comrades, we oppose some of the party's leaders; but that does not mean that we oppose the party. Also, when we oppose some leaders in the government, we are not rejecting socialism. Is it not the lack of democracy that permits those leaders freely to accuse us of being something which we are not. We must all unite to sweep Deng Xiaoping off the historical stage as soon as possible, save China and her people, and turn over a new page of democracy and freedom.

[Undated]

XLIV: *Aims of the Beijing Construction Workers' Autonomous Union*

This union is formally established on this day, May 21, 1989.

Its aim is as follows:

We are not prison laborers who happen to live in society, but legal citizens of the republic. We want democracy and freedom. The students are demonstrating for the people with their hunger strike. We, Chinese workers, have a conscience, and sympathise with our student brothers and sisters against the wicked government. We must support the students through to the end.

A national crisis lies ahead, and each individual, from both the working class and the professions, must join a union to protect our students. Deng Xiaoping and Li Peng, not knowing how to respond, must be removed by us.

May 21, 1989

XLV: An Open Letter to the Standing Committee of the National People's Congress [28]

This morning we heard that Wan Li, chairman of the Standing Committee, had returned from abroad. We are making an urgent appeal to him.

The third Plenum [of the CCP Central Committee in 1978] forecast a great economic reformation for the whole of China. However, for complex reasons, this developed into a radical economic, political and ideological transformation. We can see that every step in the development of socialism brings forth new ideas and demands for democracy in opposition to the old system and ideas. The Thirteenth Party Congress of the CCP [in 1987] discussed political reform, and adopted a gradualist position. Starting in April, however, the Democratic-Patriotic Movement of university students has generated significant change. Li Peng did not follow the historical trend and opposed the will of the people, arousing their anger and making the situation uncontrollable. Li Peng and his group, not respecting the dignity of the people, have brought shame to the government of the People's Republic of China. The situation could not be worse, and we hope that the Standing Committee will pursue a just solution.

With greatest respect...

May 24, 1989

XLVI: Declaration of the Guandong Workers' Autonomous Union

The GWAU, a local patriotic organization developed within the framework of the nationwide, Patriotic-Democratic Movement, declares itself established. It is an organization initiated by the Guandong workers, and supervised by the citizens, with the purpose of uniting as many elements as possible for the pursuit of freedom, democracy and the well-being of a long-suffering China.

Now that the soldiers have opened fire in Beijing, and the people lie bleeding, the nation has reached a critical juncture. A historical burden falls on the shoulders of every worker. We have no other choice than to oppose the violence, support the students, and promote both democracy and knowledge.

The nation is confused and disrupted, flooded with bureaucracy, with a corrupt political and economic system. The future of the nation has become the personal concern of each individual worker. The Guandong workers cannot stand by, and the GWAU urgently appeals to people from every walk of life to support and participate in the nation-wide, patriotic, Democratic Movement.

June 4, 1989

DISILLUSIONMENT IN THE PARTY

XLVII: Our Suggestions [29]

We are student party members who have taken to the streets to demonstrate with all of the other students, demanding democracy and truth. Each of us has an honest party spirit, and is deeply saddened and disgusted with the corruption, profiteering by officials, and newspaper lies.

We earnestly appeal to the government to open up a dialogue, acknowledge the significance of the Student Movement, and accelerate the process of democratization in China.

We suggest:

1) Do not use freedom of speech for personal attacks, but to discuss constitutional questions.

2) A student strike be staged, without abandoning institutions, to open democratic discussions on the future of China, and of the student autonomous associations.

3) Every party member should think seriously, act honestly, and reject self-seeking behaviour.

April 25, 1989

XLVIII: I Declare my Views [30]

I joined the CCP a few years ago out of unqualified admiration. Its objective is to represent and serve the interests of the people. However, the leaders in this time of conflict are not honest. Therefore, as water can sink the boat which floats upon it, so government can only be popular as it continues to represent the people's interests.

The CCP and our motherland are not identical; and the people love the country before they do the party. The people loved and trusted the party in the 1950's and 1960's. But how much do they trust us today? As a party member I am saddened, for it has lost the trust of the people, which has led to the creation of the Students' Movement. It does not mean that the CCP is no longer great, only that it must represent the interests of the nation if it is to rule legitimately.

Nor are the party central administration and the CCP identical. The people denounce the party centre because it suppresses and lies to the people. This does not mean that the people have ceased to love the party, but that they want immediate reform.

The students' actions are just, and from now on the question of justice follows me everywhere. All conscientious CCP members must open their hearts to the students, and speak the truth. We must defend anyone who represents the interests of the people.

Beijing University, April 30, 1989.

XLIX: The Choice Between Conscience and Party Spirit — An Open Letter to Party Members [31]

Party Comrades,

The hard-line stance of the party is obvious from the analysis of events in the *People's Daily*, and from the general attitudes of party members, which support the position of the central administration.

Deng Xiaoping says, "In Beijing, only 60,000 students have taken part in the strike. One hundred thousand are not involved. We have three million soldiers. What, therefore, do we have to fear?"

The government is probably going to use force to suppress the Democracy Movement; and it seems likely that the march and demonstration planned for tomorrow will develop into another bloody incident.

There are now only two options open to me. I can either be a conscientious Chinese, and conscientious party member, and struggle for democracy and prosperity in China; or I can be a compromised party member, safely maintaining my party membership by uncritical compliance with the demands of the party centre. How should I choose?

Comrade Zhou Enlai once said, speaking to foreign guest, "I am Chinese before I am a party member." Some people would shed blood for democracy and freedom, for the sake of reform. How trivial is party membership and personal interest from this perspective. In fact, the decision of the party centre does not represent the wishes of the party, and we must say this!

Look at the scene. In front of the Great Hall of the People three students hand in a petition, and are ignored. Where is the party spirit of our leaders? Is the party the voice of the people? Who is destroying the party?

The government would use three million soldiers, who are supposed to protect the people, against the Student Movement for freedom and democracy. Is this not dictatorship?

As party members we are not prepared to shed more tears over a corrupt regime and popular indifference. I simply want to be a good communist, working for democracy and freedom, even shedding my blood.

History will prove that those who fight for democracy are the true communists, fighting for the well-being of the nation.

May 3, 1989

L: *Support the Actions of the Students!* [32]

Today we hear much about the university students in the capital, about their persistent and just actions in the promotion of democracy. This meets with our approval, and we have the deepest respect for their actions.

We hope that those same students understand that all who have reason and a sense of justice, all political and judicial cadres concerned with the strengthening of our nation, will not submit blindly to those pig-headed leaders who oppose the students. We understand and sympathise with the students.

Our position is difficult, and we cannot take up the same stance as you, the students, in the great Democracy Movement. However, we would never go against the tide of history, nor passively watch it. We have faithfully transmitted the platforms, slogans and actions of the students to our colleagues, and have supported the students in various ways.

The students should be satisfied with our position, and history will bear witness that China's elites were not afraid to make sacrifices for the creation of a democratic, prosperous and civilised country.

May 3, 1989

LI: *Quit the Young Communist League!*

In view of the corruption within the Communist Party, and the total despair that it has bred within the people by its responses to the Student Movement, we, members of the Beijing University Young Communist League, as rational and conscientious persons, have lost hope, and show our disillusionment by quitting the League, declaring our full support for the hunger strikers, and opposing the inhuman attitude of our unresponsive government.

May 15, 1989

LII: *Communist Party Members, Step Forward!* [33]

The Patriotic-Democratic Movement has reached a crucial stage, with the hunger strike by thousands of students in Tiananmen Square having entered its seventh day. Yet our leaders have still said nothing in response to their reasonable demands. As members of the CCP we feel that the government's response has been wrong and unwise. Since April 15th we have identified with the Democracy Movement, are disgusted with the erroneous assessment of the government's leaders, and the poor image of the party thus generated.

We treasure our title, members of the Chinese Communist Party. We joined the party to promote communism and, although we have only been in the party for a few years, we value our identity with it. The party member is in the vanguard of revolution, serving the people by example. Our predecessors gave their blood and their lives to give honour to the party, whose name is today tarnished by the current demands for democracy and a rule of law. Since April 20th we have been under considerable pressure not to associate with the Movement as party members, but only as individuals, leading us to reflect deeply upon our commitment and duties as party members. We are not ashamed to stand before the students bearing the proud title of membership, for it is truth that genuine party members defend, not the reputations of particular leaders. Considering specific leaders, we say that they are not true party members. The image of the CCP is not their monopoly, but of all of us.

We assert,

1) that all CCP members should step forward and defend the right of its members to participate in the Patriotic-Democratic Movement *as party members,* which is also in the greatest interest of the people;

2) that the Movement is threatened, and party members should come forward to assist in the organization of autonomous student associations, self-consciously avoiding unnecessary losses in their numbers.

[undated]

LIII: *Urging Deng Xiaoping to Admit His Mistakes — an Open Letter to the CCP* [34]

To the Central Committee and all comrades in the party:

The students are in danger! The situation is perilous! The future of our country is at stake!

Yet the Politburo and State Council continue to ignore the reasonable demands of the student hunger strikers. The conflict is intensifying and the consequences will be dreadful.

As party members, we are immensely concerned. Therefore, we appeal to Comrade Deng Xiaoping to admit openly his mistakes, and acknowledge that his calling the Student Movement a "riot" was entirely wrong. Deng, who is head of neither the party nor of the Standing Committee of the Politburo, is not in possession of decision-making powers. That he should give orders to the whole party is a violation of the party's principles of organization. This kind of imperious behaviour makes a mockery of any claim that there is democracy in the party. We hope that Comrade Deng will value his past achievements, and consider his mistakes from the perspective of the national welfare, so as to solve this problem in perfect honesty.

We want the Politburo to show its party spirit, conscience and courage, follow the wishes of the people and the party, make truly collective decisions, immediately and unequivocally acknowledge this Patriotic-Democratic Movement, consider and comply with the legitimate demands of the students (which are simultaneously the demands of the people), and immediately set out to promote the democracy and the rule of law in our mother country.

History will not give us many chances. The Central Committee and the entire party should act immediately, and make the correct choice for the welfare of our race.

Save the students! Save the nation!

May 18, 1989

LIV: *Letter to the People* [35]

Dear Students, Citizens of the Republic, Compatriots, Communist Party Members, Soldiers of the PLA,

We must inform you, with great anger and deep sadness, that Zhao Ziyang has certainly resigned from his post as party leader, and that Li Peng has taken charge of the Politburo and ordered an immediate crackdown.

On May 13th Zhao Ziyang proposed to the Standing Committee of the Politburo a renunciation of the April 26th editorial of the *People's Daily*. The proposal was defeated. On May 15 Zhao intended to make a public statement of his views on the matter in Tiananmen Square. The central office of the CCP regarded this as a violation of party rules. Then, on May 16th Zhao presented the following six proposals to the Politburo Standing Committee which was attended by Deng Xiaoping [although he is not now a member]:

1) Repudiate the April 26th editorial.
2) Deng should accept responsibility for the editorial.
3) A special department of the People's Congress should be set up to investigate bureaucratic profiteering by the children of top cadres, including the son of Deng.
4) Provide a full biography of all top cadres.
5) Reveal the salaries and fringe benefits of all top cadres.
6) Cancel the privileges of top cadres.

The Politburo rejected these proposals, and on May 17th a decision to oust Zhao was passed with a narrow majority. Li Peng took over the leadership of the Politburo. Martial law becomes the order of the day, and the repression of May, 1976, is to be repeated.

Yet we live in a different age, and the past will not be repeated. We hear that Wan Li stands with Zhao and will call a meeting of the leaders of the National People's Congress. Li Peng threatens Wan Li with party discipline. And we hear that students are about to go on a new hunger strike. Given all of this, we appeal to all people,

1) to avoid bloodshed and refrain from violence;
2) to initiate a nationwide general strike; and
3) to remind the PLA that it is the child of the people, and should not kill them.

We demand, therefore,

1) a meeting of the Standing Committee of the National People's Congress to dismiss Li Peng from the Premier's position, and
2) a meeting of the Central Committee of the CCP to elect a new General Secretary, and to put an end to the interference of old men behind the scenes.

Dear Students, Citizens, and Compatriots, the Chinese nation is again at a dangerous juncture, with the republic and CCP facing a life and death situation. Let us immediately move to resolve the problem in a non-violent manner.

May 19, 1989

LV: Statement on Quitting the Party [36]

Firmly and unequivocally I withdraw from the Communist Party, which has been raped and dishonoured by Deng Xiaoping and Li Peng. This party has destroyed in me the hope and confidence with which I originally associated it. It now stands for opposition to the people. If Deng is the party, and Li represents the party, then I want no truck with it.

Such is my solemn declaration.

May 20, 1989

LVI: Quit the CCP and Establish a Society for the Promotion of the Chinese Democracy Movement [37]

To all Patriotic Chinese intellectuals,

The corrupt and incompetent hierarchy of the ruling CCP represses the people, regards democracy as a heresy, ignores the reasonable demands of the patriotic youth, exploits the intellectuals and adopts an attitude of enmity towards them. Therefore, we propose that all intellectuals, who have served the party to this moment, organise themselves into groups and withdraw from the party *en masse*, and establish an organization that can represent the interests of the people. This organization could be called the Society for the Promotion of the Chinese Democratic Movement (Minzhu Hwei — MZH).

The Need to Quit the CCP:

1) The CCP was once a progressive, revolutionary force, but has deteriorated under the conservatism, narrow-mindedness and stupidity of petty peasants.

2) Before it gained power the CCP collaborated with intellectuals, but thereafter, as a tactic in defence of its dictatorship, intellectuals were attacked by the party. The various Anti-Rightist campaigns have been aimed mainly at the intellectuals. Even in better times, intellectuals were used rather than respected by the CCP.

3) The CCP is insincere in its supposed policy of improving teaching conditions and expanding education budgets. Education is of no value to current leaders in their efforts to maintain control.

4) Intellectuals can no longer promote their own or the people's interest through a communist organization. Besides, the reputation of the CCP has been destroyed inside and outside of China. Intellectuals will only taint their own good reputation by being associated with it.

The Procedure for Quitting the Party:

A group of better-known individuals in the field of education and the arts, perhaps a few dozen or a couple of hundreds, must take the lead by publicly quitting the party at a press conference in Beijing. This must be done the day after applying for withdrawal from the party according to its constitution, and the event will be used to publicise the reasons for quitting.

Further, all intellectuals must follow up with a statement of withdrawal. If celebrities cannot be found to initiate the procedure, then the teachers and researchers of Beijing's main institutions of higher education could be coordinated to lead the withdrawal.

Initiation and organization of the MZH:

The CCP cannot represent the interests of the people. The various public organizations are only adjuncts of the party; so we must set up our own organization. In the early stages, mass enrollment at rallies could be used to build up membership. To accommodate intellectuals of various political dispositions the MZH should keep its objectives general — the promotion of political democratization, freedom of the press, independence of the legal system, the punishment of corrupt bureaucrats, and the improvement of education.

Struggle for the Legalization of MZH:

Certainly, the CCP will not agree to the creation of MZH. Thousands of intellectuals will have to join the society to make it an objective reality. This will resemble the Polish Solidarity Movement, which struggled relentlessly until it was recognised. Modern

Chinese history and the Democracy Movement demonstrate that without the organization and support of such a Movement the people and students will lack unity and be suppressed by the government. The most urgent duty of intellectuals at this time is to form a society to counteract the CCP. This is the wish of the people and the hope for democracy. Let us take action now.

[undated]

THE DOUBTS OF SOLDIERS

LVII: *From the Bottom of a Soldier's Heart* [38]

Dear friends,

You have suffered enough. I speak in the name of all of the generous hearted soldiers of the Third Battalion. The Patriotic Movement of students, workers and citizens has lasted one month. As soldiers, obeying orders, we cannot support you openly. But we are the sons and brothers of the people, Chinese like yourselves, with patriotic hearts. Some young soldiers have created a bad impression in people's minds, but none of us can refuse orders, even the one to advance on the capital. But we say to you: Comrades, don't abandon us, don't treat us badly, for our hearts are linked together, as common people and as Chinese.

You are struggling for democracy and freedom; but, friends, do we soldiers have any democracy and freedom? Of course, the army is different. However, even though we don't have the right to go to Beijing and talk to students, a minority have left their posts and gone into the city, in spite of the consequences. Of course, compared with the people, they amount to but a few. But they represent our general concerns for the people and the students.

Friends, don't treat us like dogs, don't hate us. We will improve your view of us by our manner and our actions. We belong to the people. You have suffered greatly, and we will not remain silent. Let this document support you. It is late, but sincere.

We are proud to be associated with such people! Thank you, friends! I salute you with the greatest respect! Take care!

May 20, 1989.

LVIII: A Statement to All Soldiers in the PLA Who Have Been Ordered to Enter Beijing [39]

I am a university teacher who is also the wife of a soldier, and the daughter of a soldier. At this moment our students are in Tiananmen Square opposing the mad ideas of Li Peng. It is reported that you are on the outskirts of Beijing. Therefore, you have probably heard of the million-strong support of the students' Patriotic-Democracy Movement. Li Peng's government having misled you, the people must tell you the truth. The people everywhere, with the students, are in a struggle with Li Peng's government, which has in its statements and actions shown itself to be useless.

I think that truth will defeat the evil. Because you were uninformed, I was extremely worried by your arrival. Now I am eager to tell you that, although I regard you with affection, I love these honest and beautiful students more; for they have placed themselves in a life and death situation, and they are supported by the millions of honest citizens of Beijing. I beg you not to fight, not to brutalise the citizens and students of our capital; for in so doing you will be changed from our saviors into the most hated persons in all history.

With tears in my eyes, as a member of your family, I beg you not to touch our students, or arouse the people's anger. Li Peng is in the wrong, but the people will forgive you. If you attack, however, you will be criminals forever.

With my son in my arms, I will stand before you; and if you move forwards, please drive over our bodies.

May 21, 1989

LIX: A Letter to all Soldiers [40]

To all soldiers in the army:

You have often said that your guns will not be used against the people. I believe this absolutely. But think about this. After you have entered Beijing, will the government stop oppressing the people as you think? Just look at what Li Peng has said recently. First he has said that the students are patriotic, then that they are causing turmoil. Given such contradictory statements, who can trust him? In all seriousness, the government is using you to suppress the people. You must not enter Beijing; for this would make you criminals of historical dimensions.

May 22, 1989

LX: An Open Letter to the Students [41]

A salute to you from an old soldier! Over the past few days I have been watching your struggle, and want to remind you that you have already achieved an incredible victory. I cannot openly support you, but I can advise you of the following.

1) *On questions of strategy:* If there are several hundred thousand people in Tiananmen Square, the much smaller number of soldiers will not be able to handle the situation. Even though we have had martial law for a few days, no military action has taken place in the square, for there are not enough soldiers and policemen. Further, because of their training, they will find it difficult to shoot the people. The ten million people of Beijing, united together, are unconquerable.

2) *On questions of tactics:*

i) *Road junctions:* That people have blocked military vehicles is unprecedented. Never retreat. Even if a few platoons get through, they will be insufficient. Therefore, improve your command system and organization here, as it is sometimes poor.

ii) *Splitting:* A familiar tactic to be used against the army. Permit say two-thirds of the soldiers to pass, and then block the remainder. Repeat this at each junction, thus cutting the army into several separate parts which cannot cooperate. In this way, the power and the initiative of the army will evaporate.

iii) *Shooting and tear gas:* In a crowd of several thousands, this can cause confusion, injuries and deaths. We must warn the army commanders who give such orders that they will be sentenced to death by courts martial. And even if Beijing can be controlled by means of a massacre, can the whole of China? We don't have enough armies.

iv) We should trust the basic qualities of the People's Army, the product of deep and detailed ideological work. Ask them not only to refrain from entering the city, but also to stand alongside the people.

Hoping for victory for the people of Beijing!

May 22, 1989

LXI: *A Letter to all Soldiers who are Ordered to Enter Beijing to Impose Martial Law* [42]

Dear Warriors,

I am also a soldier, born in a peasant family. We are brothers, from the same class, fellow soldiers in the same trench. As your senior, I want to discuss with you your responsibility as soldiers.

The PLA is the army of the people, the sons and brothers of workers and peasants, standing close to them, service to them being our main purpose, and through which we show that we are not a private army of a warlord.

If foreigners invade our country, then we will sacrifice ourselves willingly on the battlefields. In times of natural disaster, we immediately go to the aid of affected areas, risking our lives. In the hearts of our people the PLA are secure, like fish in water.

It is sad for me to tell you that you are not here to fight enemies of the people, nor to combat a disaster. You have been deceived; for the army comes to Beijing to suppress the patriotic Student Movement; and when you fight your way into Beijing, you will be starting a civil war.

The movement which has been initiated by the students, and supported by the workers, peasants, and intellectuals, affects everyone. Its goals are the promotion of reform, to attack corruption, ending bureaucratic speculation on the black market, and the improvement of the standard of living of the entire population. In an event unprecedented in world history, one million people participated in a demonstration in Beijing. This is a Movement of the same historical importance as with the May Fourth Movement of 1919. It attacks the privileged and corrupt elements, like Yang Shangkun. Yang, purged by Mao Zedong, was saved by the party, and given important powers. However, after he became Vice-Chairman of the Military Commission, he used his authority to appoint his brother, Yang Baibang, to head of the Political Department, and his son to the leadership of the 2nd Armed Battalion. To his shame, the meeting of the Military Commission has become a family affair!

The core of the CCP must agree with the patriotic views of the students, and reject the view that the Movement has created "turmoil." That would mean that it is counter-revolutionary, which is ridiculous. The core of the party supports the students' criticism of bureaucratic corruption; and the Yang brothers fear for their feudal privileges. Regardless of popular discontent, Yang and his clique openly expel Zhao Ziyang, General Secretary of the CCP. They support the ambitions of Li Peng, who has just committed the error of declaring martial law, and have usurped the power of the party by ordering 100,000 troops to surround Beijing. Their main aim is to suppress the students' Patriotic-Democracy Movement, and to organise a cover-up. Their second purpose is to foment disorder so as to establish a fascist dictatorship, a Yang dynasty. They are outrageous, obvious, and opposed by senior commanders of the PLA. Some even mouth the slogan, "Down with the new warlord!"

Given this, why do large numbers of armed soldiers, with their tanks and their guns, enter the peaceful capital? Was there a military rebellion? No! Rioting, arson, and illegality? No! There is merely a peaceful demonstration by unarmed students, a student strike, a rally, a sit-down hunger strike. If we are supposed to be tackling a small minority of bad people, why do we need 100,000 soldiers?

Brothers, you see the attitudes of the common people, as they block our convoys with their bodies, trying to save the students and intellectuals. China has reached an important historical movement, and we must be careful to avoid stupid and cruel actions. We must refuse to be servants of the Brothers Yang, refuse to be criminals, refuse to point our weapons at the students and common people. Even if we are punished, we must not be the indifferent tools for a bloody incident. The students will remember us for this, as their parents will support us, and everybody thank us. This is the viewpoint of many soldiers.

I salute you.

May 23, 1989

THE INTELLECTUALS COMMENT

LXII: Declaration of May 17, 1989 (by Yan Jiaqi, Bao Zunxin, Ni Nanyou, Lang Lujun).

Since 2:00 p.m. on May 13th, about three thousand students have been on hunger strike; that is, for more than one hundred hours. More than seven hundred have lost consciousness. This is an unprecedented tragedy in the history of our mother country. The students are asking for a denunciation of the April 26th editorial in the *People's Daily* and the live broadcast of a dialogue between student and government representatives. The children of the mother country are collapsing, and the government is ignoring their demands. So the hunger strike goes on.

Now the problems of our country are exposed to the whole world; and that problem is that an autocrat has unlimited power, with government ignoring its responsibilities and losing all humanity. Such an irresponsible and inhuman government is what we have in our People's Republic: an autocracy.

The Qing dynasty collapsed seventy-eight years ago; yet China still has an emperor, though untitled — a senile autocrat. Yesterday afternoon the General Secretary of the Party, Zhao Ziyang, declared openly that in China all important decisions must be approved by this old man [Deng Xiaoping]. Unless he agrees, the April 26th editorial cannot be denounced. After one hundred hours of starvation, we are left with no other choice than to rely on the people themselves. In this context, we can say that the hunger strike has been a remarkable victory, demonstrating not the "riot" of which the students are accused, but the birth of a Patriotic-Democratic Movement that will bury China's last autocrat and China's last imperial regime.

Let us proclaim:

Victory for the struggle of the hunger strikers! Long live the spirit of non-violent protest!

Down with autocracy! Down with the April 26th editorial! Long live the people! Long live democracy! Long live freedom!

LXIII: An Extremely Urgent Appeal to the People of Beijing [43]

The ruling clique of the military government is blatantly violating the Constitution and openly acting as the enemy of the people. It has proclaimed martial law. The Chinese people are facing a life and death situation. The people, the students and the intelligentsia are facing immediate and bloody persecution. In order to save the republic, we members of the intelligentsia are making these extremely urgent proposals.

1. We urgently call on the 10 million people in the capital to assemble at 1.30 p.m. on May 23rd at Fuxiamen and Jianguomen for a massive procession. The common slogan should be, "Lift Martial Law; Li Peng and Yang Shangkun resign!" We shall have the greatest demonstration for justice in human history, influencing world public opinion in support of our own one billion people.

2. We must strengthen and continue our propaganda work with the People's Liberation Army. Our slogan should be, "Do not stain your hands with the blood of the people." We will wage a massive all-out campaign that includes members of high schools, primary schools, and kindergartens. Our aim is to demoralise the military and convince it to take the side of the people.

3. Immediately convene an extraordinary meeting of the people's congress of the Beijing municipality; sack [Mayor] Chen Xitong;

annul all curfew orders; and elect a new government; restore the public transportation system, law and order, and create a new social order for the people.

4. Urge all the politicians and military personnel who have a conscience to make clear their position and to use their influence in the military regions to support the people of the capital, and to send immediate help to save the people's republic.

5. We must have no illusions about the ruling clique of the militarist government. We must be clearly aware of the imminence of a large-scale and bloody conflict. All the citizens should organise themselves immediately and should establish a unified network for co-ordination, directives and mobilization. We must prevent the military from being able to crush us with a few concentrated attacks. We must also be prepared to sacrifice blood, and so must organise first aid and medical facilities.

6. If the militarist government is prepared to risk the condemnation of the whole world by resorting to bloody terror to suppress the masses, and install an autocratic rule, the people in the capital must disperse immediately and try to protect the student leaders and the vanguard among the intelligentsia. The people should call for the resolute resistance by the whole nation. The ruling clique will be buried by the resistance of one billion people. When victory is gained, the violators of the Constitution will be brought to justice for their crimes, and a new era for the republic will begin.

Dear people of the capital. This is the last fight and the last hope of the republic. With all your passion and courage, defend the People's Republic with your blood and your lives.

May 22, 1989

LXIV: To All Compatriots [44]

Since April 15th, a Patriotic-Democratic Movement, instigated by the Beijing students, has swept through China, creating a following inside and outside the country. However, the development of the movement is seriously threatened by a handful of reactionaries, like Li Peng. Fellow countrymen, note that the outcome of this movement will affect us all.

The movement's aim is to combat corruption and autocracy, and to fight for democracy. However, China has entrenched problems of a centralised autocracy and a self-protective ruling clique. The right of the people to freedom of speech and participation in political life has never been realised. Lies are normal in the media. As for freedom of thought, the media have always been ruthlessly suppressed, and lies are normal in the press. The abuse of power by experts and officials becomes dominant, and the anger of the people against it is expressed in anything that is symbolically useful. At such a moment, the people of Beijing found an outlet in the ceremonies associated with the death of Hu Yaobang:

April 20th: About 100 students were vigorously beaten up by the police for laying a wreath in memory of Yu Haobang [who had died on April 15th] at Zhongnanhai.

April 22nd: Three students, holding more than 100,000 signatures, knelt on the steps before the Great Hall of the People in Tiananmen Square, requesting that Li Peng accept the petition. They were ignored, even though Li Peng and other party and government leaders were in the hall.

April 24th: The chief editor of the *World Economic Herald* was sacked, and control of the press intensified.

April 25th: After listening to a few reports by party leaders, Deng denounced the student movement as a "disturbance," a "turmoil." He also said, "we have an army of three millions," and do not have to fear the curses of anyone in the international community. His words were, "The softer we seem, the more weak we shall become." The next day, an editorial in the *People's Daily*, entitled "Oppose Disturbances Unrelentingly," was obviously based on Deng's speech. It asserted that the student movement was an anti-party and anti-socialist disturbance.

April 27th: More than 100,000 students, backed by an enraged public, broke through the blockade of the army and police and staged a demonstration of unprecedented size. Slogans like "Freedom and Democracy" and "Down with Official Corruption" were heard. They also demanded an open, sincere and equal dialogue with the central authorities; which responded by sending in the 38th Army to threaten the students.

April 29th: The authorities held a fake "dialogue" with some officially-appointed student representatives as a mode of deception, whilst continuing to denounce the Student Movement as a "turmoil."

May 4th: A demonstration spread throughout the country, supporting the *World Economic Herald,* demanding freedom and openness[45] in politics. Zhao Ziyang publicised his view that problems had to be solved by democratic means, and within the bounds of the legal system. The students agreed to return to classes, but continued to demand a dialogue.

May 13th: The government had refused to enter into dialogue. Some students were so outraged that they went on a hunger strike. Thus began the conflict that moved the world to tears.

May 18th: On the sixth day of the hunger strike more than 2000 of the hunger strikers had lost consciousness, and many were in danger of contracting sicknesses associated with malnutrition and dehydration. Millions had given their public support. On the same day, Li Peng agreed to meet student representatives, but refused to discuss the circumstances of the hunger strikers. He also said that neither the government nor the party centre had said that the students were creating a disturbance.

May 19th: At 9:00 p.m., following a visit and statement by Zhao Ziyang, the students decided to call off the hunger strike. However, one hour later, Li Peng called a meeting of party cadres at which the student movement was officially called a riot. Worse yet, 100,000 troops were mobilised and, armed to the teeth, at about midnight, began to move on Beijing with tanks, armoured cars, tear gas and high pressure water hoses. The order was not successfully carried out only because the citizens of Beijing spontaneously organised a blockade, and the troops refused to clash with the people.

May 20th: Li Peng declared martial law in Beijing. The city government shut down public transport and ordered the traffic police to quit their posts in order to accuse the students of fomenting public disorder. However, with the active intervention of the students, traffic stayed in good order. No incidents of street fighting or robbery occurred, and social order was maintained.

May 23rd: There has been the most massive popular demonstration against martial law. As for the soldiers, they are insulted by the facile arguments that they have been sent to Beijing "on manoeuvres," or to do "relief work," or, the most stupid, "to make a film." Some high ranking officials have appealed to the Military Committee[46], demanding that the troops refrain from firing on the people, and that martial law be ended. In the afternoon, millions of people, from all walks of life, marched in torrential rain to condemn the handful of persons around Li Peng for antagonising the people, creating social disorder by the cruelest means (whilst blaming the people), and choosing violence as a way of solving the problems arising within our democracy and legal system. Their contemptible goal is to usurp the highest power of the party and the State. The people are demonstrating against this, against their militarism and their willingness to disturb the peace and good order of the capital.

In this Movement, the students have put forward reasonable demands in a legal manner. They have been extremely rational, calm and disciplined, insisting that problems be solved by democratic and legal means. Conditions have degenerated to their present sorry state because of the government's failure to respond. Ignoring the students' physical well-being, distorting public information, and stubbornly upholding its mistakes, the Li Peng government has lost the support of the party and the people. Thoroughly corrupt, it cannot desist, and it will destroy the People's Republic if permitted. Therefore,

1) Determine to carry the Movement through to victory as a precondition of a solution to the present crisis and the future civilised existence of our nation.

2) Demand the earliest end of martial law and the removal of the troops from Beijing; for production, transport, and daily life are operating normally.

3) The People's National Congress or its Standing Committee must immediately convene an emergency meeting to acknowledge the Movement and condemn the April 26th editorial.

4) Li Peng should be taken from office, since he has broken the law in his dealings with the Student Movement; and the government changed.

5) The government must permit freedom of the press, and the people must be permitted to publish their own newspaper. An open political process must ensure that decisions are really made by the people.

6) We must ensure that the government carries through the on-going reforms to their conclusion, the government and people co-operating to overcome difficulties.

Compatriots, the Patriotic-Democratic Movement has been revealed. It is a new beginning in China's history, and a major element in the democratic trend that now dominates world history. Before the eyes of the world it has shown itself to reflect the vigour, strength and self-confidence of China and her people. But the democratization process is long, and the people must be determined in their commitment. Only when every Chinese raises his/her fist in righteous support will the last stronghold of the autocratic dynasty crumble into ashes before the roar of the people.

Long live the people! Long live the Republic!

May 24, 1989

A CHINESE SOLIDARITY IN THE MAKING

LXV: *Introducing the "Capital Union"*

1. The Union of all Sections of the People of Beijing is known by a shortened name "Capital Union."

2. The Capital Union is based on the present, great Patriotic-Democratic Movement. It has been spontaneously organised, and is a mass organization of the masses of workers, intellectuals, cadres of the state machinery, young students, patriotic-democratic elements, peasants and people engaged in business.

3. The goal of the Capital Union is to unite the different sections of people in the capital. We call on all patriots from different sections,

all parties and factions to take action to set up a patriotic-democratic united front, so that the democratic forces can grow and increase in strength, and the republic be taken along the road of freedom, democracy, the rule of law and civilization.

4. The immediate goal of the Capital Union is to mobilise all patriotic people to actively assist ASUBU and other autonomous organizations in the post secondary field, and to support resolutely the present Patriotic-Democratic Movement to the very end.

5. The immediate tasks of the Capital Union will include:

a) With the help of the masses of news workers, to publish an unofficial publication that will reflect the true feeling of the people — "the Voice of the People."

b) The organization of citizen patrol groups to assist the students in maintaining order in the capital, that normal life and social stability will be guaranteed.

c) The mobilization of the masses from all sections of the community to do everything possible to resist martial law, and thoroughly defeat the conspiracy of military rule imposed by the small clique of autocratic elements.

d) The study of strategy and tactics for the furthering of the Movement, providing reliable information, practical theories, and suggestions for solving the problems of all patriotic organizations.

e) The co-ordination of the patriotic elements of all sections of the community so that purposeful, prepared, organised, forceful and united actions can be undertaken against the minority of autocratic forces, and in support of the university students.

f) The collection of opinions and suggestions from all patriotic elements of the community. Endless efforts will be devoted to promote the maturity and perfection of the Capital Union.

6. The Capital Union will have the following departments: theory and research, strategy and tactics, information, fund-raising, propaganda and agitation, liaison, coordination, supply, editorial board of the "People's Voice," publication, and defense departments.

7. Capital Union bases its action on the will of the majority of China's citizens. The Capital Union supports the Constitution and will work within the Constitution, although it feels that the constitution still needs to be amended and perfected.

8. The precondition for the dissolution of the Capital Union is: — after extensive and sufficient polling of public opinion, it is found that the majority of the Chinese people no longer feel that it should continue to exist. Unless this happens, no other factors or force could bring about its dissolution. The hatred and repression by the autocratic forces will only lead to the growth and the perfection of the Union.

9. The Capital Union is in a condition of continuous development. It is hoped that patriotic elements and organizations of various sectors would give their sincere help and guidance. All help and support, in the form of material or otherwise, are welcome. All sectors of the community are also welcome to join.

Long Live Democracy! Long Live the People!
Long Live Freedom! Long Live China!
Unite and pursue the Democracy Movement to the end!

May 25, 1989

NOTES

1. The *dazibao*, sometimes translated as "big character poster," posted in a public place, is a popular vehicle for the circumvention of censorship controls and providing criticism of the government. They are usually, but not invariably, anonymous. Mao Zedong himself had used it in 1966 to in-initiate the Cultural Revolution. The Xidan Democracy Wall Movement of 1978-1979 was centred on this kind of activity.

2. The distinction here is between a professional party member, who is paid by the CCP to perform a specific task, and regular members whose occupation is with a non-party organization.

3. This pamphlet appeared under the authorship of "A Revolutionary of the Beijing Teachers' Training University."

4. Signed by a "Disciple of Marxism."

5. Anonymous big character poster at the People's University.

6. The pamphlet was prepared by the Theory and Information section of the Beijing University Preparatory Committee.

7. Presented under the authorship, "A Revolutionist of the Teachers' University."

8. Issued by the Autonomous Students' Association of the University of Education of Beijing.

9. Produced by the Xinhua students.

10. Pamphlet distributed at the military camp at Six Mile Bridge, on the western periphery of Beijing.

11. The 38th Army, initially ordered to repress the students and citizens of Beijing, was heroically reticent. Its commander-in-chief, Xu Qinxian, received a prison sentence of 18 years for checking himself into a hospital, preferring to take sick leave to the task of executioner of innocents.

12. This document appeared under the aegis of the Beijing Teachers Training University Students' Autonomous Union on May 28, 1989. It praises the authentic "workers' picket," condemning the government for organising an anti-student segment of workers, with which it should not be confused.

13. Presented by the Autonomous Students' Union of the University of Science and Technology, under the authority of "Dreaming of China's Emergence."

14. General Secretary of the CCP, removed in 1928.
15. Leader of the Fourth Front army who split with Mao in 1935 during the Long March.
16. Denounced by Mao in 1938 for promoting "formalism of a foreign origin." Wang had just returned from Moscow.
17. Referring to Liu Xiaoqi, Deng Xiaoping, and Zhou Enlai, all of whom were accused of being revisionists of different degrees during the Cultural Revolution.
18. Lin had been designated Mao's heir in 1969, but died two years later in an air crash whilst fleeing to the USSR, supposedly after an attempt to assassinate Mao. Jiang Qing was Mao's wife, member of the infamous Gang of Four, imprisoned in 1981 for heinous crimes committed during the Cultural Revolution.
19. The next three documents appeared under the authority of the "Beijing Workers' Union."
20. The CCP distrust of intellectuals was seen during the Cultural Revolution when they were called the "stinking ninth" after the other specified "class enemies,": i) landlords, ii) rich peasants, iii) counter-revolutionaries, iv) "bad elements," v) rightists, vi) renegades, vii) enemy agents, and viii) capitalist-roaders.
21. At the time of writing, Deng Xiaoping was perhaps the most powerful man in China, although his formal position was simply Chairman of the Military Commission of the CCP. Zhao Ziyang was General Secretary of the CCP (soon to be removed for being opposed to the use of military force against the demonstrators) and Li Peng was Premier of China. In an intra-party conflict between Zhao and Li, the latter was able to swing the reactionary forces behind him. Those reactionaries are typified by the other names here: Yang Shangkun (President of China), Chen Yun (85-year old chairman of the CCP Central Advisory Commission), Li Xiannian (80-year old former President), Peng Zhen (87-year old former Premier), and Jiang Zemin (62) who was to replace Zhao Ziyang as General Secretary of the CCP.
22. Signed by "A Worker."
23. Signed by "A Beijing Worker."

24. The document appears under the sponsorship of The Chinese Workers' Movement College Committee in Support of Student Action, Capital Workers' Picket Group Temporary Command Centre.
25. An obvious reference to the final lines of *The Manifesto of the Communist Party* (1848), written by Marx and Engels.
26. As presented by the Preparatory Committee of BWAF.
27. Release by BWAF.
28. Presented by "Workers' representatives."
29. By "A Group of Marxists."
30. By "a party member."
31. By a "Beijing University student CCP member."
32. By "Cadres of the Security and Judiciary Departments."
33. By student members of the CCP.
34. This piece originated in Beijing University under the authorship of "Members of the CCP."
35. By "Some Cadres of Central State Institutions."
36. By Zhu X..., "Teacher of English."
37. By "Some Teachers and Party Members of the People's University."
38. By "A Soldier of the Third Battalion of the Central Security Guards."
39. By "A Soldier's Wife."
40. By "A Member of the PLA," handed out at Beijing University.
41. By "An Old Soldier."
42. By an "Army Colonel."
43. Presented by "Intellectuals in the Capital."
44. Presented by "Intellectuals of the Capital."
45. *Glasnost*, or openness, was the official policy in the USSR, which was moving rapidly towards a position of *rapprochement* with the PRC. The Chinese students quite obviously viewed the Soviet developments as an encouraging sign. However, when Mikhail Gorbachev visited China in May, 1989, he deliberately distanced himself from the Movement, refusing comment.
46. This could refer to the Military Committee of the National People's Congress (a government body), or to the Military Commission of the CCP, the chairman of which was Deng Xiaoping at that time.

III

INTERVIEWS WITH THREE LEADING PERSONALITIES

LXVI: Two Interviews With Wuer Kaixi [1]

[Interviewer's Introduction]

Commenting on his relationship with Wang Dan, Wuer Kaixi stated that he was both a friend and comrade in arms, although it was possible that they could become political opponents. By contrast with Wang's quiet determination, Wuer presents himself energetically and forcefully, with confidence and bluntness. By contrast, Wang stands quietly to one side, lets Wuer hold forth, occasionally reminding him of a point or adding a qualification. They never quarrel or compete for power.

On May 8, 1989, Wuer had led his classmates from the Beijing University of Education to Tiananmen Square to support a demonstration being held by the Association of Chinese Reporters. He looked for Wang around the square, shouting his name, and was disappointed not to find him. After the May Fourth Demonstration Wang had said that he was going to quit the Student Movement.

Tired and depressed, he said that he would rather work on creating a Democratic Movement. However, when the hunger strike got under way the two began again to cooperate.

At 3:00 a.m. on May 21st Wuer was under tremendous pressure to quit Tiananmen Square, and did so. The rumour was that a representative of the Foundation of the Disabled (which is headed by the son of Deng Xiaoping, Deng Paofang) told him that the army was going to march into the square and kill all of the students. Wuer was not widely condemned for his action, although some students stopped supporting him. Moreover, some of the Beijing students disliked his "individualism," his love of fun, his tendency to make independent decisions, and the fact that he always had a girl in tow.

Only twenty years old, Wuer Kaixi is an ethnic Turk from Sinkiang province. His father has a modest position on a newspaper there, so it is wrong to call the young man the son of a high official. Any money he spends is earned from providing economic articles for the Sinkiang press. The greatest influence on him is his teacher in the Faculty of Chinese at the Beijing Normal University, the Doctor of Literature, Liu Xiaobo, whom Wuer admits to consulting. [2]

After the April 27th demonstration the Student Movement became quiet for some days. Student leaders, including Wuer and Wang, sought to generate an atmosphere of interest and activism for a demonstration on May 4th. Wuer went into hiding, some students claimed that their lives were in danger, and others said that they were about to be arrested by the police. Later on, after the demonstration, they admitted that this had been a strategy to ensure that the students' spirits could be easily aroused.

In Tiananmen Square both young and old approach Wuer for his autograph, even visitors from Hong Kong. Nor is it just ordinary people who admire him; for even experienced reporters ask their colleagues to get his autograph, with some words of greeting. Wuer is quite the star, and apparently enjoys it. He also has the attributes of a celebrity, with a ready smile, clever speech, delighting in the self-conscious use of his talents. He also recognises his own weaknesses, and people seem willing to accept the sincere apologies that follow his mistakes.

These interviews were conducted on June 2nd and June 3rd. It was still a peaceful situation, and his manner was relaxed. Nevertheless, his confidence, courage and faith in democracy are all evident.

The First Interview

Question: After the successful demonstrations of April 27th and May 4th, why did students take part in a hunger strike?

Answer: After demonstrations, marches, and sit-ins, this peaceful action became most significant. The idea was proposed by Wang Meng, Wang Dan, Chin Chiang, Yang Chaofai, Ma Siufang and myself. The hunger strikers demanded democracy, and were prepared to sacrifice their lives for that end. The University of Beijing and the Beijing University of Education were its organizers.

Q: How did you feel when you saw those students being carried unconscious from the square?

A: As an organiser I was, of course, anxious and sad; but their commitment had to be respected.

Q: The hunger strike lasted for seven days, and did not achieve its objectives. Was it foolish? Why was it stopped?

A: We estimated that the government would enter into a dialogue with us before the hunger strike was three days old; but it was too stupid and shameless. The students entered voluntarily into the action, and were prepared to die even if nothing were achieved.

It is not foolish to die for the future greatness of China. It is something that is to be respected. We stopped the strike once we recognised that the government was stupid and blind to that. It would have been childish and silly to use the bodies of decent students to seek change from such a government. During the strike we matured, and came to see that we must have a revolution. Our definitive slogan became, "Li Peng! Step Down!"

Q: Some intellectuals had told you to stop the strike for the sake of the students' health. Why did you ignore them?

A: They could have persuaded us if they had treated us correctly. However, they adopted an authoritarian posture, and in condescending to us aroused discontent. They should have treated us like equals. We are all citizens; and students are not simpletons.

Q: The Student Movement has been turned into a weapon employed in the power struggle amongst the top government leaders.

A: That's none of our business. We have our own agenda; and I have no faith in the view that the Student Movement can win by means of the help of a particular group of government officials. The Student Movement will have achieved its grand purpose when the Chinese people demand the resignation of the government, voicing their great dissatisfaction with the leaders of this country. This transformation of consciousness is the first step, which must then produce a democratic society. This weapon, the Student Movement, too big for the bureaucrats to cope with, directly promotes the struggle of democracy against the power of conservatism.

Q: If you had retreated after two or three days of your hunger strike, when Li Peng met the students' representatives, would you have achieved a better result?

A: If China is to move forward she must get more than "wise leaders." Political power must be controlled, and a democratic system introduced. If we had stopped the strike to talk with Li Peng, and the government had accepted our demands, such as admitting corruption, we might have shouted, "Long live Li Peng!" But this would never have led to our current demands of "freedom of the press" and "self-governing organizations."

Let me emphasise that whether Li Peng steps down or not is unimportant compared with the broad acceptance of our slogans, which will mean social pressure to place constraints upon government. If Li Peng were to step down, to be replaced by some other party figure, it would mean nothing. Even if Zhao Ziyang retains power, and is a good secretary, restraints should also be placed on him. We will have shouted the slogan, but seen no substantial change. The Democracy Movement wants to achieve: 1) democratic consciousness, and 2) a democratic institutional structure. That is the foundation upon which we must build. It will be a long and hard process, and I am prepared to devote the rest of my life to the task.

Q: But now we see a reactionary government imposing harsher controls.

A: I believe that this restrictive policy will be temporary, and that it contains a time bomb. It will generate a huge opposition. Democracy will not be achieved overnight, but our efforts can hasten its coming. I predict that there will be changes in the next three to five years.

Q: Earlier, when the students held a dialogue with Li Peng, why did you interrupt his speech?

A: We were sitting in the air-conditioned Hall of the People, on a sofa drinking tea. Outside there were hungry students sitting on the cold ground of Tiananmen Square. Li Peng began to deliver a long opening speech, treating the students like immature children. He spoke nonsense, presented no solutions, and did not respect the people's rights. He should rather treat himself as a child of the people, a civil servant of the people and the country; but he was just too proud. We were told that his son's involvement, or non-involvement, in corrupt practices was none of our business. It was all a waste of time. His behaviour as the Premier made us sick. After three minutes we had had enough, and I just had to stop him.

Q: Everyone thinks that you had a lot of guts to interrupt his speech on television. Were you treating him like a Premier?

A: [Angrily] I treated him like a citizen. To be a Premier is his work. As a citizen of the republic I am his equal. I am more honest than he; and if we are unequal, then it is I who must be his superior, not the reverse. But I think that we are equal; so I did not need to be afraid when I interrupted his speech.

Q: Some have said that you pretended to faint at that time.

A: No. I had an asthma attack because I was so angry. I lost all my strength and had to lie down for an oxygen tube to be inserted in my nose. By then the dialogue had failed with Li Peng's bad performance. Wang Dan told me to leave, and I replied, "Please carry me away."

Q: Did your questioning of Li Peng during the national broadcast have any consequences?

A: Tremendous consequences. We met as two citizens, which is natural. However, in the words of the Hou Dejian's song, "We are not used to it." In the past, to meet the Premier was a "generous gift" from the government. My performance was a beginning. People are tired of that kind of feudalism, and are delighted to see equality.

Q: Do you think that your popularity is widespread?

A: Yes, especially in Beijing. I am, however, sad when someone shouts, "Long live Wuer Kaixi." I work for the Democracy Movement, and am opposed to dictatorship and the feudal empire. Someone wanted *me* to be long-lived; but other people have suffered a great deal more.

Q: People look upon you as the student star.

A: I am willing to be a hero, which is natural, even though I'm not worthy of it. As for being a "star", what can I do about it [with a big grin]?

Q: You are criticised for being too individualistic.

A: That's the fault of the reporters, who build up an imaginary picture by emphasising my positive aspects. I have always said that I have many weaknesses. One can only aspire to perfection.

Q: People say that you overly enjoy attractive clothes, spending money, and having a good time.

A: [Angrily again]. That's stupid. I'm an ordinary person, so why can't I enjoy good clothes, good food and good company? Why must I be solemn, and look as bad as Li Peng?

Q: There are rumours that foreign countries would provide political protection for student leaders.

A: There are many such rumours, but I don't pay any attention to them. We must struggle and sacrifice, not escape, which is useless for the Democratic Movement. It is better to be in jail. But I'm willing to travel, have a look at the U.S.A., Hong Kong, Taiwan, and Macau. I want study and experience; but I never want to lose touch with China. I am closely linked with the Democratic Movement, and would devote my life to it. I think about my personal contribution, and carry out my historical responsibility as an active person who loves literature, art and life. That is my conclusion. If Wang Dan or I were to quit it would be truly irresponsible in relation to the Movement, as much as I love life.

Q: You mean, "enjoy life?"

A: [Smile]

Q: Let's talk about the interesting matter of your relationship with Wang Dan.

A: Of course. We have been friends and comrades since the beginning of the Student Movement. He is a person whose behaviour and conduct are ever exemplary. Although we don't always agree, we cooperate always for the sake of the Movement. He was not happy for a period of time, and moved from the Square to Beijing

University. However, even if we were to become political opponents, we would always be friends.

Q: Before the 1989 Student Movement, nobody knew who you were. By contrast, Wang was promoting democracy earlier with such organizations as the "Democracy Field Salon."

A: I'm not sensitive about this. As a first year student at the Beijing University of Education I have only been in university for seven or eight months.

Q: You are always optimistic — unlike Wang, who is sometimes pessimistic. Is there anything in your family background that explains this? Do your parents support you?

A: My parents have encouraged me. My mother visited me on May 17th when I had just started the hunger strike. They were concerned about my poor health; for I have a heart infection and low blood sugar. I have been in hospital on ten occasions, and lose consciousness when I get over-excited. Although I was born in Beijing, my family moved to Sinkiang in 1984. I returned in 1987 to complete my high school studies. I had also been involved in the students' union of my secondary school in Sinkiang.

Q: You have reiterated the criticism of intellectuals as "the stinking ninth." [3] Why are you unhappy with them? Would you regret the loss of their support?

A: Intellectuals have had a distorted view for thousands of years, favouring reformism rather than revolution.

Q: Does this mean that reform is impossible?

A: Is anything really impossible? People get overly pessimistic. Ten years ago the time was ripe, and still we do so little.

Q: More recently it has been said that the students and their leaders have been demoralised by divisions and sectarianism.

A: The Student Movement is fundamentally magnificent, and beyond criticism. However, since it has a highly complex membership, it is to be expected that there will be traitors within the membership. Its honesty and cohesion can be undermined by,

i) monetary donations,

ii) corruptions of power, and

iii) exaggeration of the ability of student leaders — we all must control ourselves if we are being flattered!

Q: Why don't you all leave the Square? Is it now too late?

A: Actually, we have considered retreat often. On May 28th it was discussed, then rejected. On May 30th we announced our departure, then reversed it. The main reason was that non-Beijing students were not prepared to leave. It meant that anyone who was prepared to stand as a spokesperson had to confirm the occupation of the Square. The situation is now out of control, and we are waiting, active, for the government's response.

Second Interview

Question: The situation in Beijing is very dangerous now, so I hope that this is not the last time that I can talk to you. Why did you get so involved in the Movement, becoming a student leader?

Answer: I have cared about the democratic development of China for some years. I even wrote articles, but these were not published. Now I think that we have a great Student Movement; and I feel that I have the energy and ability to devote myself to playing a leadership role.

Q: What's your opinion on the death of Hu Yaobang?

A: The death of a citizen, even of a communist, never causes much excitement; which is perhaps a problem in itself. The fact that the death of this democratic leader has led to such immense chaos shows just how unsatisfactory the situation is in China.

Q: What were your hopes upon joining the Movement?

A: Two things. First, I wanted it to be like the May Fourth Movement, and improve democratic consciousness. The Chinese have a thirst for democracy, but they lack an understanding of it. Through the Movement educational work could be promoted. Second, I hoped that we could set a good example of the skills required for democracy. At first, I had hoped that the Autonomous Students' Union of Beijing Universities (ASUBU) could gain legal status and form an opposition to the government.

Q: What were the government's errors in dealing with the Movement, and what issues developed in consequence?

A: Before the big demonstration on April 22nd students aged 18 or 19, with no proper organization, made various appeals. At that stage, if the Government had really wanted to, it could easily have handled the issue.

Q: Given the government's determination, what became the goals of the Movement?

A: One cannot be sure, but I don't think that the situation will turn into chaos.

Q: What were the other errors of the government?

A: On April 22nd the police and soldiers attacked the students. That united the students, and led to the Temporary Students' Union of April 27th. The Student Movement became markedly different as large scale organizations were set up.

Q: What do such errors tell us about the government and the future?

A: I think that the basic cause of these errors was the undemocratic attitude of the government. It is not familiar with democratic activities, like demonstrations. Its own decision-making is not democratic. In fact, all matters are decided by one person. Even Li Peng said that the Government was controlled by Deng Xiaoping. The lack of democracy and hostility to the democratic way of life is the main reason for the current situation. At the same time, another problem is the poor quality of the leaders in the top ranks of the Government.

Q: What are your motives in leading the Movement? What conceptual ideas do you use to understand democracy and the present Chinese society?

A: My motives are simple. I'm extremely dissatisfied with the society. I study Education, so I analyzed the problems there, and discovered that the situation was very serious. I recognise that solutions cannot be provided by a bad political system. Therefore, our Student Union has to promote political reforms. First, we demand protection of our rights and freedoms as defined in the Constitution. We also seek a guarantee on the continuation of economic reforms and freedom of the press. There are many problems in China's system, including corruption, bureaucracy, and dictatorship. The major problem, however, is the fact that people cannot exercise their political rights, cannot control their political and economic lives. In fact, this is a Democracy and Human Rights Movement.

Q: Has there been a personal development for you in your experience of continual dialogue and participation in a large social movement?

A: Of course. My analytical skills and powers of observation have increased considerably. This is better than reading books. I also learned that there are practical problems inside the society and the government. These may not be noted by ordinary people. For one thing, democratic consciousness cannot exist without the right environment and the people. As I have said, the greatest barriers to progress are our one billion people and five thousand years of Chinese history.

Q: From your experience in the Movement, what is China's major problem on the road to democracy?

A: There are two aspects:

1) The democratic consciousness of the people. We are promoting democracy, but the people say simply, "Li Peng step down!" The latter is not a democratic mentality.

2) Systemic hindrances mean we cannot fully promote the democratic consciousness. If the government insists upon rejecting the creation of an opposition party, there will be no counteracting political force, and no hope for reforms and democracy in China.

Q: If your theories are applied, what will be the government's response? What is the probability of your success?

A: I think we will surely win, but it's difficult in the short run. In the long run, democracy must be developed, and our actions promote this. At present, our strength is not great and we have to work harder.

Q: What are the systemic problems?

A: Looking at things in Beijing over the past couple of days, nobody could be very optimistic. We must face reality. There may occur a serious drawback to the development of democracy.

Q: My view is that the next two to five years are crucial, irrespective of government violence or whether or not Li Peng is in power. Given that, if you are free, what will you do?

A: Try to establish a political opposition. I agree, however, that Li Peng may step down, and that there could be another purge within the party.

Q: Besides the government, have you discovered any problems among the students and the public?

A: We lack the experience of democracy, or we are too deeply influenced by the bureaucratic system. In fact many student leaders are quite bureaucratic, which is a great obstacle.

Q: What is your view of the political movements of the last forty years? For example, how do you think of the May Fourth Democracy Wall Movement of 1986-1987? Have you any general comments?

A: There's no basic difference between the past and present Student Movements. In the past, however, it lacked organization, the numbers were smaller, and they could not generate the agreement and support of people. This time our greatest success has been to achieve a consensus and reaction among the citizens of Beijing, building up a great countervailing power. We're still not satisfied, and it's hard to make progress. We may lose on this occasion; but very soon another Student Movement will appear on an even larger scale, and it will be more successful.

Our generation has witnessed the open-door foreign policy of China. The contributions of Hu Yaobang and others made us become more open-minded. After this event, the university students in the nineties will have a stronger sense of democracy.

Q: We know from the newspapers that many intellectuals declared support for you, and also promoted your political ideas. Can you point out the difference between you and them?

A: In China, a few young people have done a lot for democracy. I think the young ones are more educated than the elders, and are also pure in mind. Because of the environmental influence of the feudal system for thousands of years, the intellectuals are usually compromising and weak. They may have some suggestions. But what China needs now is specific ways to strengthen the sense of individualism in the citizen. This is not just a concept, but something which must be practiced. To do this, we think the young ones are stronger and purer.

Q: My view is same as yours. For the last ten years I have noticed that intellectuals, especially those who pursued democracy and freedom, concentrated mainly in the conceptual areas. Unlike you, they did not get away from existing society.

A: Yes, you're right. Their ideas usually agreed with the so-called reformists. My view is that we don't need reforms. We have had reforms in the past, even as far back as the Qing Dynasty, but they have never succeeded. Reforms are useless. China needs revolution. Of course I don't mean a military revolution. What I mean is: intellectuals think the power should remain at the top, with Government; but it should lie among the people.

Q: What is your definition of the "people"?

A: The people cannot be treated as a single whole. It is individuals, or organizations. The people is composed of every citizen. The old concept views people as identical, but this is an insult. We must recognise complexity, which is completely different from treating one billion individuals as a single group.

LXVII: An Interview With Chai Ling [4]

Question: What is the significance of Tiananmen Square to the Student Movement in Beijing?

Answer: We can say that the Square was a symbol to the Student Movement, especially before May 13th. Since May 13th, the first day of the hunger strike, the Square has been the focus and symbol of all the Chinese people, and of everyone in the world who seeks democracy.

Q: How do the masses see Tiananmen? Does it look to government, to Maoism, or to a new China?

A: We have often heard that the masses look to the students with admiration. They identify the students with their own sons and daughters, fighting for their own interests. The transformation of the Student Movement to a Democracy Movement indicates that the Chinese people are exerting their authority, that a new China is born, one which belongs to the people.

Q: What has the atmosphere been like over the past few days?

A: There have been some management problems and some confusion; but the organization is very united, and we are confident.

Q: What are your plans now?

A: I have seen some of the bad traits present in the Movement, and have been distressed by them. I have thought of quitting. I dearly wished for competent people to come forward to lead the Movement; and it should have been able to produce other people like myself.[5] Then, I realised that this might not happen; and in the absence of persons worthy of my trust, that I should stay on. To do otherwise would be a sin against the Movement, and so I decided to remain as Commander-in-Chief, which I still am.

Q: Do you think that Deng Xiaoping, Li Peng or Zhao Ziyang are making use of the Movement?

A: Naturally. Every Movement in the past has produced governmental changes. However, the present Movement has been unique in putting itself above factional struggles. We will not get involved in them, even though they attempt to use us. Such attempts are, I think, in vain; for the aim of the Student Movement is to struggle for progress towards a modern Chinese democracy. The Movement does not choose between Li or Zhao; for we oppose every leader who stands in opposition to the people. If, however, a leader takes a popular position, reflecting the demands and interests of the people, then he will be supported by them.

Q: You place the greatest emphasis on democracy. There are probably many Chinese who don't understand what it is. In the United States, democracy means the choice of each new President by popular vote.

A: I think that democracy is a natural right. In the past, human nature in China was very restricted, and there were no rights. For example, consider the conditions in the universities. When it comes to getting a job, you must go where the party decides. Furthermore, there is no supervision over the party, the security forces, or the army. This gives rise to profiteering, corruption, decadence and all of the ills that have accompanied the last ten years of economic reform. Those who acquired wealth recently all have links to those in power. The Chinese have had an emperor to rule them for more than two thousand years. There has never been freedom of speech, freedom of the press, or personal security, and there is little hope for the future. Prior to this Movement there was a moral crisis, and nobody was interested in anything but money. Through this Movement the Chinese have regained a sense of purpose and ability to solve their own problems. We do not depend upon foreign models, but upon ourselves.

Q: Can democracy and communist-socialism co-exist?

A: I have not done any great theoretical research. My view is that democracy is a basic human need, and not contrary to the basic tenets of communism. The sort of democracy which we demand is very natural, a natural right. It is not hooked up to any specific ideology. We are fighting for control of our own lives.

Q: Do you visualise how democracy will spread in China?

A: I think that it will be a long process, possibly sixty or seventy years. My hope is that one day we might live securely in a China where people can enjoy the fruits of their labours whilst possessing the power to participate in the management of the country. We shall have power to determine the policies implemented by our leaders, feeling ourselves to be our own masters in a country that we own. It will be a powerful nation which each generation will struggle to maintain.

Q: Will your Movement have any international significance?

A: Knowledge has no barriers. Although we struggle for our own country, we can have an influence on others as members of the world community.

There has been some confusion, but the more resolute of us are now united to combat that. We have demonstrated to the world that we are orderly, reasonable and strong. I say to you from the bottom of my heart that, if this Movement fails, it will be a tragedy for the whole nation. It will mean that the people's democratic consciousness was insufficiently developed, and that it was doomed from the start. The few thousand students on the Square cannot alone prevent its failure. However, if the Movement succeeds, the victory for democracy will be a liberation of the human nature of the whole Chinese people.

Q: Are your ideas similar to those of the May Fourth Movement? Are you the descendants of the revolutionaries of that period?

A: We have inherited some things from the May Fourth Movement. There are also differences. History will judge.

Q: In the May Fourth Movement both democracy and science were important.[6] What is the importance of science to you?

A: For us, only after democracy has blossomed will science be guaranteed. I read science at university. I would argue that up to this point in time such studies have been useless, and the prospects for China hopeless. Every strata of society saw no hope for the country. Science and technological knowledge have to be converted into productive force, which cannot be done if there is no guarantee of democracy.

Q: Do you want to see a country of equality or inequality of wealth?

A: We don't have statistics; but I would say that the disparity of wealth in China today, between the privileged and the ordinary person, is as extreme as that found in capitalist countries. I would hope that, after human nature is liberated in our society, a kind of spontaneous and harmonious regulation will occur. There will be differences. For example, those who are wise and hardworking will be better off than the lazy and incompetent. This is a natural inequality and not deliberately designed. However, today China's inequalities are deliberately produced by those in power, man-made and unnatural.

The Movement has been spontaneous and non-conspiratorial. There is no ruling theoretical framework. We just follow our feelings! It is a pure and unsullied demand for democracy. In it we see that the best and most advanced elements are students, who form a vanguard for the nation.

June 3, 1989

LXVIII: *An Interview with Fang Lizhi* [7]

Question: Professor Fang, recently Hong Kong newspapers disclosed some high level internal documents of the mainland government. Yang Shangkun gave a speech on May 24th at an extended emergency meeting of the Military Commission [of the CCP], saying that the older leaders had concluded that the Student Movement had its roots within the party. This seemed to imply that there was a link between intra-party struggles and the Movement. Do you agree?

Answer: The Student Movement, especially at the start, was entirely spontaneous. That it has since been infiltrated is a possibility. Nonetheless, the students made a spontaneous call for democracy. If we look at Yang's statement in a few years we will see that he greatly distorted the character of the Movement.

Q: In your view, how does the Student Movement differ from the Cultural Revolution?

A: The Cultural Revolution was a movement initiated by the leadership from the top downward. From the first big character poster the Cultural Revolution was a manipulation of the masses by the leaders, later developing into an inner-party struggle. This time the movement moves upwards from the base, urging the leaders to change and make reforms.

Q: But Yang Shangkun said that there were two commanders of the Student Movement in the Politburo, and that Zhao Ziyang had attempted to split the party.

A: (Jocularly) That at least shows how limited their vocabulary is. I cannot say at this time whether or not Zhao Ziyang is "splitting the party." However, compared with the Soviet leaders, the mentality of China's leaders is primitive. In the USSR differences at the top levels of the party are made public, indicating a degree of openness and confidence. If one is frightened of disclosing one's own problems, it shows a lack of confidence and weakness.

Q: Government officials gave examples to illustrate how the Student Movement was re-enacting the Cultural Revolution; for example, it pointed to the millions of people demonstrating on the streets.

A: The Cultural Revolution was a movement in which the leaders hoodwinked the masses. The Student Movement this time is a spontaneous one that grounds itself in the independent judgement of a large number of people. Other comparisons are meaningless. It is like the party saying that it is against all wars, and then advocating "just" wars, when it is obvious that all wars are equally cruel.

Q: The Secretary of the Beijing Municipal Council, Li Ximin, criticised you at a meeting of the party cadres, Politburo and Military Commission on May 19th for saying that the people would take to the streets before long. Did you ever make such a remark?

A: I might have. I was asked if a discussion at a meeting had been heated, and replied that it had, and that people would shortly be taking to the streets. I was simply commenting on the character of a meeting.

Q: On what occasion did you make the remark?

A: Privately, to a few people, or perhaps over the phone during a meeting. It was not a public statement, so it must have been reported by a spy.

Q: They also thought that Zhao Ziyang's supporters were enlarging the Movement.

A: I don't know, but I feel that many of them shared the same views, particularly during the early stages of the Movement.

Q: Li Ximin also emphasised the foreign influence on the Movement.

A: More nonsense!

Q: Yuan Mu also suggested that only Fang Lizhi himself knew what role he was playing.

A: (Laughing) This is the language of struggle of the Cultural Revolution. Could I but be the instigator of such a large-scale movement I would feel very, very honored. How honorable it would be to be capable of instigating millions of people to raise their voices in a cry for democracy.

Q: Having spoken with you the Taiwanese authoress, Long Yintai, said that you had been "on the alert to avoid suspicion." Was that because you feared that others would accuse you of being the "Black Hand" behind the Student Movement?

A: My being alert is not because I have something to fear, but because I want the students to take the more active role. They want to act, and do not need my interference in their autonomy. This shows that, in China, it is not simply "a very, very small minority," such as Fang Lizhi, who ask for democracy.

Q: They repeat the word "zui" [denoting a superlative when used before an adjective] when referring to "a small minority."

A: This is the parroting of the language style of the Cultural Revolution. The repetition of "zui" five times was the innovation of a student at the Second Girls' College in a speech of congratulation to Chairman Mao. So it is not an invention of the present leaders.

Q: It is also said that Fang Lizhi is on the alert, but his wife, Li Xian, often mixes with students, and is not above suspicion.

A: She is a lecturer at Beijing University, so it is natural for her to be with her students. For her not to be with them would be abnormal. Moreover, she is a representative of the University in the National People's Congress. So it is both her duty and her obligation to be in touch with the students.

Q: Is it also her duty to be involved in the off-campus campaign?

A: She should respond to student requests, which is her duty. However, last month she was discovered to have heart disease. So of late she has done nothing at all. Following Hu Yaobang's death some students contacted her, but she didn't go to Tiananmen Square. She went to the university, naturally; but reports that she joined in the demonstrations are mistaken.

Q: Is there any direct or indirect influence from the intellectuals on the escalation of the student movement?

A: Yes, of course. But it is chiefly ideological influence. Since the beginning of the year, intellectuals have put forth demands for an amnesty for political and ideological prisoners, and have held several academic discussions. All these had some influence on student opinion; but I don't think that intellectuals have influenced the actual organization and arrangement of the campaign. At most there is the possibility that students consulted them; but I don't think that the connection is strong.

Q: Why has the slogan, "Amnesty for Political Prisoners," not been heard in the Student Movement, which seems indifferent to the signature campaign [for the release of those incarcerated in 1979]?

A: Twenty-year old students actually don't even know who Wei Jingsheng is. Compared with older people, students are less concerned about political prisoners. What concerns them is government corruption and freedom of the press. If you trace the origin of their thoughts, they are similar to ours; it is just their slogans that are different.

Q: After the May 4th demonstration the students returned to their classrooms. What was it that gave rise to the hunger strike campaign on May 13th?

A: On May 4th Yuan Mu said that a dialogue was needed; but there was no dialogue. Maybe he thought that it could be delayed indefinitely. Everyone in Beijing knew that there was still a problem, and nobody was surprised when the students rose up again. It was the hunger strike that was a surprise.

Q: A hunger strike is a powerful and new weapon.

A: At the beginning, especially on the second day when someone declared that he was going to set fire to himself, the atmosphere was very tense. We discouraged them, saying that it would be better not to stage a hunger strike.

Q: Was the hunger strike and its timing entirely the students' idea?

A: Most likely. It is also evident that it was staged for the visit of Gorbachev.

Q: Taking place when the whole world was watching the Sino-Soviet summit, the hunger strike embarrassed the high ranking government officials. We can easily imagine how angry they were. Were the students interfering deliberately?

A: I think that they expected larger numbers of reporters, local and foreign, during that time, thus creating a bigger impact. That was all. They just wanted a dialogue with officials who have decision-making power. It is no use having discussions with people like He Dongchang.[8]

Q: Li Ximin stated that overseas Chinese had made a statement at Columbia University, proposing that you be the leader of an opposition to the CCP. Is that so?

A: I know absolutely nothing about it.

Q: We know from Li Peng's speech that the government condemns the student movement for advocating a multi-party system in China. Do you think that this is the ultimate goal of the movement?

A: The student movement aims at establishing a democratic society. Concerning the degree of democratization, I don't think that the students have very clear ideas. The present consensus is to fight for freedom of the press, freedom of speech, and to solve the problem of corruption. As to whether the next step is to amend the Constitution and to have Soviet style elections, no satisfactory discussions or conclusions have been realised. I rarely went to listen to the student discussions at Beijing University. There were certainly discussions of a multi-party system on big character posters, but the main question was the demand that their autonomous organization be regarded as legal. That is very important, for it relates to the future development of independent organizations.

Q: Are the authorities soon going to break up the student organization in Tiananmen Square?

A: It's difficult to say.

Q: Should the students retreat from the Square?

A: It is difficult for me to say. Certainly they should understand, as I have often told them, that the struggle for democracy takes more than one or two months. I warned them not to let their health deteriorate, as democracy requires a long struggle, and cannot be attained by a single act. It might even take a generation, with extensive preparation.

Q: If the students retreat without a dialogue, without a renunciation of the April 26th editorial, and without Li Peng stepping down, will the movement have been a failure?

A: Not a failure. Rather an ebbing of the tide. Even if you call it a failure, one should not underestimate the impact of the Movement. It is not simply a conflict over the April 26th editorial. Since the liberation forty years ago, this has been the first time that a Movement has made the masses realise that government is properly regarded as a servant of the people, open to criticism. This is a remarkable step forward, an unprecedented achievement, crucial to the democratization of China. In its final form democracy can involve a multi-party system. What is more important now is to cultivate a psychological attitude and popular lifestyle that gives everyone the right to criticise the government. The Student Movement has had a tremendous influence in this direction.

Q: Some think that the Student Movement should be replaced by a Workers' Movement. Are you optimistic about this?

A: This time workers have already joined the Movement. Not many, and they are not as well organised as the students; but the

Movement has influenced the workers, particularly the young ones, which cannot be underestimated.

Q: Is a Solidarity Movement likely in China?

A: It is not absolutely impossible.

Q: Are you optimistic?

A: Not very. But the workers do have some of their own organizations. As to their maturity, we just don't know yet.

Q: The government officials seem sensitive to the possibility.

A: As they are to the student organizations.

Q: Is it possible that the Movement could achieve a greater press freedom?

A: Laws concerning the press are to be discussed on June 20th. This could well be the one small positive result that the Movement can achieve.

Q: Could similar movements, challenging specific policies, gain like concessions?

A: Possibly. In the past, whatever you opposed got worse, as increasing numbers of people were accused of having "polluted minds" and of being "bourgeois liberalizers." To consolidate its position the leadership had no choice but to be high-handed. Under pressure from the masses, however, the leadership itself may get polluted and liberalised.

Q: I remember that you once told reporters that Deng Xiaoping and Li Peng must step down. Is this still your position?

A: I have long said that Deng should resign. As for Li Peng, he has failed. As Director of the commission for education he achieved nothing over a long period of time, as they have admitted themselves. As Premier, he has done nothing of note.

Q: Suppose Li Peng steps down, is there a better person to replace him?

A: I can't give you a name right now, but there are certainly better people available.

Q: What are your views on Zhao Ziyang?

A: In the sphere of economics, Zhao has indeed carried out reforms. As for reforming the political system, he did less than Hu Yaobang.

However, he does seem to be prepared to deal with the Student Movement and go ahead with political reforms.

Q: People overseas have heard rumours about Zhao's demise, with accusations that he has ignored his son's corrupt activities. Any comment?

A: This might be true.

Q. Recently, people here have been concerned that the Government will take revenge upon the participants in the Movement. How likely do you think this is?

A: The scope and duration will depend on the circumstances. If they can get even with the people, they will do it. It depends.

Q: Can you take a guess?

A. It is their intention to get even with the people. For them, that is a definite must. Can they actually do it? How will they do it? That all depends upon the circumstances.

Q: Can you say for sure that there will be an element of revenge?

A. Yes, of course.

Q. At this time only two people have been named by them: Fang Lizhi and Ren Wanding. Will you be the first target?

A. Very likely.

Q: How are you preparing for this?

A: (Laughing) I'm not.

Q: Are you worried?

A: I'm not un-worried; but if the democratization of China requires sacrifices, so be it. The Chinese people are firm, and we are not afraid of official authoritarianism.

Q: Recently circulated blacklists show the number of people to be arrested as varying from twenty to more than a thousand. We also hear that the number of Solidarity members arrested in Poland now adds up to about a thousand. Is this credible?

A: The different figures are different policy options of the government. As to the one which they will adopt, I can only say again, it depends on the circumstances.

Q: By circumstances you mean the struggle of the masses, and the power struggle at the top.

A: First, the power of the masses, and how many are prepared to follow. Then, naturally, the power struggle.

Q: It is now widely thought that the authorities have shifted their focus from the Student Movement to the intra-party struggle. Has the conflict between Li Peng and Zhao Ziyang reached an end? What do you expect?

A: It is difficult to speculate, for in China the upper echelons operate behind closed doors. Compared with people like yourself, we know so little.

Q: Professor Fang, many thanks. I hope that this will not be our last interview.

A: (Laughing) It doesn't matter even if it is.

NOTES

1. These interviews were conducted by an unnamed fellow student on June 2, 1989. The introduction is an assessment by that student of Wuer's relationship to his fellow activist in Tienanmen Square, Wang Dan, and a comment on Wuer's background and personality. Wuer escaped to the USA via France after the June repression. Wang was arrested in July 1989.

2. These comments are apparently made to counteract suggestions that Wuer was receiving funds from (and being influenced by) western reporters, who could be thought to be anti-socialist sensation seekers.

3. Wuer's distrust of the intelligentsia mirrors the traditional distrust of that group by the CCP. As was indicated earlier, the intellectuals were called the "stinking ninth" after the other specified "class enemies," who were: i) landlords, ii) rich peasants, iii) counter-revolutionaries, iv) "bad elements, " v) rightists, vi) renegades, vii) enemy agents, and viii) capitalist-roaders.

4. Transcript of an interview with freelance American journalist, Phil Cunningham, June 3, 1989. Chai Ling was one of the four high profile student leaders — with Cheng Congde (her husband), Wuer Kaixi, and Wang Dan.

5. To be identified as a leader or organiser of the Movement obviously carried significant risk (such as ejection from the university and imprisonment or exile) even before the massacre. It should be remembered that people like Chai Ling were self-selected, putting themselves forward, and taking on the tasks. That they were followed was often the measure of their popular support, although elections were also held at mass meetings. We see her taking the mantle of leadership, as she describes it here, at the time of the May 13th hunger strike, in which she participated. She is also saying that she would like other people to do the same, and that not all those who took on organizational tasks were honest and/or competent.

6. The question of science has many implications in the PRC. As a vehicle for industrial modernization it is important. However, those who possess scientific credentials have

often been accused of being elitist. In the years of Mao's dominance, one of the slogans was "Better Red than Expert." We had in the sixties the interesting picture of China's nuclear scientists saying that they only succeeded in producing their bombs because of the inspiration of Mao's thoughts. We should also remember that Marxism-Leninism-Maoism claims to be scientific communism, a claim which many social and physical scientists dismiss as inappropriate; but in doing so challenge the legitimacy of a one-party rule. Finally, we should note that communist regimes have been faced with bureaucratic inhibitions to the introduction of new methods and technologies, especially when they required autonomous decision-making being given to their operators.

7. The physicist and human rights activist, Fang Lizhi, was interviewed by telephone on May 31, 1989, by a representative of the Hong Kong journal, *Liberation Monthly*. Fang took refuge in the embassy of the USA at the time of the massacre. His incarceration was otherwise inevitable, as he indicates here.

8. A low-ranking official who had met with student representatives, and to no avail.

WITNESSES TO THE MASSACRE

These might be my last words, for the situation becomes ever more serious. I am now twenty-three years of age and, coincidentally, my birthday was the day Hu Yaobang died this year. I am from Shandong province, and I came to Beijing in 1983 to study psychology. In 1987 I was admitted to Beijing Normal University to undertake further studies in child psychology.

On May 12th I made a speech in which I said, "Our generation has the courage to die. We don't want that, preferring to win and to live under the clear skies of a reformed republic." One teacher told me that my speech had brought him to tears.

At 7:30 p.m. on May 13th, we met the others at Beijing Normal University, and went to the Square to begin the hunger strike. That evening there were less than a thousand of us; but the numbers were later to increase to more than three thousand.

It is asked: Is your action inspired by Gandhi? Indeed, I had thought of this; for when demonstrations and petitions do not work, one must offer one's own life to attract the attention of others, and to move the situation forward. I was very anxious, with a sense of great responsibility for the participants. However, even after Wuer Kaixi and others of our representatives had met with Yan Mingfu, we rejected requests to abandon the hunger strike.

Li Lu said to me that if the government ignored the strike, then we should adopt even more aggressive tactics, and set ourselves on fire. Speaking from the podium in the Square, I said that I was ready to take the role of Commander-in-Chief of the Hunger Strike Group, and sacrifice myself in order that other students might live on. Later I saw unconscious students taken away in ambulances, and I felt absolutely depressed.

There was an attempt to enter the Great Hall of the People. Knowing that the security forces would take some time to arrive, I begged those hunger strikers who had the strength to stop those involved. The leadership of ASUBU then arrived to stop it. There was chaos; for some of the student leaders were not motivated by good intentions.

I felt that the Hunger Strike Group should take the lead, having been present throughout. Since adopting a leadership role I had noticed that various organizational tasks were not being carried out. There had been 182 people in various positions; meetings were convened without serious thought or purpose; the health of the students deteriorated; requests for food got less response; and sanitary conditions became terrible. Worst of all, the students were becoming short-tempered as tension mounted in response to events.

Students from all parts of the country continued to arrive in the Square, and were frequently disappointed. Many of them did not know what we were struggling for, and had come along just for the ride. I heard that some students kept money donations for themselves; and some agreed to be interviewed by reporters only if they were paid. Worst of all, some students made a deal with the government, agreeing to retreat from the Square in return for merit marks on their records. As to the numbers of informers, we have no solid evidence.

Yet the darkest day has still to come. Many students don't understand that staying in the Square is the only way left for us; if we retreat, the government will be delighted. As Commander-in-Chief I refuse to compromise. Meanwhile we see the Autonomous Union of Non-Beijing Universities and the faction which preaches surrender competing for power with ASUBU. There are many who make use of the Movement to promote their own egos — people like Liu Xiaobo.[2]

I think that the Government will retaliate upon every one of us in a crazy manner; for the Chinese have a strong orientation towards revenge. Therefore, I have no unrealistic hopes. After our first dialogue [with party leaders] was broken off, I read out our declaration on the hunger strike, hoping that it might be broadcast over all the country, so that people would know why we had undertaken it. We thought that we could influence them.

Many people who have joined the Movement possess no views, have confused thoughts. The Movement's purpose is to show our understanding and concern for democracy. The intellectuals and the theorists are lagging behind, not having put forward a single well-rounded argument. The Movement's greatness will be that it is the catalyst of the spontaneous rising of the masses.

I think that it is inevitable that the existing situation must change. As an individual I want to live and to see the great revolution that I believe must occur, and which I want to be part of. If I live, I want to see the people of China really rise up.

Talk of reform has brought the intellectuals to a dead end. Unless the people choose to save themselves, there will be repression. On May 25th, I was chatting to a plain-clothes policeman, and he told me that anyone arrested would be sentenced to between three and seventeen years in jail. When released from such a sentence, I would be forty. I cannot accept that. I think that the establishment of a system of democracy, and the use of scientific knowledge for the public welfare, will benefit every Chinese. Of course, we could escape abroad; but if our country can solve its problems, we would not have to spend our youth and our talents on foreign countries. My mother country is poor, and needs many people who will struggle and sacrifice for her. The trouble is that, with the current political system, people from all classes have no alternative to emigration.

Someone must unselfishly continue with the task; for the fate of the entire country is at issue.

May 1989

LXX: *The Massacre in Tiananmen Square* [3]

I am a twenty-year old student of Qinghua University. Last night I sat on the steps of the Monument to the People's Heroes and witnessed the whole incident in which the army shot the students and the citizens.

Some of my schoolmates were shot dead. My clothes are still stained with their blood. As an eyewitness and survivor, I disclose what I saw during the massacre to all kind and peace-loving people.

In truth, we knew that the army would actively suppress us yesterday afternoon. A person called on us at 4:00 p.m. and told us that the army would use violence to clear everybody from the Square. After we were told this we discussed the matter urgently. We decided to adopt some measures to alleviate the conflict and to avoid great bloodshed.

At that time we had 23 guns and some bombs, which were obtained from the army during the conflict which occurred in the previous two days. The Autonomous Students Union of Beijing Universities (ASUBU) decided to give these back to the army to demonstrate our principle of "Promoting Democracy by Non-Violence." Last night we contacted the army under the Tiananmen Wall. An officer replied that they could not accept the weapons by order of senior-ranking officials. Following that the students destroyed these weapons at 1:00 a.m. because the situation had turned critical, and these weapons might have been used as "evidence" of killing soldiers.

ASUBU announced that the situation was getting worse. Since bloodshed could not be avoided, some students and citizens had to leave the Square. But there were forty to fifty thousand students and a hundred thousand citizens who decided to remain behind. I also remained.

The atmosphere was very tense. The students had never experienced anything like this. They were certainly frightened, but they were fully prepared psychologically, their minds were firm, and many students thought that the soldiers would not open fire. Anyway, we were encouraged by a noble feeling that it was worthwhile to sacrifice ourselves for democracy and development in China.

After midnight, when two armoured vehicles sped through the two sides of the Square, the situation became much more serious. The loudspeakers of the army repeated an announcement that we should leave. Many soldiers in battledress invaded the Square from the surrounding streets. In the darkness, machine guns were set at the top of the Historical Museum.

All the students were forced to retreat to the area around the Monument of the People's Heroes. I remember that one-third were girls, and the rest were boys. Students from Beijing's higher educational institutions made up 30%, the rest being students from other provinces or cities.

At 4:00 a.m. the lights in the Square were extinguished. Again we were told to evacuate the Square. My heart pounded, as if it were saying: the time has come, the time has come. At that moment, some people who joined the hunger strike, including Hou Dejian (a popular songwriter), negotiated with the army. They agreed that the students could leave peacefully. However, when the students prepared to leave, the lights in the Square were turned on. Some red flares exploded in the sky at 4:40 a.m. I saw that many soldiers had occupied the area in front of the Square. A large group of them ran out from the eastern door of the Hall of the People. They wore uniforms, helmets and gas-masks, and carried guns. (At 6:00 p.m. on June 3rd, we had spoken with a regiment of soldiers outside the western door of the Hall. They had said that they were only a supporting regiment, and that later there would be an army from Sichuan which would deal with the students directly. Their spokesman guaranteed that they would not shoot. Therefore, the soldiers who now came out were in all probability from Sichuan).

When these soldiers appeared they assembled in a row ten or so machine guns, in front of the Monument. The gunmen all crouched down on the ground with their guns pointing towards the Monument. When this was done, many soldiers and armed police, carrying flashlights, rubber clubs, whips and various weapons, rushed towards the passive students. They attacked violently, forcing the students to separate into two groups, and move upwards on the Monument. I saw forty to fifty students with blood on their faces. Just at that moment, many armoured vehicles and soldiers moved forward. These vehicles totally surrounded us, only leaving a gap in the direction of the Museum.

The soldiers and armed police who followed us up to the third level of the Monument destroyed all our broadcasting equipment, printing machines and everything else. Then they hit the students and forced them to go down. We did not move, but held our hands tightly, singing the *Internationale* and shouting, "The People's Army would not hurt people." But the attack was so violent that we were eventually forced to move down.

When we reached the ground the machine guns opened fire. Some soldiers knelt down to shoot, and their bullets just flew over our heads. But others aimed low, and their bullets hit the chests and heads of the students. We had to go up the Monument again, then the machine guns stopped firing. But the soldiers there forced us down again. Once again we were shot by the machine guns.

Meanwhile, some workers and citizens dashed towards the soldiers brandishing bottles and clubs. Then the ASUBU ordered us to retreat outward from the Square. The time was a little before 5:00 a.m. Students then began to rush towards the spaces between the armoured vehicles. These were closed by other vehicles. Moreover, more than thirty armoured vehicles were driven at people. Some students were run over. The flagpoles were destroyed in this way. Thus the whole Square was in a state of chaos. I couldn't believe that the students were so brave. They rushed at the vehicles. Many were killed. Others stepped over the dead bodies and ran forward again. At last there was a gap, and something like three thousand students dashed out, reaching the Historical Museum. Only a little more than one thousand of these were to survive.

There were many citizens there. Together we tried to go north, but there was gunfire. So we went towards the Qianmen Gate at the south end of the Square. I was running and crying. There was a mass of students running out under gunfire. Many people fell down. When we reached Qianmen, soldiers rushed towards us from the Jewellery Market (Zhubao Shi). They carried large clubs and hit us fiercely. Many people fought with the soldiers, which allowed us to run towards the Beijing Railway Station. The soldiers chased us from behind.

It was 5:00 a.m. and the gunfire started to diminish. Later I met one schoolmate at the International Red Cross. He told me that only those who ran from the Square could have survived. The machine guns had been firing non-stop for about twenty minutes.

The most unforgettable person was one of my friends from the college. He was bleeding but kept on running with us. Later he collapsed and fell on my shoulders. He said: "Please help me!" At that time I was holding two female school friends and could not help him. He fell down on the ground. People stepped on him... He was certainly dead. Look! There is still blood on my back! There was blood covering half of his body!

I shall never forget how, when some students were shot, others recovered their dead bodies, or saved those who were injured. Some girls took off their clothes to bandage the injuries of others, until they had no more to take off.

At 6.30 a.m. two school friends and I went back to the Square. There were many people there, and we followed them to the Memorial Hall, at which point we could not go any further. There were several rows of vehicles and walls of soldiers. So I climbed up a tree at the roadside, noticing that some soldiers used large plastic bags to carry away the dead bodies of students and citizens. These were piled up and covered by a large piece of canvas.

I met a school friend who had left the Square later than me. He said that many people were dead. Soldiers even refused to let the ambulances of the International Red Cross help the injured people. We went to the First Aid Centre at the Gate of Peace (Hepingmen). We saw that many injured people were carried there by cycle rickshaws. A doctor told me that an ambulance was shot at by the soldiers and was on fire. Some injured students said that many injured students were still lying in the Square.

Around 7:20 a.m. I went back to the Square and talked with several people. They said that corpses were lying all over the Square. Soldiers covered them with cloth so that nobody could look at them. Vehicles were carrying the bodies to some unknown place. About 7:30 a.m. the soldiers suddenly shot tear gas towards the people around the Square, then they rushed towards them. I ran to the

Beijing Railway Station again. I saw several students there, all crying.

ASUBU had given us Beijing students an assignment: to lead students from other places to the Railway Station. I took them to the Waiting Room, but the staff told us that all trains were cancelled. We were leaving when some citizens approached us, saying that they would take the students to their homes for protection. Many people were in deep sorrow and cried. The citizens of Beijing are really good.

How many people were killed? I'm not certain. But I believe that some day the killers must pay!

Pessimistic? No, I'm not, because I have seen China's future in the goodness of the people! Some of my schoolmates are dead, and many are injured. But I'm alive, I know how to live, and I'll remember all of the dead students. I surely know that all righteous people in the world will understand and will support us!

June 4, 1989

LXXI: Concerning June 3-4, 1989 [4]

During the massacre of June 3-4 I was part of a student patrol, which passed by many places, including Xidan, Xinhuamen, the Beijing Hotel and the main entrances to Tiananmen Square where the slaughter was greatest. I did not stay long in any one place, which is why I saw a lot that night, too much for me to remember everything clearly. However, the picture engraved on my mind is that of an abattoir, a slaughterhouse which would shock anyone.

We had already had a warning of the bloodbath which was to occur some three days before the massacre. On June 1st, when I was at a meeting with some students, we heard reports that violence would be used. Students saw troops, in groups of ten or so, dressed in civilian clothes, come out of the Imperial Palace and the Great Hall of the People. However, their size and posture gave them away as soldiers. They surveyed Tiananmen Square, looking at the tents, making notes and taking photographs. We suspected an attack, but we didn't expect things to develop so quickly. Also, at the time, the students were totally immersed in the problems of finance and administration.

Small scale clashes between troops and civilians began on June 2nd. There were reports of looting and of troops intimidating civilians. Furthermore, an old man arrived in the square in bandages, saying that he had been attacked by either a civilian patrol squad or students. However, at the temporary hospital where we removed his bandages, we discovered no injuries. The old man said that he had been forced to perform the charade.

In addition, there were small scale anti-student demonstrations by peasants in the suburbs of Beijing. The truth was that the Beijing municipal authorities promised ten yuan to any demonstrator; and that anyone who did not demonstrate would be punished with fines. Soon after this the Beijing University students demonstrated with satirical slogans — such as, "Quash Democracy," "Combat Freedom," "Fully Support Government Corruption," and "Follow Li Peng and Earn Nine-Yuan-Nine." All of this was a prelude to the massacre, as Li Peng fabricated excuses for it by trying to create the impression that civilians were against the students.

The situation got worse on the night of June 2nd-3rd. Some troops began to break into the Square. Strange things happened. For example, trucks carrying soldiers from Xidan began to force their way forward towards the Square. They were confronted because they threatened the safety of the thousands of people in there. The soldiers then got down and ran away. Students, not aware that it was a trick, climbed on the trucks and picked up the guns which were in them, and took them to our headquarters. As soon as the Union leaders saw them, they immediately warned the students that this was a trap, and they sent the guns to the police. That night, however, the radio stated that ruffians had stolen the guns. Such is the kind of shameful, fascist tactic used to exploit the innocence of the students.

Moreover, disguised in civilian clothes, perhaps two companies of troops arrived in the Square on the evening of June 2nd. Mingling with the students, it was difficult to recognise them. However, we knew they were there, and many students became anxious. Announcements over the loudspeakers told everyone to remain calm, and the intruders later departed in groups of two or three. However, they left behind military clothing. Not suspecting a trap, some students put on the clothing, and even took photographs. Later on the radio announced that ruffians had stolen military clothing, bullets and bombs. Yet I was there, and saw what happened. It was a set-up.

The massacre began at 10.00 p.m. on June 3rd. In the Square we didn't know exactly what was happening, for the troops were still some distance away at Jianguomen and Xidan. We received news from the campuses that shooting directed at civilians had begun. A student who blocked a truck, and tried to lecture the soldiers on democracy, was shot down by dozens of soldiers. A fleet of army trucks moved from the Beijing Hotel in our direction, and a girl who tried to communicate with them, saying, "The PLA are the brothers and sons of the people," was shot dead in a fusillade. Later, Wuer Kaixi held her, weeping bitterly. But this was just one case of brutal murder.

The worst of the massacre began at 2:00 a.m. on June 4th. Tracer bullets reddened the Square, and the shooting was coming from its periphery. I waited and spoke with the close friends that I had made during the ten days that I had been in Beijing. For two hours we planned our tactics, the possibility of death, how to rush forward, distract the police, and protect the girls. Meanwhile, the machine guns had already opened fire upon our fellow students at Xidan, and the tanks were rolling towards the Square, faced only by unarmed students and citizens, their arms linked, forming a human wall against the military vanguard.

Tanks advanced, stopped, and troops climbed down from them, immediately aiming their weapons at us. Students refused to let them pass, shouting slogans like, "Down with Fascism" and "Overthrow Dictatorship." In response, the tanks machine-gunned us. The front row died instantly. The troops then opened fire, then the tanks rolled forward over the bodies of the fallen, leaving behind blood and mutilation. In the screaming and gunfire it was hard to understand it all. I was leading a rush whilst others were retreating. A student next to me fell sideways, and I grabbed at him to stop him falling. I looked, and could not recognise him as his head was smashed in. All the students I had been with were lost. I dropped to the ground and rolled back towards the crowd as a tank passed beside me.

The troops holding submachine guns fired at whoever shouted slogans. Some citizens threw bricks and stones at the armoured personnel carriers. The weapons used against us were various, including tanks, armoured personnel carriers, anti-aircraft guns, submachine guns, tear gas, iron bars, wooden clubs and bayonets.

I moved away and arrived at Jianguomen, where I saw many students being killed by gunfire. Then tanks rolled over them, and they ceased to be recognizable as human beings. It was chaotic there. There were sounds of gunfire and screaming, and it was difficult to know if those who had fallen down were dead or alive. I saw a girl student with long hair being stabbed in the chest by a soldier. After she had fallen down, the soldier stabbed her in the back until she died.

The cruellest killings were at the Xidan approach and the area opposite the Military Museum. Some students who managed to get out [from the Square] collapsed exhausted; and then tanks ran over them. Submachine guns raked through every person in their path. More than twenty girls from one of the universities were crushed to death when blocking military vehicles. Those who survived the first bullet were killed by a second or third volley.

The massacre on the edge of the Square lasted for hours. Anyone sat in the Square could hear the shooting, screaming and rumbling of tanks. The Monument to the People's Heroes was lit up with the red light of tracer bullets. By 4:00 a.m. most of those on the periphery of the Square were dead. At the same time, the atmosphere in the Square was calm. They all sat peacefully under the Monument, contemplating death, expecting it, accepting it.

I remember having said earlier at a student meeting that a massacre might be the best result that we could hope for. Now, everyone was prepared to die, so we shouted, "Fellow Students! Don't panic. We swear to die defending the Square, defending democracy and the dignity of China with our blood."

I remember shouting, "Hou Dejian, Liu Xiaobo and two others declared a hunger strike on June 2nd to support our Patriotic Movement, and they have been under the monument throughout the slaughter."

When Hou found out about the massacre, it shocked him and stirred his conscience to say, over the loudspeaker system, "Officers and soldiers imposing martial law, I am Hou Dejian, and I represent the Four-Man Hunger Strike Group. Let us speak with you to arrange the safe retreat of the students." But he was ignored. Later, weeping, Hou went with students to the martial law headquarters, pleading with them to let the remaining students, some ten thousand, leave in peace. We were shut in by soldiers, and surrounded by the dead on the periphery of the Square. He negotiated, and eventually they agreed to let us leave from the south-east of the Square, but to be quick about it.

I had witnessed many killings, including some of the hunger strikers of May. I was not angry or sad, just numb. I had no tears. I went from the periphery to the Monument, thinking on the cruelty of killings, so many of them my friends, and began to choke back tears. I could never forget the death of my friend with a shattered head, whom I lay gently onto the ground; and now I was waiting for my own death, determined to sacrifice myself with the remaining ten thousand.

When Hou returned he said, "My student friends, I have done something silly, and I hope that you will forgive me. But I also hope that you will retreat now." There was no response from us, so he continued, "We have shed enough blood, and can expect nothing from this party and government. Don't wait to be massacred, save yourself for tomorrow. Leave now."

There was dead silence. As he spoke the army was moving near, and the students were furious. A student of the Autonomous Union of Non-Beijing Students stood up cursing, "Hou, get out, you bastard! You should not have done it. Leave by yourself." and then sat down. Hou shouted to us again, but we remained motionless as the army moved towards us, raking the Monument with their bullets.

Then Wuer Kaixi spoke, saying, "My fellow students, don't just sit there. Calm down and make a decision." Hou made another appeal, saying that he knew that we were not afraid to die. Many wept. The lights in the Square went out. And then the troops were upon us.

I was in the second row. The police were confronting us. Hou made a final appeal, saying he would stay until the last student had left; and some students did stand up and move towards the south-east corner of the Square. As this happened, and as we were retreating, the police opened fire. Those with clubs beat us. Girl students were shot, their flesh torn and bleeding, their clothes ripped, trampled under soldiers' feet. The soldiers would not let us retreat peacefully, but used their guns on us instead.

There were many tents, large and small, erected by students from more than four hundred universities from throughout the country, including the [more than seventy] Beijing institutions and Hong Kong. There must have been hundreds of students sleeping in the tents, exhausted because of the many sleepless nights preceding. Having faced death every day, denied the opportunity to sleep, they fell asleep as soon as they lay down, and no sound could wake them. Many of these sleeping students were crushed to death by the movement of the tanks, there being no time to save them. Side by side the tanks rolled over their bodies, grinding them to pieces, as did the personnel carriers. If I had moved a minute later than I did, I too would have been crushed.

I was retreating at a run with some students. I saw a girl from Beijing University, her face covered with blood, clothes torn, with no shoes, lying unconscious. I rushed forward and picked her up. Guns were fired at us, those with clubs chased us.

I left the group and ran towards the History Museum. Tanks had crushed all the tents and were now circling the Square. I carried the girl up an alley. When some citizens saw us they could not control their emotions, and yelled, "Down with the fascist bastards," screaming so hard that they lost their voices. Then, as tanks approached, they took to their heels, pursued by gunfire and soldiers. I crawled along the ground with the girl in my arms. Later I settled the girl student in a citizen's home. When she regained consciousness she screamed. I helped calm her down with the residents of the household.

A report on the radio stated that a citizen was burned to death by ruffians in Jianguomen. The actual facts are these: Five heavily-armed soldiers killed many old people and children. Then, when they lost contact with the other troops, an angry crowd surrounded them. Their ammunition exhausted, the crowd rushed forward and burned one of them to death; but only after he himself had murdered many people.

As for the reported murder of a child, that was done by a soldier using a bayonet. The old chap with the child shouted, "Fascists!" The soldier then shot him dead on the spot. The child was seven years old, the man fifty-plus. They were from Henan province.

According to Red Cross estimates, more than three thousand were dead in the hospitals before I left Beijing, including not less than fifty of their own medical workers. Two research students told me that many students who had tried to give first aid were killed. Also, in addition to those crushed to death, every time a group of people had been shot, soldiers surrounded them, and no-one could see what was happening to the victims.

I was worried about getting back to school, concerned that the students would not know what was happening; so I decided to leave Beijing. However, I first wanted to send a telegram, and on the way met some angry citizens. They asked me if I was a student, and advised me to get out of Beijing as soon as possible. The fiancee of a young man who was with them had been killed. They told me that, having heard gunfire during the night, they went to the Public Security Bureau on Changan Avenue to find out what was happening. Walking in a group, speaking in a Beijing dialect, eager to ask questions and be informed, they were answered with gunshots, and the girl was killed on the spot.

When I arrived at the Telegraph Office a sign informed me that there was "No telegraph or telephone service." When I asked why this was the case the staff said, "Are you crazy? Get away from here. There is nothing that you can do." So I left, went to the railroad station, bought a ticket, and hid in the washroom.

None of the Beijing workers are going to their jobs. The army is occupying the educational centres. Soldiers are beating up students, and even those who simply distributed pamphlets are being targeted. Even when I was leaving you could still hear the sound of gunshots.

Someone has asked me to comment on the rumours that the soldiers had been injected with stimulants. Who can say? I did see a girl from the Beijing Normal University shot dead when she was trying to reason with the troops. Even old women were killed when they tried to talk to the soldiers. Even at 10.00 p.m. on June 3rd, before the start of the massacre, when I spoke to the soldiers at the entrance of the Military Museum, saying, "If you really must open fire, then fire over our heads to avoid an act of murder," a soldier pointed his gun directly at me. Not having received the order to fire, he simply said,

"Get out of here. If you don't, then I'll have to get rough."

The university student standing beside me at the time said, "Without your uniforms you are the same as us. We are both citizens, and we both suffer." The soldier, pointing the barrel of his gun at the student's chest, said, "Get out of here, or else I will shoot you." I felt that all of the soldiers were insane and inhuman. They had simply no feeling for others. They were bastards whose murderous actions would be condemned anywhere.

Women university students died miserably under the gunfire. People could not bear to watch the cruelty. Those who did not experience it cannot imagine that cruelty, with blood and remains everywhere. That blood, shed by the students, should not be wasted. Those children of the Chinese people have died for good reason, saving future generations from otherwise inevitable sorrow, making their death the greatest moment in the history of China.

I hope that all of the survivors of this bloodbath are not killed in the same way as the students, and can make the students' suffering worthwhile; i.e., utilising their strength.

Although I am still alive, I am miserable, feeling that my fellow students have died for me, that I should also be dead. This regime is prepared to kill those who know the truth, and I know what happened in the Square. I also hope that something like that will happen again, to give me the chance to die in the same cause. The citizens of Beijing know this already, but what about the other parts of China? I hope that students there will do the same thing, which is why I write now, so that they will know the truth and the infamy of the government. The students who died in Tiananmen Square should be remembered forever!

LXXII: Statement of ASUBU to Compatriots Everywhere

On June 4, 1989, one month after the seventieth anniversary of the May Fourth Movement, patriotic fighters for democracy once more soaked the flag of the People's Republic with their blood in the capital city. Blood flowed in the streets and mourning songs echoed through the city. We have reached a critical moment and must, whilst saluting the republic and the fate of those killed and wounded in the struggle, broadcast the following hard facts to the Chinese people and the world:

On April 15th [the day of the death of Hu Yaobang], the huge Patriotic-Democratic Movement was born.

On April 22nd, students in Beijing went to a rally to commemorate our late comrade, Hu Yaobang, in Tiananmen Square, in defiance of official prohibition. After the rally some students remained, kneeling before the Great Hall of the People, hoping that the authorities would accept a petition. They were simply ignored.

On April 26th an editorial in the *People's Daily* viciously described the mass movement of students as a "riot." To protest this vicious smear, the Beijing institutions of higher education organised another demonstration, for the following day. People from all parts of Beijing gave enthusiastic support. A million people took to the streets. People and students from all over the country responded enthusiastically, pushing the Democracy Movement to new levels.

Faced with popular demands and the power of the Democracy Movement, the government resorted to its usual tactics of double talk, avoiding responsibility, and trying to divide the students and the people. They refused to talk with the legitimate representatives of the students, or even discuss conditions for such a dialogue. From the first instance the students and people of Beijing handled the situation with sophistication, orderliness and restraint. In circumstances involving massive numbers of people, where the government initiated disruptive and provocative actions in the hope of creating mistrust of the movement, the protesters maintained peace and stability in the capital; and the authorities refused to listen.

On May 13th, finding the situation intolerable, one thousand students spontaneously organised a hunger strike. Within two days the number went up to more than three thousand. The whole country gave evidence of solidarity and support, demanding that the government meet the conditions put forward by the hunger strikers and engage in an open and equal dialogue with them.

On May 19th, early in the day, Zhao Ziyang, Li Peng, and other senior officials appeared in the square, speaking briefly with the students. They said that they were confident of the patriotic motives of the students, and that the party centre had never suspected us of riotous intent. They promised that there would be no retaliatory actions against the members of the student movement. *However*, on the evening of that very same day, Li Peng and Yang Shangkun summoned a meeting of party, military and government leaders, and came to the conclusion that the movement was indeed riotous, and that emergency steps must be taken to curb it.

The next day, May 20th, martial law was declared by the State Council [of the National People's Congress] and municipal government of Beijing. Several hundred thousand soldiers were assembled on the outskirts of Beijing, and the smell of blood was in the air.

As soon as the army moved on the city, the students and citizens flocked to the city approaches to talk to the soldiers of the People's Liberation Army. They talked to the soldiers about politics, exchanging ideas. The tension generated by the authorities was eased. The soldiers and the people were on friendly terms, with the citizens of this wonderful city carrying on their lives in a normal manner. According to the media, there were fewer crimes, traffic violations, and even fires, during these days. However, the planned atrocity of the government against the innocent students was under way.

On June 2nd, a speeding army truck knocked down several people in Beijing, killing three, and seriously wounding one more. The bloody suppression instigated by the reactionary government entered its preliminary stage.

On June 3rd, in the early morning, troops in civilian clothes moved towards the centre of the city on public transport. Citizens and students tried to stop them. On the approach roads to Tiananmen Square the army, using gas and rubber bullets, injured many. In one incident a seven-year-old child was stabbed to death by a soldier.

On June 3rd, in the evening, armoured cars, riot police, and gas were used to clear the way for soldiers who moved upon Tiananmen Square from all directions. As they progressed, the soldiers fired indiscriminately on unarmed students and citizens with machine guns and automatic rifles. Around Muxidi casualties numbered approximately 400, with soldiers firing at those trying to rescue the wounded.

On June 4th, in the early morning, three armoured cars travelling at high speed down Xidan Road hit a bus which was in the centre of the road [as a barricade]. From the direction of the Military Museum, those in the Square could hear the roaring of trucks and continuous shooting. According to the retreating students, many of them had been killed and wounded.

In the first hour after midnight, soldiers about 500 metres down Xidan Road shot a great deal of tear gas. The crowd was forced to lie on the ground. Some cars were set afire, obviously by policemen out of uniform, with the intent of giving the authorities an excuse for carrying out a massacre. Ten minutes later, a large force of riot police, yelling, "Shoot! Shoot!", fired at the assembled civilians, who were totally surprised and absolutely vulnerable. Suddenly there were students and citizens lying everywhere on the street, dead or wounded. Those who managed to escape down narrow side-roads were shot at as soon as they were spotted by soldiers, who spared nobody, young or old.

At about 1:00 a.m. army trucks full of soldiers raced towards the end of Xidan Road. People ran up from side-roads to see what was happening, and were shot at by soldiers, who also beat those in their way with rifle butts. A student from the Second Beijing College of Foreign Languages was so badly beaten that his legs were useless bloody lumps. He also reported that five of his school-mates were shot whilst trying to rescue a female colleague. Then, some three hours later, when the soldiers had passed them, the surviving students headed for Tiananmen Square. However, the roads were blocked by soldiers who did not hesitate to open fire on the approaching crowd, even firing upon those who were running away. Where slogans were shouted, shooting followed.

From 3:00 a.m. to 6:00 a.m. on June 4th, there was a sound of shooting from Tiananmen Square and the connecting streets. Blood could be seen wherever the soldiers went by. Casualties were many, and cries and screaming filled the air. It was a horrifying scene. In the Square there were many army trucks, and tanks rolled everywhere. The preliminary estimates of dead and injured were 3000 and 7000 respectively. As the massacre continued the figure was expected to increase. Large numbers of students and citizens were drenched in blood; for they were unarmed and totally vulnerable. The only protection they had was a cloth mask, for the worst they expected was tear gas and rubber bullets. These innocent students and citizens never expected the Li Peng government to be so inhuman. From the first volley they were left wondering why they had to die. And these were the people whom the Li Peng government accused of being counter-revolutionary rioters!

Actually, what happened on June 3rd and 4th, the premeditated massacre and bloodbath, was evidence of the real counter-revolution. The people of the world will not forgive the Li Peng government the bloody debt which must now be paid.

The movement which began in Beijing on April 15th, and then spread across the whole country was honorable, patriotic, and democratic. Young students raised the banner of freedom and democracy, demanding an end to dictatorship and autocracy, which reflected the wishes of the one billion Chinese people. The movement inherited and furthered the spirit of the May Fourth Movement, and turned a new page in the struggle for freedom and democracy in Chinese history. However, a small handful who are opposed to both the party and the people, headed by Deng Xiaoping, Li Peng, and Yang Shangkun feared and hated it in the extreme. They hid the truth to protect their own interests at the expense of the people and the country. To do that they shamelessly accused this movement for democracy of being a counter-revolutionary riot. Having used threats and bribery from the beginning, they finally resorted to the bloody slaughter of unarmed students and citizens, and created a tragedy of global significance. The events reveal the horrible and corrupt nature of persons who can in no way be regarded as the government of the people. Rather it is the cruelest and most autocratic government in the world. Deng, Li, Yang and their like have shown themselves to be criminals of historic proportions, corrupted elements of our race, and the common enemies of everyone.

The fascist government has lifted its hypocritical veil and the dictators have revealed their disgusting intentions. A black cloud covers the vast landmass of China, and bloodshed fills the air of Beijing. But history has already shown that the people, democracy, and freedom will win. We, the college and university students of Beijing, will never make the slightest compromise with this evil authority, and will struggle to the end. We swear to the people of China and the world, with our youth and our blood, that we will not shame our forbears of May 4th, nor the martyrs of June 4th, nor the people of our time. At this critical moment in our nation's history, we appeal to the Chinese people to unite to overthrow the Deng-Li-Yang reactionary government, these inhuman fascists who ruthlessly slaughtered the people, these dictators who unashamedly tramped on the will of the people. We also appeal to all countries and peoples in the world who are peace-loving, and who treasure freedom and democracy, to use effective economic and diplomatic sanctions to support the Chinese students and people in their fight against the fascist atrocities of the Chinese government. Let democracy and human rights prevail. The Chinese and the people of the world must unite in the struggle for democracy and freedom. Down with autocracy! Down with fascists! Long live Democracy! Long live Freedom! Long live the People!

June 4, 1989

LXXIII: *This is How They Died in Tiananmen Square* [5]

I work for the Capital Iron and Steel Company. I arrived at Tiananmen Square at 6:00 p.m. on June 3rd to see what was going on there. Although I did not feel much sympathy for the government, I did not think that it would go to extremes. So I stayed with the students, and gave them my support.

At 1:10 a.m. on June 4th, gunshots sounded in Tiananmen. I told the students not to be frightened, that the shots would be fired in the air, and that they should neither panic nor get hold of sticks or clubs. I argued that we should talk to the soldiers and persuade them that they would meet no resistance from us; and that if we reasoned with them we could leave the square peacefully, or even be escorted out by them, with nobody hurt.

At 1:40 a.m. shots were fired. Police cars and armoured vehicles rumbled towards us from the east. At 2:00 a.m. they confronted us. I could not see if it was policemen or soldiers who fired on the crowd. At the time, everyone believed that they would use rubber bullets. I kept holding the students back and urging them not to fight, thinking that if I could restrain even one person it would be the right thing. Believing in pacifism, alone in the square, I confronted neither vehicle nor soldier; but I believed that the soldiers could be persuaded by words.

Then my faith was shattered in a burst of gunfire. The People's Liberation Army was firing at the people. The crowd was stunned to see row upon row of people falling down. They tried to get out of the way, some running wildly about, with many falling down.

As the gunfire died down trucks and armoured vehicles rolled straight towards the crowd. The Square was very crowded, and many more lost their lives.

I hid to one side, and counted the dead. In that one small spot, from 2:10 a.m. to 3:05 a.m., twenty-nine people lay in a pool of blood.

Most tragic of all were the deaths of a young woman and her younger brother. The dead boy was pulled out of a pool of blood. Seeing him, his sister lit a cigarette, and prepared to rush at the troops. The crowd restrained her, saying that the soldiers were no longer human. She promised not to do so, smoked cigarettes, until losing control of her emotions, ran at the troops.

Seeing her example, some young men rushed forwards too. At first the troops did not fire; then they shot at the crowd, and all the youths fell. The woman continued forward, ignoring her own safety. I shouted to the troops that it was a woman, and that no soldier would kill a woman. After all, she was a girl with a cigarette in her hand, not a grenade. Had the soldiers possessed any humanity, they would have arrested her when she reached them. But they shot right at her. Ten strides from the soldiers she stiffened, blood running all over her body. We rushed forward to rescue her, and where she had fallen we left a large pool of blood.

She was a tall woman, dressed in pink, in her early twenties. For her, everything was now over.

Wherever you looked there were pools of blood; and on the walls of the Imperial Palace blood stains were everywhere. Those who were wounded needed medical attention, but the soldiers did not make way. A vehicle flying a first-aid flag was prevented from entering the square by gunfire, its windows shattered. An ambulance was then denied entry. I saw with my own eyes people laying in their own blood, waiting for help, which was denied to them. Many people wanted to enter the Square to help the wounded, but they were prevented from doing so. The wounded and dying were then shot again.

What can we do in response? Nothing but a nationwide strike will be effective. Knowing what has happened, how can anyone say that the student movement is a counter-revolution? But you know what the official news report will say this morning.

June 4, 1989

LXXIV: *Chai Ling, "I Am Still Alive"* [6]

Today is June 8th, 1989. It is now 4:00 p.m. I am Chai Ling, Commander-in-Chief in Tiananmen Square. I am still alive.

I believe I am the best qualified witness to the situation in the Square during the period from June 2nd to 4th June, and I also have the responsibility to tell that truth to everyone, every single country-man, every single citizen.

At about 10 p.m. on the night of June 2nd, the first warning of what was to come was given when a police car knocked down four innocent persons, three of whom died. The second signal immediately followed when soldiers abandoned whole truckloads of armaments, military uniforms and other equipment, leaving them behind for the people and my college mates who had blocked their way. We were very suspicious of this act; so we immediately collected together everything that had been abandoned and sent them to the Public Security Bureau, retaining a receipt as proof. The third signal occurred at 2:10 p.m. on June 3rd, when large numbers of military police beat up students and citizens at Xinhuamen. At that time, the students were standing on top of cars, using microphones to cry out to the police: "The people's police love the people," "The people's police won't beat people up." Instantly, a soldier rushed towards a student, kicked him in the stomach, and scoffed: "Who loves you?" He then gave him another bash in the head and the student collapsed.

Now, let me briefly describe our position. I was Commander-in-Chief in the Square, where at that time there was a broadcasting station for the hunger strike group. I stayed there throughout, directing the activities of all the students in the Square. Of course, the commanding unit consisted of other people, such as Li Lu and Feng Zhende. We received constant and urgent messages, from every direction, that students and citizens were being beaten and harassed. That night from 8:00 p.m. until 10:00 p.m., we watched the situation get increasingly worse, as at least ten reports kept us informed of developments.

Around 7:00 or 8:00 p.m. we, the commanding unit, had held a press conference, and told both local and foreign reporters as much as we knew of the situation. There were not many foreign reporters, and we heard that this was because hotels where the reporters lived were controlled by troops, and that their rooms had been searched. So only a few foreign reporters came to the Square. The commanding unit made one statement, saying that the only slogan we held was, "Down with Li Peng's false Government."

At 9:00 p.m. sharp, all of the students in the Square stood up and with their right hands raised, declared: "I vow that, for the promotion of our nation's process of democratization, for the true prosperity of our nation, for our great nation, for defense against a handful of schemers, for the salvation of our 1.1 billion countrymen from White Terror,[7] that I will give up my young life to protect Tiananmen Square, to protect the Republic. Heads can fall, blood can run, but the people's Square can never be abandoned. We are willing to sacrifice our young lives in a fight to the death of the very last person."

At 10:00 p.m. sharp, the Democratic University was formally established in the Square, with vice-commander Jiang Deli becoming the principal, and people from all sides celebrated the occasion enthusiastically. At that time, the commanding unit was receiving many urgent warnings, as the situation became very tense. On one hand, there was the thunderous applause for the establishment of our Democratic University in the northern part of the Square near the Statue of the Goddess of Liberty; whereas along the Boulevard of Eternal Peace at the eastern edge of the Square, there was a river of blood. Murderers, those soldiers of the 27th Battalion, used tanks, heavy machine guns, bayonets (tear gas being already outdated) on people who did no more than utter a slogan, or throw a stone. They chased after the people, shooting with their machine guns. All the corpses along the Boulevard of Eternal Peace bled heavily from their chests; and all the students who ran to us were bleeding in the arms, chests and legs. They did this to their own countrymen, taking their life's blood. The students were very angry and held their dead friends in their arms.

After 10:00 p.m. we, the commanding unit, made a request based upon the principle that our Patriotic-Democratic Movement, as both a Student Movement and People's Movement, had always been to demonstrate peacefully. In opposition, therefore, to the many students and citizens who angrily declared that it was time to use weapons, we proposed the supreme principle of peace and sacrifice.

In this way, hands joined together, shoulder to shoulder, singing "The International," we slowly came out from our tents. Hands joined, we came to the western, northern and the southern sides of the Monument of the People's Heroes, and sat there quietly, with serenity in our eyes, waiting for the attack by murderers. What we were involved in was a battle between love and hate, not one between violence and military force. We all knew that if we used things like clubs, gasoline bottles and the like (which are hardly weapons) against those soldiers, who were holding machine guns or riding in tanks, and who were out of their minds, then this would have been the greatest tragedy for our Democracy Movement.

So the students sat there silently, waiting to give up their lives. There were loudspeakers next to the commanding unit's tent playing "The Descendants of the Dragon." We sang along with it, with tears in our eyes. We embraced each other, shook hands, because we knew that the last moment of our lives, the moment to give up our lives for our nation, had arrived.

There was this student called Wang Li, who was fifteen. He had written his will. I have forgotten the exact wording, but I remember him saying: "Life is strange. The difference between life and death is just a split second. If you see an insect crawling toward you, all you have to do is to think about killing it and the insect will instantly stop crawling." He was only fifteen, and yet he was thinking about death. People of the Republic, you must not forget the children who fought for you.

Between 2:00 and 3:00 a.m. on June 4th, we had to abandon our headquarters at the bottom of the Monument and move to the Monument's platform to continue our command of the Square. As Commander-in-Chief, I went with my deputy, Li Lu, to visit the students around the Monument, to give them moral support. The students just sat there quietly. They told me they would sit there in the first row, steadfast and immovable. Students in the back row said they, too, would remain steadfast. "We would not be afraid even if the front row of students was beaten and killed. We would continue to sit still and not withdraw. We would not retaliate and kill."

I chatted with the students and told them the old story that goes: "There were these 1.1 billion ants living on a mountain top. One day, the mountain was ablaze. To survive, the ants had to get down the mountain. They gathered themselves into a giant ball and rolled down the mountain. The ants on the outside were burnt to death. But the lives of many more were saved. My fellow students, we at the Square are the outermost layer, because in our hearts we understand that only by dying can we ensure the survival of the Republic." The students sang the *Internationale* again and again. They held hands tightly. Finally, the four hunger strikers — Hou Dejian, Liu Xiaobo, Zhou Duo and Gao Xin — couldn't stand it any more. They said, "Children, don't sacrifice yourselves this way." But each student was determined. The hunger strikers went to negotiate with the soldiers, with the so-called Martial Law Command Post, to tell them we were leaving. It was hoped that they would ensure the students' safety and peaceful retreat. Our headquarters consulted students on whether to leave or to stay. We decided to leave.

But the executioners didn't keep their word. As students were leaving, armed troops charged up to the third level of the Monument. They didn't wait for us to inform everyone of the decision to leave. They had already shot our loudspeakers to pieces. That was the Monument to the People's Heroes. They dared to open fire at the Monument. Most of the students withdrew. With tears in our eyes, we started to leave the Square. People told us not to cry. We said we would be back, because this is the People's Square. We only found out later, that some students still had hope in the Government and they thought that, at worst, they would be removed.

Then the tanks made "mincemeat" of them. Some say more than 200 students died. Some say more than 4000 died in the Square alone. I don't know the total. But the members of the Independent Workers' Union were on the outside. They stood their ground and they're all dead. There were twenty to thirty of them. I heard that, after the students left, tanks and armoured personnel carriers flattened tents with bodies inside.

They poured gasoline over them and burned them. Then they washed away the traces with water. Our movement's symbol, the Goddess of Democracy, was crushed to bits.

With locked arms, we went around Chairman Mao's Memorial toward the south of the Square. That was when we first saw tens of thousands of helmeted soldiers. The students ran toward them and yelled: "Dogs. Fascists." So we headed west, and saw ranks upon ranks of soldiers running toward the Square. Civilians, students, though hoarse from all the yelling, continued to shout: "Fascists, dogs, beasts." But they were ignored by the soldiers, who kept on running toward "our" Square.

We got to Xinhuamen, all of us from the headquarters in the front row. Xinhuamen was where the first bloody battle took place in the afternoon of June 3. Debris was all over the place. From Xinhuamen, we ran along the blood-slick Changan Avenue. All we saw were burnt-out vehicles, fallen concrete and debris — signs of a hard-fought battle. We later found out that, as these fascists machine-gunned people, other soldiers would pick up the dead and wounded and throw them onto buses. Some were still alive but later suffocated to death. That's how the fascists tried to hide their disgusting actions.

We wanted to go back to the Square. But the people tried to stop us. They said: "Children, don't you know they've set up machine guns over there? Please don't go back to die!" We then went north along Xidan Avenue toward the university area. Along the way, I saw a mother crying bitterly. Her son was dead. We also saw the corpses of four soldiers who had been beaten to death by citizens. We continued north, and as we neared the campuses everyone had tears in their eyes. Some people said: "Did I buy bonds to let them buy bullets to kill innocent people? To kill innocent children?"

First hand reports from students and civilians stated that these executioners acted in a calculating manner. They aimed at residential areas along Changan Avenue and fired rockets at them. Children and old people were killed. What were their crimes? They didn't even chant any slogans. A friend told me he was blocking tanks on Changan Avenue at 2:00 a.m. He saw a girl, not very tall, standing in front of a tank, waving her right hand. The vehicle rolled over her body. She was crushed into "mincemeat." My friend said the students to both his right and left were killed by gunfire. He literally came back from the dead.

On our way, we saw a mother looking for her son. She said he was alive yesterday. Is he still alive? Wives were looking for husbands, teachers looking for students. Government buildings still displayed banners calling for support of the correct policies of the party leadership. In anger, the students tore them down, and burned them.

The radio kept saying that the troops had come to Beijing to deal with riotous elements and to maintain order in the capital. I think I'm most qualified to say that we students are not riotous elements. Anyone with a conscience should put his hand on his chest and think of children, arm in arm, shoulder to shoulder, sitting quietly under the Monument, their eyes awaiting the executioner's blade. Can they be riotous elements? If they were riotous elements, would they sit there quietly? How far have the fascists gone? They can turn their backs on their conscience and tell the biggest lie under the sky. If you say soldiers who kill innocent people with their rifles are animals, what do you call those who sit in front of the camera and lie?

As we left the Square, arm in arm, as we walked along Changan Avenue, a tank charged at us and fired tear gas at the students. Then the tank rolled toward us, rolled over the students' heads, and legs. We couldn't find any of our classmates' bodies intact. Who's the riotous element? In spite of this, we in the front continued on our way. Students put on masks because the tear gas hurt their throats. What can we do to bring back those students who were sacrificed? Their souls will always remain on Changan Avenue. We who walked away from Tiananmen Square, arrived at Beijing University, still alive. Many students from other universities, students from out of town, had prepared beds to welcome us. But we were very, very sad. We were alive. Many more were left in the Square, and on Changan Avenue. They'll never come back. Some of them were very young. They will never come back.

As we entered Beijing University, our hunger strike turned sit-in, our peaceful protest, came to an end. Later we heard that Li Peng, at 10 p.m. on June 3rd, had handed down three orders: First, troops can open fire. Second, military vehicles must go forward without stopping. They must take back the Square by June 4th. Third, the leaders and organizers of the Movement must be killed.

My compatriots, this is the frenzied, puppet government that initiated a slaughter and is still commanding troops and ruling China. But my compatriots, even at the darkest moment, dawn will still break. Even with the frenzied, fascist crackdown, a true people's democratic republic will be born. The critical moment has come. My compatriots, all Chinese nationals with a conscience, all Chinese people, wake up! The ultimate victory must be the people's! Yang Shangkun, Li Peng, Wang Zhen and Bo Yibo, the final hour of your puppet regime is near!

> *Down with Fascism!*
> *Down with Military Rule!*
> *Long Live the Republic!*

June 8, 1989.

LXXV: *After The Massacre* [8]

Life seemed to be normal, undisturbed by the massacre in Tiananmen. Perhaps Guangzhou [north of Hong Kong] is too far from the site of the killings. That was the impression when I stepped down from the train on July 3rd. Friends were so excited to see me. Everybody is hungry for news from the outside world. My friend's house became a small library when others found out that I had managed to smuggle out some Hong Kong newspapers to this isolated world. Yet my friends became very cautious as more people arrived. In Guangzhou people are more open-minded and less likely to follow the government's instruction to report "counter-revolutionary activities." However, I could detect my friend's anxiety — in a community where "the Street Organization" has complete control over people's lives and keeps everybody under surveillance, only fools take things for granted.

In a mere month the atmosphere of the city has changed. It is like going back to the "old days." The propaganda machinery is in full swing again. According to the Deng-Li-Yang clique, the cause of the recent "rebellion" is a serious negligence in "ideological education" and the "toleration" given to capitalism. So "ideological education" once again becomes the core activity of one's daily routine. I tried to call a few people, but everyone was behind closed doors, busily engaging in "Studying the Speeches of Deng Xiaoping."

Prices for luxury goods such as stereos, refrigerators, and even furniture, have been slashed. Everybody is saving up for the forthcoming economic crisis. People are uncertain of the future. It is obvious that the government is short of cash. In the rural areas the government has issued IOU certificates instead of paying cash for crops. The farmers are insisting that they want cash, not bits of white paper. So it is thought that the government will start printing money next month, making inflation inevitable. Therefore, people are faced with a dilemma. If they do not spend their money now, it will become useless paper in the future. Yet the future is so uncertain that people are no longer in the "spending mood" of a few months ago. Some people are hoarding gold bars.

The streets are less crowded compared with the pre-massacre period. There are hardly any tourists from Hong Kong. The large flow of business people, migrant workers and visitors from other parts of China has ceased. People are afraid to travel. According to my friends, there have been many train accidents. Some trains were blown up, some were derailed. One train plunged into the gorges near Xion. However, the news of train accidents were suppressed along with other news so as not to further jeopardise the debilitated tourist industry.

Travellers also take the risk of being wrongly identified as one of the people on the wanted list. At every station the police search through luggage as if seeking a needle in a haystack. They also carefully match faces with those on the wanted list. We are living in a society where those who are in authority have absolute control over the fate of those unfortunates who are wrongly arrested simply because their faces resemble those of "counter-revolutionaries." They could end up in jail, or even with a bullet in the back of the skull.[9] Except for the most urgent reasons, nobody wants to travel in the environment of a spreading "White Terror." I was planning to move on to Chungdao, but my friends literally begged me not to go. "If you insist upon going, then I will risk my life by accompanying you. I will not allow you to travel alone at this time." So I cancelled my trip.

The roads are relatively quiet, the buses not crowded. I even got a seat on the bus! Life seems to carry on undisturbed. However, stories of people being secretly executed, of people failing to show up for work, of the arrest of student leaders and intellectuals, all generate uneasiness. People suffer in silent anger. Tension and anxiety are mounting.

NOTES

1. This essay was written during the May hunger strike, and its conclusion was almost illegible because of the physical exhaustion of the author.
2. Liu, born in 1954, was a lecturer at Beijing Normal University, mentor of Wuer Kaixi, arrested on June 6, 1989.
3. By "A Student Who Survived."
4. The student was a member of the Students' Autonomous Union of Non-Beijing Universities who escaped from Beijing and returned to his campus. The following is an edited recording of his statements at a meeting there broadcast by Radio-Television Hong Kong on June 22, 1989.
5. By "An Eyewitness."
6. This text was taken from a tape smuggled to Hong Kong.
7. A reference to reactionary violence by the government. The term, "White" has indicated this to all raised in Marxist-Leninist societies since the time of the Russian Civil War (1918-1921), when the Red Army of the Bolsheviks fought and won against various White Armies trying to overthrow them.
8. Reproduced from *Echoes From Tiananmen*, No. 2 (August, 1989), published by the Friends of Chinese Minshu, Hong Kong. Written by A Guangzhou resident in July 1989, after his return from Hong Kong, the author must of course, remain anonymous.
9. This is not a paranoid mentality. As Jasper Becker stated in a report from Beijing, "Security forces are routinely torturing the thousands of detainees seized in the weeks after the army crushed the student democracy movement, according to diplomatic sources... Those who die under interrogation are reported to have had an accident and quietly buried... It is not known how many have been arrested or sentenced during the past six weeks, but most estimates are upwards of 30,000." See "China reported to be torturing detainees, " *Manchester Guardian Weekly*, July 30, 1989.

BLACK ROSE BOOKS
has published the following books of related interests

Peter Kropotkin, Memoirs of a Revolutionist, introduction by George Woodcock
Peter Kropotkin, Mutual Aid, introductionby George Woodcock
Peter Kropotkin, The Great French Revolution, introduction by George Woodcock
Peter Kropotkin, The Conquest of Bread, introduction by George Woodcock
    other books by Peter Kropotkin are forthcoming in this series
Marie Fleming, The Geography of Freedom: The Odyssey of Elisée Reclus,
    introduction by George Woodcock
William R. McKercher, Freedom and Authority
Noam Chomsky, Language and Politics, edited by C.P. Otero
Noam Chomsky, Radical Priorities, edited by C.P. Otero
George Woodcock, Pierre-Joseph Proudhon, a biography
Murray Bookchin, Remaking Society
Murray Bookchin, Toward an Ecological Society
Murray Bookchin, Post-Scarcity Anarchism
Murray Bookchin, The Limits of the City
Murray Bookchin, The Modern Crisis
Edith Thomas, Louise Michel, a biography
Walter Johnson, Trade Unions and the State
John Clark, The Anarchist Moment: Reflections on Culture, Nature and Power
Sam Dolgoff, Bakunin on Anarchism
Sam Dolgoff, The Anarchist Collectives in Spain, 1936-39
Sam Dolgoff, The Cuban Revolution: A critical perspective
Thom Holterman, Law and Anarchism
Etienne de la Boétie, The Politics of Obedience
Stephen Schecter, The Politics of Urban Liberation
Abel Paz, Durruti, the people armed
Juan Gomez Casas, Anarchist Organisation, the history of the F.A.I.
Voline, The Unknown Revolution
Dimitrios Roussopoulos, The Anarchist Papers
Dimitrios Roussopoulos, The Anarchist Papers 2

send for our free complete catalogue of books
BLACK ROSE BOOKS
3981 boul. St-Laurent, #444
Montréal, Québec H2W 1Y5 Canada

Printed by
the workers of
Editions Marquis, Montmagny, Québec
for
Black Rose Books Ltd.